The Mythology of America's Seasonal Holidays

"Arthur George's *The Mythology of our Seasonal Holidays* offers an impressively-researched and scholarly-yet-accessible study that details the historical, cultural, and mythological underpinnings of our most celebrated American holidays. George offers to both the interested scholar and general public a 'hermeneutic key' that opens one up to the *mytho-poetic* and symbolic dimensions of numerous traditional celebrations. In doing so, he offers his readers the gift of a deeper, more meaningful engagement – with both our seasonal rituals and our daily lives"
—David M. Odorisio, Associate Core Faculty, Mythological Studies, and Director, the Retreat, Pacifica Graduate Institute, USA

"Arthur George sifts through a mountain of evidence about ancient and modern myths and rituals, paying attention to both the forest and the trees. The result, meticulously researched and lucidly explained, is a treasure trove of fascinating historical, mythological, and psychological insights into the often obscure religious backgrounds of American holidays and Christian holy days."
—Robert J. Miller, Rosenberger Professor of Religious Studies and Christian Thought, Juniata College, USA

"A spellbinding myth-critical gaze into the underpinnings of our common calendric cycle. Arthur George offers deep insight into how and why holiday traditions transform through the ages and still order our contemporary lives."
—Richard C. Miller, Author of *Resurrection and Reception in Early*
ity (2015)

Arthur George

The Mythology of America's Seasonal Holidays

The Dance of the Horae

Arthur George
Solvang, CA, USA

ISBN 978-3-030-46915-3   ISBN 978-3-030-46916-0   (eBook)
https://doi.org/10.1007/978-3-030-46916-0

Cover illustration: "Horae Serenae," Edward John Poynter
Contributor: Historic Collection / Alamy Stock Photo

This Palgrave Macmillan imprint is published by the registered company Springer Nature
Switzerland AG.
The registered company address is: Gewerbestrasse 11, 6330 Cham, Switzerland

The Horae, coming to earth in their own proper forms,
with clasped hands are dancing the year through its course ...
How they sing, and how they whirl in the dance!
Philostratus the Elder, *Imagines*, 2.34

To my dear wife and muse
Elena

PREFACE

There are many ways to study holidays, and many ways to celebrate them. Ideally, the way in which we celebrate them should reflect what we have learned about them as a result of some study and thought, and then our holiday experience will be deeper. This book is aimed at that goal.

The particular makeup of any culture's menu of annual holidays can be a study in itself, as can be comparing holidays across cultures and over time. We also can study the historical evolution of any given holiday, seeing how its meaning and rituals have evolved. This historical approach is the one taken by most books about holidays, whether about single holidays or the entire cycle of annual holidays. Many books about holidays give us such historical information; they can be found in the Bibliography.

My own interest in holidays, however, concerns more fundamental questions. Why do we need holidays at all? What human psychological needs do they satisfy? How do they relate to the natural environment and cosmos in which we live, and to the seasons? Why do we have the particular holidays that we have and not others? Why are the rituals of various holidays so similar in many cases? Why are the rituals for the *same* holiday (e.g., New Year's) so similar across cultures and over time? Most books and Internet writings about holidays do not consider such questions, but this book engages with them.

Further, holidays tend to be based on myths, the myths contain corresponding symbols that appear in holiday celebrations, and the original holiday rituals also are derived from the myths (although our modern holiday rituals have often strayed from the original myths). Yet, at least outside the academic world and sometimes even within it, scant attention has been paid to analyzing the mythology underlying our seasonal holidays. This book endeavors to do just that.

And finally, holidays are moments of sacred time, spent outside our normal workaday or even recreational routine. They should have special meaning to us, not just be a day off to engage in some unrelated activity. It was the original mythology underpinning holidays which made them sacred in the past. But as we know, the customs of many of our modern holidays have been commercialized or have otherwise departed from the original myth, with the result that our holidays as currently celebrated are no longer so sacred, and therefore do not satisfy our psychological needs as well as they once did. Much of the spiritual component of holidays has been lost. Just as the ordinary, "corporate" version of vacation travel is dumbed-down,[1] so too is the usual understanding of our holidays and how we typically celebrate them. For our own good, this situation should be remedied. This book strives toward that end.

But these days we cannot do this by simplistically returning to what people originally believed about the myths on which holidays were based. The world has moved on, and so too has our understanding of those myths. But the myths should not be dismissed simply because they are unhistorical. The myths took hold not because they were true but because they were meaningful: They resonated with our psyche. And the makeup of our psyche has not changed. This book contends that by understanding the myths underlying our holidays, we can better appreciate what our holidays are really about and why they should still be important to us. They should be taken seriously and be celebrated with an appreciation of their original mythological meaning, even as we view them with a modern understanding. If we do so, celebrating our holidays can become a more meaningful and spiritual exercise.

As an example, it is often said that we should "put Christ back in Christmas," as an antidote to the holiday's commercialization or to its relativization alongside other end-of-year/solstice holidays of other religions. For people who take the biblical stories of Jesus's birth literally, putting Christ back in Christmas means that the way in which we celebrate the holiday should be anchored in those stories on the assumption that they are historically true. But most people these days, including most professional New Testament scholars, don't consider those stories to be historical, that they are, well, myth. But from my point of view, that juncture – where we recognize them as myth – is precisely the point where the stories can become most valuable and meaningful to people in the modern world. Thus, as I explain in the final chapter about Christmas, it really is important to "put Christ back into Christmas," but in a sense that recognizes the true mythological and psychological meaning of the Christmas story, which actually brings out its spiritual essence more authentically than if one simply takes the story literally.

This, then, is what I have endeavored to achieve in this book. It is ultimately an effort to show how our holidays can be celebrated in a revitalized and more spiritual way, by understanding their mythological roots in the past and applying the myths to the holidays according to our modern understanding of myths.

I need to say a word about my choice of holidays covered in this book. I am interested in those holidays which have mythological underpinnings, and as it turns out most major American holidays do have such underpinnings. Further, the holidays which have a mythological background tend to reflect the annual cycle of the seasons and the traditional human activities which are determined by this cycle. Therefore, this book is about the *mythology* of our *seasonal* holidays, as its title indicates. As a result, holidays that are neither seasonal nor based significantly in myth are not covered, such as Presidents' Day, Mother's Day, Father's Day, Martin Luther King Day, Memorial Day, Labor Day, and Veterans' Day. Where the mythology and related holidays of minority cultures or religions are relevant, I bring those into the discussion, such as the Celtic Beltane and Samhain (still observed by many), and the Jewish Day of Atonement (Yom Kippur), Feast of Booths (Sukkoth), and Purim, though not others where such content is lacking (e.g., Hanukkah (based on the defeat of the Seleucid forces and the rededication of the Second Temple) and Cinco de Mayo).

I am also interested in holidays which reflect our own mythmaking about ourselves. In this respect, our 4th of July holiday and Thanksgiving are important (the latter also is seasonal in nature). They are peculiarly American, are rooted in our young nation's history, or more importantly in our traditional collective version of that history: Both holidays reflect myths that we have created about ourselves and our country. An honest study of these myths and their symbols in relation to these holidays can teach us a lot about ourselves as Americans; it is an introspective exercise in self-knowledge. Those myths and symbols are especially valuable because they call upon us to be our better selves as individuals, and likewise call upon our nation to be its better self and a more perfect union. Those holidays annually remind us to do that, and we need it.

On technical matters, I use an author-date style of citation keyed into the Bibliography and the List of Abbreviations. The style of the endnotes, Bibliography, and abbreviations is a blend of the *Chicago Manual of Style* (16th edition) and (for biblical material) the Society of Biblical Literature's *Handbook of Style* (2nd edition), with some concessions to make them more understandable to the general reader. Credits for the Figures appear in their captions. Quotations of biblical passages are from the New Revised Standard Version translation unless otherwise noted.

I wish to thank my loving wife Elena for her patience, for her many helpful suggestions, and for reading and commenting on the manuscript. She was my muse who inspired me to get it done. This book would not be what it is without her.

Solvang, CA, USA   Arthur George

NOTE

1. Steves 2018, p. 11.

CONTENTS

ABBREVIATIONS

ABD   *The Anchor Bible Dictionary.* Edited by David L. Freedman. 6 vols. New York: Doubleday, 1992.

ANET   *Ancient Near Eastern Texts Relating to the Old Testament.* Edited by James Pritchard. 2nd ed. Princeton University Press, 1955.

BDAG   Danker, Frederick, ed. *A Greek-English Lexicon of the New Testament and Early Christian Literature.* 3rd ed. Chicago: University of Chicago Press (2000).

CCC   *Catechism of the Catholic Church.* 2nd ed. New York: Doubleday, 1995. The citations refer to the numbered paragraphs.

CW   *The Collected Works of C.J. Jung.* 20 vols. Princeton: Princeton University Press (1954–1979). Dates given to cited material are to the dates of the *CW* volume in which they are reproduced rather then the date when the works originally appeared. Cites are to page numbers rather than the numbered paragraphs.

DSS   *The Dead Sea Scrolls.* Translated and edited by Michael Wise, Martin Abegg, Jr., and Edward Cook. San Francisco: HarperSanFrancisco, 1999.

ER   *The Encyclopedia of Religion.* 16 vols. Edited by Mircea Eliade, New York: Macmillan, 2005.

HBD   *HarperCollins Bible Dictionary.* Edited by Paul Achtemier et al. 2nd ed. San Francisco: HarperSanFrancisco, 1996.

HTR   *Harvard Theological Review*

JAF   *Journal of American Folklore*

JBL   *Journal of Biblical Literature*

JEA   *Journal of Egyptian Archaeology*

JSS   *Journal of Semitic Studies*

LSJ   *A Greek-English Lexicon.* 9th ed. with revised supplement. Edited by
          Henry Liddell and Robert Scott, revised by Sir Henry Stuart Jones.
          Oxford: Clarendon Press, 1996.
NCE   *New Catholic Encyclopedia.* 2nd ed. Edited by Thomas Carson and
          Joann Cerrito. Farmington Hills, Mich.: Thomson Gale, 2003.
NOAB   *New Oxford Annotated Bible.* 4th ed. Edited by Michael Coogan.
          Oxford: Oxford University Press, 2010 (uses NRSV translation).
NRSV   New Revised Standard Version of the Bible.
OCD   *Oxford Classical Dictionary.* Edited by N. G. L. Hammond and
          H.H. Scullard. 2nd ed. Oxford: Clarendon Press, 1970.
OCY   Blackburn and Holford-Strevens 1999.
SJOT   *Scandinavian Journal of the Old Testament*
SR   *Sociology of Religion*

LIST OF FIGURES

CHAPTER 1

Introduction: Why We Have Holidays

Our days of the week are named after Norse and other Germanic gods and goddesses, together with heavenly bodies formerly associated with deities.[1] Eight of our months are named after two Roman gods (Janus and Mars), three Greek and Roman goddesses (Aphrodite, Maia, and Juno),[2] a Roman holiday of purification rituals (the Februa), and two Roman rulers who were mythologized and considered divine (Julius Caesar and Augustus). In light of this, we can rightly suspect that our calendar and its seasonal holidays have mythical origins and meanings, and further that the seasonal holiday cycle was celebrated within a mythical framework.

No culture's calendar marks merely the running of time. Calendars incorporate sacred moments. Our seasonal cycle is "the patterned unfolding of sacred moments" around which people "plot their lives, in accord with an inheritance of memories that matter and a cycle of rituals that revisit them."[3] Such holy moments are packaged with myths, rituals, and symbols which form chapters in the progression of the sacred master-narrative of the year. Holiday rituals, at least traditionally, have mediated and placed us between the human and the divine, and they still can and should. The mythology and symbolism of our holy days also lends them an artistic character, which over history has inspired some of humankind's greatest art.

In ancient Greek myth, the course of the year was overseen by a triad of goddesses called the Horae ("the Seasons") representing the three traditional seasons of the ancient Greek year (spring, summer, autumn).[4] The

A. George, *The Mythology of America's Seasonal Holidays*,
https://doi.org/10.1007/978-3-030-46916-0_1

Greeks called the course of the seasons the dance of the Horae.[5] The characteristics of the Horae evolved in a manner similar to the seasonal holidays themselves. In their earliest known form, the Horae were closely tied to the seasonal cycle of vegetation and reflected people's concerns about fertility, as reflected in their early names:

- **Thallo**, meaning blossoming, especially of fruit trees, was a goddess of spring, budding and blossoming, and of youth, representing the return to life during this season, and also was a protector of youth.
- **Auxo (or Auxesia)**, meaning growth and increase, personified summer, and was the protector of vegetation, growth, and fertility.
- **Carpo**, referring to bearing and harvesting fruit, was responsible for autumn and its processes of ripening and harvesting the crops.

As one would expect, this ancient triad was dear to early Greek farmers. As Greek culture became more urban and city-states emerged, and Greek mythology became Olympian, however, a different triad of Horae evolved. While they were still tied to the seasons, they also took on roles associated with higher urban civilization and culture.[6] This is evident from their parentage: They were all daughters of Zeus and Themis. Themis, daughter of Uranus (heaven) and Gaia (earth), was a Titaness counselor who personified divine order, law and order, human social order and norms, propriety, and morality. These characteristics were reflected in her daughters, the Horae, who brought such gifts into our world:

- **Eunomia**, meaning both good *(eu)* green pastures *(nomia)* and good law *(nomos)*, was the spring goddess of green pastures, but also the goddess of governance according to good laws.
- **Eirene**, meaning peace, was the goddess of peace and wealth. She was associated with late spring, because this was the military campaigning season when peace was at stake.
- **Dike**, meaning "justice" as well as "just retribution," was the enemy of falsehood and the protector of the wise administration of justice. She wrought just punishment on the wicked and rewarded the virtuous.

While still personifying nature and seasons, the Horae also had become keepers of order in our world, serving to "mind the works of mortal men,"[7] as Hesiod put it. So too, they guarded the gates to Mt. Olympus, which is to say the gates of Heaven.

Dike is especially instructive. She represented the way of the universe as a whole, as well as of each thing comprising it, which way is manifested in the course of the seasons. She was the natural law and "way of life" of the cosmos to which everything, including humans, should conform,[8] much like the goddess Maat in Egypt. Dike called upon people to live in harmony with the universe, and live nobly according to high principles.[9] Robert Graves called Dike "an artificial deity invented by the early philosophers."[10]

This evolution of the Horae from more primitive associations with nature and vegetation to higher, abstract concepts dealing with human conduct and ways of being, right up to individual spiritual experiences and practices, is typical of the evolution of myths, religion, and, as occurred in Greece, philosophy as well. This same kind of evolution is also reflected in the history of our seasonal holidays. Now we have our own dance of our own Horae.

THE NATURE OF THINGS HOLY, INCLUDING DAYS

Humans have always had holidays. Why? How did they first appear long ago? And why are there so many of them? Why do holidays always have rituals? Which vestiges of old holiday rituals can be seen in our holidays today? Why have such rituals persisted when we no longer understand their meaning? What mix of pagan, Judeo-Christian, and modern secular traditions do our holidays exhibit? The list of important and interesting questions could go on and on. This book considers them by focusing on the principal mythological underpinnings of holidays.

We need only reflect for a moment on these questions to realize that holidays are somehow essential to the human experience, that they are rooted in our very being. They have always functioned to help develop and maintain the structure and integrity of human communities, as well as the health of our individual psyches and spiritual life. Nevertheless, we don't often think about holidays in such terms. This book asks us to do so.

The perspective of this book can be seen in the very meanings of "myth" and "holiday." For our purposes, a myth can be understood as a narrative story that is not historically accurate but conveys an important sacred truth, and which usually but not always involves divine figures, heroes, or supernatural events. There is something holy about a myth that resonates with our souls or psyches. And "holiday," as we can easily guess, means "holy day." Holidays are conceived of as sacred time set apart from everyday profane life. There is normally at least one myth associated with any holiday, which either purports to explain its origin or enhances its meaning and makes it more sacred. Myths and holidays go together.

To glimpse how holidays function in this way, we need only consider the example of our vacations. We take them to get away from it all, and we come back from them to our normal lives refreshed, with our "batteries recharged." (Actually, in British English the usual term for vacation is "holiday," which better expresses the dynamic at work.) Vacations are our personalized, extended holidays. Our traditional seasonal holidays, though usually spanning only one day, serve a similar purpose as days set apart to have a more meaningful experience of life. But because of their mythical character, holidays are more powerful than typical vacation days.

What does it mean for a particular day – or anything else – to be considered holy or sacred? How and why does this come about? To understand this, we must look back into our ancient past, before there was anything that we might recognize as religion, and before anthropomorphic deities, and consider what may have happened in light of human psychology. In ancient times when the rituals that developed into holiday festivals first emerged, people did not yet have developed ideas of religion or a writing system in which to express any such ideas. While our holidays did derive from perceptions of the divine that later resulted in religions, they were not originally established on the basis of ideas, beliefs, or creeds. Rather, the primitive rituals from which our holiday celebrations arose came directly from our ancestors' confrontations with the overwhelming powers and mysteries in nature that they did not understand or control, powers which could be either harmful or beneficial. Their reactions of awe and terror to such forces and unknowns were highly emotional, often irrational. People developed rituals in an attempt to control or placate these powers. Rituals were based on divine models, or archetypes.[11] Holidays too emerged at times of the year when people developed rituals for confronting, honoring, and trying to control these powers, together with myths to understand and explain them.

Many holidays commemorate what we think were historical sacred, perhaps mythical events that occurred only once, for example the creation of the world (New Year's Day), Christmas as the birth of Christ and Easter as his resurrection, Jewish Sukkoth (Feast of Booths) to commemorate the Hebrews' Exodus and 40-year stay in the wilderness under Yahweh's protection, and the Islamic New Year commemorating Muhammad's flight from Mecca to Medina (the Hegira). Other holidays mark not one-time events but those which recur each year (whether naturally or by human designation) and in which divine forces or deities are especially active. These include the sprouting of new vegetation in the spring (also sowing) (as in Easter and May Day), harvest time, the annual appearance of our ancestors' ghosts (Halloween), and any number of winter and summer solstice holidays. Other holidays are more purely human creations, arising in order to satisfy psychological needs that build up over a period of ordinary time between other holidays. Examples are Groundhog Day, Valentine's Day and Carnival, together bridging New Year's and the arrival of spring celebrated during Easter and May Day. It seems that we need holidays frequently. The fact that we manufacture some holidays strictly out of need and desire can give us insight into their underlying nature and shows that psychological factors are at work, even when there are ostensible external (e.g., historical) pegs on which to hang a holiday. Finally, other holidays are more purely socio-political, which almost by definition are modern and are based on traditions that have acquired a nearly mythical character (e.g., Independence Day, Thanksgiving).

The Sociology and Psychology of Holidays

One does not have to be a psychologist to see that humans like to envelop themselves in sacred time and space (reality) fairly often. One cannot live in that realm constantly, however, so we set aside special times of the year for such experiences.

Holidays used to be communal affairs that strengthened human bonds within what the mythologist Joseph Campbell called the "mythologically instructed community"[12] and socialized people into sharing community values and responsibilities, leading to what the anthropologist Victor Turner called *communitas.* This social process in turn supported the individual. Formerly the important communities were villages and church congregations, which often amounted to the same thing. In today's urbanized society where we hardly know our next-door neighbor and most of our acquaintances are from the workplace, usually a commercial organization with commercialized values in which employees are disposable and come and go, we lack this former sense of community. As a result, holidays no longer serve this communal function, except within the family and, with religious holidays, dwindling church congregations.

Nevertheless, even in our modern secular culture, our holiday celebrations remain a refuge, because they are just about the only occasions when we all drop our everyday routines in order to live, albeit briefly, in sacred time. What are we to do with it?

In the final chapter of *The Hero with a Thousand Faces,* Campbell addresses this situation where the mysteries associated with the old myths have been lost. Unlike ancient peoples, we no longer view animals with reverence, nor is the reappearance of vegetation in the spring or the growth of crops a divine process. Even that last refuge of the divine mystery, the heavens, has been found to be susceptible to explanation by science and human exploration. These trends affect our holidays and how we can celebrate them. The communities in which holidays used to be celebrated and gave them meaning either no longer exist or are declining. Essentially, we are left only with the human community of the whole planet on the one hand, and the individual on the other.

While it is important for the entire human community to come together as one for many purposes, when it comes to celebrating sacred time on holidays the individual is now paramount. Campbell recognized that the human psyche is both our most important remaining mystery and the realm in which one can experience the divine in sacred time and space, even in the conditions of contemporary society.

The leading twentieth-century scholar of comparative religion Mircea Eliade described humans as by nature "religious man."[13] In a similar vein, the nineteenth-century Russian writer Anton Chekov once observed that if a man does not believe in God, it is only because he believes in something else. This explains why most people who abandon traditional organized religion still pursue spirituality in some alternative way, or they might find meaning by founding or joining a noble social or political movement, which activity meets similar psychological needs. This behavior shows that people need to generate and experience positive psychic energy (libido) to achieve a healthy state of mind. Accessing and experiencing the "sacred" serves this purpose. The need to experience the sacred is a trait that evolved in us over time because it must have had evolutionary (survival) value, although it is hard to pinpoint what exactly that was in prehistoric times.[14] The clear result, however, is that we seek and inevitably detect the sacred in our world. Establishing and celebrating holy days during which we can enter a sacred dimension is part of this spiritual quest.

ARCHETYPAL RITUAL TRADITIONS IN HOLIDAYS

We color eggs on Easter, but so did Iranians on New Year's,[15] and people in Gaelic lands on May Day. We have our house-to-house trick-or-treat ritual on Halloween, but so did ancient Romans at some of their festivals, as did the English, Irish, and Scots on various holidays. In many ancient and modern holidays people make a lot of noise as part of the ritual, use fire, make offerings or sacrifices, and share meals. People held similar bonfire rituals at Easter, on May Day (Beltane), on midsummer night, and on the holiday marking the transition to winter (e.g., Samhain). Many holiday rituals involve role reversals in society, such as masters serving their slaves, and appointing temporary mock Kings and Popes. Many involve rites of purification and catharsis. In almost all cases, business, governmental, and other ordinary activities cease on holidays. Why do so many holiday rituals repeat themselves across various holidays in so many places and cultures over time?

The field of depth psychology as developed by Carl Jung, James Hillman,[16] Lionel Corbett,[17] and others provides a persuasive explanation. In this view, the ways in which we perceive, experience, and act in the world and the way in which we think are governed by psychic patterns called archetypes. These lie in the unconscious part of our psyche as part of its essential make-up as it evolved over time; archetypes can be studied through their impact on our behavior. People across cultures and over time share these common archetypes, leading to similar sacred experiences (hierophanies) in response to the same phenomena of nature, including the seasonal cycle. As a result, hierophanies tend to fall into common patterns. Our reactions in response to similar objects or events will be similar, so similar elements will be found in the rituals and holidays associated with them, both across cultures and over time. So, for example, as we shall see:

- The cycle of the year suggests an end followed by a new beginning or renewal, so New Year's rituals reflect mythologies of the creation, and reenact the creation.
- The appearance of renewed vegetation in the spring was experienced as a mysterious and divinely caused event, leading to rituals of thanks on the one hand and others designed to encourage and protect fertility (i.e., control nature) from danger.
- Certain holidays in the annual seasonal cycle besides New Year's mark a transition, such as from winter to spring, the final coming of

summer, and the transition into winter. These can be times of celebration, but they are also liminal times of unusual supernatural activity and of danger to humans and their property, livestock, and crops. The rituals in all such holidays similarly are designed to counter threats to our well-being.

- Many holidays involve some struggle between opposites: dark and light, chaos and order, good vs. evil, or one's own community vs. some enemy, in which the community is of course victorious and a spirit of renewal and bonding prevails. So New Year's is a victory over the old and bad, replacing it; Easter is victory over evil and death; May Day and Halloween counteract evil spirits and ghosts; and national independence and revolution holidays mark victories over enemies (projections), reaffirming the goodness and superiority of one's own community.

These and other archetypal patterns in holidays will be traced in the course of this book.

The actions through which we honor and reenact the sacred are called rituals, while in language we convey the sacred through myth. Both rituals and myth are built out of symbols, which are images pregnant with value and meaning. Symbols originate in the archetypes of our unconscious psyche, hence so too rituals and myths, and therefore also the impulse for creating holidays. Myths, rituals, and holidays are thus usually closely related. Some scholars have concluded that rituals developed first as a form of magic, and that subsequently etiological and other myths were developed to explain what people were already doing. (This is called the "ritual school of myth.") That this sometimes happened is evident from Ovid's *Fasti*, in which he put forth myths to explain some Roman holiday rituals, which myths clearly came after the fact. On the other hand, in many other cases myths developed without any accompanying ritual, or at least existed before any accompanying ritual developed.[18] In the case of our holidays, we normally have elements of both ritual and an accompanying myth, which have been developing and fusing together over time. For example, the Christmas nativity and Easter stories were generated in the first century CE, Christians then developed rituals aligned with these stories; then the focus both in the stories and in the rituals changed over time. Moreover, as we shall see, the original Christian stories were based to some extent on existing mythological motifs in the Jewish and Greco-Roman world, and the original holiday rituals later merged with many pagan holiday rituals.

THE DEVELOPMENT OF HOLIDAYS
IN PRE-LITERATE SOCIETIES

We know next to nothing of holidays that existed prior to the emergence of literate societies. Yet the human concerns and psychology that generated these early, unknown holidays and their rituals would have been much the same as those which generated holidays in later, literate societies. Indeed, many ancient holidays of which we are aware appear to have been derived from festivals in pre-literate societies. Therefore, before discussing the holidays that we know about in the ensuing chapters, we must say something about what most likely happened before them.

We don't know what holiday festivals may have been held in Paleolithic and Neolithic times, before the invention of writing. We do, however, see evidence of the human concerns that later became the subject matter of holidays. For example, even in the Paleolithic period people had begun to track the phases of the moon, so they were thinking in terms of cyclical time, in particular that of life, death, and renewal. Burials evidenced a belief in an afterlife or perhaps a resurrection in some sense. People were concerned with having enough food, so they performed rituals designed to bring success to the hunt, as well as to ensure ongoing fertility and fecundity among the animal populations on which the people depended. Feeling a kinship with animals and having a psychological need to deal with having to kill them, some peoples rationalized that their prey would be reborn, so that the killing was not permanent. In these developments we see the notion of rebirth or resurrection, and a recognition of the cycle of life and death. Presumably these people analogized the seasonal cycle to life and death. Further, Paleolithic cave art depicts what people hoped would be a successful result of the hunt, meaning that the rituals were designed to *cause* this to happen, an early appearance of magic. Magical aspects of rituals later appeared in most known holidays. The many anthropomorphic goddess figurines from Paleolithic times point to a concern for human fertility, and rituals must have developed out of that, apparently centered around the lunar cycle (which equates with the menstrual cycle) and also the coming of spring, as evidenced in our later holidays. Finally, we can assume that other rituals came to depict (reenact) key historical or mythical events in the sacred oral lore of the community which had to be remembered, retold, and celebrated periodically, generating primitive versions of holidays.

In the Neolithic period, when people became agricultural and dependent on the soil, rain, and crops, people became concerned with these things rather than the hunt, and with agricultural fertility in addition to human and animal fertility. In an agricultural society people became more dependent on the *solar* seasonal cycles, and learned astronomy to keep track of them. This provided one basis for having *seasonal* holidays. The rituals centered around sowing and generation, protecting crops from harm, ensuring rain, and the harvest. In this cultural context, at first an Earth-Mother-Goddess representing the soil, life, and the crops developed into the dominant deity. Originally, she was self-generating and self-fertilizing and therefore independent. The resurgence of vegetation and its eventual dying off in the barren months was sometimes symbolized as a son-lover of the Goddess, who was born and died in the seasonal cycle, which also generated corresponding myths and seasonal rituals. In the early stages of agriculture, women were especially important, but men became more important once agriculture grew more sophisticated and increasingly demanded heavy labor, as in ploughing and in constructing and operating irrigation systems. With this and the development of astronomy the notion of a heavenly father/sky-god developed, who among other things produced the rain that fell from the skies and fertilized Mother Earth. Eventually the sky-gods (e.g., Marduk, Yahweh, Zeus) became dominant, and the Goddess was relegated to secondary status, often as the wife or consort of the sky-god. Multiple goddesses and gods sprang up, each representing and addressing particular human concerns. Having multiple deities facilitated having multiple seasonal festivals, with particular deities being the patrons of particular festivals and being venerated at them.

The above process brought us to the point where literate societies emerged. We can read about their already existing seasonal festivals, including their corresponding rituals and myths. To some extent we can also read back into where they came from.

The Inevitable Fate of Holidays and their Rituals

Holidays and their accompanying rituals and myths have arisen in response to the concerns of humans in a particular historical timeframe and cultural context. But history does not stand still. Civilization progresses, so that what concerned us at one time in a later era may no longer be a problem, while new challenges arise. What concerns people and what they consider important to celebrate evolves over time. For example, many traditional festivals were agricultural in origin, being concerned over the well-being of crops, but as farming methods improved and societies urbanized this was no longer was a problem for most people. Even in the ancient classical world, the urbanized citizens of Athens and Rome no longer understood the origins and meanings of their original holiday rituals rooted in agriculture; the meanings of the holidays and their rituals began to change. Much the same has happened in our modern world, and continues. Many of the original values and concerns reflected in our holidays are not so important today, so the holidays and their rituals have been changing, much like the Horae changed. We rightly wonder, for example, what the commercialized aspects of contemporary Christmas have to do with the meaning of the birth of Christ, or what the real St. Nicholas had to do with either. As we shall see, various archetypal festival rituals get grafted onto any holiday that is receptive to them, so that similar rituals appear across various holidays. By the same token, the nature of this process leaves open the possibility of developing new holidays.

The Structure of the Course of the Seasons and this Book

As matters have evolved over the past couple of millennia, our seasonal holidays have fallen into three groups of sequences. This book is organized according to them.

The first sequence, revolving around the winter solstice and thus the shortest of the three periods, is the time of most fundamental transition, from the death of the old year to the beginning of the new one. It includes both New Year's and, in Christian cultures, Christmas. This is the underlying mythical reason why the Western Christian liturgical year begins with the Christmas season. I considered beginning with Christmas in this book too, but decided to keep to our secular calendar because New Year's serves this purpose well enough and because Christmas, being a solstice holiday, also looks *toward* the next year.

The second sequence runs from the first hopes, expectations, and signs of the coming spring, beginning in February, through spring's end and the beginning of summer. It is a time of the resurrection of life, of love, and of youth. The holidays here are Groundhog Day (Imbolc/St. Brigid's Day), Valentine's Day, Carnival, Easter, and May Day (Beltane).

The third sequence runs from the summer solstice to the transition into winter (the period of death), when the sun is fading, the crops are harvested, and people confront the coming of winter. The holidays covered here are Halloween (Samhain/All Saints' Eve), Thanksgiving, and Christmas. Christmas, as a winter solstice holiday, also marks a turning point toward the new year.

I deviate from the seasonal emphasis to include American Independence Day, because it and other countries' national days and anniversaries of revolutions have archetypal characteristics and generate modern myths, though not based on the seasonal cycle. Thanksgiving likewise illustrates mythmaking in action.

In some chapters (especially those about Easter and Christmas) I discuss in some detail the psychological aspects of the myths and rituals underlying how we conceive of and celebrate out holidays. There are many potentially valid psychological approaches to the subject, especially from the field of depth psychology, but within the scope of this book there is insufficient space to discuss them all. Therefore, I utilize mainly the work of Carl Jung and so-called post-Jungians, stripped down to the bare essentials. I find that this approach has the most explanatory power in the cases of key holidays. For discussions of other possible approaches, as well as evaluations of the Jungian approach, I refer readers to two classic treatments of the various theories about the psychology of religion, David Wulff's *Psychology of Religion: Classic and Contemporary*, and Andrew Fuller's *Psychology & Religion: Eight Points of View*.[19]

CHAPTER 2

New Year's Day: Creation Renewed and Re-lived

New Year's Day is the most celebrated holiday in the world, and the only truly global one. It has been universal since the dawn of civilization. From this worldwide historical standpoint, and also from the anthropological and psychological standpoints, it is humanity's most important holiday, because it resonates with something inside us all, regardless of time or culture. New Year's also features many themes and rituals that reappear in other holidays as well, making it the mother of all holidays.

How Do We Decide When Is the New Year?

Since times immemorial people have kept track of the cycle of the moon, and early cultures created months to mirror this cycle, the names of which often corresponded to the seasonal events and human activities during a particular month. Originally our fundamental cycle of time was lunar, which is more obvious to people than the more gradual and subtle changes in the positioning of the sun; and it also corresponded with the female menstrual cycle. The trouble is that using lunar months doesn't enable us to track the seasons because 12 such months, which average about 29.5 days each, yield a "year" of only 354 days, so within a few years the seasons would go askew.

The rise of agriculture during Neolithic times altered our sense of time reckoning. If farmers relied solely on a lunar calendar, they would not know when to plant or harvest. The times of holidays also would

© The Author(s) 2020
A. George, *The Mythology of America's Seasonal Holidays*,
https://doi.org/10.1007/978-3-030-46916-0_2

constantly move. (This is why the date of Easter fluctuates: Its date is linked to the first full moon after the vernal equinox.) The ancients initially attempted to adjust for this either by annually adding a few days to each lunar-based year of 354 days or by adding an extra "month" every few years, a process called intercalation. But eventually people concluded that it is better to adopt the solar year as the fundamental cycle of time; the months (except February) were lengthened to accommodate the change to a solar year. This was first done in Egypt, but was most effectively achieved when Julius Caesar (with Egyptian help) adopted the Julian calendar in 46 BCE. That's one reason why the Roman Senate re-named a month in his honor: July.

Moving to a solar year was one thing, but deciding when the year ends and a new one begins is another. There are many possible ways to decide this. One way is to use annual astronomical phenomena, such as dating the New Year on or around a solstice or equinox. The Chinese and the Incas, for example, celebrated New Year's around the winter solstice (the Incas' being June 21, since they were in the southern hemisphere). An astronomical date could be full of symbolic meaning. For example, the winter solstice marks the beginning of the return of the sun, and therefore of fertility, and warm months. Mythologically speaking, this renewal symbolizes the sun's victory in the struggle between cosmic and chaotic powers. But this astronomical and mythological concept does not necessarily have anything to do with the annual cycles of human activity, and celebrating New Year's, say, on June 21 could interfere with work in a busy period of the year. Thus, an alternative approach was to base New Year's on the annual cycle of important human activities. In agricultural societies, the obvious choices in this regard were related to the vegetation cycle: just before sowing crops or just after the harvest. These two times of year were crucial in religious life, because the crops and the food supply were at stake, so at these times rituals were performed and deities were venerated and placated. Therefore, ancient civilizations usually marked the New Year based on the agricultural cycle. As this turns out, the sowing and harvesting seasons occur roughly around the spring and fall equinoxes, when both the earthly patterns of nature and astronomical patterns reverse themselves, so it was both feasible and logical to date this holiday of beginnings, endings, and transformation at these times. So some cultures dated New Year's in March when vegetation was sprouting and crops were sowed, as in Babylon,[1] ancient Greece, and (originally) the Roman Republic, while others celebrated New Year's in the autumn after the harvest was brought in, as in ancient Assyria, Israel and other Semitic cultures.

Originally the ancient Romans had only 10 months running from March to December, with no months in the winter (our January and February) because it was the "dead" time of the year when nothing of importance transpired. (This is why our months September–December mean the seventh through tenth months.) According to Roman tradition, January and February were added by Rome's second king, Numa (reigned 715–673 BCE), but we cannot be certain of this. In any event, the next important development came in 153 BCE (if not earlier), when January 1 was declared the beginning of the calendar year. Previously it had been March 1, being connected with the renewal of vegetation in the spring and the upcoming agricultural and military campaigning season. This new date for beginning the year served mainly civil governmental and legal purposes (e.g., newly elected Consuls took office then); the dates of the traditional March holiday festivals of religious significance remained unchanged. Changing them would have been impossible, bound as they were to the seasonal cycles of human activity and concerns.

Roman practice set the tone for New Year's in medieval and modern Western civilization. Most medieval Europeans in Christendom followed Rome in celebrating the New Year's on January 1. As Rome declined, the holiday retained its original pagan flavor (described below), so much so that in 567 CE the church's Second Council of Tours abolished January 1 as the beginning of the year, making that date instead the Feast of the Circumcision of Christ. For over 1000 years thereafter practice in Christian Europe varied widely. Depending on the time and place, the New Year was observed on December 25 (the birth of Jesus), on the Feast of the Annunciation (March 1 or 25), or at Easter. Finally, in 1582 Pope Gregory XIII established the Gregorian Calendar and restored January 1 as the beginning of the year. Most Europeans fell into line rather quickly, but in England March 25 (essentially the spring equinox, and the English Feast of the Annunciation) remained New Year's until 1752. This change applied to England's North American colonies too. So most of our founding fathers were born celebrating New Year's in March but celebrated it in January after American independence.

In order to understand New Year's rituals better we must first understand the mythological concepts and meanings underlying this holiday.

A Holiday of Recreation, Beginnings and Endings, and Transformations

The Romans named January after the god Janus, an ancient Italic (perhaps Sabine) god who predated the Romans, and who had no ancient Greek counterpart. It was he who welcomed in the New Year, which made eminent sense, as his essence and functions embodied its meaning. He was first and foremost a god of transitions. This made him a god of time, seeing the past and the future, and presiding over all sorts of endings and beginnings whether abstract or concrete, sacred or profane. These included sowing and harvesting, marriages, births and deaths, journeys, exchanges, and the beginnings of all months (which he presided over with the goddess Juno). Thus, he was portrayed as having two faces, on the front and back of his head, symbolizing his ability to see in both directions and hence too his awareness. As an aware god of beginnings, he was also a god of omens and auspices, and so he was invoked to ward off evil at beginnings, symbolized by the white thorn rod that he held in his right hand. (Thorn plants were thought to repel evil spirits.) Symbolizing passages and transitions, he was portrayed as holding a key in his left hand, making him an opener and closer of doors;[2] indeed, his name led to one Latin word for "door" or "gate" (ianua).[3] Thus, according to the Roman poet Ovid,[4] Janus presided at the doors of heaven together with the Horae, meaning that he was the means of access to all other deities; even Jupiter went in and out of heaven through his good offices. So when Romans invoked other deities, they first made offerings of incense and wine to Janus. He was an ubiquitous presence in religious ceremonies throughout the year, regardless of the deity principally being honored on each occasion. He served as the guardian of the universe: Whatever one sees – sky, sea, clouds – is closed up and opened by Janus. The Romans invoked and blessed Janus before the commencement of any significant activity, as when commencing war and reaching peace. His cult center was at Rome's Janiculum hill named after him. The structure, said to be built by king Numa, had an archway at each end through which the Roman armies marched on their way to and from war. Its gates remained open during wartime (so that the way back would lie open and allow easy access for making offerings to the god) and were closed during peacetime (so that peace would not leave). On each side it had 12 windows in a 4 x 3 pattern representing the four seasons of three months. Inside were 12 altars, one for each month, and a statue of Janus with his right hand bearing the number 300 and his left the number 65, together representing the number of days in the solar year. On New Year's Day sweet offerings (dates and wrinkled figs) were given to him so that the whole year would be a sweet journey, as well as coins to ensure continued prosperity.[5]

Ovid[6] tells a myth about Janus that is a key to the mythological underpinning of New Year's. He wrote that originally Janus was a primitive phenomenon that used to be personalized as Chaos. That is, originally Janus was a formless mass that developed into form having a multiplicity of features, so that he could take on the identifiable characteristics of a god. Whereas the primordial substance that would become the cosmos was, as Ovid put it, originally "just one heap," the creation process that *was* Janus enabled the primary elements (air, fire, water, and earth) to separate and form the objects and beings of the cosmos. Ovid then remarks, in an etiology that is probably fanciful, that Janus's two faces recall his original chaotic form when he once looked the same from any standpoint. This reflects the earliest type of creation myth in which the first deity constitutes and arises from the substance of primordial chaos and then self-evolves into the ordered cosmos. Thus, in an Egyptian creation myth the god Atum self-generates himself as a god from formless primeval waters so as to create other gods and ultimately the cosmos. In ancient Sumer, it was a primeval goddess, Nammu, who did much the same. In ancient Greece too Chaos was the first of the primeval deities, who then produced the other components of the universe represented by other divinities.[7]

In the somewhat later archetypal ancient creation myth, the creation of the cosmos is an ordering process in which the primordial formless substance (chaos), usually represented as water (since it lacks form), is brought into order and multiplicity by a sky-creator god. In mythological terms this process was often represented by such god engaging in a battle with a serpent monster or dragon (usually from the sea) that represented primordial chaos, known as the "dragon-fight motif." The sky-god vanquishes the chaos monster, after which he proceeds to create the cosmos (including humankind) by ordering it. The creation is finally complete when the creator-god decrees names and the destinies of humans and his other creations. The classic example is the Babylonian creation myth known as *Enuma Elish,* in which the Babylonian sky-god Marduk vanquishes the female chaos monster Tiamat, and forms the earth and the sky from the two halves of her corpse.

But in these myths chaos can never be permanently destroyed. Thus, in *Enuma Elish* a haunting feeling remains that Tiamat (chaos) has not been finally destroyed, that this cosmic struggle never really ends. Tiamat might resurrect and return at any time, so the myth ends by looking forward with hope to a future in which this will not happen:

> *May he [Marduk] vanquish Tiamat; may her life be strait and short!*
> *Into the future of mankind, when days have grown old,*
> *May she recede without cease and stay away forever.*[8]

Why do creation myths have this archetypal motif of bringing chaos into order? There are two main theories. The first, best articulated by the Dutch scholar Arent Wensinck nearly a century ago,[9] focuses on the fact that ancient peoples observed the seasonal cycles in nature in which healthy growing seasons of life would be preceded and followed again by periods of withering in the wintertime and/or parching summers, both periods characterized by a falling apart of the seasons of life and descent into death. Then a healthy world of water and life would come together again. According to this theory, people projected this experience onto the whole cosmos and backward in time to the process of creation. These seasonal cycles likewise determined a culture's seasonal holidays, first and foremost New Year's.

The other theory accounting for the archetypal chaos-into-order motif comes from depth psychology.[10] According to this view, the motif derives from our own experience of how we come into consciousness from an unconscious state, in which there is not much form or order, cause and effect are weakly linked, and time and space are not clear, which is why water is a typical symbol of the unconscious. We experience this when we wake up each day, and when we as young children are still developing a sense of our conscious self. Our development from a lower state of consciousness into full ego consciousness was also a historical fact in human evolution, an event symbolized in various myths, including, as I have argued elsewhere,[11] when Adam and Eve gained higher knowledge (of "good and evil") from eating the forbidden fruit. Such myths reflect our psyche experiencing ego consciousness coming into being as "world-becoming." As Marie-Louise von Franz put it, creation myths "describe not the origin of our cosmos, but the origin of man's conscious awareness of the world."[12] That is, from the perspective of our psyche, our becoming aware of the world and the world coming into existence are one and the same. Our ego consciousness wants to preserve this higher psychic state and fears slipping back into a murky unconscious state (which would mark the ego's destruction), while our unconscious psyche wants to pull our psyche back into its own realm (think about trying to wake up in the morning!), and thus threatens ego consciousness. In myths, this tension is represented as the primordial yet eternal struggle between order and formlessness, primeval chaos vs. cosmos, and heaven vs. the underworld. In human moral terms, the conflict is conceived of as one between good and evil. A god like Janus (likewise, e.g., Marduk and Yahweh) who brings and preserves order is therefore good and is to be venerated, while chaos and the unconscious are treated as evil spirits and ghosts of the underworld which threaten our existence and well-being. Hence the evil spirits who were thought to be active before New Year's and other points of transition during the year must be placated and temporarily repelled, but, just as in the case of Tiamat, they can never be finally destroyed, because the unconscious will never be destroyed but will continue to reassert itself.

The New Year naturally came to be conceived of in terms of this creation mythology. The coming around of the sun and the stars each year to the same position when the same eternal seasonal cycle of natural events begins again is obviously a cosmic ending and a new beginning. What ended and began again on New Year's was nothing less than the cosmos itself, the idea being that if the same cosmos were continuing there would be no such repetition. The New Year's holiday was not so much an annual memorial to the initial creation as literally a *renewal or re-creation of the cosmos*.[13] Since the New Year period entails the old cosmos ending, inevitably primordial chaos rears its head and gains the upper hand temporarily before the new cosmos (order) is established. In the end, the establishment of the New Year means that the creator god has overcome chaos again, re-creating and regaining control of the cosmos, which is good.

Conceiving of this transition from the old year to the new in cosmic terms enabled ancient peoples to locate themselves, for the period of the holiday, outside of everyday, profane earthly time and space and instead in a sacred cosmic realm. During this festival, they were with the gods in another reality, re-experiencing the most important and sacred event that ever happened. Since people experienced this every year, New Year's became the prime example of what Mircea Eliade called "the myth of the eternal return."[14] Thus, in the experience of the participants, the New Year's rituals do not so much *memorialize* the original creation as *repeat* it.[15] As we shall see, many other holidays also partake of this concept and thus have similar rituals. Therefore, it is helpful to review some key archetypal concepts and rituals at this point so that we may recognize them in our discussions of New Year's as well as other holidays.

Archetypal Patterns in New Year's Rituals

Before people can celebrate the New Year, they must first confront and dispose of the baggage from the old year (chaos), especially whatever taint of the bad that has remained. Further, people thought that during any such liminal time of transition, evil spirits were particularly active and had to be placated and/or repelled in order to keep them from tainting the New Year. Naturally, people conducted rituals to achieve this.

First, in many New Year's festivals people portrayed in rituals the negative aspects of the outgoing year as it was about to end. In its classic form, the situation at the end of the old year would be portrayed and experienced as a form of chaos. Sometimes the ritual was literally cosmogonic, as we shall see in the case of Babylon, while in other cases it was a milder expression of the same underlying idea. In some cultures, deities (especially patron deities of cities) were deemed to have gone out of the city or into the underworld (the realm of chaos, evil, and death), so in rituals people temporarily removed the statues of these deities from the city, or buried them, and then cleaned them up and brought them back for New Year's. In many cases hearth and ritual fires were put out (rendering the environment dark rather than light), to be rekindled once the New Year arrived. Another example was people acting out role reversals in society that symbolized a temporary breakdown in the social and political order, a form of chaos. Thus, a political ruler or high religious official would temporarily lose his powers, sometimes being replaced by a mock king or Pope. Our contemporary tradition of excessive drinking on New Year's Eve fits this pattern, which of course is experienced as disorder!

Another archetypal ritual was to purge any existing or threatened elements of contamination or evil (manifestations of chaos) before the New Year, in order to safeguard people and their possessions in the coming year. This was done mainly through ritual purifications of the environment, communities of people, and individuals. Individuals, for example, might tend to confess their sins, fast or undergo other deprivations, or ceremonially wash themselves, while communities tended toward purifying sacred community spaces (e.g., temples) and driving out evil spirits. In the ancient world, "purification" was not so much individually spiritual in nature as being directed toward eliminating evil spirits and their maleficent influence on the community.[16] The purifications were carried out by various common methods, such as:

- Sweeping and cleaning a temple with water, which symbolically clears the dust and dirt of the old year
- Using fire to burn away evil and frighten away evil spirits
- Burning incense to produce smoke that purifies the air
- Conducting sacrifices to purify places and expiate evil, and also to placate deities
- Scapegoat rituals to carry away the evil that had settled on the community during the old year
- Raising a din (especially rattling and banging noises) to scare away evil spirits and ghosts
- Cleaning the cult statues of key deities in advance of the New Year
- Smearing doors and doorframes with apotropaic substances to keep evil spirits out

These traditional rituals are still reflected in our modern New Year's rituals. The ancient tradition of raising a din is reflected in our custom of blowing horns, using other noisemakers, and ringing bells on New Year's Eve and at midnight. According to one superstition, you should sweep out (i.e., purify) your house before midnight on New Year's Eve, otherwise the old year's dirt will be carried into the new. Another says that you should pay your bills (again a type of purification) before January 1, lest you be in debt during the New Year.[17]

The struggle between good and evil on New Year's was sometimes symbolized and reenacted thorough sporting events or other contests (fights) between two teams. Inevitably, good would win, in order to guarantee a good next year. This is actually the precedent for our staging of football games on New Year's.

Once the necessary rituals for ending the old year were completed, people were ready to meet the New Year. This was literally the ominous moment when past and future meet, called the "witching hour."[18] Naturally, it was common to engage in divination and augury, because people wanted to know what the New Year would bring. Thus, in Rome the College of Augurs would look for omens and advise the populace.[19] Our tradition of New Year's resolutions derives from such omen rituals, but reflects a proactive approach of controlling our own destiny rather than relying on external signs.

Once the tension-filled moments had safely passed, people could celebrate with banquets and drinking, congratulations, visits, and gift giving. A flip side was that for so long as the New Year was being celebrated, one should not engage in the kind of end-of-year purifications that were just completed. This is reflected in some of our modern New Year superstitions, such as not to throw anything away or wash anything on New Year's (or you'll wash a family member away).[20]

We can now review how these archetypal patterns were exemplified in the mythologies underlying the New Year's festivals in the ancient, medieval, and modern worlds. Due to space considerations, I cannot carry out such a detailed culture-by-culture comparison with the other holidays, but it is important to do so in the case of New Year's because the holiday is so fundamentally important, because the comparisons bring out the various common themes and their meanings in concrete cultural contexts, and because some of these same themes and rituals reappear in connection with other holidays.

New Year's Festivals in the Ancient World

The New Year's festivals in the ancient world embodied aspects of the mythology described above. I cannot discuss all of them, so I cover only Babylon, Egypt, Israel, Greece, and Rome, because they all contain the above-mentioned archetypal elements, which are also present in our own New Year's celebrations.

Babylon

The best ancient example of the above mythology is the New Year's festival in Babylon. The Babylonians thought of their city as the sacred center of the world where the creation had occurred, and so was called a *duranki*, meaning "the bond of heaven and earth" or "the place where heaven and earth meet," giving its people access to the gods.[21] We see this idea in action in their New Year's festival.

In Babylon, where Marduk was the city's patron deity, the New Year was celebrated in the spring, close to the equinox during the first 11 days of the month of Nisan (approximately our March). This is when the inactivity of winter was ending and vegetation was returning – signs of renewal and rebirth. The Babylonians were about to sow their new crops in antici-pation of spring rains. A new cycle was beginning, making it an appropri-ate time for New Year's.

The New Year's festival, called the Akitu festival, began with three days of purifications at the city's temple of Marduk, the Esagila ("the lofty house"). The means of purification included water, smoke, fire, recitation of spells, and smearing the temple doors with resin. These purifications served to eliminate evil from the temple precinct so that the ensuing ritu-als would be uncontaminated and effective.

On the fourth day, after morning prayers, a blessing of the temple, and an evening meal, the High Priest recited *Enuma Elish* (the Babylonian creation myth) in its entirety, reading it to a statue of Marduk. This liturgy served to recall the primordial chaos that existed before the creation of the cosmos, before earthly time and the cycle of the seasons came into being. Indeed, until day seven of the festival, Marduk was deemed to be confined in the underworld, here thought of as being inside a mountain, which was represented in the city by a ziggurat next to the Esagila temple called the Etemenanki ("temple of the foundation of heaven and earth"). He seems to have been incarcerated in the company of criminals there.[22] As such, he was caught in the realm of primordial chaos and therefore of death, deprived of the sun. Correspondingly, since he, the creator god, had dis-appeared from the cosmos, affairs back on earth in the city likewise were deemed to have fallen into the throes of chaos. The populace wandered through the city streets asking, "Where is he held captive?" They thought of themselves as descending into the underworld to look for him, which was represented by their laments and wailings. This was quite literally life back in the primordial realm before (another) creation, when Marduk would re-create order, literally a new cosmos.

The fifth day was one of atonement and further purification. It began with an exorcist purifying the Esagila temple, most particularly the shrine of Marduk's son Nabu within it, where a statue of Nabu would soon be placed temporarily as part of the ritual. After an exorcist cleaned the shrine, he summoned a slaughterer, who ritually slaughtered (sacrificed) a sheep.[23] The carcass of the sheep, a kind of scapegoat bearing the bad from the old year, was then cast into the Euphrates. Since the exorcist and the slaugh-terer were now considered unclean (having taken upon themselves the taint of the victim), they went out to the countryside (i.e., into the realm of chaos, much as in the Israelite scapegoat ritual) until the festival was over, so as not to re-contaminate the temple.

Later that day came a ritual humiliation of the king before the statue of Marduk.[24] As the head of the kingdom, which is the most important part of the earthly order, the king must have his power restored on New Year's, and for this to happen he must be out of power for a brief period when chaos prevails. Thus, the king's experience during the festival conceptually paralleled Marduk's. In the ritual, the high priest stripped the king of his scepter, ring, scimitar, and crown, which were placed before the statue of Marduk. The priest then struck the king on the cheek, made him kneel, and dragged him by the ears before Marduk. The king, as Marduk's steward on earth, then recited a negative declaration of innocence, in which he affirmed that over the last year he had not sinned, had not been negligent before Marduk, had tended the Esagila and not forgotten the rituals, had not harmed those under his protection, and had done nothing to cause the destruction of Babylon. The king then provisionally regained his regalia, hence too his dignity and powers, but the judgment of Marduk now awaited. The priest struck him once more on the cheek, hard. If tears flowed, this meant that Marduk had accepted the declaration; if not, then Marduk was angry and the king would meet his downfall. In this ritual, therefore, the chaos swamping the earth was thus seen to reach the very summit of human society,[25] but this also set the stage for beginning the New Year (new creation) on a proper basis.

On day six Marduk's son Nabu was led to the Esagila. On the way there he was taken to a pigsty to inspect boars. They apparently represented the criminals with whom Marduk was imprisoned, and Nabu had them killed (thus too the criminals in the underworld). When Nabu arrived at the temple, he was then enthroned on the Throne of Destiny. From this position, on the seventh day Nabu and the other gods completed their defeat of the underworld forces of death and liberated Marduk.

On day eight the gods assembled to determine the destiny of the liberated Marduk. As in *Enuma Elish*, Marduk was assigned to fight Tiamat. He again stood at the head of the pantheon, and Nabu's role in the festival was essentially over. Marduk then rode in a procession to the Akitu House,[26] a temple outside the city walls where he took his seat. (One of Marduk's epithets was "The Lord who sits in the midst of Tiamat at the Akitu festival.") The temple and its precinct outside the city (i.e., outside ordered civilization) seem to have represented the realm of primordial chaos, since that necessarily is where Marduk fights Tiamat. The Akitu House was probably decorated with motifs from *Enuma Elish*, and we know that when Marduk arrived there his statute was placed on a dais representing the primordial sea.[27]

Marduk remained at the Akitu House until the 11th and climactic day of the festival. That morning the gods held a banquet to celebrate Marduk's victory over Tiamat. Then Marduk rode in a procession celebrating his triumphant return to his city. Once there, Marduk took his throne and the gods assembled to decree the destinies of the Babylonians for the coming year. This probably replicated the episode in *Enuma Elish* when, after defeating Tiamat, Marduk created humankind and decreed its destiny. Finally, a sacred marriage ritual between Marduk and his wife Sarpanitum was enacted, designed to ensure fertility of the crops, animals, and humans. The period in which life in nature had been suspended was now over, and the activities of the New Year could begin. The people could now go out into their fields and sow the crops.

The myth and ritual in the Babylonian New Year's festival show that the New Year entailed nothing less than a new creation of the world, in this case according to the archetypal dragon-fight motif. People actually believed this was happening, and they had the privilege of experiencing this holy event in sacred time and space. We also see various archetypal forms of purification from the taint of the old year, followed by a happy outcome that enabled people to celebrate and then safely and confidently undertake their activities in the New Year.

Egypt

In ancient Egypt the rhythm of the agricultural year was different than anywhere else, which made the timing of its New Year as well as its rituals somewhat distinctive. Unlike in Mesopotamia and Syria-Palestine, Egypt was not dependent on the rains, which in that desert land were insufficient to support agriculture. Rather, Egyptian civilization depended on the annual inundation of the Nile, which brought water for the crops (which Egyptians stored in irrigation systems) and also deposited fresh, fertile silt in which to grow the new crops each year. Thus, Egypt did not need or have rain gods, but many deities were associated with the Nile, its inundation, and the animals and plants living in it. The timing and volume of the inundation varied from year to year. Too little water and there would not be enough for the crops, while too much flooding would overwhelm and damage the fields and irrigation systems, and sweep away animals and buildings. The inundation usually started at the end of May or early June, its height was usually in early August, and the floodwaters receded by mid-September or early October. At that point farmers could sow the crops in the new, moist soil.

As a result of this cycle, Egypt had three seasons of four months each, called Inundation, Coming Forth (referring to the sprouting of newly sown crops), and Harvest. The original Egyptian calendar placed the beginning of the year on the day when the brightest star in the sky, Sirius (Sothis in Greek, Sepdet in Egyptian), first appeared in the pre-dawn sky after an absence of some 70 days. The exact date of this heliacal rising shifted over the centuries: In 3100 BCE it was on June 20, but by 145 BCE it occurred on July 19 or 20.[28] Originally this date was near the first day of the first month of the Inundation season.

Just as the Egyptians had various creation myths, they had varying understandings of what and when was the New Year, because the New Year was viewed as a new creation on the anniversary of the original creation. In one understanding, which took an astronomical approach, the day of the rising of Sirius was considered the anniversary of the creation of the world.[29] Since this was the first day of the cosmos, it was also the day in which the sun-god Ra rose for the first time, so it was Ra's birthday and was celebrated as the Feast of the Birth of Ra. One of Ra's epithets was "opener of the year."[30] Sirius was personified and deified as the goddess Sepdet. Originally, she was considered a messenger of Isis, informing the Egyptians that Osiris had arisen from the dead. Egyptians made this link to Isis because Sirius rose low in the sky near the Nile itself, in the early morning hours much like Venus, with which Isis was identified. Indeed, the resurrection of Osiris (symbolizing renewed life and victory over death) was associated with the rising of the Nile waters. According to Egyptian myth, it was the tears of Isis from mourning over Osiris that were responsible for the swelling of the river, and which helped resurrect him.[31] New Year's was thus tied to the inundation, which by then was getting into full swing. By this time the anxious Egyptians could tell whether the waters would be too little or too much, either of which would mean that chaos is getting the upper hand. This meant that, as of New Year's, the Egyptians could determine the destiny of the New Year.

According to the Egyptian Heliopolitan creation myth, the world emerged from the primordial waters (*nun*) as a primeval mound of earth. Egyptologists believe this concept came from Egyptians observing the annual emergence of new fertile soil when the floodwaters of the Nile receded. This event marked the first day of earthly time, and hence was the beginning of the first year. Egyptians logically marked this event, occurring on the first day of the first month of the Coming Forth season, as the beginning of the New Year, since by then the floodwaters were receding and crops could be sown. Egyptian kings came to link the formal beginning of their own reigns with this new creation of the world, a cosmic cycle in nature. Accordingly, new kings scheduled their formal coronations on this New Year.

There is a corresponding mythology behind coronating the king on New Year's. The new cosmic order commencing on New Year's included the human socio-political order, which had at its apex the king, who was divine. The creator god Ra, the ultimate king of the cosmos, including earth, was thought to have delegated his powers over Egypt to the king, thought of as his son and in whom the god Horus was incarnate. Thus, on his coronation on New Year's, the king was thought to become Horus and take his office on the Throne of the Living.[32] This was thought to create on earth a new era of order and justice *(maat)*.

On New Year's Eve, which was the last day of the Inundation season, a ritual was held in which the god Osiris was interred, and then a *djed* pillar representing Osiris was raised with ropes by priests and the king (or his delegate). The internment probably was thought of as the sowing of the seeds, while the raising of the *djed* pillar represented the resurrection of Osiris and so too the sprouting of the crops.[33] The two rituals were linked, because in Egypt the ritual of internment facilitated resurrection in the hereafter, hence the ritual's application to the planting and sprouting of seeds. Performing these rituals was a prerequisite for the well-being of Egypt in the coming year.

New Year's Day, the first day of the Coming Forth season, was celebrated with the Nehebkau feast,[34] named after the serpent-god Nehebkau. His name means "uniter of the kas."[35] The ka is the vital spark or life force of being and sustenance that everything in existence has, including gods and even plants and plain objects which today we (unlike the Egyptians) think of as inanimate. Their ka is the source of continuing in the state of being. It is lost upon death, so its loss is the mark of death. Thus, when a king dies, his ka (that of Horus) leaves his body until the body is interred, which ritual marked the reuniting of the ka (now that of Osiris) with his body and his resurrection into the hereafter. In line with the creation mythology, regardless of when the king actually died, his internment ritual was not carried out until this New Year's period. At that point Horus (including his ka) could become incarnate in the new king. Accordingly, at his coronation on New Year's the new king adopted his "Horus name" as part of his royal title. At that point both the kas of the old king and Osiris, as well as those of the new king and Horus, were finally correspondingly united. Annually on New Year's, the anniversary of the king's coronation was celebrated, and the ritual was thought to reconfirm his vitality and power. By analogy, what happened to the king was extended to all of Egypt, including its people and vegetation, all of which had kas. Nehebkau's magic was thought to be the agency for all this, so he was venerated at the New Year's feast held in his name.

The Egyptian New Year is another illustration of ancient Egypt's uniqueness. Unlike in Mesopotamia, there was no atonement or similar cleansing ritual, no humiliation or confession of the king, no sacred marriage, and no determination of destinies. The only period of chaos was between the death of a king in the prior year and the new king's coronation. But in both cases New Year's was linked to the king's renewal and the sowing of new crops.

Israel

The ancient Israelites had two traditional New Year's festivals, both in the autumn, which eventually were combined into a single holiday period. One came from pre-Israelite Canaan and was agricultural in character, while the other was derived from the nomadic tradition outside Canaan.

The agricultural New Year's was already a traditional Canaanite festival long before the emergence of Israel. It was an autumn harvest festival, in Israelite times called the Feast of the Ingathering. It occurred after the olive and grape harvest had been pressed, around the autumnal equinox. The holiday was celebrated over seven days, mainly in the vineyards but culminating in the local sanctuary/temple, where a ritual meal was held. As in the case of the Dionysian festivals of ancient Greece, in Canaan vineyards, grapes, and wine lent themselves to this type of festival. Wine was important to the Canaanite economy and the people's welfare. Vineyards represented life, fertility, and well-being, and were connected with divinity. Having a successful vineyard was considered a divine blessing, for which offerings and thanks were due during the festival.

The festival was celebrated right in the vineyards. There the celebrants built and stayed in temporary booths made of freshly cut leafy branches, to symbolize life and fertility – booths of life. While the festival included solemn ritual and prayer, it also featured ecstatic merrymaking thought to achieve union with the divine, including dances by young women (Judg 21: 21), intoxication from wine, feasting, nakedness, and sex. The intoxication from imbibing wine was seen as divine inspiration and a divine experience. A key part of the festival, in traditional Canaanite practice and at least in the early Israelite period, was the sacred marriage rite involving ritual intercourse, thought to connect the participants and the community with the divine and ensure fertility in the coming year.

Only at a late stage did the priestly establishment in Jerusalem associate the holiday with Exodus ideology, calling it the Feast of Booths (Sukkoth), which from then on could be celebrated only in Jerusalem. In the new official theology, instead of New Year's being a harvest festival, it commemorated the Exodus and the 40-year sojourn in the wilderness, and no sacred marriage ritual was held. The booths were now taken to symbolize the tents in which the Hebrews lived in the Sinai wilderness before entering Canaan, and living in the booths during the festival was designed to inspire people to reflect on that legendary past.

Since the festival celebrated the New Year, naturally it was associated with creation, so a mythological account of creation (or re-creation) would be recited or perhaps reenacted on the occasion. Originally in the Canaanite festival, the mythological combat utilized was most likely the traditional Canaanite myth of Baal defeating the sea monster Yam (again the dragon-fight motif), vestiges of which appear in the Hebrew Bible.[36] It is less clear how this myth was handled in Israelite times, but some scholars have suggested that Psalm 104, which among other things celebrates Yahweh setting the earth on its secure foundations and controlling the primordial waters of chaos and setting boundaries for them so that they will never (again) engulf the earth, was used in Jerusalem temple liturgy,[37] and so probably was sung at this festival. The festival became associated with Moses's consecration of the Tabernacle in the Sinai and Yahweh's glory filling the Tabernacle, which was said to have occurred at New Year's (Exod 40: 2–34). Likewise, Solomon consecrated his temple at the time of this festival. Naturally, the culmination of the festival was the enthronement of Yahweh in the temple, much like that of Marduk at the end of the Akitu festival. Mythologically speaking, the consecration of the temple and the enthronement of Yahweh were thought to mark the culmination of the creation, which at this point in Israelite history likely meant the seven-day creation myth in Genesis 1. Some scholars believe that Genesis 1 has a liturgical nature and may have been recited as part of the seven-day festival's ritual,[38] even if vestiges of Canaanite creation myths remained.

More generally, outside the formal priestly liturgy, the holiday celebrated the fertility bestowed on this Promised Land by Yahweh, including "wine to gladden the human heart" (Ps 104: 15). In still later tradition, New Year's Day (Rosh Hashanah) came to be considered the anniversary of the creation of Adam and Eve.

The original harvest New Year's festival probably included some element of purification but we don't know what that was. New Year's purification rituals become visible only in the Israelite period, when they were performed for 10 days after New Year's culminating on the Day of Atonement (Yom Kippur); the cleansing was finally completed five days later, when people celebrated the Feast of Booths (Sukkoth). This is where the nomadic/wilderness tradition makes itself felt, it being represented in Leviticus 16. This day was one of fasting and prayer in which a scapegoat was assigned to the demon Azazel to bear the community's accumulated sins of the past year. The scapegoat was expelled into the desert wilderness (i.e., back into chaos) to carry away all sins, while another goat was sacrificed as a sin offering to Yahweh, and the carcass was then destroyed "outside the camp" (later outside Jerusalem). The priest who conducted this ritual, much like the one in the Babylonian sheep sacrifice ritual, was now deemed tainted, and he and his clothes had to undergo an ablution before returning to the community. The Israelite New Year's festival is unlike most New Year's festivals in that the purifications occur not at the end of the old year but at the onset of the new year, but the purpose was the same.

Greece

New Year's in Athens[39] was also the city's birthday and name day (Panathenaia), which was the subject of an etiological myth portrayed on the west pediment of the Parthenon. Soon after the city was founded, it needed to adopt a patron deity. Both Athena and Poseidon coveted the role, and since Zeus could not resolve the dispute the gods agreed to let the city itself, through its king Cecrops, choose which deity it wanted, based on what gift each would give to the city. Poseidon struck his trident on a rock to produce a spring of seawater that formed the Sea of Erekhtheis, meaning that the gift was one of navigation and naval power. Athena gave the olive tree on the Acropolis, a symbol of agriculture and peace (hence our "olive branch"). The city chose Athena. This points to the political and propagandistic nature of the Athenian New Year's holiday.

The New Year began with the first new moon after the summer solstice, which was the first day of the first month, Hecatombaion (normally in our early July).[40] This month and others were named after a festival held during the particular month. Some were old agricultural festivals that reflected the rhythm of seasonal activity, while others reflected the urbanized life of the polis. New Year's rituals in classical Athens mostly fell into the latter category. During the weeks leading up to it, several minor festivals served in whole or in part to wind down the old year and set the stage for the New Year's celebrations, in the archetypal manner that we have already seen in other cultures, especially in respect of purification rituals.[41]

The first of these rituals was at the Thargelia, celebrated in late May-early June.[42] This was a cleansing of the city for the upcoming New Year by means of a scapegoat ritual. A convicted criminal who was already condemned to death was selected to be a *pharmakos* ("magic man"), since such a person already had evil upon him.[43] After first being feasted on barley cakes and cheese, he was led through the city streets and flogged with wild fig branches, leeks, and other wild plants, which was done to the accompanying music of flutes. This beating was thought to help expel evil from the city. Leeks and fig sprigs were used because they have strong smells, which were considered purgative.[44] Thus, hanging a leek over one's door was thought to ward off evil. At the end of the ritual, the *pharmakos* was either killed or permanently expelled, the main point being that he was so infected and tabooed that he could never return to the city. Once this was done and the feelings of the Athenians were relieved, the city could undertake the more particular purifications in subsequent holidays leading up to the New Year.

The next step was to cleanse and re-dress the city's ancient wooden image of Athena in the Plynteria ("washing") festival on the 22nd of Thargelion (sometime in our June). The statue was ceremonially veiled, undressed and stripped of its gear, and taken down to the sea to be washed in its water. This was all done by women. In the procession to the sea, called the Hegeteria, the women carried cakes of figs. Since the city was now temporarily unprotected by its patron deity, this period was considered impure, so all temples were closed and no business was done, lest chaos arise. Athena was brought back to the city as part of the Kallynteria festival, when she was re-dressed, re-decked, and beautified. The festival's name comes from the Greek words for broom *(kalluntron)* and to sweep or beautify *(kalluno)*, and refers to sweeping out Athena's temple to purify it before she is brought back. The Kallynteria involved purifying not only Athena's temple but all sacred places in the city.

Next came the nocturnal Arrephoria festival on the 3rd of the last month of the year, Skirophorion (late June or the beginning of July). In the ritual, two maidens[45] of noble parentage between 7 and 11 years old who had lived for nearly a year on the Acropolis preparing for this moment were each given a covered basket with a sacred object in it unknown to them. Starting at the Erechtheum where Athena's sacred olive tree grew, they descended down the north slope of the Acropolis into an underground passage, where they left the baskets without uncovering them. While there, they picked up another item wrapped in a veil and brought it to the surface, at which point they were discharged from their duties; other maidens continued the festival ritual. What exactly they carried each way remains unknown to us, but apparently it served to placate and keep away evil chthonic spirits or ghosts for the next year, so as to protect the city. The leading theory is that they were snake images, which would confront and confound the troublesome underground spirits, since they too were conceived of as snakes, so this would have been an exercise in sympathetic magic.[46]

Later in the month of Skirophorion came the Skirophoria festival. It was mainly a festival of dissolution prior to New Year's, but it was also designed to renew the soil and prepare it for the autumnal sowing. The festival began with a procession from the Erechtheum in Athens to Skiron near Eleusis, where there was a temple to Demeter and Kore, and another to Athena. The procession was led by the priestess of Athena and the priests of Poseidon and Helios, who walked under a white canopy *(skiron)*. (Correspondingly, the Erechtheum, a joint temple of Athena and Poseidon, was closed.) During the middle of the festival reigned some form of wantonness and dissolution (although we don't know the details) marking chaos at the end of the old year. On the final (third) day of the festival an ox was sacrificed on the Acropolis in Athens, through which evil and collective guilt were expiated.

On the 12th of the first month of the New Year, Hecatombaion, Athenians held the Kronia festival, in honor of the Titan Kronos, who was thought to have ruled the cosmos during the Golden Age, when social distinctions and oppression did not exist. Thus, this too was a festival of dissolution followed by cleansing. The fixed order of society was suspended and people's roles were reversed. Slaves were invited to banquets of their owners and they played games together, and the owners waited on their servants. Slaves ran through the streets making noise. The original concept of the dissolution as representing primordial chaos was altered to symbolize socio-political harmony in Athens. For good measure there was probably a sacrifice; also, much as in the Thargelia, a criminal who had already been condemned to death was led out, fed food and wine, and then slain.

The final preliminary festival, on the 16th of Hecatombaion, was the Sunoikia, which led into the political aspects of New Year's. It celebrated the unification of the towns of Attica under Athens by Theseus (the *sunoikismos*), according to myth. Its main ritual was a sacrifice to the goddess Eirene ("Peace") on the Acropolis. This festival brought Attica into a unified and stable state following the prior festivals of dissolution and purification, ready to celebrate New Year's.

The Panathenaia, which lasted several days beginning on the third day from the end of Hecatombaion, started with solemn, symbolic ceremonies and then became purely a celebration of the city's splendor. At sunrise a torch was kindled at the grove of Akademos outside the city, where a sacrifice to Eros and Athena was made. The torch was then carried to the Dipylon Gate of Athens, where a procession formed from all elements of the population proceeded up to the altar of Athena on the Acropolis. There a new robe made by the women of Athens was presented to the statue of Athena, the motif of which was the battle with the Gigantes, representing victory over the chaotic forces outside civilization. Then numerous animals including 100 oxen were sacrificed, the meat from which was distributed to the populace in the marketplace *(agora)* during a banquet on the final night of the festival called the Pannychis, meaning "all-nighter." The celebrations included the Panathenaic Games involving various athletic contests highlighted by a chariot/foot race. Poetry and music competitions were also held.

Rome

Originally the Romans celebrated New Year's on March 1. When it was moved to January 1, this date was used mainly for civil and political purposes, and as described above mythologically was associated with Janus. The traditional, mainly agricultural, festivals connected with the old New Year in March did not and could not change, tied as they were to the cycle of the seasons and farming. March was named after the god Mars, who was not only the god of war but (from much earlier) also that of agriculture. March was named after him because that is the month of the reawakening of life and vegetation after the long sleep of winter, when farmers were again becoming active and needed divine protection. An old farmer's prayer reported to us by Cato the Elder in his book *On Agriculture* (ca. 160 BCE) captures the farmer's state of mind:

> Father Mars, I pray and beseech thee that thou mayest be propitious and well-disposed to me, our home and household, for which cause I have ordered the offering of pig, sheep, and ox to be led round my field, my land, and my farm, that thou might prevent, ward off and avert diseases, visible and invisible, barrenness and waste, accident and bad water, that thou wouldest permit the crop and fruit of the earth, the vines and shrubs to wax great and prosper, [and] that thou wouldest preserve the shepherds and their flocks in safety and give prosperity and health to me and our house and household.[47]

Thus, Ovid begins his account of March by telling Mars to lay down his arms for a while, and release his shining hair from his helmet. That's how he had come upon the Vestal Silvia, who bore for him Romulus. According to Ovid, it was Romulus who named March after his father.[48]

Much as in Greece, the period before (old) New Year's had a series of purification festivals. This month, February, was named after pieces of wool or other items *(februum,* plural *februa)* used in these purification rituals.[49] The preparatory February festivals were as follows:

Parentalia (our February 13–21). This was when people honored and placated the ghosts of their dead ancestors. On the first day, a Vestal Virgin performed a public ceremony in honor of the dead, but otherwise the rituals were held privately within each family. The public ceremony seems to have been motivated by the legend in which a Vestal, Tarpeia, betrayed Rome to the Sabines and was crushed to death because of her treachery, so her ghost was thought to be malevolent unless appeased in a Vestal ritual.[50]

Lupercalia (February 15, during but not part of the Parentalia). At the cave of the Lupercal, where Romulus and Remus were said to have been nurtured by the she-wolf, two goats (known for fertility) were sacrificed and two youths from the two colleges of priests in Rome (Luperci) were smeared on the forehead with the blood of the victims, which they wiped off with wool dipped in milk, after which they had to laugh. Then they dressed in the two fleeces of the sacrificed goats, from which they each also cut two strips for *februa* and which they held in each hand. (The Lupercalia may have subsumed an older spring cleaning festival called the Februa.) They proceeded to run around the walls of the Palatine, thereby protecting and purifying the border of the old town. While doing so, they struck women in the palms of their hands with the *februa*, the women offering themselves for this purpose. The *februa* were thought to have magical power, so that the beating chased away evil spirits and promoted the fertility of the stricken women. This festival lasted until at least the end of the fifth century CE, when, at least according to tradition, Pope Gelasius suppressed it and converted it into the Feast of the Purification of the Virgin Mary (or possibly the feast of St. Valentine).[51]

Feralia (February 21). On the last day of the Parentalia, the gods were deemed to be inactive and the temples were closed, so that attention could be focused on the placation of ghosts. The name appears to derive from the Latin *ferre* (also Greek *ferō*) meaning "to carry," referring to offerings that families carried to the tombs. Another ritual involved an old hag who, while sitting with girls, performed a magical rite with a fish head and black beans. Its purpose seems to have been to silence potentially hostile tongues of spirits from harming the living.

Caristia (February 22). Having just placated the dead at the Parentalia, the living now turned to each other to renew and firm up ties, and patch up any old quarrels. A family feast was held in which each member brought his or her own contribution. (Any truly wicked people were not invited.) The *Lares* (guardian spirits) of the household were also honored with offerings. The Catholic Church later converted this family feast into the Feast of St. Peter.[52]

Regifugium. This ritual, meaning "flight of the king," fell six days before March 1. The name may hark back to the historical expulsion of the tyrannical King Tarquinius, which resulted in the establishment of the Republic in 509 BCE. So it seems to have been a kind of independence (or revolution anniversary) day, which traditionally involves a cleansing of the community from impure elements. In the ritual, the *rex sacrorum* (a priest who was the only "rex" in the Republic), conducted a sacrifice at the Comitia (public assembly) and then made a hasty exit. While the political interpretation was in the back of Romans' minds, the real origin of the ritual probably lay in the sacrifice made just before New Year's.[53]

New Year's on March 1 was a day of renewal featuring a festival in honor of Mars, whose birthday fell on this date. The sacred Vestal fire was tended and fresh laurels (sacred to Mars) were affixed to prominent buildings around the city, including at the shrine of Mars at the Regia. The main ritual was the dance of his priests called the Salii ("leapers"). They were patrician men whose parents were still alive. They assumed military dress, wore swords, and carried shields and spears. They walked in procession through the city beating their shields with their swords, stopping at places to perform dances to flute music and sing a hymn. In the evening they hung up their weapons and went to an elaborate banquet. Most likely this ritual was originally agricultural in nature and became militarized over time. The beating was designed to drive away evil spirits, while the dance and song may have served to promote the growth of the crops (soon to be sown).[54]

March 1 was also devoted to Juno Lucina, and rituals were held at her temple in her ancient grove in connection with her role as goddess of childbirth. To women, this day was also known as the Matronalia. The epithet Lucina probably comes from *lux* ("light"), referring to babies being born into the light. Women participating in the ritual had to unbind their hair, not wear any belts, and untie any knots on their clothing, so as to symbolically eliminate anything that might hamper childbirth. Husbands gave their wives presents, and the wives dressed and entertained and fed their slaves (who had the day off).[55] The Matronalia may have originated our tradition of New Year's babies.

New Year's in Post-Roman Europe

Celtic New Year's

In Celtic Europe the year had only summer and winter seasons, beginning respectively on May 1 and November 1. (The major holidays were not on or around the solstices and equinoxes.) New Year's was November 1, well after the harvest when people were ready to turn their attention to winter. On the occasion the Celts, at least in Ireland, celebrated the three-day feast of Samhain, their main holiday of the year. The death of the old year was marked by extinguishing all fires in the land, and the New Year was ushered in by lighting new fires.

I discuss Samhain in more detail in Chap. 9 since it relates more to Halloween.

The Effect of Christianization

The native festivals in Europe gradually changed under the influence of Rome and then the Catholic Church. In Christendom New Year's was folded into the Christian holiday period connected with the Christian Feast of the Nativity, December 25, which later became known as Christmas, and initially confusion resulted.[56] In 567 the Second Council of Tours declared that the whole period of 12 days between the Nativity and Epiphany was a single festal cycle, which became known as the "12 days of Christmas." The Council confirmed that the old Roman Kalendae (January 1–3) would be part of it, as days of fasting. But the old festive New Year's tradition would not die, and people still celebrated in the old way. In the eighth century the church tried to Christianize the occasion, declaring January 1 to be the Feast of the Circumcision of Christ. This established the holiday cycle of December 25, January 1, and January 6 that still exists today.[57]

New Year's in the British Isles

Since it is not feasible to discuss New Year's across all of modern Europe, I focus here on what are now the British Isles, since they reflect both Celtic and Christian influence, and in turn most directly influenced celebrations in the United States.

Easter remained the principal annual festival in southern Europe and the Mediterranean, but in northern Europe, where the darkness and cold of midwinter were more pronounced and the pre-Christian pattern of winter solstice celebrations was traditionally strong, the occasion of the Nativity became more prominent. Further, in what had been Roman Britain, the January 1 new year date and its celebration survived. In 1155 the English Crown reverted to the early Roman month of March as beginning the New Year, picking the 25th because this was already the Feast of the Annunciation. This was not changed back to January 1 until the above-mentioned reform of 1752.

The ideas and rituals of New Year's varied somewhat as between England, Wales, Scotland, and Ireland, but there were also many similarities. Many traditions fall under the broad category of rituals known as "wassailing." The word wassail comes from a toast meaning, "Be in good health." During New Year's, wassailing rituals were designed to ensure the good health and well-being of people and their possessions, crops, and animals for the coming year.

Thus, in England, at least, a form of the Celtic New Year's bonfires remained in the form of "fire wassailing," usually a set of 12 fires around fields. The explanations behind these fires came to vary widely, but the underlying idea seems to have been to scare away evil spirits, witches, and other enemies that come out on New Year's Eve, so that the crops would be protected from blight.[58] In the Scottish highlands, people also hung up holly in their houses to keep out the fairies.

Another ritual was "orchard wassailing," practiced in the cider producing areas of England to ensure the health of the apple trees over the next year. Groups of people would visit an apple orchard on New Year's Night. While gathered around a particular tree, the partiers would toast and pray for a good apple crop, sing songs, and pour some cider over the roots of the tree.[59] Thus, one such wassailing song ran:

> Stand fast root, bear well top
> Pray the God send us a howling good crop.
> Every twig, apples big,
> Every bough, apples now.[60]

Then, like the ancients, the celebrants would raise a din with their voices and by rattling tin lids and bird scarers, in order to ward off evil spirits.[61]

The other popular form of wassailing was visiting households. Groups of people would walk around the village on New Year's Eve, visiting each home. They carried a wassailing bowl decorated with greenery and ribbons and containing ale, roasted apples, and other fruits to distribute to the householders. These visitors would confer blessings and good luck on the households for the New Year. In return, they expected some gift of food or money.

Similarly, in Scotland and northern England villagers conducted the "first footing" New Year's ritual. The people gathered in village squares and waited until midnight, when the New Year's bells would ring, and then the revelries would begin. After some initial celebrations, a group led by a tall, handsome, dark-haired man would go from house to house. Such a man was deemed to reinforce the good qualities in a man that a woman of the house would most desire in the household. He would set the "first foot" of the year in a house, conferring these qualities on the household. When doing so, he would bring in a piece of coal and a piece of cake or bun in to each house, symbolizing warmth and food for the household in the next year. He might also circle the kitchen table three times sunwise (clockwise) while reciting a rhyme to bring good luck. The first footing process went on all night until all houses in the village had been visited and blessed.

OUR NEW YEAR'S

Today we no longer believe in evil spirits who come out around New Year's and might impede us, nor do we need to purify our crops or cities anymore. But we can still reflect on our faults over the past year and purify and renew ourselves. As we have seen in the New Year's myths, the occasion provides us an opening and special opportunity to shape our future. And it starts by cycling out the bad. New Year's addresses our psychological need to have a second chance and fashion a renewed self that we can feel good about. That's a complicated and ongoing process, but New Year's offers a good place to start, or assess our progress and recharge. Even in our age, New Year's has a liminal character, and as such is an occasion to reflect upon where we are going in our lives, consider what changes may be in order, and plan accordingly. Our modern tradition of making New Year's resolutions is right in line with the mythical tradition. Janus still holds the door of opportunity open for us, and we should leap through it.[62]

CHAPTER 3

Groundhog Day: Prophecy, Rebirth, and Renewal

Groundhog Day is our first holiday that formally looks forward to spring weather, optimistically reminding us that it will come sooner or later, the pressing question being which it will be. The equivalent holiday worked likewise for our ancestors centuries ago, with one difference: Technically it was actually the beginning of spring. Today we regard Groundhog Day as quaint and secular, but in centuries past its equivalent was mythological and religious, featuring rituals that were taken seriously.

WHY WE CELEBRATE FEBRUARY 2ND

The importance of what is now the beginning of February goes back to Neolithic times. In Ireland we find Neolithic monuments that align with the rising sun on this date, which became the festival of Imbolc. According to the Irish myth *Tochmarc Emire* ("The Wooing of Emer"), the maiden Emer named the calendar points of the year, including Imbolc, when setting up a challenge to her half-divine suitor, the hero Cú Chulainn, to remain awake for an entire year in order to win her. She divided the seasons of the year according to the four days which fall roughly halfway between the solstices and equinoxes (called "cross-quarter" days), now the first days of February, May, August, and November. So February 1 was the first day of spring. Emer called the opening of spring Imbolc, after the lactation and milking of ewes which began at that time of year.[1] Thus, for Ireland anyway, was created what is commonly called the Celtic calendar.

© The Author(s) 2020
A. George, *The Mythology of America's Seasonal Holidays*,
https://doi.org/10.1007/978-3-030-46916-0_3

Our current practice of dividing the seasons at the equinoxes and solstices is relatively recent, coming to full fruition only in the twentieth century, following the lead of America.[2] But even today in America, we still have three holidays marking the old seasonal divisions: Groundhog Day, May Day, and Halloween. The Irish first-fruits of harvest festival of August 1 (Lughnasadh) is not observed in our American industrialized society, but it continues in some places, such as Lughnasa in Ireland.

Since the day began and ended at sunset, Imbolc was celebrated on the night of our January 31 and February 1. Unlike Beltane (May 1, discussed in Chap. 7), which was a very public event with large bonfires, Imbolc was more of a domestic affair involving hearth fires, candles, and possibly a bonfire representing the lengthening sunlight and other signs of spring. Divination, especially of the weather, and spring cleansing (purification) were also customary. At some point February 1 became associated with the goddess Brigid, who with the arrival of Christianity became St. Brigid. Over time, the holiday transformed into St. Brigid's Day. In both her pagan and Christian guise, she was associated with food production, including crops and livestock, especially preparations for spring sowing. The Saint's day featured having her bless people, their homes, and their livestock, and other rituals designed to bring healthy crops and good fortune, some of them quite superstitious.[3] In this context, weather signs were also important, so among other things people noted the wind direction and the sky. To see a hedgehog (which hibernates) was also a good sign. If it stayed out rather than returning to hibernate more, it meant that the weather will be mild. On the other hand, while the day should show signs of improving seasonal weather, an exceptionally fine day was regarded as an ill omen of poor weather to come.[4]

The first time a European holiday became fixed on February 2 rather than February 1 was with the advent of the feast of Candlemas. February 2 falls 40 days after the December 25 Christmas holiday. This was significant in Christianity because of the episode in the gospel of Luke in which Joseph and Mary went to the Jerusalem temple 40 days after Jesus's birth for the dual purposes of their purification and to present Jesus at the temple.[5] On this basis, starting no later than the fourth century in the Eastern Roman empire when the Feast of the Nativity had become established on December 25, February 2 was celebrated as the feast of the Purification of the Virgin Mary (typical in the West), the feast of the Presentation of Jesus at the Temple (typical in the East), or both.[6] It brought the Christmas season to an end. The holiday's ritual came to include a procession in which celebrants held candles, the idea being that Jesus as the true, divine light had entered the world, initially into the Jerusalem temple but more broadly as a "light for revelation to the Gentiles."[7] Accordingly, the holiday came to be called Candlemas in Catholic lands. The details of the feast's central ritual varied according to location and over time, but generally it involved bringing candles to church to be blessed and then lighting them, though some were taken home. In theory, the ritual represented the appearance of the divine light of Jesus, but in practice the candles also were thought to ward off evil and bad luck, and were used as good luck charms and for healing at home. In Ireland, Candlemas was also the occasion for weather forecasts, which has nothing to do with Christianity but much to do with farming and husbandry. A fine day meant bad weather for the rest of February.[8] While it is hard to document a clear and direct connection between pagan practices and the establishment of Candlemas and its candle ritual,[9] it must have resonated with the traditional fire rituals and imagery from pagan festivals at this time of year, where the idea was more one of purification, cleansing, and warding off evil.[10] It was precisely because of the festival's association with superstitions that Protestants opposed Candlemas, with the result that in most Protestant countries this Christian feast had faded away by the mid-eighteenth century,[11] although to some extent the candle rituals merely retreated into the home, where in some locations such as Wales the candles were used for divination.[12]

Stripping away the Christian aspects only left people with whatever beginning-of-February pagan rituals had survived, whence the groundhog. And the February 2 date stuck.

The Original Meaning of the Holiday, and How it Came to Involve a Groundhog

In Celtic Europe, all four cross-quarter days were considered days of transition, liminal times when the veils between the normal and supernatural worlds were thin. So it was natural that people practiced divination on these holidays, which pertained not just to when the warm weather would arrive, but also more generally to the season's crops, prospects for marriage, and other matters of human concern. People also sought supernatural blessings for protection against sickness, blight, evil spirits, and other nasty things. For this purpose, protective fires, in the form of bonfires, torches, and candles were also part of rituals, because they had a protective, purifying, and cleansing function. As we have seen, in Ireland Brigid/St. Brigid mediated this purpose.[13]

Divination of the weather also became a tradition on February 1. People used various mediums to make a forecast, including animals, which was natural: Any farmer or herdsman can predict the weather by watching the animals. Beginning in ancient times, people attributed magical powers to animals that changed their behavior at key points of the seasonal cycle.[14] Most important were hibernating animals, which emerge from their winter sleep in the spring, as we have seen in the case of the hedgehog on St. Brigid's day. The focus on the hedgehog (or badger) for divining the weather was most pronounced in Germany, which is how this holiday ritual made it to America via the so-called Pennsylvania "Dutch," which was originally "Deutsch" since these immigrants were really Germans, who then adopted the American groundhog as the oracular animal. It was from Germany that the idea spread that the animal seeing his shadow on February 1 meant a continuation of winter for several weeks, whereas seeing no shadow meant that the warm weather was about to come, in which case the animal should remain out of hibernation.

People are often puzzled regarding why a sunny Groundhog's Day, when the groundhog can see its shadow, means that winter will continue, whereas cloudy or bad weather, when no shadow is cast, portends that spring weather is nearly upon us. Doesn't this seem backwards? The answer lies in the original mythology lying behind this ritual.

In Europe, the animal originally associated with this holiday ritual was not a hedgehog, but the bear.[15] (The original Latin taxonomic term for the groundhog was *arctomys monax*, *arctomys* meaning "bear-mouse," indicating a miniature bear.[16]) Only when the population of bears in Europe diminished did people turn to hedgehogs as a substitute for divination on this day. In principle, any hibernating animal who "returns to life" in the spring could work for this purpose, but bears worked best while they lasted.

The bear was the largest, most powerful and magnificent creature in Europe, the king of the beasts, like lions in more southern climes. Venerated since prehistoric times, the bear probably was the oldest zoomorphic deity,[17] and it have figured prominently in myths, folktales, and art.[18] Some of their traits are similar to humans, so they were viewed in anthropomorphic (including totemic) terms, often considered the ancestors of humans.[19] Importantly, they also were considered spirit or soul animals and were identified with spiritual well-being.[20] Since ancient times their shadow has been thought of as their soul. These beliefs arose from the bear's practice of hibernation, which has inspired much mythology and folklore. The point of this mythology is not simply that the cave (or underworld) is associated with death, but that it represents a sacred place and a world unto itself which incorporates alternative modes of existence.[21] Thus, bears were thought to move between worlds, and so could instruct shamans.[22] In depth psychology, the bear can serve as a symbol for the Self,[23] and spiritual awakening or reawakening entails agitation in the dark recesses of the psyche, sometimes involving bear imagery in dreams and visions. Similarly, in alchemy the bear symbolized the darkness of the *prima materia* that was transmuted on the path to enlightenment.[24]

Because bears ate honey, they were considered wise and to have prophetic powers. This is because honey was thought to be a divine substance. It was the source of the first intoxicating drink, mead, through which intoxicated humans thought they were experiencing divinity. In myths divinities often consumed honey and mead. In ancient Greece, honey was associated with nectar, the drink of the gods, and ambrosia, the food of the gods. In the Eleusinian Mysteries honey was given to the higher initiates as a sign of new life. Through its association with honey, the bear was thought to have godlike insight.

The process of hibernating in the winter and emerging back into the world in the spring was viewed in terms of death and rebirth,[25] much like the seasonal death and rebirth of plants reflected in so many myths. In the winter, life goes back into the womb of the earth (death), only to be reborn. If the bear is ready to be reborn from its "little death,"[26] then death, symbolically its shadow, will remain behind when it emerges back into the world. Therefore, if it emerges from hibernation and sees its shadow *on earth,* its emergence was premature because death is still with it. It must return to the underworld for a few more weeks because it has not yet completed the sleep of death and rebirth. In parallel, spring weather too must await. On the other hand, if the bear sees no shadow (because it has remained in the underworld), then it has fully completed the cycle of death and rebirth and is truly alive again, so spring can begin and the bear can remain above ground.[27]

Before describing particular hibernation myths, it is first important to discuss the mythological significance of the caves in which hibernation occurs, focusing on the example of ancient Greece. The entrances to caves are liminal. When you enter a cave, you cross from the familiar everyday world into a mysterious, numinous world. The Roman philosopher Seneca wrote that in a cave "your soul is seized by a religious apprehension."[28] Sometimes the cave is thought of as the underworld, sometimes as a womb, sometimes the dwelling of a deity. Scientific studies show that being in a cave alters one's consciousness and can even cause hallucinations, mainly because of sensory deprivation but in some cases also because of noxious gases coming from within the earth, as appears to have been the case with the (underground) oracle at Delphi.[29]

For such reasons, caves were sought out as places where one could have religious experiences and receive revelations of divine knowledge, beyond what is accessible using our normal conscious mind. Caves as well as grottoes (both natural and man-made) were often used as oracles. For the ancient Greeks, this was part of their quest to attain absolute wisdom and ultimate truth, by any means possible.[30] The transformational cave experience was an initiation, which is why initiations in mystery cults were held in the dark, underground chambers (e.g., the Eleusinian and Mithraic mysteries). Orpheus himself was initiated in the Idaean cave by Dactyls.[31] Once so initiated, one could be a seer and prophet, or a shaman. Accordingly, in Greek myths caves were inhabited by divine beings associated with prophecy, such as, nymphs, Sibyls, and Pan (whose name connotes altered consciousness, and who taught prophecy to Apollo). Prophets and seers were often said to have been born of a nymph (e.g., a Sibyl). Cassandra was said to have acquired her prophetical powers from being in a cave.[32] The founders of many philosophical schools, such as Pythagoras, Parmenides, Epimenides, and Empedocles, made it a practice to spend time in caves and had their students do the same. Pythagoras had his own grotto for such purposes at his school on Samos.[33]

Such human cave experiences were projected upon the bear as it hibernated and then emerged into the world in the spring. As a result, peoples the world over had bear rituals in which a candidate, such as a boy ready to become an adult, becomes a bear and emerges from the initiation as a new personality.[34] Symbolic hibernation was also the subject of numerous myths along these lines. Since in ancient times cultures north of the Mediterranean were pre-literate, we must look to ancient Greece for the earliest surviving bear mythology. One, known as the Zalmoxis myth, came from Thracian tribes called the Getae, from along the lower Danube in what is now northern Bulgaria and southern Romania.[35] Zalmoxis was said to have been a slave of Pythagoras from whom he gained higher knowledge, including celestial lore, and after gaining his freedom and returning to Thrace he became a successful and leading local figure. He hosted prominent people at his hall, and while providing hospitality taught a doctrine of immortality. Meanwhile, he was building an underground cave dwelling for himself in the mountains. When it was completed, he disappeared from society and lived there for three years. He was said to have worn a bearskin then; indeed, his name comes from the Thracian word for hide, *zalmo*.[36] People thought he had died, but in the fourth year he reappeared, after which people considered his doctrine of immortality credible. He then became a co-regent of the king and priest of the chief god of the Getae; eventually he was considered to be that god himself, apparently a bear deity.[37] Herodotus reports that the Getae thought that they do not really die, but rather go to the spirit *(daimon)* Zalmoxis.[38] After some time Zalmoxis moved back to his mountains, rarely communicating with anyone but the king and his ministers. Among other things, he was famous for his meteorological predictions.[39] Zalmoxis worshippers would shoot arrows at thunder and lightning, apparently a ritual of weather magic. So here we have a bear immortality cult in which the divine bear figure, among other things, prophesizes the weather.

Further to the south in Boeotia was the famous Trophonian cave oracle, named after the legendary oracular *daimon* Trophonius (meaning "Nourisher of the Mind"). Once human, he was supposedly swallowed up by the earth and transformed into the *daimon* of the cave, where he still dwelled and communicated to enquirers. Thus, this cave was said to be the only oracle where querents received oracles directly (from being inside the cave itself) rather than through a medium.[40] The querents made a sacrifice to Trophonius, feasted with the meat, were given a purification bath in the river Herkyma by boys titled Hermes, were anointed with oil, drank water from the fountains of Forgetfulness and Remembrance, and finally were dressed in white linen.[41] Then they descended into the cave (underworld), stayed there for some duration, and returned transformed and enlightened. In one case reported by Plutarch, a querent named Timarchus remained in the cave two nights and his family had given him up for dead, but while they were mourning him he emerged radiant at dawn on the third day.[42] The philosopher-wizard Apollonius of Tyana was said to have descended into this cave in his philosopher's garb for seven days in order to ask what is the purest philosophy, and he emerged with the answer: a large volume of the tenets of Pythagoras,[43] who also taught a doctrine of immortality, thus implying that the oracle agreed with Pythagorean teachings. These stories are not merely about oracular prophecy, but also describe an initiation ritual of symbolic death and resurrection to a new mode of being.[44]

A similar myth is associated with the seventh or sixth century BCE Cretan seer Epimenides, who was reportedly very hairy, like a bear. According to the myth, one day he went looking for a lost sheep and fell asleep in a cave sacred to Zeus on the slopes of Mt. Ida. He slept there for 57 years. When he awoke, he thought that he had taken only a nap, and so continued looking for his sheep. But when he returned to his village everything and everyone was unfamiliar. Soon he and everyone realized what had happened. Thereafter he was considered to be a prophet under divine protection, and people sacrificed to him as to a god. He hardly needed to eat, and his soul could go in and out of his body at will. So he claimed to have returned to life several times. He also purified Athens after a pestilence (marking an atonement) for the 47th Olympiad. He was said to have lived an extraordinarily long life, from 154 to 299 years.[45] According to one legend, Pythagoras also descended into the Idaean cave, for 27 days;[46] in another, he descended all the way to Hades with a supernatural guide.[47]

Many analogous ancient myths involved descent into a cave or another version of the underworld, a womb from which one could be reborn. These include the myths of Inanna, Persephone, Aeneas' descent to the underworld in the *Aeneid,* Odysseus being held in the cave of the Cyclops, and even Zeus being born and raised by nymphs in a cave on the slopes of Mt. Ida, until he was ready to fight the Titans and claim his position as the preeminent god. Given that Orpheus often was depicted as a bear, his descent into and return from the underworld may have been modeled on ancient bear rituals.[48]

Such cave lore appears in the myths of other cultures too, including in all three Abrahamic religions. In the Hebrew Bible, the prophet Elijah stayed in a cave and the voice of Yahweh came to him, who instructed Elijah on what to do (1 Kings 19:9–18). The early church historian Eusebius related an early Christian tradition that Christ gave secret revelations to his disciples in a cave on the Mount of Olives.[49] Then too we have Christ's descent into the underworld in order to free souls deserving resurrection and eternal life (see pp. 91–92), as well as the later tradition that he himself was born in a cave (see p. 236). And finally, Muhammad was said to have received his first revelation and the first verses of the Qur'an from the archangel Gabriel while in the Cave of Hira during one of his retreats to the mountains. Muhammad generally could not read or write, but under divine inspiration in a cave he could.

MYTHOLOGY IN THE FILM *GROUNDHOG DAY*

The above hibernation and cave mythology helps us to understand the meaning of the insightful Bill Murray film, *Groundhog Day.* There Murray's character is equated with the groundhog: He is named Phil, like the groundhog Punxsutawney Phil, and they are both weathermen. The groundhog predicts a longer winter, whereas Phil the weatherman fails to predict the wintry weather that will descend on him that day, setting up his personal initiation ordeal. He gets what he deserves. He is stuck in Punxsutawney in the winter in a hotel, so he is figuratively in hibernation in his hotel room (cave), in a state of spiritual death. This is paralleled by the groundhog in the film having a shadow, and therefore not being ready to resurrect. So in one scene in the hotel's breakfast room, when another guest learns that the weatherman's name is Phil, the guest warns him, "Watch out for your shadow." This is a psychological reference: In order to emerge from his spiritual death, Phil must, among other things, confront and deal with his own shadow.

Thus, while potentially Phil could emerge from his plight on Groundhog Day in accordance with the traditional mythology, he is not yet spiritually ready to do so. Therefore, he must re-emerge from his hotel-room-cave each morning to re-live Groundhog Day over and over again, like the bear who has not yet undergone transformation. He must keep returning to re-hibernate until he gains in wisdom and is worthy, so that his old soul can be left behind when he awakes and goes outdoors on Groundhog Day morning. His process is much like that of karma and reincarnation: Indeed, in one sequence of the film, he literally does die (by suicide) each day and is reborn the next morning, only to keep trying until he learns the right way to live and gain his release. In the end, by eventually learning to love and be authentic, and to think of and help others rather than be self-centered, he is reborn, both physically and spiritually, into a new day and a new way of life filled with love.

Today, Groundhog Day is but a shadow (so to speak) of its former self: It is no longer observed at the beginning of spring, there is no bear, the original mythology has been lost, and the ritual is simply taken in jest. But at least we have a fine film to remind us in part of what this occasion originally meant to people, and what the holiday can still mean for us.

CHAPTER 4

Valentine's Day: How a Saint Became Eros

The most enduring symbol of Valentine's Day is a heart pierced by the arrow of Cupid, called Eros in ancient Greece. It is not obvious, however, what this pagan image and the mythology that lies behind it should have to do with the third-century CE Christian martyr, St. Valentine. The connection between Eros and the Saint and thence to our holiday that bears his name is as tortuous as it is fascinating. As we shall see, at all points along the road to this holiday—except in relation to Valentine himself—the idea has been about celebrating the spring season and the various themes that it has evoked in myth, literature, philosophy, and art. The themes of love and matchmaking are more recent.

Eros in Ancient Greece

Originally in Greek myth, Eros was not the cute cherub that we see today. In fact, originally he could hardly be visualized at all because he was not even a deity, so at first he was represented simply by a herm.[1] According to Hesiod's *Theogony*, Eros self-generated into existence once Chaos and Earth (Gaia) came into being.[2] Eros then became the driving force behind the subsequent creation of the universe, and so too the motor of generation and procreation. Eros is usually translated as "Love" because Eros as a force manifests itself in humans as the passionate desire that drives physical love, and hence procreation. Eros was thought to strike our hearts because in the ancient world the heart was considered the repository of thought as well as of the affective powers (e.g., emotions, intuition, wisdom), as evidenced by our heart pounding when we are excited and inspired. This primal power of Eros was overwhelming and could not be resisted by humans, gods or goddesses, or anything else. The result is what we see in nature: fertility, life, and the seasons.

Eventually Eros came to be represented as an Erote, a type of winged sprite *(ker)* that both symbolizes and mediates the coming of life, and so too of spring. Hence the sixth century BCE poet Theognis wrote:

> *Love [Eros] comes at this hour, comes with the flowers of spring,*
> *Leaving the land of his birth, leaving Cyprus, beautiful isle.*
> *Love comes, scattering seed for man upon earth.*[3]

Indeed, Eros as an Erote was usually depicted holding sprigs of foliage or sprays of flowers (Fig. 4.1), and also could be seen watering flowers in a garden.[4] Eros later evolved from an Erote into a fully formed, handsome youth *(ephēbos)* with golden wings, and his power was represented by the arrows that he sent into the hearts of humans and gods alike.

The Greek philosophers also got hold of Eros, making him the inspiration for lofty philosophical ideas. The most famous example is the discussion about the nature of Love (Eros) in Plato's *Symposium*. To understand that dialogue properly we must put aside our contemporary notions of love and appreciate that Plato's symposiasts were debating the question against the above-mentioned mythology of Eros; Hesiod's above-mentioned creation myth is even quoted near the beginning.[5] At the end of the dialogue, we learn that the primal power of Eros can serve as a starting point to inspire and guide a person in realizing beauty in earthly nature, and on that basis move further to realize pure, heavenly beauty— "beauty's very self"—so that when such person "has brought forth and reared this perfect virtue, he shall be called the friend of god, and, and if ever it is given to man to put on immortality, it shall be given to him."[6] Somewhat analogously, Eros played a key role in the Orphic mysteries, mediating the initiations.[7]

Saint Valentine

Having discussed Eros as a harbinger of spring, and as the inspiration of love and the experience of the divine, we can turn to that real man of God said to lead us into love, St. Valentine. In fact, we know almost nothing

Fig. 4.1 Eros as an Erote bearing a blooming lotus flower, a sign of spring. Drawing from painting on the Kachrylion Kylix, ca. 510 BCE

reliable about this murky figure. His name derives from the Latin *valens*, meaning strong, powerful, potent, or vigorous. Most probably he was a bishop in Terni, Italy, who was martyred about 269 CE, purportedly on February 14. Catholic tradition also describes a second St. Valentine, supposedly a priest in Rome who also was martyred the same year on February 14. Most scholars today think that the bishop of Terni is the real historical personage, but that his figure was then cloned in Rome and mythologized onto that of the nonexistent Roman priest.[8] In turn, apocryphal stories about this priest were then attributed back to the bishop, which explains why several stories about them are so similar.[9] For example, both were said to heal people, whom they converted, thus arousing the ire of the Roman authorities. As a healer, he was said to have cured crippled children, and in particular became the patron of epileptics.[10] Another legend arose that, after being arrested to be interrogated, he healed the blind daughter of his jailer, as a result of which the jailer's whole household converted to Christianity. This was said to be the event which prompted the Romans to behead him on February 14, which became the date of the Saint's feast.[11]

But with one possible exception, neither the earliest stories nor those from nearly the next thousand years contained or even prefigured the love and matchmaking customs now associated with Valentine's Day.[12] The possible exception is the legend that, after Emperor Claudius II supposedly prohibited soldiers from marrying,[13] the Saint defied the ban and began marrying young lovers in secret, for which he was arrested and eventually executed. This of course could account for his being associated with romance, love, and marriage, but there is no evidence that this story (and we don't know when it arose) had any role in the Saint's feast day or its evolution into a holiday of romance.[14] Rather, we had to await the age of chivalry and the genius of Geoffrey Chaucer (c. 1343–1400), who has been called "the original mythmaker" in this regard,[15] to make the romance connection and bring in Eros. Chaucer put Valentine's Day on the map with his poem, *Parliament of Fowls,* in which birds gather on February 14 to choose their mates:

> *You well know how on Saint Valentine's day,*
> *By my statute and through my ordinance,*
> *You come to choose your mates,*
> *As I prick you with sweet pain,*
> *And then fly on your way.*[16]

Scholars over the centuries have tried long and hard to figure out how Chaucer got the idea of linking the Saint with the coming of spring, but they have never been able to find an earlier tradition that he could have relied upon.[17] The troubadours, for instance, wrote about love, birds, and the spring, but never mentioned or made a connection with St. Valentine. Rather, it seems that Chaucer's creative genius simply combined existing bird lore and traditions of spring with the coincidence of St. Valentine's feast day falling on the fitting date of February 14. As mentioned earlier (pp. 41–42), there was already a tradition of spring beginning on February 1; but other medieval calendars and sources marked the beginning of spring in mid-February when the sun moved into Pisces.[18] Indeed, by mid-February signs of spring were appearing, not only birds singing and

mating but also some spring flowers; some farming activities also had commenced such as the pruning and grafting of trees and vines. An observant
poet like Chaucer would not miss this.

Once Chaucer had penned his poem, a cascade of other literature followed connecting the Saint with love. Inspired by his friend Chaucer, Sir
John Clanvowe (1341–91) wrote a debate poem entitled *The Book of
Cupid, God of Love,* in which a nightingale and a cuckoo respectively extol
and mock love.[19] John Gower (1330–1408) and the monk John Lydgate
(1370–1451) both wrote that birds choose their mates on Valentine's
Day, Lydgate also associating the Saint with the "Valentine," the genre of
poem which he established.[20] He also authored a poem called *Kalendare*
covering various feast days, in which he introduced St. Valentine for
February 14 and associated him with love and romance, in some rather
racy lines for a monk:

> *Be of good comfort and joy now, heart mine,*
> *Well may you glad and very lusty be,*
> *For as I hope truly, Saint Valentine*
> *Will show us love, and dancing be with me.*[21]

Soon members of the aristocracy in England and France were writing
love notes on Valentine's Day, and the custom reached the commoners by
the late seventeenth century. From the outset Valentines were decorated,
most commonly with hearts and cupids. The connection between Eros
and the Saint was now secure.

MYTH AND VALENTINE'S DAY TRADITIONS

Once Valentine's Day had become a holiday tradition, further mythmaking about the Saint followed. For example, the story of the Saint healing
the blind daughter of his jailer was now embellished to add that on the eve
of his martyrdom the he wrote a farewell note to the young lady (implying
that he was in love with her), thus supposedly accounting for the origin of
Valentine notes.[22] As another example, the idea of connecting the origin
of some Valentine's Day traditions (matchmaking and love-notes) with the
Roman February festival of Lupercalia (described in Chap. 2, pp. 34–35),
celebrated on February 15 also surfaced, beginning in a 1756 century
book by Alban Butler and embellished in 1807 by Francis Douce. Under
that theory, the Lupercalia was a celebration of love involving

matchmaking and the sending of love notes. Pope Gelasius supposedly prohibited the festival in 495–96 and replaced it with the Christian Feast of the Purification of the Virgin Mary[23] (or possibly the Feast of St. Valentine),[24] although the Lupercalia traditions were thought to have persisted through the centuries. Scholars long ago demonstrated that there is no evidence that the Lupercalia had such a character or that Gelasius ended it.[25] The festival's rituals were different and served different purposes,[26] and while Gelasius opposed the holiday there is no evidence that he actually forbade it, which should be obvious because only the Senate had jurisdiction to eliminate that or any other state holiday.[27] The most that Gelasius could have done is forbid Christians from participating in it. Nevertheless, this claim persists in some modern books and on the Internet.[28] The Lupercalia was, however, yet another example of a February holiday designed around purification for spring and encouraging fertility.

In America, the English Valentine's Day traditions had a rocky start because puritanical Protestantism dominated early colonial culture, but some Valentine traditions occasionally surfaced. In fact, even John Winthrop, a founder and eventually governor of the Massachusetts Bay Colony, once wrote a letter to his wife dated February 14 in which he said, "thou must be my valentine for none hath challenged me."[29] But in the 1840s after Puritan influence had faded, the English custom of sending Valentine notes became a fad, and the holiday was securely established in America; it even trickled down to children. The holiday's popularity and near-universal participation may have arisen because it is playful, is grounded in the universal emotion of love, and is not associated with anything potentially divisive, such as religion (whether Christian or pagan), nationality, or politics. By the early twentieth century, commercial greeting card producers, confectioners, jewelers, and florists developed Valentine's Day products that helped shape the holiday's rituals and meaning.[30]

The growth of such media to carry the holiday ritual led to the symbols from the mythology becoming established images of the holiday: The heart because originally it was the seat of emotions. Eros/Cupid because in the myths in which he is the agent of the love goddess (Aphrodite/Venus), he strikes love suddenly into people's hearts. Flowers because they symbolize spring, new life, and romance. Then came lace, because it is characteristic of undergarments, and thus is suggestive of romance and sexual intimacy; it is also associated with beauty. Red because it is the color of libido, passion, and life energy. But red was also combined with white, which can signify purity and innocence, as well as eternity, the absolute, and the infinite (thus embracing and uniting opposites, including man and woman[31]), possibly too the lingering signs of winter.[32] The image of love-birds goes back to Chaucer. In this process, the Saint was just along for the ride.

Valentine's Day's place in the calendar prompts us to reflect on what in many ways is its opposite, Halloween. Halloween is on the eve of the traditional beginning of winter, while Valentine's Day is just after the traditional beginning of spring. Halloween is full of images and rituals about death, while Valentine's Day is all about the passions of life. Halloween imagery is of harvested crops and the dying autumn foliage; Valentine's Day has spring flowers and other symbols of life, such as the red heart. Halloween pranks are typically performed by males, while Valentine's Day is mostly about the female.[33] As the Horae dance through the year, the holiday symbols usually reflect the seasons.

Quite apart from what Saint Valentine really did, today's Valentine's Day in important ways can and does reflect the Greek concept of Eros. The occasion of this holiday can inspire us not only to celebrate our bond with our beloved, but also to appreciate beauty and turn the force of our love and compassion toward the highest ends. At the same time, history shows us that this holiday, as a celebration of life, also marks the coming of spring.

CHAPTER 5

Unmasking Carnival

Carnival is the most jovial of holidays. Others can't match the inventive masks and costumes, float parades, the irreverent atmosphere, and the psychological release that it can provide. We see this in America's principal version of Carnival, Mardi Gras in New Orleans. But the experience and meaning go beyond just the fun. As it turns out, a lot of myth underlies Carnival's rituals, which points to the psychology behind the holiday and also explains why it originated in and still flourishes mainly in southern Europe. In our Christian tradition, Carnival is usually thought of as a last chance to feast and make merry before the privations of Lent, but the roots of the holiday are deeper and older, reaching into ancient times. And like Groundhog Day and Valentine's Day, Carnival also relates to the transition from winter to spring.

HOLIDAYS OF DISSOLUTION AND REVERSAL

Carnivals typically include such rituals as an irreverent parade/procession, excessive feasting and drunkenness, masks and costumes (masquerade), contests, sexual license, and role reversals in which people of lower social rank temporarily gain stature and authority; they are free to speak their mind and are served by their usual masters, who for the moment must obey them. This reversal also typically includes the temporary removal of the ruler and appointment of a temporary mock ruler, who is then removed at Carnival's end—in some ancient cultures he was killed as a sacrifice.[1]

© The Author(s) 2020
A. George, *The Mythology of America's Seasonal Holidays*,
https://doi.org/10.1007/978-3-030-46916-0_5

Holidays featuring such rituals are known as holidays or festivals of dissolution (or of reversal or inversion). They normally occur during a seasonal transition from one state of being into another, whether astronomical in nature (e.g., solstice, equinox) or in terms of human activity (e.g., sowing, harvest). As we have seen, the most important such festival is New Year's, but the transition from winter to spring, with its rebirth of nature and the stronger sun, inspires the dissolution of Carnival. Many countries which don't celebrate "Carnival" as such have similar if not equivalent festivals of reversal and dissolution around this time of year. One is Butter Week in Russia and other Slavic domains, a period of revelry and license likewise preceding Lent. Another is Purim among the Jews. In the British Isles and other countries in northern Europe it is called Shrovetide, culminating on Shrove Tuesday (also called Pancake Tuesday). These commonalities make it important to examine their shared archetypal nature.

The concept behind festivals of dissolution derives from ancient creation myths. The ancients conceived of the creation process as one of instilling order and structure into pre-existing formless chaos, so as to produce the cosmos as we know it. Thus, for example, Genesis 1:2 depicts a formless and dark void existing before God began the creative process. The created cosmos features multiplicity, time, rational space, cause and effect, hierarchy, and distinctions, especially opposites. In the human sphere this led to, among other things, social distinctions and stratification, and in particular the institution of kingship, thought of as a divinely ordained form of order that maintains order in the world. Holidays of dissolution temporarily undo all this.

As we saw in Chap. 2, the mythology behind New Year's is that the date marks a re-creation of the cosmos. That made it the classic festival of dissolution. But other seasonal transitions constitute mini re-creations, so their corresponding festivals also can feature elements of dissolution. The annual progression through the seasons and astronomical alignments—the dance of the Horae—was thought of as a journey through distinct stages and modes of being. The coming into being of a new stage, such as spring, also was viewed to some extent as a new creation. But in order to make way for such a new creation, the prior stage (e.g., the old year, winter) must be dismantled and reduced to chaos. As mentioned earlier (p. 19), this recurring pattern of a reversion to a primordial state followed by new creation in myth-based rituals is known as "the myth of the eternal return." During the period of the festival, ordinary, profane time is suspended. A festival of dissolution thus serves to assist time, to usher in the next phase of the dance. When people are temporarily outside normal time, they are also beyond all ordinary rules and curses, meaning they may do whatever they want and be whomever they want, without consequences. (We saw this in the film *Groundhog Day.*) This idea is reflected in a myth about the birth of the Egyptian god Osiris. In the story, the sun god Ra cursed the goddess Nut, saying that she can have children in no month of the year. But the god Thoth circumvented the curse by playing cards and winning a portion of each day of the 360-day year until he accumulated five epagomenal days. This period existed outside out of normal time and therefore was beyond the curse, so Nut was able to bear Osiris and her other children during these days without violating the curse.[2]

ANCIENT GREEK ORIGINS OF CARNIVAL

Although some elements of Carnival stretch back into the ancient Near East and Egypt, the holiday has its more direct origins in the classical Greek and Roman world. In Greece the principal festival of dissolution was the Kronia, held after the summer harvest and thus representing the transition into the post-harvest regime of life heading towards winter. It is named after the Titan Kronos, who according to myth ruled the universe during the Golden Age of mankind, when there was no hunger, death, sickness, social distinctions, or oppression. But then Zeus established the Olympian order of the cosmos by defeating Kronos and the other Titans in battle. Zeus imprisoned Kronos for a while in the underworld realm of Tartarus, but eventually let him out and assigned him to rule over the Elysian Islands, a paradise of the dead where, among other things, again there was a primordial equality and other features of the Golden Age.

Kronia reflects this legacy of Kronos (as well as perhaps his originally being a harvest god—he did, after all, wield a sickle). During this festival the usual order of society was suspended. Among other things, slaves banqueted and played games with their owners, who waited on their slaves. Slaves also ran riot through the streets raising a din. These reversals represented a reversion to the Golden Age of Kronos when oppression and social distinctions did not exist.[3] At the end of the festival, a criminal who had previously been condemned to death (a mark of chaos and disorder) was led out, given wine, and slain.[4] This purification ritual marked the end of dissolution and the moment of transition into the next seasonal modality of being.

As seen below, Kronos and the features of the Kronia later appear in Roman festivals.

ROMAN ORIGINS OF CARNIVAL

The Origins of Carnival Time in the Roman Calendar

Carnival's ties with ancient Roman myth, religion, and ritual are extensive. In order to appreciate how this came about, it is necessary to understand something about how the ancient Roman calendar worked and changed over time, especially in our Carnival month of February. Originally the Roman year attributed to Romulus began on March 1 and had 10 months, the last being December (*decem* meaning "ten") making for a "year" of only 304 days; there were no months during what is now January and February. For the Romans this was a time of relative inactivity during which people waited and prepared for the coming of the spring sun and vegetation, planting, and the start of the military campaigning season. March 1 was the New Year because the agricultural season started in March, and Mars, after whom the month was named, was in part an agricultural deity. Eventually, during the reign of king Numa (traditionally 715–693 BCE) if not somewhat before, the months of January and February were added. The revised calendar year had 355 days.[5] Later, in 153 BCE if not earlier, the civil (though in theory not the religious) New Year was changed from March 1 to January 1. In 46 BCE Julius Caesar established a 365-day calendar, with a leap year every fourth year, the approach that remains today. But whereas we insert February 29 on leap year, the Romans inserted an additional February 24th,[6] so as not to disturb the dates of the traditional pre-New Year holidays, the Regifugium on February 24 (here the second 24th) and the Equirria on February 27, which had to be a fixed number of days before the Ides of March (March 1).

February normally had 28 days, but it consisted of 2 parts: February proper consisting of days 1–23, which were stable, and days 24–28, which were epagomenal.[7] February 23rd was called the Terminalia because in an important sense it was both the end of the month and of the old year; it was the last day in which any religious festival in the old year was held. The festival on the 23rd was called the Terminalia, named after the ancient Roman god of boundaries, Terminus, who normally was associated with physical land boundaries (his name comes from *termini,* "boundary stones"); but in this case the boundary in question was temporal.[8] This epagomenal period of February 24–28 had a special liminal status of being outside normal time, between the end of the old year and the beginning of the new. It is in these epagomenal days that we find the origins of the concept behind and the rituals of Carnival at this time of year.

The Late-February Roman Festivals

We've already seen in prior chapters how the mid-February festival of Lupercalia originally was oriented around purification and fertility in preparation for the New Year, and as such it was not really a festival of dissolution. Subsequent February holidays served this purpose.

On February 24, the first day of the epagomenal period, the Romans celebrated the above-mentioned (p. 35) Regifugium, meaning the "flight of the king." That day the official exercising the highest priestly functions conducted an important ritual. During the ancient period of the kingship, the king held these priestly functions and would have performed them. During the Republic (after abolition of the kingship) this official was the *rex sacrorum*, who was the highest priest and the only figure entitled *rex* ("king"). An etiological legend arose during the Republic that the holiday celebrated the expulsion of the tyrannical King Tarquinius, which resulted in the establishment of the Republic in 509 BCE, making the 24th a kind of national independence day. But the story is dubious and cannot have been the holiday's origin;[9] its roots go deeper.

On that day, the *rex* made a sacrifice at the Comitia (public assembly) in Rome, and then made a hasty exit from the city, not to return until the New Year on March 1. We know that the Vestal fire, which burned in the Forum all year, was re-lit on March 1, which raises the question of when it had been extinguished. No extant ancient sources specify this, but scholars generally think that extinguishing the fire must have been part of the ritual performed by the *rex* on the 24th, being connected with the sacrifice and his flight from the city for the epagomenal period,[10] during which the fire would have remained out. Originally, the king's absence must have entailed a shutdown of governmental and priestly functions during this period.[11] Whether in form or effect, this constituted a temporary abdication of the king. Some scholars believe that during this period power was handed over to a temporary (mock) king who costumed himself like the real one, and that he was then dethroned, expelled or perhaps (at least originally) sacrificed at the end of the epagomenal period; further, the period was characterized by unruly celebrations and drunkenness.[12]

The Equirria, celebrated on February 27, was more of a public holiday than the Regifugium. The main event, for which the holiday was named, consisted of horse races on the Field of Mars outside the city limits. At first, these may have been horse races, not necessarily chariot races.[13] According to the etiological myth, Romulus instituted these in honor of his father, Mars, whose month would soon start on March 1. On the practical level, it has been noted that these races served to exercise the animals and riders in preparation for the upcoming military campaigning season,[14] but there was another opportunity to do that at a second Equirria on March 14, so this military aspect may not explain the origin and initial meaning of the holiday. In any event, it was a festive day reflecting the carnival nature of the epagomenal period, and it is possible that the races were the predecessor to Carnival processions.[15]

The Regifugium and Equirria served as festivals of dissolution just before the March 1 New Year, but in 153 BCE the civil New Year was transferred from March 1 to January 1. It seems to have been after this that the Saturnalia in late December evolved into its classic form as a festival of dissolution.

The Romans identified their god Saturn with the Greek Kronos, who, according to Virgil's mythical account, became an exile after being defeated by Zeus, and landed in Italy.[16] Historically, his cult may have ended up in Rome through Greek influence on Etruria, where he may originally have been an agricultural deity, especially of sowing and harvesting. Saturn's festival, called the Saturnalia, was on December 17–23, which was both just after the winter sowing and just before the winter solstice. Originally the festival probably had an agricultural character. But after 153 BCE, at least in urban Rome, the Saturnalia also began to serve as the end-of-year festival of dissolution. Even though the Saturnalia is in December rather than in what became Carnival season, it became important for Carnival because many Carnival (and Christmas) rituals can be traced back to the Saturnalia. These customs survived best where Roman culture penetrated deepest and was most lasting, in what is now Italy, southern France, and southern Spain, and that's where Carnival originated and remains strongest in Europe today.

At the start of the Saturnalia, the cult statue of Saturn, which was bound by woolen fetters all year, was released, signifying a time of liberation. After a sacrifice to him and a banquet open to all people on December 17, the celebrations became a festival of reversal and dissolution, which like in the Kronia was a reversion to the Golden Age, when Saturn ruled.[17]

Masters waited on their slaves, who ate before their masters did. The formal toga was shunned in favor of colored Greek-style clothing (the *synthesis*), and both master and slave wore the conical felt cap *(pilleus)* which was the mark of a freedman (i.e., slaves, being not free, could not normally wear it, meaning that they were "free" for the period of the festival). Slaves were also entitled to free speech, and they could disrespect their masters. Slaves and masters gambled together, and there was also gambling on the streets. Women played a more prominent role than usual. People also wore masks and costumes. Overeating and drunkenness was the rule. Within the family a mock king *(Saturnalicius princeps)* was appointed for the duration of the festival, whose orders had to be followed.[18]

Shrovetide traditions in Britain and Ireland also seem to have roots in the pagan feasts of Bacchus, who was venerated in Roman Britain. At Eton, until the nineteenth century students would write poems in honor of Bacchus on Shrovetide, and displayed them at the school.[19]

CARNIVAL IN EUROPE AND AMERICA

The European Carnival originated in Italy and harks back to Roman traditions, but its precise development in medieval times remains unclear. The main theories are that it either evolved from pagan holidays (including holdover Roman traditions) serving to transition from winter to spring which were then Christianized into Carnival, or that it was more directly a creation of the church as a lead-up to Lent, which also utilized Roman traditions. For the church, the holiday also had a didactic function, showing what would happen to society if the Devil and his henchmen were to rule our lives. In any event, once Christianity took hold, the Lenten season leading into Easter matched the transition into spring in timing and in spirit, and Carnival became our institutionalized pre-Lenten festival of dissolution. At the practical level, it was also an opportunity to eat up the last winter stores of meat which would soon be spoiling in the warmer weather. (The word Carnival probably comes from the Italian *carne levare,* meaning to take away meat.[20]) Likewise, it was a last chance to eat cheese, milk, and eggs, which were forbidden during Lent. This was accomplished by making pancakes for the occasion, which also symbolized the spring sun, and they became a traditional Carnival food.

The first post-Roman record of Carnival comes from Venice in 1268. It spread from Italy into southern France (of which the Nice Carnival, first held in 1294, is a legacy) and the Iberian Peninsula. From France it spread to New Orleans (Mardi Gras) and from Iberia to Rio. On Mardi Gras, we still have a mock king who rules the French Quarter of New Orleans until midnight on Ash Wednesday. In the north of Europe, Carnival as such did not become such a typical tradition, but equivalent rituals of dissolution, including masquerades, developed on Shrove Tuesday, especially in the British Isles. The Jewish festival of Purim gained its masquerading and dissolution tradition among Jews in fifteenth-century Italy, influenced by Carnival there.

As Carnival evolved in Venice and elsewhere into a party, the masquerade became its central feature. In fact, among the peoples of the Caribbean, carnivals, as well as their participants, are called Mas, from masquerade since the celebrants dress in masks and costumes.[21] Masks and masquerade are full of meaning. In both preliterate and later cultures, masks symbolized the presence of supernatural beings. They allowed spirits or deities to be personified, and enabled the person wearing them to feel transformed; the person took on the qualities of the spirits or deities. In psychological terms, of course, the "deity" is already inside, so the mask serves to encourage them to become manifest and be experienced consciously. Thus, a mask is not just a face to the outer world, but forces one to look inward as well. It facilitates access to experiences not ordinarily available to the conscious mind. At the same time, our masks and costumes guide us in how to behave with others during this temporary time of transformation. The disidentification that masks and costumes afford also facilitates our temporary escape from authority, so as to allow archetypal emotions to come forth resulting in a catharsis. As Oscar Wilde quipped, "Man is least himself when he talks in his own person. Give him a mask, and he will tell the truth." Indeed, masquerade etiquette forbids overt recognition of mask wearers, although in practice it is often possible to recognize them. The experience is heightened by music, dancing, and drinking.

Which brings us finally to the experience of play. In medieval times when Carnival first developed, the church was strict and life was dreary, so the holiday served as an important, psychologically necessary outlet for playful irreverence. Play is important for our creativity and overall psychological health. Schiller once said that play stands at the beginning of all culture because it has no practical value, and that we are completely human only when we play. If we suppress our natural need for play, the consequences will come out later in pernicious forms. Today, when we are so serious and work so hard at our jobs and at raising families, the need to take time out for play is critical. Mass spectator sports satisfy only some of this need, because the experience is vicarious, and many of us are not interested in such sports. Of our holidays, for adults Carnival even more than Halloween can best serve as this outlet. This holiday deserves more attention than it gets in America.

As we don our Carnival masks, we can remember that this ritual is not only part of the transformation from winter to spring, but is also our own temporary transformation into another archetypal being in sacred time, as well as an opportunity to engage in play.

CHAPTER 6

Easter and Our Resurrection

Easter celebrates the central stories on which Christianity is based, concerning the most influential figure in Western civilization, yet its mythical theme of death-and-resurrection is universal. Easter also comes at a most propitious time of year, when springtime renewal and rebirth are in the air, a cyclical occurrence which itself has spawned innumerable myths in many cultures, some of which have influenced the development of Easter. These factors have combined to make Easter Western civilization's most mythologically rich, meaningful, and important holiday. The Easter story is rightly known as "the greatest story ever told." So we must do it justice by exploring it in detail.

The archetypal motif of death-and-resurrection has existed all over the world since time immemorial, and is expressed principally in the form of myths and related symbols. Likewise with Easter. Although the Easter story contains profound ideas that came to be expressed as doctrine, in practice Christians express Easter's meaning through its myth and corresponding symbols and rituals.[1] As we shall see, this is because its meaning originates from deep within the human psyche.

In this mythology, rebirth depends on death. That's how the lunar cycle spawned myths, for example. Similarly, vegetation dies during winter, while the vernal equinox brings spring, the rebirth of vegetation, and the renewed dominance of the sun, a cycle symbolized in world myths. The Christian aspects of the Easter season likewise center on death and rebirth: Good Friday (crucifixion and death), Holy Saturday (Christ in the tomb, and his descent into the underworld), and Easter Sunday (resurrection). Earlier we saw much the same dynamic at work in the mythology behind Groundhog Day.

It is thus appropriate to begin by discussing an aspect of Easter that combines these similar and related mythologies—the holiday's name.

Myth and the Holiday's Name

In most of both Eastern Orthodox and Western Christianity, the name for Easter is derived from the Greek word *pascha* (from the Aramaic cousin of the Hebrew *pesah*), which refers to the Jewish Passover festival, and also to the "paschal lamb" sacrificed during that festival, which became a metaphor for the sacrificed Christ.[2] Further, the Greek verb *paschō* means "to suffer" and the Latin noun *passio* means "suffering," which is why in English we call Christ's suffering the "passion."

The name "Easter," however, is confined principally to Anglo-Saxon countries, such as Germany, the British Isles, the United States, and Canada. The word ultimately derives from the Proto-Indo-European root *aus meaning "to shine," especially in relation to the dawn, which is the etymology of Eos (Homer's famous "rosy-fingered dawn"[3]) and Aurora, respectively the Greek and Roman goddesses of dawn. This root eventually led to the Proto-Germanic *aust ("east," or "toward the sunrise") and *austron ("dawn"). In England this etymology was reflected in the name of Eostre (also Eastre), a purported goddess, and Eosturmonath (possibly "Eostre month," later "Easter month").[4] In German lands she was called Ostara. Eostre reportedly was the goddess of dawn, and so too a goddess of spring and fertility.

Our tradition is that "Easter" comes from Eostre and/or Eosturmonath. The earliest known expression of this idea comes from the English Christian ecclesiastical historian Bede, in *The Reckoning of Time*, written in the early eighth century after England had been nominally Christianized. Among the English people, he writes,

> Eosturmonath has a name which is now translated "Paschal month," and which was once called after a goddess of theirs [i.e., the English] named Eostre, in whose honor feasts were celebrated in that month. Now they designated that Paschal season by her name, calling the joys of the new rite by the time-honored name of the old observance.[5]

Eosturmonath being named after Eostre may be paralleled by Charlemagne later naming this same month Ostarmanoth (after Ostara) in his realm, as reported in Einhard's *Life of Charlemagne* (ninth century CE).[6] After Bede and into the nineteenth century numerous English, Dutch, and German scholars (including theologians and clerics) also wrote about this goddess.[7] An early nineteenth-century writer said that under Charlemagne "the spring festival of the goddess Ostara was replaced by the resurrection feast of the Savior of the world, which was called by the name Ostern (Easter) because the Saxons would have been then more disposed towards Christianity."[8] That is, Charlemagne retained the goddess-based name as an accommodation. Later in the nineteenth century, Jacob Grimm, one of the famous brothers Grimm, in his monumental study of Germanic mythology, concluded that there is evidence of this same goddess in northern continental Europe under the etymologically related name Ostara:

> The great Christian festival, which usually falls in April or the end of March, bears in the oldest of [Old High German] remains the name ôstarâ. . . . This Ostara, like the [Anglo-Saxon] *Eástre,* must in the heathen religion have denoted a higher being, whose worship was so firmly rooted, that the Christian teachers tolerated the name, and applied it to one of their own grandest anniversaries. . . . Ostara, Eastre seems therefore to have been the divinity of the radiant dawn, of upspringing light, a spectacle that brings joy and blessing, whose meaning could be easily adapted by the resurrection-day of the christian's God.[9]

Unfortunately he does not cite any direct evidence for the goddess; since Bede's account had become well-known on the Continent, much of Grimm's account might ultimately be derived from it.[10] Beginning in the nineteenth century and into the twentieth, several commentators argued that Bede either had made up this goddess or was simply wrong, a suspicion that continues today in some quarters.[11] But neither has anyone adduced sufficient evidence to disprove the existence of Eostre,[12] nor is there a convincing alternative explanation for the origin of the name of the month Eosturmonath and hence of our holiday. We are still faced with the problem of why we use Easter and not Pascha in Anglo-Saxon lands.[13] Fortunately, we have more than old unsubstantiated writings to go on.

In 1958 we learned more about this potential goddess from an archeological discovery just northwest of Cologne, Germany. Archaeologists found over 150 votive inscriptions from around 150–250 CE dedicated to

deities referred to as the "matronae Austriahenae," which name is etymologically connected with Eostre/Ostara.[14] The Austriahenae seem to have
been goddesses associated with the east and dawn, like Eos and Aurora.
This tantalizing find, however, only suggests rather than establishes an
ancestral link between these matrons and Eostre/Ostara.[15]

The literature on Eostre/Ostara going back centuries is also filled with
numerous names and descriptions of sacred places traditionally associated
with Eostre/Ostara,[16] as well as medieval field-blessing poems mentioning
her as a mother or fertility goddess.[17] Unfortunately, however, many of the
items mentioned no longer exist, in which cases we are not in a position to
evaluate the descriptions of the older authors. The name Eostre may also
be associated with names of some towns in England (such as Eastry in
Kent, Eastrea in Cambridgeshire, and Eastrington in Yorkshire), as well as
with several personal names (e.g., Estrild, Austrovald),[18] but again the
evidence is inconclusive. Arguably some of the place names refer to "east"
rather than to the goddess, but this would not explain the personal names.

In summary, our word Easter probably took its name most directly
from Eosturmonath, the month in which our holiday most commonly
fell.[19] The name Eosturmonath, in turn, may relate to Eostre/Ostara and/
or to a festival of hers in that month which gave the month its name, much
as the ancient Athenians named months after festivals in them. Likewise,
naming the Christian holiday after the month in which it most commonly
fell would have made good sense.[20] While the existence of Eostre has not
been decisively established by direct evidence, there is clearly a pagan *tradition* about Eostre going back into early medieval times, possibly earlier.
So even if there is no goddess, this tradition still explains the origins of
"Easter."

The dual etymology of the name for our holiday (Pascha/Easter) suggests that our Easter traditions are derived partly from the stories about
the passion and resurrection of Christ and partly from European paganism, which as we shall see is indeed the case. We'll start with the mythology pertaining to the original Eastertime events—the passion and
resurrection of Christ.

Myth and the Original Eastertime Events

In approaching the biblical Easter events from the standpoint of myth, we
confront the possibility, recognized in mainstream biblical scholarship,
that none of these events ever happened. The main reason is that the

earliest evidence (sources) that we think we have concerning the historical Jesus gives no indication that it happened, or even any reason why it would have happened. The earliest evidence is known as the Q source (from the German "Quelle," meaning "source"), which most New Testament scholars believe was a written collection of sayings of Jesus that Matthew, Luke, and possibly Mark later used in writing their Gospels.[21] They include familiar sayings: needing to remove the splinter from one's own eye, the blind leading the blind, the tiny mustard seed growing, the Son of Man having nowhere to lay his head, and so on. Q scholars have identified three strata in Q representing three phases in the development of Q and in the life of the Galileans who wrote it down and used it (called the "Q people"). The earliest stratum of sayings (known as Q^1) probably dates from not long after Jesus's lifetime and includes only wise aphorisms together with instructions from Jesus on how to live in their nascent community and how to behave and dress when advocating their beliefs and lifestyle to others. The second layer (Q^2) was added by the 50s or 60s CE, after the Q people had experienced rejection of their message and lifestyle by others (principally Jews) and had grown infuriated enough about this to commit their frustrations to writing. Perhaps they knew or imagined that Jesus had suffered much the same rejection. Thus, Q^2 portrays Jesus as an apocalyptic prophet pronouncing judgment on others such as Pharisees who don't accept his (i.e., the Q community's) message and prophesizing the end of the world. The third stratum (Q^3) was added in the wake of the failed revolt against Rome (66–73 CE), commonly known as the Jewish War. Q^3 is more conciliatory and reconciles the Q people to living with other communities in the world as it is until the end times; here Jesus is upgraded to a divine being.[22]

Q^1 is our earliest known source about Jesus, and is as close as we can get to the historical Jesus.[23] It is important in analyzing mythmaking in connection with Easter because it portrays a different Jesus than the one in the Gospels which we celebrate at Easter. The Jesus of Q^1 simply engages in social and religious commentary, talks about the Kingdom of God, and gives advice on how to live a modest, countercultural lifestyle set apart from society's norm. Jesus performs no miracles, and there are no named disciples. By all appearances he is entirely human, not divine, so he is called simply Jesus, not Christ, the Messiah, Lord, or king. There is no mention of the Holy Spirit. Nothing is said about his death or any resurrection. Except for one reference to Solomon, Jesus mentions nothing having to do with Judaism, Jewish scriptures, the Jerusalem temple or its priests and scribes, or (even in Q^2 and Q^3) about him ever going to Jerusalem. One barely recognizes him or his God as Jewish. Jesus does not prophesize, debate with Pharisees (who are not mentioned), or have a social reform program. He refers to the "son of man," but this figure is not divine; the term seems to be just another word for human being (including for Jesus himself). The Kingdom (or rule) of God appears to refer to a way of life in the present shared among the Q people, not to an apocalyptic kingdom to be established after the end times; this idea of sharing in such a present Kingdom seems to have been the attraction around which the Q people formed as a social and religious group. In one intriguing saying, he teaches, "Whoever does not take up his cross and so become my follower, cannot be my disciple."[24] The reference to bearing one's cross was probably a common metaphor for the philosopher with integrity undergoing voluntary suffering by standing up for his beliefs under criticism and condemnation,[25] for he makes this point in the context of talking about a community member alienating his family and losing his social position because of his new Jesus-based beliefs. So it is not an allusion to Jesus being crucified. Indeed, in Q^1 Jesus says and does nothing to violate Roman law, much less anything justifying crucifixion by the Romans, who are not even mentioned. Still, years later such a statement could have been used to develop the notion that he had been crucified, as appears to be the case in the Gospels.[26] In the end, according to some scholars, Jesus comes across as being similar to a Cynic sage.[27] Q^1 contains no myth, and even in Q^2 and Q^3 there is still no crucifixion and resurrection. In short, the Q people don't look like Christians. If the above is a more accurate portrayal of the real life of Jesus than what we read in the Gospels, then the Gospel narratives, including the Easter events, are myth.[28]

The above portrait is corroborated by what we know about the other early groups of Jesus followers in Palestine and southern Syria. For example, the earliest information that we have about the Jesus group in Jerusalem formed by Peter, James and others says nothing about any belief on their part about Jesus's crucifixion and resurrection, or that he was divine, or that he was an apocalypticist.[29] Nor do the pre-Markan parables, conflict-and-pronouncement stories, or miracle stories circulating among early Jesus groups that found their way into the earliest Gospel (Mark) say anything about any Easter events.[30] The earliest we hear about belief in the death and resurrection of a divine Christ (called the "Christ myth") is in St. Paul's epistles from the 50s CE, in which he characterized these notions as creeds that had been passed down to him (see next paragraph). Such belief appears to have developed among groups in certain Hellenistic cities of northern Syria and Asia Minor (e.g., Antioch). We are used to these groups being called "churches," but the Greek term used by Paul for such groups was *ecclesia*, which simply means "assembly," "gathering," "meeting," or "congregation"; the more descriptive term preferred by some scholars for such groups is "Christ cults" because they venerated him as divine.[31] When Paul first encountered Christ cults, he rejected their beliefs and persecuted their members, but then he experienced his famous revelation (or insight) that changed his mind, and he went on to found churches and evangelize across the Mediterranean world.

Perhaps the earliest formulation of this Christ myth is visible in Romans 3:21–26, where Paul restates an earlier creed. It merely states that Christ died as a sacrifice for the sins of the gentiles, who can be redeemed through recognizing Christ's sacrifice and having faith in him. In this scenario, Christ dies a martyr's death for a cause, belief in which may have been inspired by the popular Greco-Roman motif of a noble death (discussed below p. 90).[32] Note that in this formulation no resurrection is mentioned or needed; the sacrifice is effective and Christ is vindicated simply because God accepted it. No other details are given about his death. The other main early formulation of the Christ myth that Paul had received was that restated in 1 Corinthians 15:3–5. Here again Christ died for "our sins," but the creed adds that he was buried and then raised on the third day; Paul then lists various post-resurrection appearances of Christ. These appearances imply a resurrection, but no narrative of Christ's death or resurrection is given which could serve as our Easter story. In Galatians Paul again mentions the crucifixion in which Christ "gave himself for our sins," as well as that God had raised him from the dead (1:1, 4), but again there is no narrative. The final tradition that Paul says he received concerns the ritual meal, set forth in 1 Corinthians 11:23–25. It reports that on the night when Jesus was "handed over" he was dining with companions, broke bread which he said was his body, and said "do this in remembrance of me." He said the same regarding the cup of wine, which he likened to his blood. This refers to his anticipated execution, but says nothing about redemption (from sins or otherwise), and does not mention any anticipated resurrection. This is may be an etiological myth explaining the origin of the Christ cult's fellowship meal ritual, in which the continuing presence of the divine Christ is felt and contemplated. (Ritual meals were central to Hellenistic private fellowships organized around various purposes and interests, and such groups typically had a patron deity or deified hero, such as Dionysus or Heracles, that they honored at the meal,[33] so the Christian congregations similarly may have been motivated to deify their founding figure.) In summary, a few places Paul does mention Christ's crucifixion, cross, and resurrection, but he gives no narrative context.[34] So the above Christ myth contains only the most basic fragments of what would become our Easter story. The Easter story appears first in the Gospel of Mark, probably written in the 70s CE. The subsequent Gospels, in respect to the passion and resurrection narrative, are largely variations on Mark.

In light of the above, when analyzing the mythology of Easter we must begin by recognizing the real possibility that the Easter story is a myth created by Mark based on elements of the earlier Christ myth and motivated by the concerns of Mark's own Jesus community, which his Gospel endeavors to resolve. Specifically, it appears that, due to their novel behavior (e.g., not obeying Jewish purity requirements) and their odd ideas about the Kingdom of God based on what they thought were Jesus's own teachings and example, by sometime in the 60s CE, if not before, Mark's people were expelled from the synagogues after long and acrimonious debates and conflict, a fate similar to that of the Q people reflected in Q². They then needed a founding myth to justify their existence as an independent social and religious group with its own way of life. A perfect opportunity to write it came with the destruction of the Jerusalem temple and its priestly establishment in the Jewish War in 70 CE, which Mark interpreted as divine punishment of the Jewish religious establishment. He portrayed Jesus as having suffered condemnation as Mark's own community had, in turn condemning the pre-War Jewish establishment. Expanding upon the Christ figure previously developed in the Christ myth, and based on earlier Jewish apocalyptic literature and perhaps Q² and Q³, Mark portrayed Jesus as a divine agent of God sent to render judgment at the end of the world and bring justice in a future earthly Kingdom of God. Such a post-War turn of thought appears to be reflected in Q³, where Jesus says, "You who have followed me will sit on thrones, judging the twelve tribes of Israel."[35] This myth provided a founding rationale for Mark's community and hope to its members. They only had to remain in the group (not defect like the disciples in the Gospel) and be obedient (like Christ in the Gospel) until judgment day. In fleshing out this myth, Mark himself may well have made up most of the Easter story.[36]

Were we to stop with simply declaring the Easter story a fiction, however, this chapter would be very short and fail to account for our holiday.

Easter is based on the Gospels, so in examining fully the mythology of Easter we must leave Q[1] and much other pre-Gospel evidence aside. Indeed, some fragments of the myth are corroborated by Paul, such as the crucifixion and resurrection, and the existence of Peter. And a substantial number of New Testament scholars even outside the fundamentalist/evangelical orbit consider at least the crucifixion if not the full details of the passion story (not including the resurrection) to be historical. Therefore, the discussion below focuses on the Easter story of the Gospels.

For our purposes the Eastertime events fall into two categories. The first is the sequence of events from Jesus's entry into Jerusalem through his trial, suffering, and death on the cross (collectively called the "passion"). These events are in principle historical in nature, so their historicity can be scrutinized by historians using the historian's toolkit, although, as we shall see, mythical features appear throughout the story. The second category is the resurrection, which by definition is a miraculous event not susceptible to analysis using historiographical methods, and so it is mythical by its very nature. Belief in the resurrection is a matter of faith. Therefore, each category is discussed separately below, starting with the passion.

Myth and the Passion of Christ

According to the Gospels, Jesus was crucified outside the walls of Jerusalem after being convicted of sedition against Rome. That is the best attested part of the story. But once we get into the details of his entry into Jerusalem, actions in Jerusalem, arrest, trial, and crucifixion, and resurrection, things get messy and confusing. The four canonical Gospel accounts often contain or stress different details, some of which flatly contradict each other. Take, for example, just the short scene in which women discover the empty tomb, an Easter tradition which in principle could have been derived from eyewitness testimony:

- How many women came to Jesus's tomb, and who were they? Mark 16.1 says three (Mary Magdalene and Mary the mother of James and Salome); Matthew 28:1 says two (Mary Magdalene and "the other Mary"); John 20:1 says one (Mary Magdalene); Luke (23:55–56 and 24:1, 10) says apparently three or more ("the women who had come with him from Galilee").

- How early did they come? Matthew 28:1 and John 20:1 say when it was still dark; Mark 16:2 and Luke 24:1 say at daybreak.
- Why did they come? John 20:1 does not say why they came; Matthew 28:1 only says to inspect the tomb, and does not say they had spices to anoint the body; Mark 15:1–2 and Luke 24:1 say to anoint his body with spices. Luke 23:54–46 says they already had the spices on Friday before the Sabbath, but Mark 16:1 says they bought them after the Sabbath was over.
- Who greeted the woman/women at the tomb, where were they, and how were they positioned? Mark 16:5 says a young man, sitting inside the tomb; Matthew 28:2–5 says an angel from heaven, sitting outside the tomb on the stone that he had rolled back from the tomb's entrance; Luke 24:4 says two men standing inside the tomb; John 20:1–2 says two angels sitting inside the tomb where Jesus had lain, one at his head and the other at his feet.
- When was the stone in front of the tomb rolled back? In Mark 16:4, Luke 24:2, and John 20:2 it had been rolled back before the women arrived, but in Matthew 28:2 the angel rolled it back while they watched.
- What did the women do after finding the tomb empty? Mark 16:8 (original ending) says they ran away and told no one; the other Gospels and the longer ending to Mark say they ran and told the disciples (Mt 28:7; Lk 24:9; Jn 20:2; Mk 16:10).
- To whom did the resurrected Jesus first appear? John 20:14 and Mark 16:9 say Mary Magdalene alone; Matthew (28:1, 9) says Mary Magdalene and "the other Mary"; Luke (24:13, 15, 18) says Cleopas and another disciple.

But there are broader, more important inconsistencies. The accounts differ because the four evangelists had somewhat differing theologies, wrote in different places and times and faced different issues that they wanted to address in their accounts, and so wrote for differing audiences. As a result, the Gospel accounts have an anachronistic element to them, because the evangelists were structuring their accounts of the Easter event in order to address contemporary concerns among members of Christian communities, potential converts, and Roman authorities. The trial of Jesus in particular is a challenge, because much of the action took place behind closed doors solely among Jewish and then Roman officials, meaning that the Gospel narratives of the trial cannot have been based on eyewitness testimony. This gave the evangelists creative license to describe what they thought should have happened. As a result of such factors, New Testament scholars consider the passion and resurrection narratives (together with the infancy narratives, see p. 197) the most historically unreliable parts of the Gospels.[37]

The result, as one would expect, is that the truly historical parts of the passion narratives are few; otherwise the evangelists were creating myth, and to some extent different, inconsistent myths. The following sections of this chapter analyze this process, but we begin with some historical background about Jesus. There are far too many details and questions relating to the passion than can be addressed here, so I only touch upon some of ways in which it was mythologized in order to illustrate what dynamics were at work in creating our Easter traditions.

The Historical Jesus
In the current state of the evidence, we can know very little about the historical Jesus with confidence. But for purposes of discussing the passion story, we will posit that Jesus was convicted of the capital crime of sedition against Rome, for which he was crucified. The issue, for Rome, was whether he claimed to be the King of the Jews. Pilate obviously decided yes, and so the plaque on the cross (which Romans typically used to inform onlookers about the nature of the crime) read, "King of the Jews." Further, reportedly he was crucified together with other criminals *(lestai)*.[38] Mark and Luke say that Barabbas, whom Pilate infamously released instead of Jesus, was being held with insurgents who had committed murder during a recent insurrection,[39] so he was probably one of them.

The above information is helpful in analyzing what Jesus may have been about and how the evangelists may have changed the story, because these facts presumably bear some relation to his ideas and activities. If Jesus were simply a peaceful sage conveying such wisdom as "love your neighbor" and "turn the other cheek," the Romans would not have cared and they would not have nailed him to a cross. Moreover, the Romans typically did not get involved with internal Jewish religious disputes; they cared only when someone's actions threatened the peace, the collection of taxes, or the system of Roman power. For example, they would not have cared about Jesus's differences with the Pharisees about the interpretation of the Torah (e.g., whether it is permissible to heal on the Sabbath). They would, however, care if he considered himself the Messiah, or if enough people believed he was the same to the point that there arose a risk of public disorder or revolt. The Romans also cared about the continued stability of the temple and its priesthood, with which they had a cooperative relationship. Any threat to the temple establishment would also be a threat to the Roman scheme of power in Judea. In the Gospels, this is the specter raised by Jesus's visit to Jerusalem.

Sedition against Rome was treasonous, but one does not have to take up arms or be leading a public revolt to be guilty of it. Although some have argued that Jesus was a politically active leader,[40] there is virtually no evidence for this, and few New Testament scholars consider him to have been such. Nevertheless, it is clear that he opposed the status quo in Palestine, most particularly the Jerusalem temple priesthood and the Roman regime (although, for reasons discussed below, according to the Gospels he hardly talked about Rome). He was also concerned about social injustice, and in the Gospel of Mark promised that justice would be coming soon, in what he called the "Kingdom of God." The question was how this would happen. What kind of Jesus thinks he is the Messiah and in some sense King of the Jews, tells his audience that evil will be defeated and justice will be done (and soon), and that the temple priesthood (and by implication Roman power) will be overcome, but does not resort to rabble rousing or armed revolt to achieve this? Numerous would-be messiahs in Judea and Galilee had tried armed revolt in the first century CE before and after Jesus, and they were captured and executed by Rome. So if the Kingdom of God was not to be realized by revolutionary means, then how?

The dominant answer among New Testament scholars throughout most of the twentieth century[41] was that Jesus thought that God would do it, very soon, and that Jesus considered himself to be God's agent who would set the process in motion and later rule the Kingdom of God once it was established. This approach is called apocalypticism. It has deep roots in Judaism, and by Jesus's time it was playing an increasingly important role in Jewish thinking. For our purposes, we can skip that background and move right to what, according to this view, was Jesus's own version of apocalypticism, which is well summarized by professor Bart Ehrman:

Jesus fully expected that the history of the world as we know it . . . was going to come to a screeching halt, that God was soon going to intervene in the affairs of this world, overthrow the forces of evil in a cosmic act of judgment, destroy huge masses of humanity, and abolish existing human political and religious institutions. All this would be a prelude to the arrival of a new order on earth, the Kingdom of God. Moreover, Jesus expected that this cataclysmic end of history would come in his own generation, at least during the lifetime of his disciples.[42]

As part of this process there would be a general resurrection of the dead so that all people, whether living or dead, would be judged, and the elect would then live in the Kingdom. In the Kingdom there would be no hunger, poverty, death, evil, or even marriage. Correspondingly, in in his miraculous actions, such as exorcising devils, feeding the hungry, and raising the dead, Jesus was demonstrating that the Kingdom was starting to come (often called "realized eschatology"). And finally, Jesus would reign as king of the Kingdom, with his 12 disciples governing each of the 12 tribes of Israel, which would be reconstituted.[43] This apocalyptic vision is most clearly set forth in the Gospel of Mark.

The earlier evidence discussed above cuts against the above view, however. As noted, the Jesus of Q^1 was not apocalyptic; apocalypticism emerged only in Q^2. But it is possible that even the Jesus of Q^1 spoke of the Kingdom of God in terms that led some people to think that he had an apocalyptic vision in mind. Further, some Q scholars don't agree that Q was stratified as discussed above, in which case the apocalypticism of "Q^2" may have been in Jesus's own thinking. As for St. Paul, writing in the 50s CE, his churches (Christ cults) were portrayed as apocalyptic communities, but it is not necessarily the case that they *began* that way. The above-mentioned Christ myth according to which such Christ cults lived was not originally based on an apocalyptic message. Apocalypticism rears its head only when you have some good ideal to live by but it is being frustrated by external circumstances rather than realized; the apocalyptic solution promises to leapfrog over the problems, as we saw happen in the Q^2 community when their original conception of the Kingdom of God was threatened.[44] Paul seems to have introduced apocalypticism as an adjunct to the preexisting Christ myth, as a defensive move to address particular concerns that arose. But he envisioned a different kind of kingdom. Unlike Mark, Paul did not talk of an earthly Kingdom of God. Rather, there would simply be a second coming of Christ and a wrathful judgment day at the end of time (which was thought to be imminent), where only the faithful Christians would be saved and whisked up to heaven for eternal life. Paul wielded his eschatology as a club to secure faithful, moral behavior in the interim period (misbehavior was becoming a problem), and as a way to resolve certain knotty problems, such as what happens to church members who die (they will be raised at the end of time, Paul promises in 1 Thessalonians).[45] None of this is evidence for an apocalyptic historical Jesus; Paul wrote virtually nothing about the teachings of the historical Jesus.

One might think the apocalyptic viewpoint portrayed in Mark was apolitical because Jesus was not preaching about or engaging in any revolutionary activity: God would be responsible for the apocalypse. But that is not how the Romans would have seen it. Clearly the Romans were among the "forces of evil" that would be destroyed, together with the temple and its priesthood. And even though Jesus was not proclaiming himself King in this world but only in the future Kingdom of God, the Romans wouldn't have cared one wit. Such an agenda still stirred people up against Rome and the temple priesthood, and anyone leading such a movement would be considered a traitor. That's what Pilate's interrogation of Jesus was aimed at.

Early Christians in gentile Roman society faced a set of seemingly insurmountable problems in converting people and growing their religion. Their obscure Messiah had been crucified as a political criminal by Rome, and so presumably had opposed Rome. The Kingdom of God, predicted to be imminent, had not come, so it was logical to conclude that Jesus had been wrong. He had not achieved anything that the Messiah, however previously defined, was supposed to accomplish. And Jews were in disrepute, especially after the Jewish War, which was a problem since many of the earliest Christians were from the Jewish diaspora, and in people's minds Christianity was associated with the Jews and Judaism.

Christian leaders addressed these challenges by mythologizing Jesus, recasting him as less-apocalyptic, apolitical, peace-loving, non-threatening to Rome, opposed to the Jewish establishment, and innocent of his alleged crime. Because of the miracle of Christ's resurrection, Christians increasingly believed that Jesus the Messiah came not to end oppression on earth, but to save people for eternal life in heaven. Christians blamed the Jews rather than Rome for his death. Further, they claimed that his crucifixion and resurrection were predicted by scripture and were part of God's grand plan. As a result of the Jewish War, the temple was destroyed and the "mother church" of Jerusalem that had been tied to the Jewish Law was gone, together with its nominal control over other worshippers of Christ. Therefore, Christians were now free to divorce themselves from Judaism and transform Jesus into a peaceful teacher and divine being whose Kingdom was not of this world.[46] Christians could redefine what messiahship meant, and claim that the Jews didn't understand their own scriptures. Christian evangelism now focused more than ever on gentiles. This break with Judaism was well symbolized by the veil in the temple being torn in two at the moment of Jesus's death, thus allowing direct access to God and ending the dominance of the Law (Mk 15:38; Mt. 27:51). Now much of Jesus's Jewishness also could be made to disappear. Christians had to find their place within Greco-Roman society and culture and develop their religion within its framework; the center of Christianity drifted toward Rome. The theme of holding up under persecution, originally the result of Jesus movements being rejected and thrown out of the synagogues in Syria-Palestine, was now reworked to apply to Roman persecution of Christians throughout the Mediterranean world.

Let's examine more specifically how the above tactics were used to mythologize the passion events that we celebrate at Easter.

Fitting the Passion into Jewish Scripture and Tradition
The evangelists had at their disposal centuries of Jewish scriptures, including mythical material, into which they desired to fit their positions and narratives in order to give the Jesus story the stamp of prophetic authority, and also to show to skeptical gentiles that Christianity was not something entirely novel but had ancient and venerable roots going back at least to Moses, before even Homer.[47] In particular, they often referred to Hebrew Bible stories and prophecies to show that events in Jesus's life, including the crucifixion and resurrection, were fulfilling scripture.

Early Jewish Christians had a well-known scriptural model (and mythological motif) to work from when recasting Jesus. Numerous stories in the Hebrew Bible told of the persecution and vindication of an innocent, pious, and just person. Such stories were popular and reassuring because Israel itself had suffered so much over its history. According to New Testament scholar George Nickelsburg, such stories form a literary genre, called the "wisdom tale." Its elements usually include a wise, innocent person who is the object of a conspiracy, is consigned to death (though not always killed), and finally is rescued, vindicated, and exalted.[48] Examples include the stories of Joseph, Susanna,[49] Mordecai in the book of Esther, the three Jewish courtiers in Daniel 3, Daniel himself in Daniel

6, and the righteous man in Wisdom of Solomon 2–5 (although the conspiracy was only conceived, not acted upon).[50] Needless to say, these stories were full of myth and legend, and some, like Esther,[51] were probably entirely fictitious.

Mark portrayed the passion and resurrection using this mythological template,[52] and the other Gospels followed. Interestingly, however, one text that the evangelists relied upon (*as if* it fit this template) for prophesizing Jesus and his passion was Isaiah 53, which describes a suffering servant who was "despised and rejected," was silent when oppressed (like Jesus at his trial), was "like a lamb that is led to the slaughter," and who "was numbered with the transgressors" [cf. Luke 22:37]; yet he bore the sin of many." The problem with this, as recognized by most biblical scholars, is that here the suffering servant was not an individual but Israel itself, as is evident from the preceding verse 49:3—"You are my servant, Israel".[53] Also, as a historical matter, the suffering in question (Babylonian captivity) had already happened.[54] Nevertheless, the evangelists calculated that referring to this passage would help mollify discomfort with Jesus having been crucified, and it evidently worked.

The evangelists also relied on scriptural prophecies to craft the passion narrative. One interesting example relates to Jesus's triumphant entry into Jerusalem. A prophecy in Zechariah 9:9 portrays the arrival of the triumphant King of Israel on a donkey. It was utilized in all four Gospels to describe Jesus arriving in Jerusalem as King to the cheers of an adoring crowd. Zechariah's prophecy reads:

Humble and riding on a donkey,
on a colt, the foal of a donkey.

This is a form of Hebrew (and earlier Canaanite) poetry, known as synonymous parallelism, in which the second line reiterates the substance of the first line in different words. Mark, Luke, and John, understood that the same donkey was referenced in both lines,[55] but Matthew either did not understand or was unsure, so he said that Jesus sent for *both* a donkey and a colt, and that Jesus rode *both of them* into Jerusalem (Mt 21:2, 5–7)! A belt and suspenders approach.[56]

This strategy of relying on Jewish scripture extended down to the small details. In Mark 15:29, Jews mocking Jesus at the cross wagging their heads fulfils Psalms 22:7 and 109:25. In John 19:23, Roman soldiers at the foot of the cross take Jesus's clothes and cast lots for them, in fulfillment of Psalm 22:18. Sometimes the evangelists used different scriptures to support contradictory elements in their stories. Thus, in Mark 15:34 and Matthew 27:46, Jesus on the cross utters words from Psalm 22:1, "My God, my God, why have you forsaken me?" Luke 23:46, however, has him say, "Father, into your hands I commend my spirit," which quotes Psalm 31:5. (In John 19:23 he says simply, "It is finished," there being no apparent reference to scripture.)

While a prophecy might indeed turn out to correspond with an actual future historical event, scholars rightly suspect that these cases the evangelists made up facts to fit the prophecy. Further, many of these "proof citations" don't fit well in the contexts in which an evangelist uses them,[57] or the scripture referenced turns out to be nonexistent.[58] And finally, no Jewish scripture predicts the suffering and execution of the Messiah. So the evangelists had to get creative.

Portraying Jesus and Christianity as Apolitical, Innocent, and no Threat to Rome

The lives of Christians in the Roman empire could fall into jeopardy at any moment, so they learned to keep a low profile and live exemplary lives in order to give no occasion for criticism or arrest. Several of the New Testament epistles (e.g., 1 and 2 Timothy, Titus) exhort their readers to behave in this way. And as told in Paul's epistle to Philemon, when Philemon's runaway slave joined Paul's company seeking his freedom in the Christ cult, Paul sent him back to Philemon. Paul and his churches had no interest in calling Greco-Roman institutions into question.

But in the Gospel of Mark Jesus opposed the Jewish establishment, and he went to Jerusalem in order to provoke matters, specifically to initiate the end times and bring on the Kingdom of God. So his turning over the tables of the moneychangers and driving people from the temple was probably intended as a way to begin the cleansing of Israel to make way for the Kingdom, and also to symbolize the coming destruction of the temple and its priesthood.[59] To some this made Jesus look like a troublemaker, implicitly opposing the Roman power scheme in Judea, but Mark was careful to dampen any such impression. The plot to destroy Jesus was hatched early in his Galilean ministry (Mk 3:6), and Jesus knew his fate ahead of time, considered it part of God's plan, and so went to Jerusalem in order to sacrifice himself. Thus, only a minimal, symbolic provocation was needed as a pretext to arrest him, for which the incident at the temple sufficed. The rest of the time he was peacefully teaching at the temple and said nothing against Rome directly. Thus, according to Luke 23:2, the priests told Pilate that Jesus was forbidding Jews to pay taxes to the emperor, but Jesus is portrayed teaching on the temple steps shortly before his arrest and affirming that it is acceptable to pay taxes to Rome—"Pay to Caesar what belongs to Caesar."[60]

In another example, when Jesus was arrested at Gethsemane, the arresting party was armed (and in John included Roman soldiers), but the evangelists have Jesus say, "Have you come out with swords and clubs to arrest me as though were an insurgent? Day after day I was with you in the temple teaching, and you did not arrest me" (Mk 14:48–49). Jesus is thus portrayed as not being an insurrectionist. This is stressed again a moment later when Jesus chastises one of his disciples for cutting off the ear of the chief priest's slave: "Put your sword back into its place; for all who take the sword will perish by the sword" (Mt 26:52). In Luke 22:51 he even heals the victim's ear.

During his trial, Jesus is portrayed as innocent of sedition, and Pilate agrees. So does Herod Antipas (Lk 23:15). At his trial Jesus never admits to considering himself the King of the Jews, which in all Gospels was Pilate's principal question and the only charge against him. According to Matthew 27:24, Pilate, seeing that he would have to submit to the will of the crowd lest a riot ensue, literally took some water and washed his hands, saying "I am innocent of this man's blood; see to it yourselves." (This refers to Jewish ritual hand washing described in Deuteronomy 21:5–7 and Psalm 73:13—"I have kept my heart clean and washed my hands in innocence.") Then the people "as a whole answered, 'His blood be on us and on our children!'" (Mt 27:25). They then force Pilate to free the murderer Barabbas and crucify Jesus. So according to the Gospels, it was not the Romans who were to blame, but the Jews.[61] In the Gospels, the scandal of the crucified Messiah is lessened by the fact that, at least on the earthly legal level that would have been concern to the audience, it was all a big mistake.

And finally it helped to portray Romans as accepting Jesus. So as Jesus breathed his last, the Roman centurion guarding the cross exclaimed, "Truly this man was God's Son!" (Mk 15:39; Mt. 27:54). Luke 23:47 instead has him say, "Certainly this man was innocent!"

Addressing the Scandal of a Crucified Messiah

Although the Jesus of the Gospels may have thought of himself as the Messiah and his followers believed this, in fact he did not achieve anything that the Messiah was supposed to achieve, no matter which Jewish definition of the Messiah one uses. Instead, he was crucified as a criminal. Therefore, to the normal Jewish mind, calling Jesus the Messiah was scandalous. For them, a principal scriptural problem was Deuteronomy 21:22–23, which says that anyone convicted of a capital crime and hung on a tree (i.e., crucified) is cursed by God. So how could Christ be worshipped when his crucifixion rendered him cursed by God and invalidated any claim that he was the Messiah? Gentiles too considered the Christian claim foolish. Cicero had written, "The mere mention of the word 'cross' is shameful to a Roman citizen and a free man."[62] A graphic example is found in the famous Alexamenos Graffito discovered in Rome (probably from the early third century), which mockingly depicts a figure in the form of a donkey being crucified and is captioned, "Alexamenos worships his god" (Fig. 6.1).

As a result, the crucifixion was a roadblock for early Christians in recruiting potential converts. St. Paul admitted the problem, characterizing the crucifixion as "a stumbling block to Jews and foolishness to Gentiles" (1 Cor 1:23). The fact that the crucifixion was such an embarrassment is why many scholars believe it must have happened, on the ground that no one would make up such an embarrassing tale.

So how did Christians endeavor to mythologize around the problem? For starters, portraying Jesus as innocent as described above arguably avoided the Deuteronomy problem and aligned the passion story instead with the traditional wisdom tale discussed above. Another part of the solution was to claim that Christ was resurrected, that his disciples and others saw him after the resurrection but before his ascension into heaven, and further that he will return soon to complete his and God's work. For Mark, Christ's sacrifice set the apocalypse in motion. So actually he had defeated death, was vindicated, and will prevail in the end. St. Paul gave yet another explanation. He argued that Jesus was the second Adam who willingly sacrificed himself on behalf of all humanity to remove the curse of original sin and thus bring salvation to everyone who accepts Christ (Rom 5:12; 1 Cor 15:21–22). Yes, there was a curse as Deuteronomy said, but Christ, being born without the taint of original sin and sinless himself, was willingly bearing the curse resulting from the sins of all others. People

Fig. 6.1 Drawing from Alexamenos Graffito, ca. 200 CE, originally in the quarters of the Imperial Pages on the Palatine, now at Palatine Hill Museum. Alamy stock photo

can be redeemed by accepting him and his sacrifice on their behalf. The creative doctrine of original sin actually had no solid basis in prior scripture and Jews rightly had never interpreted their scripture in that way,[63] but this new idea successfully served the purpose of recasting Jesus. Christians claimed that the crucifixion was simply part of God's grand plan. In order to help prove this, they argued that the crucifixion was predicted by scripture (see above) and that Jesus himself repeatedly had predicted it and his resurrection (e.g., three times in Mark alone: 8:31; 9:30–31; and 10:33–34).

Appealing to Gentiles Using Classical Mythical Parallels
Once Christianity moved outside Judaism after the Jewish War, in order for the Christ story to appeal to a Mediterranean gentile audience, it would help if it had a familiar a ring. As Bart Ehrman noted, Christians "increasingly shaped the stories so that Jesus looked more and more like

the divine men commonly talked about in the Roman world."[64] Indeed, many aspects of the Gospels parallel traditional myths from the Mediterranean world, especially in connection with the passion and resurrection. The point here is not necessarily that the evangelists and others were consciously patterning the Jesus story after particular Greco-Roman myths in each case, which is hard to prove. Rather, it is sufficient that the evangelists followed common mythological motifs with which the gentile audience was familiar in order to make Christ appealing.[65] As M. David Litwa put it, "the Christian promotion of Jesus [was] a modification of a broader theme of deification in the ancient Mediterranean world."[66] Early church fathers recognized the comparisons and based some of their arguments on them. For example, Justin Martyr famously argued, "When we say that . . . He was crucified and died and rose again and ascended into heaven, we propound nothing new beyond [what you believe] concerning those whom you call the sons of Zeus."[67] He then listed several classical figures who bore some parallels to the Christ story, including Asclepius, Dionysus, Heracles, the Dioscuri,[68] Perseus, Bellerophon, Ariadne, and Roman emperors deified after their death. (He also argued that, since Moses was the most ancient writer, these classical myths actually copied Jewish scripture![69]) Origen also mentions that Christianity's opponents were claiming that Christ's resurrection story was like those of various Greco-Roman figures such as Zalmoxis and Pythagoras, and therefore should be discounted.[70] So we can see that such comparisons were being made at the time; they are not the brainchilds of modern scholars.

One New Testament scholar, professor Dennis MacDonald, points to interesting examples of parallels from Homer. He argues that many episodes in the Synoptic Gospels are modeled on episodes from Homer's *Iliad* and *Odyssey* that would have been familiar to the Mediterranean audience, in order to make Jesus look even better than the Homeric heroes. These include several episodes in the passion story, such as:

- Jesus's anointing in Bethany being modeled on Eurycleia's washing of Odysseus's feet
- Jesus's entry into Jerusalem being modeled on Odysseus's entry into the city of the Phaeacians and Aeneas's entry into Carthage
- Overturning the tables of the moneychangers in the temple being modeled on Odysseus's clearing his palace of Penelope's suitors
- Judas's treachery being modeled on Odysseus's disloyal slave Melanthius, who sided with Penelope's suitors

- The Last Supper being modeled on the Laestrygonian cannibals' feast
- The heroic death of Jesus and his abandonment by everyone around him being modeled on the death of Hector and his abandonment by Deïphobos and Apollo
- Joseph of Arimathea's rescuing Jesus's corpse being modeled on King Priam's rescue of Hector's corpse
- The mourning women at Jesus's tomb being modeled on the lamentations of Hector's mother Hecuba, his wife Andromache, and Helen[71]

Also, the symbolic cup of which Jesus spoke in the garden Gethsemane may have been modeled on Socrates drinking his cup of hemlock.[72]

Finally, the story of Christ's death and martyrdom may be modeled on the popular Greek motif of the "noble death," which was applied to various warriors, athletes, and in particular to Socrates and other philosophers. The concept was fundamental to Greek views of citizenship, honor, and virtue. To be willing to die as a martyr for a noble cause (obedience to one's teachings, beliefs) was the ultimate test of virtue and strength of character.[73] This motif complements the Jewish wisdom tale tradition discussed above (pp. 83–84).

The most important parallel with Greco-Roman mythical figures, as well as with deified Roman emperors, however, was in connection with the resurrection. So let's turn to that.

Myth and the Resurrection of Christ

In the Christian tradition the resurrection of Christ is considered a historical event. Without it, there would be no Christianity. As St. Paul put it, "if Christ has not been raised, then our proclamation has been in vain and your faith has been in vain" (1 Cor 15:14).

Some aspects of the resurrection story point to its mythical character. Take for example, the report that Christ died and then rose on the third day. Did this actually happen, or was this just the way a resurrection was "supposed" to happen? After all, Jewish tradition held that a dead person's spirit/soul remains for three days and then departs,[74] so perhaps Jesus's resurrection was simply supposed to take that long anyway. More generally, in Jewish scripture three days can be an idiomatic expression meaning a short period of time,[75] just as 40 days (or years) meant a long period of time. But for polemical purposes, it had to be three days in order to fulfil a specific scripture: Both Luke (24:46) and Paul (1 Cor 15:4) invoked Hosea 6:1–3, which had spoken of a raising on the third day. Hosea himself, however, may have meant only a short period of time.[76]

But such explanations do not get to the bottom of the question: Why do we have a three-day motif in the first place, and in the context of death and resurrection? A mythological approach yields the deeper answer. The three-day motif in such a context reflects lunar mythology based on the lunar cycle.[77] Traditionally, the period in which the waning moon dies, the moon is not visible (is dead), and the waxing moon appears (is reborn) is viewed as three days (although astronomically it can vary from this).[78] Since the cycle is known to everyone worldwide, the mythological motif is archetypal. Three days is the period in which mythical figures are dead or dormant before being revived, such as in the Mesopotamian myth of Inanna's/Ishtar's descent, Osiris according to Plutarch,[79] or Jonah's captivity in the belly of the whale (probably a metaphor for the underworld).[80] In Chap. 3 (p. 47) we saw how Timarchus emerged alive from the Trophonian cave on the third day. St. Paul was said to have undergone an analogous experience, when as a result of having his vision of Jesus, he was blinded (and he fasted) for three days, and then regained his sight (Acts 9:9). So it is natural that the three-day motif appears in Christ's resurrection as well.

This three-day lunar motif is also reflected in the notion of Christ's descent into the underworld on Holy Saturday, known as the Harrowing of Hell. The scriptural basis for belief in this is Ephesians 4:9, which says that Christ "descended into the lower parts of the earth," and 1 Peter 4:6, which says that "the gospel was proclaimed even to the dead" (though without expressly specifying by whom). While this scriptural reed is thin (and also late among New Testament writings), it is logical that, once dead, Christ would first go to the realm of the dead (in order to be finally dead) before resurrecting. Indeed, the Catholic Church argues that, given that he resurrected, his descent to the underworld must be presupposed.[81] According to this doctrine, Christ brought back with him the risen righteous dead, who would now reside in heaven.

The descent of a hero or goddess into the underworld and reappearance is an ubiquitous mythological motif.[82] Sometimes the underworld journey of the person or deity to be resurrected is specifically a three-day affair, as noted in the cases of Inanna, Jonah, and Osiris. Also, the figure who descends, like Christ, often saves and brings back someone who has been trapped in the underworld. Thus, Heracles raised Theseus and

Ascalaphus from Hades in his 12th labor, and so overcame death himself; Hermes retrieved Persephone to save humanity from starvation; Dionysus rescued his dead mother Semele from Hades,[83] while in Aristophanes's *Frogs he* brought the playwright Aeschylus back from Hades to save Greek tragedy; Orpheus almost rescued Eurydice this way. Christ's descent follows a common mythological pattern.

Why and how would belief in Christ's resurrection arise in the first place? There seem to be two possibilities. The first is that such belief arose among Jesus's disciples and other followers who knew him.[84] Arguably, no one else would have known about Jesus or have cared enough to advance such a proposition. One explanation, psychological in nature, would be that they experienced bereavement and saw visions of the resurrected Christ, a possibility that is taken up below in connection with the reported post-resurrection appearances of Christ (p. 97). But we don't need that explanation if Jesus was indeed an apocalyptic prophet. In that case, his resurrection would be a logical consequence of his apocalyptic teachings. Specifically, Jesus, as portrayed in the Gospel of Mark, taught that when the end of the world comes, all of the dead would be resurrected so that they could be judged and possibly enter and live eternally in the Kingdom of God. The judge was to be the Son of Man sent by God, who will carry out the last judgment and then establish and rule the Kingdom. In this case, logically he should be the *first* to be resurrected so he could judge all others. That's why St. Paul called Christ's resurrection the "first fruits of those who have died" (1 Cor. 15:20), that is, the beginning of the general resurrection. Finally, since Jesus and others who are resurrected will be living on earth in the Kingdom, it follows that they will be resurrected bodily, not as incorporeal spirits. His resurrection and the post-resurrection appearances also serve as the final vindication and exaltation stages in the traditional Jewish wisdom tales discussed earlier (pp. 83–84).[85]

The other possibility is based on pre-Markan evidence. As we have seen, the Jesus of Q¹, as opposed to that of Mark, was not apocalyptic, in which case the above logic does not apply. So the first actual evidence for a resurrected Christ is in the Christ myth, as described in Paul's epistles. While the original martyrdom aspect of the Christ myth would not necessarily require a resurrection, once Paul introduced apocalypticism as a secondary aspect of the myth, then the resurrection of Christ would follow according to the apocalyptic logic explained above. Mark would then have borrowed from this later, Pauline version of the Christ myth.

In evaluating whether or to what extent the resurrection story is a myth, we must consider whether it really happened as a historical matter. When a historian endeavors to verify the historicity of miraculous events such as the miracles and resurrection of Christ, he or she faces a conundrum. By their very nature, supernatural miracles have virtually a zero probability of occurring. That's why they are called miracles. No historian using normal historical methods has access to the kind of information that would establish whether a reported ancient "miracle" actually happened as described. Virtually any alternative non-supernatural explanation has a greater likelihood of being true, in this case, for example, that Jesus survived the crucifixion, that the body had been moved (stolen), that the women went to the wrong tomb, or that there was no tomb to begin with, making it impractical to find his body. From the historian's perspective, these explanations would first have to be eliminated before accepting a supernatural explanation that by its very nature is less probable. Belief in the resurrection is therefore a matter of faith. If it didn't happen, then we have a myth. But even if it did happen, the event (and post-resurrection events) could still have been mythologized like so much of Jesus's life, as we have seen.

Be that as it may, let's consider what evidence for the resurrection has been proffered. The best evidence, and indeed almost all of it, is contained in the four canonical Gospels and certain epistles of St. Paul. It falls into two separate categories, the first being known as the "empty tomb" tradition, in which women discover that Jesus's tomb is empty, and the second being the "appearances" tradition, according to which various disciples, St. Paul, and some others claimed to have encountered Jesus after the crucifixion and, in some cases, watched him ascend to heaven (known as the ascension). Each tradition needs to be addressed separately.

Before looking at each in turn, however, it is important to discuss briefly a Greco-Roman mythical tradition known as "translation fables," in which a human, demigod, or god living on earth dies and then is resurrected (deified in the case of humans) into heaven (i.e., "translated"). There are dozens of such stories, including about Romulus, Heracles (and his mother Alcmene), Aeneas, the Dioscuri, and Apollonius of Tyana.[86] Much as the mythological hero cycle[87] and the related "birth of the hero" motif (see pp. 201–04) contain standardized elements, so did the classical translation fables. In analyzing 77 examples of such fables, New Testament scholar Richard Miller identified 15 common elements often present in them. These include:

- The translation rectifying an injustice, undoing a tragic loss, or vindicating the person
- A vanished or missing body
- One or more post-translation appearances by the translated individual, particularly on a road, seen by one or more eyewitnesses
- A post-translation didactic speech by the translated individual
- An ascension, often by winds or into the clouds[88]

Miller concluded that Mark utilized this template in composing his Easter story. Christ's resurrection indeed fits several standard elements in it: He was executed as an innocent man, and his resurrection vindicated him. His tomb was found empty and the body was nowhere to be found. Then he appeared to the disciples, when he provided further teachings and instructions. And finally he ascended into a cloud (Acts 1:9). These elements are detailed further below (pp. 104–06).

The Empty Tomb Tradition

Although historically an empty tomb would have to precede any appearances, most scholars believe that the appearances tradition arose first.[89] Paul, who wrote well before the Gospels were composed, never mentions an empty tomb. The first mention of the empty tomb appears in Mark, written in the wake of the Jewish War, just when Christian evangelists had already shifted their focus from Jews to gentiles. The empty tomb stories seem to have arisen as part of an argument to prove that Christ was resurrected bodily, not merely in spirit, in accordance with the apocalyptic idea noted above and to refute the traditional Greek belief that during life the spirit is imprisoned in the body and is released upon death and goes to the Elysian Fields.[90] The Greeks thought that upon death the spirit and body separate; the body was too profane to ascend to heaven, the realm of the ideal (cf. Plato). St. Paul argued for bodily resurrection to his Greek listeners but ran into difficulty convincing them, as exemplified by his unsuccessful speech to the Athenians (Acts 17:32: "When they heard of the resurrection of the dead, some scoffed") and doubts about the claim among some in Corinth (1 Cor 15:12, 35).[91] An empty tomb story would help shore up the Christian position since, as a matter of common sense, it presumes bodily resurrection, because the stone had to be rolled away in order for the bodily resurrected Jesus to be able exit the tomb.[92] There was also a Greek mythological precedent for the stone, from when Heracles rolled aside the stone that had kept Ascalaphus imprisoned in Hades.[93]

The empty tomb stories face a threshold historical problem because the notion of there being a tomb for anyone crucified by Rome contradicts standard Roman crucifixion practice. The Romans let the corpses remain on the cross for a while in order to further humiliate the offenders and deter other people from committing such crimes. The flesh would be eaten by scavengers, the corpses would decompose for a while, and eventually the remains would be tossed into a common grave.[94] (To make the point, the eminent Catholic New Testament scholar John Dominic Crossan colorfully argued that Jesus's corpse was probably eaten by dogs.[95]) The only exception to this practice that we know of is reported by Philo of Alexandria, who noted that if the criminal was executed on the emperor's birthday then the body might be given back to family members at their request.[96] But Easter was not on the emperor's birthday (Tiberius was born in November), nor do the Gospels report that family members of Jesus (who were from Galilee) were present and requested and were given the body. So it is not likely that there was a tomb to be empty in the first place.[97]

But assuming there was a tomb, the story then becomes more fantastic from a historian's perspective. In all three Synoptic Gospels, when the women arrive at the empty tomb, they encounter one or two angelic beings dressed in white, one of whom reports that Jesus is no longer there and has been raised (Mt 28:5–6; Mk 16:5–6; Lk 24:4–5); in John the resurrection is implied by the neatly folded burial head cloth found in the tomb (Jn 20:7), which presumably would not have been there or in that state had the body simply been moved.[98] New Testament scholars generally view the Synoptic Gospels as historically more reliable than John, but what is a historian to do when the only potential eyewitness testimony that Jesus was resurrected comes from an angelic being? That only adds another problematic supernatural layer to the story.

Nor did the people featured in the empty tomb stories accept them as evidence of Christ's resurrection. In the Gospels, with the possible exception of the women who discovered the empty tomb, none of the characters believed that Jesus had risen based on the empty tomb. (They came to believe this only as a result of subsequently reported appearances of Jesus, discussed below.) So the question arises, why bother to include this story when it fails to convince the parties involved? The answer appears to be that it would nevertheless be convincing to the gentile audience, because it fits well within Greco-Roman mythical traditions.

As mentioned above, a key feature of translation fables is that the body of the deceased disappears. This "missing body" element is what demonstrates that the deceased has been taken up by a god; the absence of decaying remains helped to view the person as not mortal, and also avoided the ignominy of not having had a proper burial rite.[99] Mark may have modeled his empty tomb story on this mythical tradition so that Jesus's resurrection story would be familiar and persuasive.[100] For this purpose, Christ's body being left on the cross for some time according to Roman practice would not work. Also, in some of the translation fables, like those of Romulus and Aristeas of Proconesus, it was clear that the deceased was resurrected bodily, which examples would be helpful in convincing potential converts of the bodily resurrection of Christ.

The Appearances Tradition

The stories of post-resurrection appearances were designed to prove that the resurrection had occurred, demonstrate that Christ had resurrected bodily, and convey additional teachings and instructions from him. The case for bodily resurrection is made especially strongly in Luke, where the resurrected Christ tells the disciples, "Look at my hands and my feet; see that it is I myself. Touch me and see; for a ghost does not have flesh and bones as you see that I have." He then showed them his hands and feet, and ate a piece of broiled fish (Lk 24:39–42). Similarly, in John 20:27–28 Christ tells doubting Thomas to look at the nail marks in his hands and to insert his hand into his side (where the spear had punctured it), and Thomas comes to believe in the resurrection, and that this Christ is no ghost.

Like the resurrection itself, the reported post-resurrection appearances of Christ also are supernatural events that a historian cannot verify (or disprove) using usual historical methods. While we might accept that someone has had a vision, this does not mean that the vision reflects external reality. Nor does a vision of Christ necessarily imply the kind of bodily resurrection that Christians were claiming.

The stories of post-resurrection appearances in the Gospels and Acts are not from first-hand eyewitnesses, so under usual criteria of historicity one could dismiss them as simply legendary traditions. In Paul's case, however, we have the report of a first-hand witness who claims to have had a vision of the crucified Christ (1 Cor 15:8; Gal 1:11–12), though not necessarily one walking the Earth. This kind of claim must be addressed differently. Paul could have made it up, of course, which is plausible because he was competing for apostolic status with and arguing about doctrinal issues with Jesus's followers in Jerusalem and elsewhere who not only knew Jesus while he was alive but also may have already claimed to have seen the risen Christ. Paul wanted and needed information not derived from those apostles to give him that authority and status, and then, lo and behold, he received a revelation directly from Christ himself! But as an alternative to both Paul consciously making it up and a supernatural explanation, scholars and other commentators have evaluated Paul's report, and also the other reports of appearances, on the basis of modern psychology.

According to the psychological approach, these visionary experiences of Paul and others, assuming they were not intentionally made up, were most likely visions or hallucinations resulting from psychological factors. In the case of Jesus's original followers, this could have resulted from bereavement, in which situation people even today report visions of recently deceased people close to them. Such visions also could have been prompted to some extent by their apocalyptic expectations of resurrection as discussed above. So the power of suggestion may have been at work here. Also, to the extent that the disciples did not expect or could not accept Jesus's death or resurrection, the visions could have been a case of cognitive dissonance reduction,[101] in which the shock of the crucifixion and seemingly shameful end of their Messiah was compensated for by convincing themselves that Jesus had been resurrected and was seen again. This indeed has happened when the prophecies of modern messiahs have not worked out and they unexpectedly died. This was recently the case in the Jewish Lubavitch eschatological cult when their messianic leader who was supposed to usher in the end times died,[102] and this dynamic also has been documented in the reaction of UFO cult members when their charismatic leader's prediction of the end of the world failed to materialize.[103] Importantly, both of these modern cases involved the unraveling of imminent end-of-world predictions, which an apocalyptic Jesus too would have made.

In the case of Paul, there is a different psychological twist: Having violently persecuted Christians (Gal 1:13) while gaining familiarity with their beliefs, at some point he became sympathetic to them and experienced not only guilt but outright fear that he would be among the condemned on judgment day as predicted by Jesus, so he did an about-face and repented, in which case his ensuing vision-experience of the crucified Christ is explained by modern psychology. In the account in Acts, after all, out of all things that Jesus could have told Paul (i.e., what Paul perceived he had heard), Jesus said, "why do you persecute me? . . . I am Jesus, whom you are persecuting" (Acts 9:4–5). Thus, Carl Jung concluded, "the apparition of Christ came to St. Paul not from the historical Jesus but from the depths of his own unconscious."[104] From the historian's standpoint this explanation has a much greater probability of being correct than a supernatural explanation or concluding that Paul consciously made the story up.

In sum, from the historian's standpoint, while the crucifixion is generally regarded as historical, the subsequent stories of the resurrection and post-resurrection appearances cannot be confirmed as historically authentic. Outside the peculiar field of biblical studies, there isn't a single instance in which any modern scholars have concluded that an event was historical on the basis of a supernatural explanation. If someone believes that the resurrection occurred, it is not because of what any historian would consider to be solid historical evidence, but because of his or her theological beliefs and faith. That fact in itself raises mytho-psychological questions. In such a case the mythologist (and historian) must examine what myth people were living by, and why. In this case the above-mentioned mythology of an imminent apocalypse involving a general resurrection appears to provide the most likely answer. Jesus's apocalypticism (or an understanding that he was an apocalypticist) *required* physical resurrection of the dead, so when Jesus died, logically he *had* to be resurrected. Thus, rather than having to abandon belief in their Messiah after the crucifixion, Jesus's followers could have assumed that Jesus had been raised from the dead, so that the end times could commence. Such belief in turn would have functioned as the power of suggestion and encouraged visions among some.

The appearances tradition also fits into the Greco-Roman mythical "translation fables" discussed above. Many of those stories include episodes in which the resurrected figure is later seen on earth by eyewitnesses, who report the event to others. Figures who so appeared include Romulus, the emperor Claudius, Aristeas of Proconesus, and Drusilla.[105] This would have made Christ's reported appearances familiar and more persuasive to the gentile audience.

After his appearances and ascension Christ did not return, and the apocalypse did not happen imminently, within the lifetimes of people whom Jesus knew as promised. By the Jewish War most of them had probably died. As the apocalyptic vision faded, the church was gradually organized into a permanent institution. Christians could no longer live deprived lives waiting for an imminent apocalypse, but had to get on with their lives, marry, support the family by working at normal jobs, and plan for the future. But the resurrection was already the central belief and tradition in Christianity, and was not about to be abandoned. So the myth had to be taken out of its original apocalyptic context and given new meaning. Originally, the significance of Christ's resurrection was as the beginning of the general resurrection, which was a cosmic and collective affair, although each individual did have to repent for one's sins. Now, however, salvation had become entirely an individual affair. The resurrection was now interpreted to demonstrate that Christ is alive and there for each of us, in heaven, and that anyone who has faith in him will be saved and overcome death (and hell) and instead enjoy eternal life in heaven rather than in a Kingdom of God on earth. This is the version that we celebrate at Easter. In many countries the standard Easter greeting is, "Christ has risen!"

Influences from Non-Classical Myths
Insofar as the Easter resurrection story has a mythical character, it becomes important to distinguish which aspects of the myth partake of motifs common to other myths, and which aspects are more unique to Christian Easter. We can then see which aspects may be archetypal and which are more particular to Judaism and Christianity. The body of myths is full of heroes and gods who die and are then reborn or resurrected, or who, like King Arthur and Quetzalcoatl, are supposed to return someday. The themes of dying gods, resurrecting gods, and gods returning after death and resurrection are all standard motifs in Thompson's *Motif-Index,*[106] which suggests that these motifs are not particular even to the ancient Near Eastern or Mediterranean worlds.

In this connection, one claim originating with James Frazer which we often hear in popular books and on the Internet is that Christ is just one of many "dying-and-rising gods," such as Dumuzi/Tammuz, Baal, Osiris, Adonis, and Attis.[107] It is important to consider such claims not only because they are common and popular, but because doing so helps us clarify what kind of myth we really have in the Easter story, and its true underlying basis.

Scholars in recent decades have challenged the very validity of the "category" of dying-and-rising gods, on the ground that there is not enough meaningful commonality in the myths.[108] I believe the category can be valid so long as we understand clearly the similarities and differences in these myths, and why they exist. One potential explanation for their superficial similarity with the Christ story is that the dying-and-rising god motif diffused into Palestine and remained a factor in Christ's time, resulting in a genealogical relationship among these myths. In Israel, for example, one of the abominations that Ezekiel mentioned was women weeping for Tammuz at the north gate of the Temple (Ez 8:14), which would have been on September 17, 592 BCE,[109] when Babylon (where Tammuz was from) was threatening. The (only) other biblical mentions of such gods concern various versions of Baal, who in Canaanite mythology died and was brought back to life. If outside influence from this motif were the hypothesis for how the Christ resurrection story arose over 600 years later, however, the question to analyze must not merely be whether Baal and this motif were present in Jewish religious thought in the first century CE, but also whether it was influential specifically on either the illiterate Jewish followers of Jesus or members of the Hellenistic Christ cults, i.e., the people who generated the resurrection story. As seen below, in both cases the answer must be no. Rather than one dying-and-rising god myth being derivative of another, they are archetypal responses to parallel religious situations.[110] As discussed below, there is a large psychological component to this.

My own view on dying-and-rising gods is similar to that of Tryggve Mettinger, who in 2001 wrote what is now the leading study on the matter. He restricts the category to certain ancient Near Eastern gods who die and are reborn in connection with the seasonal agricultural cycle, excluding even the Egyptian Osiris because of differences in the underlying myths (he dies but remained in the underworld where he became god of the dead, but from where he still bestows his agricultural bounty and blessings to the people of Egypt; it is a separate deity who rises to life on earth, his son Horus).[111] I consider the category valid if it is restricted to ancient Near Eastern agricultural deities and Osiris (because of because of his similar connection with the crop cycle), but believe that the Christ death and resurrection story is not derived from or otherwise validly connected with this category. There are, however, relevant parallels between the Christ myth and figures in the above-mentioned Greco-Roman translation fables which probably influenced the development of the Easter myth. I elaborate on these points below.

"Dying-and-Rising Gods" Compared with the Resurrection of Christ

It is important to distinguish the content of the Christ resurrection story from that of the pre-Greco-Roman dying-and-rising god motif in at least five respects:

- The dying-and-rising god myths were based on the seasonal agricultural cycle. The god is dead for a considerable portion of the year before coming back to life, and the cycle repeats each year. And he comes back to life on earth (or inside it); he is never borne up to heaven. He is always a god, at no stage a human. Dying-and-rising gods also were the consorts or sons of goddesses (e.g., Inanna/Ishtar, Cybele, and Isis). Christ differs from these gods in all of these respects: no relationship to vegetation; no repeated yearly cycle but was resurrected just once and for all time; no long period of being dead, but instead rose on the third day (so lunar not seasonal mythology); he was a human figure rather than a god while on earth (which is why he could die);[112] when he resurrected he left the earth for heaven; and he was not married to, the son of, or otherwise associated with any goddess but was borne of a mortal woman and thought of as the son of the male Jewish god.
- Unlike the dying-and-rising gods who thought and taught nothing, Jesus had ideas and teachings that he acted upon, and for which was punished by execution, by humans. These were in principle historical, not mythical, events. Dying-and-rising gods were not executed, much less by humans. They died so spring could come again. Their deaths were not sacrifices. They had nothing to do with morals, individual spirituality, human salvation, apocalypticism, or any kingdom of God. Dying-and-rising gods were not messiahs.
- Myths are closely related to accompanying rituals. Differences in the rituals illustrate how the underlying myths differ. Indeed, the rituals in early Christianity and the cases of dying-and-rising agricultural gods were different and unrelated. The annual festival of Osiris, for example, celebrated when the Nile's flood waters were about to recede so the crops could sprout, featured the building of "Osiris beds," filled with soil and sown with seed. Similarly, participants held "corn mummies" made of soil and seeds and wrapped in linen; some were ithyphallic, alluding to his ability to father Horus after his death.[113]

There is nothing of the kind in Christianity. More generally, the rituals for dying-and-rising gods featured annual periods of mourning during the *infertile* part of the year; Christ died and rose over three days in the spring. Ritual in early Christian communities was largely limited to baptism, the Eucharist, and the weekly communal meal.

- Christ was a Jew, and so were his followers. Late Second Temple Judaism was solidly monotheistic, no dying-and-rising gods existed in it, and the religion and mythology was no longer tied to agricultural cycles. There is no sign that dying-and-rising god myths had any presence among Jews (as distinct from Romans) in Judea or Galilee during Jesus's time. To the Jews, Yahweh himself provided all agricultural bounty (there were no subsidiary agricultural/seasonal deities) and he never disappeared for part of the year. Nor was the Jewish Messiah, however understood, ever portrayed as a dying-and-rising god. Reza Aslan rightly observed that "belief in a dying-and-rising messiah simply did not exist in Judaism."[114]

- By Jesus's time the notion of the bodily resurrection of *humans* (not gods) had already become established among certain communities of Jews. The notion of resurrection of humans first became prominent during the Maccabean revolt when martyrs died defending the Law; some Jews came to believe that these heroes would be recompensed by enjoying bodily resurrection.[115] The Pharisees also seem to have believed in bodily resurrection,[116] and the apocalypticism of Jesus held that there would be a general resurrection of all dead humans at the end of times;[117] a general resurrection is also envisaged in Daniel 12:2. That is, in apocalyptic thought, including that concerning Jesus, resurrection did not function in regard to particular individuals (whether humans or gods), but rather was a single *collective* eschatological moment at the end of the age. In this scheme, *all humans* were going to be resurrected and face judgment, after which the elect living in the Kingdom along with Christ would not suffer death (whereas rising gods die again). Given the above, there is no need to appeal to ancient notions of dying-and-rising agricultural gods to establish how Jesus's followers got the idea that he had been resurrected. Rather, as we have seen, Christ's death and resurrection were interpreted within an apocalyptic framework. There were no concerns about agriculture. After all, the existing world was about to come to an end, and in the Kingdom of God there would be no hunger.

In light of the above, as a historical matter the resurrection story could not have *originated* based on traditional "dying-and-rising god" myths. Nevertheless, some exemplars of the dying-and-rising god motif may well have played a background stimulating role in the *subsequent spread* of Christianity among some gentiles in the Greco-Roman world. For example, the cult of Magna Mater (Cybele) and Attis became popular in Rome itself.[118] The emperor Claudius (reigned 41–54 CE), because he fancied himself a descendant of the Trojans from Asia Minor, declared Attis a Roman god, and instituted a two-week vernal equinox festival known as the Hilaria.[119] As part of the festival ritual, Attis "died" by a pine tree on March 22, a large pine log with an image of Attis on it was brought to the Magna Mater temple in Rome, and he was reborn on March 25,[120] the date of the vernal equinox. This holiday arose too late and too far away from Judea to have influenced the origin of the belief in Christ's resurrection, but later on it might have influenced people in Rome who would become Christian converts. Similarly, the example of Dionysus, who was resurrected and was venerated in Palestine and throughout the Mediterranean, may have played a role. This is hard to prove, however.

Also relevant here is the notion of death and rebirth in Greek and Roman mystery cults, which involved initiates experiencing a spiritual form of dying (to one's prior self) and rebirth. But these mystery rituals were not generally modeled on "dying-and-rising gods." The Eleusinian mysteries were modeled on the myth of Demeter and Persephone also Dionysus, and the Mithraic mysteries were modeled on Mithras, who never actually died. There was a mystery cult of Isis in Rome by the first century CE, but not of Osiris—by then her partner was Sarapis. Christianity offered an analogous alternative through the initiation of baptism, entry into a new way of life, and the promise of salvation. Outsiders often viewed Christianity as a mystery cult.

The mystery cults lead to an important psychological consideration. Specifically, dying-and-rising god myths, the Christ resurrection myth, and the mysteries all may be expressions of the same archetypal process within the human psyche, simply being expressed in somewhat different ways according to the differing cultures and situations. In discussing the psychology of the notion of rebirth, Carl Jung argued that the similarities of dying-and-rising gods derive from archetypes of the collective unconscious and represent an effort of the psyche to experience a "permanence and continuity of life which outlasts all changes of form," which helps develop the wholeness of one's Self.[121] Thus, as discussed below, he viewed the Christ figure as a symbol of the Self.[122] Scholars of the ancient Near East have acknowledged the explanatory value of a psychological approach to such myths.[123] From this perspective, the point is that the Christ resurrection myth did not "copy" the dying-and-rising god motif, but rather that resurrection myths in general emerge from same structures within the human psyche. This archetypal character of the Christian resurrection myth helps explain the appeal and ultimate success of Christianity in the Greco-Roman world, a point on which I will elaborate at the end of this chapter.

In light of the above, the afore-mentioned Greco-Roman translation fables may offer a much stronger parallel and source of influence on Christ's resurrection story. Let's explore one example of that.

Greco-Roman Heroes and Deities in Translation Fables

Space does not permit discussing many of the Greco-Roman heroes and deities who resurrected (or humans who were deified), such as Heracles, Dionysus, Asclepius, and others. Rather, I'll focus on one specific to Rome since the evangelists' audience was Roman and knew Rome's myths well. The story of Christ's resurrection and later appearances bears several key resemblances to the mythologization of Romulus, the eponymous founder of Rome, dear to the Romans, and probably their most famous figure. He was conceived when Mars slept with a vestal virgin and so was the son of a god, and whereas Romulus founded the kingdom of Rome, Jesus proclaimed the Kingdom of God. According to the story of Romulus's death, once he had put Rome on firm foundations, his father, the god Mars, decided that it was time to take him back up to heaven. According to the fable, one day when Romulus was reviewing his troops on the Field of Mars, he disappeared; the fable claimed that Mars had raised him up.[124] Just in relation to the Easter events, we find at least the following parallels:[125]

- Like Jesus (as the Word) in the Gospel of John, Romulus was preexistent and divine, came from the divine realm to incarnate for a specific earthly mission, and returned to heaven.[126]
- As Romulus was dying on the Field of Mars, clouds came, the sun disappeared and the sky went dark, and thunder clapped;[127] he disappeared in a mist or cloud.[128] When Jesus was dying, darkness came

over the land, and at the moment of his death the earth shook (Mt 27:45, 51). He ascended to heaven in a cloud (Acts 1:9).

- When Romulus died, his body (and clothing) disappeared and people wondered what had happened. Some suspected that certain Senators had killed him and spirited away the body[129] (although no ancient source takes this position). After Jesus died, his body could not be found in the tomb, and people apparently suspected that the disciples had stolen it. So Matthew countered that notion by having Pilate station guards at the tomb (27:63–66). After the body nevertheless disappeared, the guards were bribed to claim that the disciples stole it while they were asleep (28:12:13).

- After Romulus disappeared and his body could not be found, the confused people hurried away from the Field of Mars.[130] This aspect of the event was so famous and important that the day was celebrated as a holiday annually in the Roman world as the day of "The People's Flight" *(Poplifugia)*, thus ensconcing Romulus's ascension as the quintessential resurrection story in the Roman world.[131] The original ending of Mark, where the women fled the tomb upon discovering that the body was missing, may be modeled on this tradition, thus also implying that Jesus was taken up.[132]

- The people concluded that Romulus had ascended to heaven and become a god, and they began to worship him.[133] This parallels Jesus's resurrection and ascension, and subsequent worship of him (e.g., Mt. 28:17; Luke 24:45–53; Acts 1:1–8). In both cases there are eyewitnesses to the ascension (see immediately below).

- After the death of Romulus, his intimate friend Julius Proculus reported that while traveling on the road he had seen Romulus coming toward him. When he asked Romulus what had happened, Romulus replied, "It was the pleasure of the gods, O Proculus, from whom I came, that I should be with mankind only a short time, and that after founding a city destined to be the greatest on earth for empire and glory, I should dwell again in heaven. . . . And I will be your propitious deity, [called] Quirinus."[134] Sightings of resurrected humans, particularly on a road, were a common feature in translation fables.[135] This recalls the encounter of two disciples with the resurrected Christ on the road to Emmaus (Lk 24:13–49).

- Romulus offers Proculus (and Rome generally) parting advice and instructions.[136] This parallels the parting instructions that the resurrected Christ gave to his disciples (Mk 16:14–18; Mt. 28:18–20; Jn 20:21). Both Romulus and Christ rose to heaven after giving their instructions.[137]
- In both cases, their admirers recognized his divinity after his death and resurrection, calling him the son of God (of Mars in Romulus's case).[138]
- Both Romulus and Christ were resurrected and immortalized bodily (corporeally). This was a useful parallel because the Christians taught that the resurrected Christ existed in bodily as well as spiritual form, whereas the Greeks in general thought that the soul is immaterial and that an immortal exists only as spirit after death. As noted, this issue had proved a stumbling block for St. Paul.

Interestingly, after relating the story of Romulus's death, Plutarch raises doubts about its historicity because it appears to parallel similar stories that were told about various Greek men and women who disappeared upon dying, including Alcmene (mother of Heracles), Aristeas of Proconnesus, and Cleomedes of Astypaleia; in other words, because the story was following familiar mythological motifs.[139] The church father Tertullian also noted that both Romulus and Jesus reportedly were taken up to heaven in a cloud, but claimed that this was "far more certain" to have occurred Christ's case than in that of Romulus.[140]

Deification of Roman Emperors

In the first century BCE, Romans began regarding some of their emperors[141] (the good ones) as divine. Sometimes emperors were considered divine while still alive, but more commonly they were deified after their death; sometimes they claimed divine ancestry. In this capacity, the emperor was called the "Son of God"; Augustus put this title on coinage bearing his image.

The practice of deifying emperors presented a challenge for Christians. When Christ's followers decided that he was the divine Son of God, this placed Christ in direct competition with the emperors. For Christians, Christ rather than any emperor was the divine Son of God, and this competition shaped how Christians packaged their myth. As Bart Ehrman observed, Christians were elevating Christ to divinity "under the influence and in dialogue with the environment in which they lived."[142] Christ had to be portrayed as greater than any emperor. One consequence was that the moment when he became divine was pushed back further and further in time.[143] Instead of becoming divine upon his resurrection as seems to have been the case initially (Rom 1:4; Acts 13:33), the moment when he became divine was pushed back to his baptism, then to his conception in Mary's womb, and finally to even before the creation when he was a divinity in heaven (Jn 1:1–3).[144] He was seated at the right hand of God. No emperor could match that.

THE EVOLUTION OF EASTER IN EUROPE

The Easter holiday became firmly established in Rome during the reign of Constantine. Further, Constantine insisted on a uniform date for the holiday, because it was being celebrated on differing dates in various parts of the empire. The holiday's date relates not to the supposed actual date of Christ's resurrection, but rather to both to the vernal equinox and the lunar cycle, like Passover. The date of Easter became established as the first Sunday after the first astronomical full moon after the spring equinox.

When the holiday spread with Christianity itself into pagan Europe, the essential Easter *myth* remained largely unaffected by European pagan myths. In contrast, pagan holidays and rituals relating to the vernal equinox and the coming of spring, which reflected in the underlying pagan mythology and religion, did influence Easter *rituals*. These pagan influences were most pronounced in peasant village customs, but some of them were felt even in official church rituals. As a result, Easter celebrations became mixed with pagan traditions pertaining to the equinox and the coming of spring. Thus, although the Easter myth narrative is not pagan, the way in which Easter was celebrated became somewhat pagan. These influences are still with us today. It is not feasible to discuss all of these (which differ from place to place) in detail, so I will cover just one example; some others appear in connection with the Easter symbols discussed further below.

The Easter liturgical ritual utilizes fire. Mythologically speaking, fire symbolizes life, renewal, transformation, and purification. In the form of the sun, it was worshipped as a deity, but Christianity denied the sun itself such status and instead used it and light to symbolize Christ (e.g., Jn 8:12). The use of fire in Easter rituals centers on the Paschal Candle, which goes back to the late fourth century in Rome.[145] It represents the divinity and purity of Christ, and Christ as the light that brings salvation. But where did the fire that lights this candle come from? It came from a new fire kindled outdoors next to the church; kindled not from the embers of an existing fire but by new and different means, such as flint and steel. It is blessed before it is used to light the Paschal Candle. This kindling and blessing of the new fire has its own ritual called the blessing of the New Fire, and its roots are pagan, apparently originating in pre-Christian Ireland. The Irish made sacred bonfires on important holidays such as Beltane and Samhain, and apparently also around the time of Easter (equinox, coming of spring vegetation); so did various pagan cultures on continental Europe.[146] These fires symbolized renewal, purification, and the triumph of life over death; thus, in many such bonfire traditions a figure of Death was incinerated during the ritual.[147] These were always new, pure fires, kindled not from existing fires but by rubbing sticks together, using lenses, or by flint and steel. Rites of renewal were performed at the bonfire. Initially Christians opposed the bonfire custom, but eventually they adopted it into their rituals, especially at Easter. Thus, St. Patrick recorded that large bonfires were lit in Ireland on the eve of Easter. The pagan bonfires became Easter bonfires throughout Europe. In some places an effigy of Judas (or a figure called "the Easter Man") was now incinerated instead of the old figure of Death.[148] On the next day, the ashes of the fire were spread on the fields to consecrate them, protect them, and bring fertility.[149] Out of this bonfire tradition, by the seventh century but possibly as far back as St. Patrick's time, arose in Ireland the Easter ritual of the blessing of the New Fire. From Ireland the ritual made its way through the Carolingian Empire to Rome.[150] Thus, the means by which the Paschal Candle was lit originated in pagan spring bonfire traditions.

Having covered the Easter-related myths and some rituals, we are now in a position to discuss the more important symbols of Easter.

EASTER SYMBOLS

In our Easter celebrations, we participate in the myth through symbols, which come from both the original myth as well as from pagan cultures.

Easter Eggs

Eggs were especially fascinating to early humans. They were seemingly inanimate objects, yet they produced life, rendering them a mystery. Accordingly, they were thought to possess the divine life force—a force of creation—and so they were revered. Eating them enabled us to partake of that force. And so even in prehistoric times, people placed real or clay eggs in burials, apparently to nourish the deceased in the next world—some were found in King Tutankhamen's tomb for this purpose—or to prompt the person's rebirth. Burial pithoi and tombs were often fashioned in an egg shape.[151] In Boeotia figures of Dionysus (a resurrecting god) holding an egg have been found, to symbolize and aid the return to life.[152] The egg became a symbol of immortality.

Once humans came to think more abstractly, the egg became a symbol of the creation of the cosmos in numerous world mythologies. Either it represented the state of primordial chaos and when it hatched the cosmos came into being, or it was an intermediate stage between chaos and the orderly cosmos, such as in Egyptian myth when the god Khnum was born from an egg and then, in his turn, began to create by shaping eggs.[153] The egg's parts were often thought to make up the essential parts of the cosmos: the two halves of the shell being earth and heaven, with the yolk being the sun and the white the moon as in the Finnish epic poem *The Kalevala*,[154] or alternatively the female moisture/ovum and semen respectively.[155] The egg represented not just creation, but perhaps more importantly the periodic re-creation of the cosmos,[156] in the sense discussed above in connection with New Year's. Thus, in Vedic writings, the cosmic egg has a spirit (or energy) within it, which will be born, die, and be born again.[157]

Eggs thus became associated with the rebirth of life in the springtime. Once people began to practice agriculture, eggs became part of sowing rituals, in order to guarantee successful crops. Eggs were placed in the plowed earth, or were kept in one's pocket at plowing time, or would be thrown in the air before plowing. As such, eggs were an offering to the Earth Goddess or other agricultural deities. They were also rolled on top of the ground, which is the origin of our modern Easter egg rolling games, most famously held on the White House lawn. Because eggs represent renewal, they were also used in New Year's rituals and feasts of the dead.[158]

As far back as Upper Paleolithic times eggs (or representations of them) were colored or otherwise decorated in order enhance their symbolic qualities. Thus, in Neolithic Europe, spirals or square crosses painted on them represented the divine energy within them.[159] They were sometimes colored red because red (from blood) represented life[160] and the birthing process (hence too the Goddess), the same reason why red ochre pigment was often used in tombs. Other colors would represent the colors of spring (e.g., green symbolizing new spring foliage). But such decoration was not always merely symbolic. Sometimes decorating was an exercise in magic intended to give eggs protective powers against evil, death, witches, etc.[161]

In light of the above traditions, once belief in Christ's resurrection arose and the Easter holiday was established, eggs naturally became a symbol of the resurrection and part of the holiday ritual. In Christian eyes, the egg also symbolized the tomb from which Christ broke forth.[162] Red-colored eggs were now interpreted to symbolize the blood of Christ, but various other colors were used as well, continuing the springtime connotations. Eventually Christianity broadly embraced eggs and their symbolism in rituals, holidays, and art[163]

As Christianity spread, the pagan myths and rituals syncretized with those of Christianity, and many hybrid rituals and superstitions arose. For example, in German and Slavic areas, a mixture of eggs, bread, and flour was smeared on the plow on the Thursday before Easter.[164] In many parts of Europe Easter eggs were considered magical good luck charms (amulets), repelling evil and death and protecting the crops. Priests would bless them for this purpose.[165] Easter eggs, especially those sanctified in church, were placed in fields, orchards, and vineyards. In parts of England an egg laid on Good Friday and eaten on Easter Sunday was a charm against evil spirits and death, and protected crops.[166]

In our Easter tradition, it is a bunny that brings the Easter eggs and hides them. Let's now explore why.

The Easter Bunny

Originally the symbolic animal of Easter was the hare, not a rabbit; the rabbit became associated with Easter in America because hares are not so common here whereas rabbits are ubiquitous. The Easter symbolism of the hare is not derived from Jewish or early Christian tradition. For Jews it was an unclean animal, nor for Christians did it have any original connection with Christ. Rather, it came from pagan Europe and became part of Easter rituals in medieval times.

The hare is an extremely fertile animal. They begin mating while young, and females can have several litters per year. Accordingly, hares became associated with spring, and so too with the moon, most specifically its rebirth/resurrection. Also, the gestation period for hares is 28–30 days, like the lunar cycle. So too, the hare became associated with goddesses, especially moon goddesses such a Freya, Holda, and Eostre.[167] For this reason Christians also came to associate hares with witches. On the other hand, a white hare was often portrayed at the feet of the Virgin Mary, to symbolize her virginity and the triumph over lust.[168]

In light of the symbolism of eggs in spring and at Easter, the hare was thought to lay these eggs. This tradition appears to have arisen because eggs were often found in bushes where hares also lived; the bushes protected them both. That is the origin of our Easter egg hunt, because the hare's eggs were naturally hidden in bushes. Later, however, a ritual tradition arose of the Easter hare distributing eggs to children who had been good over the past year (the hare knew who had been naughty and nice).[169] Eggs and the hare (later the Easter bunny) are thus mutually reinforcing symbols.

Easter Lamb

Why is lamb the traditional meal at Easter? It derives from Christ's association with Passover, and is based on an etiological myth. According to the Synoptic Gospels the Last Supper was a Passover meal, for which lamb was the traditional dish. This tradition arose because, according to the Hebrew Bible, the Hebrews while in Egypt painted the blood of sacrificed lambs on their doorposts so that they would be "passed over" by Yahweh when he was killing all firstborn sons in Egypt by plague; Yahweh also told them to eat the lambs that evening (Exod 12:7–8). Thus, sacrificing paschal lambs at Passover and eating lamb for the Passover meal became Jewish traditions, carried over by Christians to Easter because the crucified Christ was portrayed as a sacrificed paschal lamb.

New Clothes and Easter Bonnets

The tradition of wearing new clothes on Easter goes back to the early Christian Easter celebrations, when Easter was the prime time for baptizing converts. After emerging from the baptismal waters, the initiate was given a set of new white garments, which symbolized his or her purity given that all sins had just been forgiven. On such occasions, even previously baptized onlookers might don new clothes on Easter as a reminder,[170] a way of annually celebrating one's new life in Christ. So wearing new clothes on Easter became a tradition. In Great Britain, wearing new clothes on Easter was thought to bring good luck.[171]

Fast forwarding to the United States, in the late nineteenth century people would wear new clothes to the Easter church service, and socialize afterwards. In particular, in New York City by the 1870s it had become traditional to stroll along Fifth Avenue in one's Easter finery, which for women now included an Easter bonnet. This was rather conspicuous consumption and made the clothing merchants happy, but such ostentation was criticized in some Protestant circles. This procession eventually developed into the Easter Parade,[172] memorialized in the film of that name starring Fred Astaire and Judy Garland.

Easter Lilies

Among the new plants of spring are flowers, which we see in abundance at Easter. The Easter lily takes first place among them. The particular lily in question, called the Bermuda lily *(Lilium longiflorum)*, is native to Japan but became cultivated in Bermuda. Once Easter became popular in the United States, in the 1880s it became established as the Easter flower because other kinds of lilies would not bloom in time for Easter. So it was widely adopted in churches.[173]

The lily symbolizes various things in Christianity, including purity and innocence, as in reference to Mary (particularly in paintings of the Annunciation), and hence also the Immaculate Conception and the virginal conception of Jesus. In connection with Easter, lilies symbolize the resurrection (since they bloom around Easter), and their trumpet shape represents triumph (through the resurrection). Lilies appear in the New Testament only in one dialogue where Jesus asks, "Why do you worry about clothing?" He then analogizes to lilies as doing just fine as they are under God's care, looking more splendid than even Solomon in his fine clothes. So since God cares so much more about people than about lilies, faithful Christians should not be concerned about the future, which for them will be in the imminent Kingdom of God (Mt 6:28–33; Lk 12:27–31). That is, people should place themselves in God's hands without reservation. Fine clothes are not needed.

THE MODERN MYTHO-PSYCHOLOGICAL MEANING OF THE RESURRECTION

As noted above (pp. 103–04), dying-and-rising god myths, translation fables, mystery cults in which initiates underwent a personal transformation ("death" and rebirth), and the Christian resurrection story may share a common archetypal psychological underpinning that is also reflected in the mythical symbolism of the vernal equinox and the rebirth of life in spring. These mythologies can be viewed as varied but similar expressions of the same inner psychic conditions.[174] With this background in mind, below I explore the full modern meaning of the Easter experience, not as a matter of Christian doctrine or interpretation of scripture, but in mytho-psychological terms.

In short, from the mytho-psychological and spiritual perspectives, the birth, life, and teachings of Jesus together with his suffering and resurrection can be understood as symbolizing the integration of our total psyche (the "Self," capitalized), namely the integration of the unconscious part of our psyche with the conscious part (the "self").[175] Carl Jung called this process "individuation," and it results in a person being more whole—psychologically balanced, self-aware, and spiritually more advanced. This endeavor can be termed "religious" in nature because at the deepest level of our collective (transpersonal) unconscious lies an archetype of unity and totality that Jung calls the "God-image," which is the deepest source of our numinous experiences of "divinity." Numinous experiences have a lasting emotional impact on us and drive much of our thinking and behavior, including in the individuation process. This happens in everyone, atheists included, and it is the realm that mystics from various religious and non-religious traditions access during their sacred experiences, including in some forms of meditation.

The Evolution of the God Image

Jung held that there was a long evolution of the God-image before ancient Mediterranean culture could reach the point where the Christ figure could resonate with people's psyches and emerge in myth, so that Christianity could emerge, become viable, and even dominate our culture. As Jung observed, "If ever anything had been historically prepared, and sustained and supported by the existing *Weltanschauung*, Christianity would be a classic example."[176]

As seen in Chap. 2 (pp. 18–19), in creation myths the creation symbolizes the emergence of ego consciousness, by which we were able to see opposites, as exemplified by Adam and Eve gaining the "knowledge of good and evil" in the Eden myth. Later, Jesus was seen as a second Adam (Rom 5:12–14; 1 Cor 15:21–22, 45), marking a kind of second creation, and also another stage in human consciousness and spirituality. What happened in between these two events that made the Christ figure possible and relevant? As Jung explained in *Answer to Job,* it is because our God-image had evolved.[177]

At its deepest level in the unconscious, the God-image is an undifferentiated unity, with no opposites yet emerging. According to Jung, Yahweh, portrayed as the single Israelite god, originally encompassed all aspects of divinity, including opposites such as the masculine and feminine, which were still combined in their latent forms. Thus, Yahweh was considered ineffable, he was not thought of in sexual terms, he could not be represented, and his name could not be written or spoken. But this meant that he did not function in terms of opposites. Accordingly, in the book of Job he insisted that humans cannot possibly understand how he thinks and operates, so they must unquestioningly submit to him. Yahweh was temperamental, impulsive, and unpredictable. While sometimes loving and merciful, he was just as easily unjust and cruel and often changed his mind, reflecting a lack of self-awareness and a failure to consult his own omniscience. For example, he violated many of the Ten Commandments, and he broke his Davidic Covenant in which he had promised that a descendant of David would forever be king over Israel. Accordingly, Jung described Yahweh as "unconscious," especially in having a dark, shadow side of which he was unaware and which was not integrated with his consciousness. Yet Yahweh increasingly needed humankind (our consciousness) to support his identity, to the point where he would need and want to share in being human.[178] This was really our own restless "divine" unconscious seeking to make itself conscious (human).

According to Jung, the turning point came when Yahweh let his shadow side (Satan) mistreat Job, who then protested Yahweh's injustice, inflicting a moral defeat on Yahweh from which he would never recover.[179] The God-image began to splinter as opposites emerged. His divine wisdom became personified separately as feminine Sophia, needed by Yahweh for self-reflection and to accommodate to some extent the feminine side of the psyche.[180] Also, according to Jung, in the books of Ezekiel, Daniel, and 1 Enoch, Yahweh drew closer to humanity as his consciousness developed, being represented in each of these books by quaternity symbolism[181] of the Self. Each of those books also featured the "Son of Man" figure, a divine out-growth of Yahweh embodying wisdom, righteousness, and justice. According to Jewish apocalyptic literature, he would arrive soon as Israel's (or even humankind's) savior, an intimation that Yahweh's incarnation lies in the near future.[182] (That's why the Gospels later would call Jesus the Son of Man.) Finally, the figure of Satan, rather than being an appendage of Yahweh, was now split off from Yahweh as a symbol of evil, psychologically representing our shadow (hence too Yahweh's). Inevitably, that would necessitate in response an opposing figure of goodness, justice, and love (eventually the Christian God and his son, Jesus Christ). In short, the God-image was becom-ing differentiated, changing from an unconscious totality of all divinity into conscious opposites represented by corresponding mythical figures. In actual-ity, this evolutionary process was that of our own increasing psychological self-awareness, necessary to achieve integrated wholeness. Because the Christ figure is rooted in and symbolizes the Self, the emergence and popularity of the Christ myth was a natural human psychological process; we should not necessarily expect to find the events of the myth in the historical record.

Meanwhile, in the everyday earthly world, by the time of Jesus people in Palestine were dominated by the Roman military and governmental machine on the one hand, and by a strict and dry Jewish legalism managed by an aloof and compromised priesthood on the other. People were taxed by both, monetarily and spiritually. Both trends were manifestations of ego consciousness run rampant, to the point where too many people's lives had no experience of the divinity that comes from within; conscious-ness and the unconscious had become dissociated. The result was what psychologists term a "loss of soul,"[183] the result of our rejection of numi-nous unconscious content reaching out to make itself known and be inte-grated. Individuals and the society at large come to operate only at the level of everyday ego consciousness, at the expense of inner spiritual life.[184] In such a state we lack psychic energy, which comes from the unconscious (whereas ego consciousness only sucks it up). This "loss of soul" problem is commonly reflected in myths, such as where Wolfram's Grail hero Parzival encounters a "wasteland" kingdom, and proceeds to heal it,[185] much as the apocalyptic Jesus thought would happen when Roman Palestine (and beyond) would be transformed into the coming Kingdom of God. Something had to change. The old pagan Roman and Greek gods were in disrepute and no longer appealing, so they offered no alternative.

Nor did the new emperor's cult resonate with people because it was too politically oriented (being a product of ego consciousness) and because it limited divinity to one individual rather than letting each person experience divinity, so it was psychologically sterile.[186]

In contrast, Jesus had taught his followers, "You are gods" (Jn 10:34, quoting Ps 82:6). Indeed, true divine experiences of renewal and rebirth come from an infusion of psychic energy and content emanating from the unconscious.[187] In the Greco-Roman world, one way to accomplish this was through participation in one of the increasingly popular mystery cults, in which initiates experienced transformation (rebirth). In these rituals an initiate was transformed through participation in the fate of the deity, as also would be the case with Christ in Christianity. These developments evidenced a growing yearning for a more individualized spirituality of transformation that would provide a more meaningful experience of the sacred, but the mysteries (and Gnosticism) were confined to a small, sophisticated part of the population, and mostly to men. As Jung mentioned (p. 113), the situation was ripe for a break-out religion that would answer to the archetypal spiritual needs of people in general.

Christ as a Symbol of the Self, and the Meaning of the Incarnation

In order for a new religion to take hold, it must resonate with our inner being, not just our rational ego consciousness. This is because religious experience is not rational, but is highly psychological, being rooted in the depths of our unconscious. It is when we dip into that realm, where there are no limits of space or time,[188] that we feel not subject to annihilation, sense immortality, encounter God, and can feel at one with the cosmos. The intersection of the unconscious and conscious parts of the Self is personified (projected) in myths and symbols, sometimes as a pair, such as the Greek Dioscuri (one mortal and the other immortal), or alternatively in a single God-man figure such as Christ.[189] In either case, the God-man lives within each of us as a mediating force between the human and divine (conscious and unconscious), and gets expressed by corresponding mythological symbols. The God-man must be projected as a figure in order to be visible and more comprehensible to our ego consciousness.[190] The more we can let the "divine" unconscious come forth (though not to excess) and provide psychic energy, the more we will feel renewal (resurrection), our spiritual lives will be deeper and more satisfying, and we will avoid loss of soul. This individuation process leads to wholeness of the Self. A whole Self has its corresponding symbols of totality and wholeness, which include the mandala, the circle, and the cross.

This process of integration manifested itself mythologically as God incarnating his divinity into humanity (consciousness), symbolized by the mythical figure of the God-man. Thus, as Jung observed, the Christ figure is a symbol of the Self.[191] But we must be careful about what this means. First, As Jung also recognized, Christ is not a "snapshot" of anyone's entire Self at any point in time. The God-image now having split into various aspects, Christ represented only light, consciousness, goodness, love, and justice. He lacked, in particular, both the feminine element and any dark side, elements carried by Mary (in part) and Satan respectively. But he did integrate the human and the divine. Therefore, we may view Christ as a mediating figure[192] who symbolizes the Self as it goes through the dynamic process of the incarnation of "God" coming from the God-image into consciousness, as the Self becomes better integrated.[193] Thus, Christ represents both the *process* of the "divine" integrating (incarnating) into ego consciousness as well as the *result,* a more integrated Self. As Jung expressed this, "The drama of the archetypal life of Christ describes in symbolic images the events of the conscious life—as well as in the life that transcends consciousness—of a man who has been transformed by his higher destiny."[194]

Christ's Suffering

This brings us to the meaning of the passion of Christ. According to St. Paul, Christ suffered and died for our sins, eliminating the taint of original sin and making possible our salvation. The Gnostics differed. They didn't doubt that Jesus was nailed to a cross, but for them the crucifixion was unimportant because what made Jesus a savior were his teachings, according to which to be saved one must find one's inner, divine spark, which is what you really are. According to the Gospel of Thomas, which in part seems to reflect Gnostic views, Jesus taught:

> Seek and do not stop seeking until you find.
> When you find, you will be troubled.
> When you are troubled, you will marvel and rule over all,
> And having ruled, you will rest.[195]

The mytho-psychological perspective sheds light on the above passage and offers a similar spiritual interpretation. When numinous unconscious content confronts the ego, the ego suffers. From this standpoint, the passion of Christ symbolizes this suffering. Thus, in the Gospel accounts, Jesus collides with the Roman juggernaut, the Pharisees, and the temple priesthood (Sadduces). They are dominated by ego consciousness, as shown by their zealous interpretation of technical rules and concern for preserving their power. Jesus's suffering at their hands symbolizes the confrontation of divine spirit with ego consciousness, and the suffering of the ego that this process entails. As Jung wrote, "crucifixion is the beginning of individuation."[196]

Through the Christ myth, our old God-image also suffered, and as a result was transformed. Yahweh's own sin against Job was redeemed. Aspects of divinity that had been repressed and suppressed in our unconscious came forward and were differentiated. God became a divinity of justice and love. Yahweh's shadow aspect came into full view as Satan. The feminine aspect of the God-image came forth in the figures of Mary mother of Jesus, Mary Magdelene, and Elizabeth, mother of John the Baptist. The Holy Spirit (psychic energy) emerged more clearly and took on a more defined role (see pp. 243–45). Christ appeared as a divine-human figure who mediates and symbolizes the individuation process, and also represents the more integrated Self.

The Meaning of the Resurrection

Unpacking the above mythology, however, is only a start because the resulting mythical figures are still projections. We cannot let them remain as such. Likewise, the traditional story of Christ's resurrection is a projection onto the figure of Christ of the realization of the Self.[197] Because these mythical figures and the resurrection itself represent archetypal elements of our inner psyche, they should be integrated within us rather than remaining as external figures and events. Indeed, when we examine Jesus's actual teachings, we see that they focused on a person's inner life and encouraged the individuation process.[198] As Luke's Jesus said, "the kingdom is within you" (7:21). Likewise in the Gospel of Thomas he said, "If you bring forth what is within you, what you have will save you."[199] In psychological terms, Jesus was demanding a commitment to and a transcendent relationship with the Self.[200] So in truth the resurrection is a potential experience that already lies within us. As Alan Watts observed, "the Christ story can only find its way into the human heart because a place for it has already been prepared."[201] By letting "Christ" in, we can find and integrate our "divine" nature and be resurrected as Christ.

That the Christ figure has archetypal psychological roots is demonstrated by the rapid archetypal mythologization of the historical Jesus. For that very reason the historical Jesus quickly became nearly unrecognizable and unknowable, and for religious purposes in an important sense irrelevant.[202] The stories about Jesus's birth, acts, death, and resurrection became more mythical and legendary over time, his biography in many ways taking on the archetypal features of other mythical heroes, as we have seen.[203] The resurrection became the focal point, yet for a long time (including in all four canonical Gospels and in Paul) there was no narration of the resurrection event itself. That was natural not only because there was no information about it, but also because the motif of resurrection, being derived from the unconscious, is difficult to express, except symbolically and mythically. Thus, when the resurrection was finally narrated, in the apocryphal Gospel of Peter (late second century CE), the reported events themselves defied any rationality: The heavens opened in a great brightness and two angels descended to the tomb and escorted Jesus out of it between them. As they came out, the height of the angels reached to heaven, while Jesus stood still higher. (His massive size may have been designed to compare favorably with the superhuman size of the resurrected and deified Romulus, Asclepius, and Heracles.[204]) They were followed by a walking, talking cross affirming to a voice from heaven that Jesus had "preached to those who sleep."[205] The susceptibility of the Christ figure to mythologization, made possible by his archetypal nature, accounts in large part for why Christianity spread (and in its many forms) and eventually succeeded.

In light of the above, we can see that actually any religion that hits the right archetypal notes in our psyche will work to achieve essentially the same spiritual results, a fact borne out by history, comparative religious studies, and various spiritual practices and traditions. It is in this essential sense that various religions can be said to be all alike. But this is equally why a "non-religious" approach to one's spirituality and "resurrection" (Easter) also can work. This, in fact, is becoming more important in the modern world as the old religious doctrines have become stale and are losing their hold on people. While the traditional approach may indeed still work best for some, others will prefer to manage one's resurrection directly and mindfully, recognizing who the God-man really is rather than being carried off by projections that constellate him as an outside being and interpreting mythical metaphors as historical events.[206] Thus, Eastern spiritual traditions have long utilized forms of introversion (e.g., meditation) to realize the godhead within.[207] From the objective standpoint, neurological brain studies indicate that the psychic experience from deep non-religious meditation in the Eastern tradition and the experiences of "God" among Christian and Islamic mystics are essentially the same.[208]

We can work on our own resurrection any day of the year, but Easter offers us an annual reminder to focus on it. In the Synoptic Gospel accounts, when Jesus died the temple veil was rent in two (Mt 27:51; Mk15:38; Lk 23:45). It had separated people from God, so its renting meant that we can access the divine directly ourselves,[209] now that the God-image was transformed to include a mediator. Easter can be an opportunity to rend our own veil of ego and let divinity in. We all want and need to be resurrected, and Easter in springtime reminds us to just do it.

CHAPTER 7

May Day: Beltane Fires and the May Queen-Goddess

May Day does not get much attention in America, but our culture has deep mythological roots in this holiday going back to our European ancestors and even to the ancient classical world. May Day festivities as we know them today come to us largely from the nineteenth-century revival of the holiday, and they differ markedly from the more meaningful original celebrations in northern continental Europe and the British Isles that I cover here. In Gaelic lands the festival was called Beltane. The original May Day was not celebrated in colonial America. Early attempts to celebrate it here after European settlement were frowned upon by the Puritanical establishment, just as in Cromwellian England; the holiday was revived there after the Restoration, and was associated with it as a symbol of the traditional order of Church and State.[1] May Day gained some traction in America only as socio-political holiday in connection with workers' rights, labor unions, and Communism in the aftermath of the bombing of the Chicago Haymarket demonstration in 1886, but I do not cover that here because of our focus on mythology. Today May Day is celebrated most enthusiastically by neopagans, enthusiasts of Celtic culture, Wiccans, and some New Agers, but as discussed at the end of this chapter it also has a Catholic Christian component; after all, May Day falls within the Easter liturgical season.

Since May 1 lies about halfway between the vernal equinox and the summer solstice, it was a good time to mark the transition into summer. Indeed, in most of medieval northern Europe, May 1 *was* the beginning

© The Author(s) 2020
A. George, *The Mythology of America's Seasonal Holidays*,
https://doi.org/10.1007/978-3-030-46916-0_7

of summer. In northern Europe, by then the seeds for crops had just been sown, so farmers and their laborers could take a short break, while for pastoralists it was time to drive cattle and sheep out to their summer pastures. Both the sprouting crops and the soon-to-be pastured livestock needed divine protection from the dangers of the natural and supernatural worlds, which is why May Day developed as a holiday and took on the associated rituals and mythology that it did. And a goddess was a good figure to deal with such human concerns.

THE GODDESS MYTHOLOGY BEHIND MAY DAY

The Goddess of what is now May Day goes back to ancient times, in Anatolia, Greece, and Rome. Spring goddesses came to be venerated at two Roman holiday festivals that led to our May Day. The Roman Empire is important here because it took over much of Europe and the British Isles. Roman mythology, associated rituals, and holidays spread there and were assimilated into local religion, mythology, holidays, and customs.

The Greeks held an annual spring festival for Rhea, the Titaness who was considered the mother of the first gods, including several Olympians, and so she was the Great Mother called Queen of Heaven. We don't know much about her festival, but eventually she became identified with the Phrygian goddess Cybele, whose mythology and ritual is better known, especially from the period after she entered Rome, to which we can now turn.

Cybele, in Rome known primarily as Magna Mater ("Great Mother"), was venerated at the Hilaria festival (from Greek *hilareia/hilaria* ("rejoicing") and Latin *hilaris* ("cheerful")), held between the vernal equinox and April 1. In the Roman version of her myth,[2] she had a son-lover, Attis, who was mortally gored by a boar, and bled to death under a pine tree. Cybele knew that he had not died for eternity but that his spirit simply had taken refuge in the pine tree for the winter, and that he would be reborn from the tree in the spring, on the vernal equinox. When Cybele was introduced in Rome, she was given her temple of Magna Mater on the Palatine Hill and also a holiday with corresponding rituals. In her festival, a pine tree (that of Attis) was cut and stripped of its branches, wrapped in linen like a mummy, and decorated with violets (Cybele's flower, because in the myth violets were said to have sprung from the blood of Attis). It was then brought before Cybele's temple on wagons in what resembled a funeral cortege, since Attis was "dead" inside the tree. This was followed by days of frenzied grief and mourning (including scourging) known as the "blood days," when the tree was symbolically buried in a "tomb." Attis then resurrected (rose out of the tree) on the day of Hilaria (March 25, the date of the equinox in Rome) and was reunited with Cybele, symbolizing the beginning of spring. The tree was then erected before Cybele's temple, and the people celebrated around it. The celebrations ended on April 1, which may account for the origin of our April Fool's day (a "hilarious" celebration). This ritual has obvious parallels with the Maypole and May Day celebrations.

The second of these spring holidays was the Floralia, named after Flora, goddess of flowers and spring. Originally, she may have been a Sabine goddess, about whom we know nothing other than that she had a spring month named after her on the Sabine calendar (Flusalis, linguistically related to Floralia) and that supposedly an altar to her in Rome was established by the Sabine king Tatius during the legendary period of his joint rule of Rome with Romulus. But none of her Sabine mythology has survived. In Rome Flora acquired her entire surviving mythology from the Greek spring goddess Chloris (from *chloros*—"pale green"), who, as Ovid tells us,[3] was originally a beautiful nymph in the Elysian Fields catering to the pleasures of the fortunate dead. There she also attracted the attention of Zephyrus, the god of the West Wind and of spring, who quickly had his way with her. He married her, in what turned out to be a happy, loving marriage. As a wedding gift he filled her fields (her dowry in the marriage) with flower gardens, flowers which were said to spring from the wounds of Attis and Adonis. Zephyrus, as the West Wind, also brings the spring rains that grow the flowers. Thus, Virgil wrote that "the meadows ungirdle to the Zephyr's balmy breeze; the tender moisture avails for all."[4] Chloris also bore from Zephryus a son, Karpos, in Greek meaning "fruit" or "crop." Through Zephyrus's wedding gift Chloris became the goddess having jurisdiction over flowers, which she spread (by spreading their seeds) all over the Earth, which until then was monochrome. She also became the goddess of spring. In Rome, where she was called Flora, in the late third century BCE a festival was instituted in her honor that lasted from April 28 to May 2. It included theater, a sacrifice to Flora, a procession in which a statue of Flora was carried, as well as competitions and other spectacles at the Circus Maximus. These events included releasing hares and goats (both noted for their fertility) into the Circus, and scattering beans, vetches, and lupins (all fertility symbols) into the crowd. The celebrants wore multi-colored clothing symbolizing flowers and spring, as later was customary on May Day in Europe, and as famously portrayed in Botticelli's rendering of Flora's dress in his painting *Primavera* ("Spring"). As one views that painting, on our far right is Zephyros catching Chloris/ Flora. To their left is Primavera, into whom the nymph Chloris had been transformed following her marriage. She is depicted spreading flowers over the ground, wearing a multicolored flowery dress as in her myth, based on that of Aphrodite (Venus). According to Fragment 6 of the Greek epic *Cypria,* when Aphrodite was born from the foamy sea, she was clothed in garments that the Graces and Horae had made for her, colored in the flowers of spring.

Goddesses also appear in the May Day festivals in medieval and pre-modern northern continental Europe and the British Isles. Scotland had a goddess of winter called Cailleach (meaning "hag" or "old woman") or Beira, and correspondingly a summer goddess Brìgde. On May 1 there was a festival marking Brìgde's arrival. Similar is the Slavic myth of Vesna, the Slavic goddess of spring and fertility. (The Russian word for spring is *vesna.*) She was typically paired with the winter and death goddess Morena (also called Marzanna). Vesna was venerated each spring for having defeated death and winter. In the spring ritual, her battle with and defeat of Morena was reenacted by setting an effigy of Morena on fire. Vesna's name also seems to signify light, like Eostre marking the return of light after the period of winter darkness. In more northern climates where Eostre and Vesna flourished, the winter darkness is more pronounced than around the Mediterranean, hence the importance of the motif.

This annual spring transition of goddesses forms the background to the tradition of the May Queen. On May Day the May Queen and the Queen of Winter, together with their companies, would engage in a ritual battle, and the result was never in doubt. After the May Queen won, she would be crowned. In this crowning ritual the May Queen would be married to the May King in a ceremony that harks back to ancient sacred marriage rituals, and also to the annual reunion of Cybele and Attis discussed above. Depending on the culture, the May King was variously known as the "Green Man," "Leaf King," the "Grass King," "Green George," "Father May," etc.[5] He was typically a young man dressed in green foliage. In the tradition of Flora, May Day festivities also involved picking flowers, making them into garlands, spreading the garlands and flowers throughout each village, and (as with the tree of Attis) decorating the Maypole with flowers (including violets).

The goddess background to May Day also took on Christian trim-
mings. In Germany, on May Eve (April 30), called *Hexennacht* ("Witches
Night"), famously dramatized by Goethe in *Faust*, witches were said to
gather on the Brocken, the highest peak in the Harz Mountains, to foment
their evil plans. After the advent of Christianity, the witches were said to
meet with the Devil, but their plans were foiled through apotropaic May
Day rituals. Eventually that Eve became known instead as Walpurgis
Night, named after the abbess St. Walpurga (ca. 710–778), who is said to
have been instrumental in bringing Christianity to Germany in the eighth
century. Further, the Catholic Church developed a May Day "Crowning
an Image of the Blessed Virgin Mary" ritual, which I discuss at the end of
this chapter.

THE BONFIRE RITUALS OF MAY EVE

In Gaelic lands, the main Beltane festival ritual was the bonfire on what is
now May Eve, whereas in the non-Gaelic areas of the British Isles (i.e., of
English language and influence) Maypole rituals (discussed below) dominated.[6] The bonfires were especially important to pastoralists dependent
on their herds of cattle and sheep that were about to be pastured for the
summer.[7]

In the colder climate of Northern Europe, May 1 was a perilous but
ultimately optimistic moment of transition from the old to the new, from
the winter to the summer season. Whereas the February and vernal equinox holidays are dedicated to the *anticipated* victory of spring and fertility,
May Day, being halfway between the equinox and the summer solstice
when the sun's waxing light and warmth is more clearly felt, *celebrates and
guarantees* the full-blown forces of summer. At this point winter is finally
defeated and left behind and summer begins. This transformation process
necessitated rituals of cleansing and renewal, for which task fire was per-
fectly suited.

Generally in mythology, fire is a purifying and cleansing agent, which
enables it to destroy the causes and manifestations of evil. Fire is therefore
an agent of transformation, a notion that goes back as far as Heraclitus.[8]
The sun is thought to be made of fire, meaning that fire on earth is just a
lesser manifestation and representation of the same solar substance, which
is divine by nature. Of the traditional four ancient essential elements, fire
was the only one which humans could participate in creating, which connected them to the divine. Building such a fire on earth was a ritual of

sympathetic magic designed to ensure the supply of light and heat from the sun and stimulate the growth of crops. Since the sun can grow crops, people reasoned, so can fires because the substance is the same. A complimentary use of the bonfire ritual was apotropaic, to ward off evil and protect people, livestock, and crops. At least as far back as the ancient Near East, fire was used in incantations to thwart evil spells and sorcery. The ancient Greeks too had a ritual of running over hot coals *(pyrobasia)*, which appears to have originated as a springtime purification ritual like those described below. The most relevant springtime fire ritual in the Classical world, however, was that of the Parilia festival in Rome.

The Parilia, celebrated on April 21, was the pastoral festival of Pales, the deity or deities[9] of shepherds and sheep, and it goes back to pre-Republican times. Held just prior to putting the sheep out to pasture for the summer season, it was intended to protect shepherds, sheep, and their stalls from harm. As reported by Ovid in *Fasti*, the original ritual involved cleaning out the sheep pens and decorating them with green branches and garlands of flowers. A bonfire was then lit, and the shepherds would leap through the flames with their sheep in tow. Offerings of cakes and milk were made to Pales, and then the shepherds wet (i.e., purified) their hands with dew, prayed, and consumed a beverage that was a mixture of milk and boiled wine. Then they would leap through the flames three more times.[10]

In medieval Europe, similar May Day bonfire rituals were observed both in northern continental Europe and the British Isles, with the Gaelic Beltane bonfires in Scotland, Ireland, Wales, and the Isle of Man being the most emblematic. The word "Beltane" means "bright fire," "Bel" being derived ultimately from the Proto-Indo-European root *bhel*, meaning to shine, flash, or burn.

People thought that on May Eve (April 30), a liminal moment of transition, the veils between the ordinary world and the divine Otherworld (see pp. 159–61) were thin, making it easier to cross from one world to the other. Thus, at this time witches and evil spirits were hatching their evil plans for the people, livestock, and newly planted crops, and trying to carry them out. In response, people built bonfires and performed rituals around them to counteract this evil. The process began when all hearth fires and candles in people's homes were put out, so that the village bonfire could then be kindled. Typically, the bonfire was started by the most primitive means possible, by rubbing two wooden sticks together (or by plank and wimble) to produce sparks emanating from the wood. (The rubbing also had sexual overtones.) Kindling a bonfire in this way rather than from an existing fire made it most sacred. Afterwards, the people took embers from the bonfire to re-start their hearth fires at home, thus conferring the fire's sacredness onto the household for the next year. Ashes from the bonfire also were scattered over the newly sprouting crops.

Other aspects of the European bonfire ritual resemble those of the Parilia. The herders led their cattle around the bonfire; alternatively, there were two bonfires and they would pass between them. The smoke and heat were considered agents of purgation and protection that would drive out any winter disease and protect the livestock and the farmers from harm during the summer. In some cases bones were thrown into the fire, because the foul smoke that they emitted was considered especially effective for driving away evil spirits. (A fire that consumes bones is the etymological origin of our word "bonfire.") To supplement the bonfire, people gathered and scattered yellow primrose and orange rowan (the colors of which suggested fire) before their doorways to protect the interiors of their houses; rowan was also hung on doorways of cow-houses, farm equipment, and livestock.[11]

In most cases the bonfire ritual also involved preparing and bringing some cakes or pies, at least one piece of which was darker than the others (or was marked to be such). The pieces were distributed randomly among the participants, and the unlucky person(s) with the dark portions had to leap over the fire three times, and bore a stigma for the rest of the ritual and even into the following year. This act, performed on behalf of all the villagers, likewise ensured protection, though more for crops than for livestock. Some commentators see in this rite evidence of earlier human sacrifice.

Today the May Eve bonfire rituals are celebrated by neopagans and others in several festivals around the world. The most important is the Beltane Fire Festival held in Edinburgh, now a tourist attraction.

MAY DAY MAYPOLE AND RELATED RITUALS

The Maypole lay at the center of a broader set of rituals known as "Maying." On May Eve youths of both sexes would go to the woods. Besides having sex, they would gather foliage and flowers (especially violets and daisies), boughs of newly flowering hawthorn or blackthorn, and a tree trunk for the Maypole to be erected the next day. (If the Maypole was large, it would be brought in on oxcarts, or simply dragged by oxen.) Many of the flowers were made into garlands used in processions or simply for decoration. The tree trunk was stripped of its branches, though in some locations the branches and leaves at the very crown of the tree were left intact as a reminder that they were dealing not simply with a representation of life but with something sacred which has a divine spirit behind it. This serves to remind us to pause and reflect on certain mythological aspects of trees.

Trees are the tallest and most venerable living things on earth. Their lives span many human generations, and so they represent longevity. They are green, and either remain so all year (evergreens) or grow new foliage each spring. They therefore represent life and its preservation and renewal. And since life was divine, trees were associated with one or another deity (male or female) or tree/vegetation spirit. Importantly, trees exist not only in the surface realm of "earth" but also grow their roots into the ground toward the divine realm of the underworld; conversely, they grow their branches upwards toward the heavens, also a divine realm. Trees thus serve as a means of accessing divinity in both heaven and the underworld; in both cases they are conduits to the divine. Therefore, trees also were oracles, used in divination. Tree veneration was ubiquitous both in the ancient world and in pre-modern Europe, so it was natural to utilize trees and their foliage in a spring/summer festival dedicated to the renewal and preservation of life.[12] The Maypole represented the coming of summer and its attendant fertility, together with the associated divine forces that were at work, so it served as the focal point of the day's rituals.[13]

The Maypole was brought from the forest and decorated with painted spirals or horizontal rings, then festooned with flowers and ribbons (Fig. 7.1). It was then erected on the village green. In some locations, smaller Maypoles were placed in front of people's houses. Normally, Maypoles were used just once, but as time went on Maypoles in large cities tended to become permanent, being reused each year until they had to be replaced. The largest known Maypole was erected in 1661 in London on the Strand, stood over 134 feet high, and lasted over 50 years. When it was taken down, Sir Isaac Newton purchased it and put it to the novel, scientific use of supporting Huygen's new large reflecting telescope. More commonly, once taken down, Maypoles were employed as ladders or as beams in buildings.

Along with Maypoles themselves, in some localities the celebrants would also cut and similarly decorate a thorn bush (even if it was already flowering) with flowers, ribbons, and bright shells, which became known as the May Bush. As with the Maypole, May Bushes could be both

Fig. 7.1 Engraving of C. Cousen based on Joseph Nash painting entitled *The May-pole*, 1866. Alamy stock photo

household and communal (for the whole village, on the village green). Thorn bushes were symbolically important for at least two reasons. First, the combination of thorns and blossoms on bushes and thistles represented opposites, in this case the opposites of winter and summer. Thorns typically represent adversity, suffering (cf. Christ's crown of thorns), and tribulation, and so are symbolic of winter. Decorating them in a spring/

summer motif was not merely symbolic of the transition to summer, but apparently was a ritual of sympathetic magic designed to facilitate that transition. Second, in Gaelic lands thorn bushes were associated with the sí, or fairies. The good fairies were seen as helping to bring on and protect summer and vegetation, so they needed to be encouraged.

On May Morn women would rise early and rush to the fields, meadows, and forests to gather the morning dew, which was thought to have magical healing and cosmetic properties, and applied it to their faces. For the wealthy, venturing out on May Day morning was an involved affair; England's kings and queens did it. In Thomas Malory's *Le Morte D'Arthur*, Queen Guinevere went out on May Morn in cavalcade with her ladies and knights, dressed in green clothes; they returned "dashed with herbs, mosses and flowers."[14]

Also on May Morn the youths who had been out in the forest all night would make the rounds of the village, decorating the outside of people's houses with flowers, garlands, and boughs while singing songs and blowing horns. In some places they would also carry a miniature representation of the Maypole and a doll representing the May Queen, both of which ultimately represented the divine forces at work in the trees and thorn bushes. Sometimes the main Maypole was decorated with women's clothes and/or a similar doll was hung on the Maypole, making the connection clearer.

As the youths visited each home, they expected to receive a token gift from the homeowners. The idea here was one of mutually beneficial and socially useful exchange and reciprocity: The youths were mediators conferring through the flowers, boughs, and dolls divine blessings, good luck, and protection for households and their crops and animals. In this way the entire village, house-by-house in a private, family-specific manner, came under divine protection. Since the youths were doing a service for the community as a whole and each individual in it, they expected to be rewarded with gifts in return. The gifts were rather nominal and symbolic and included eggs, tea, bacon, sausage, cream, cakes, and money, but it was still thought that the generosity of the gift to the youths (and ultimately to the divinities) would influence the magnitude of the blessing conferred. A homeowner who refused to provide a gift would be warned that his crops and livestock would not prosper. The youths assumed the right to punish the niggardly because they were divine messengers: They are the first to see spring, they bring and reveal it to the community, and establish and hasten it through their rituals. Avarice is dangerous to a community and was frowned upon, so holiday rituals developed to discourage it. The villagers depend upon one another, and so they must share with each another.[15]

As the day wore on, the villagers would gather around the Maypole, where the organized communal rituals took place. They would typically include some contest in which summer defeats winter, as when the May Queen defeats the Queen of Winter and she marries the May King. Then the pair would be crowned, marking the renewal of fertility at the base of a symbol with obvious phallic significance. After that the villagers celebrated with dancing and singing around the Maypole. The elaborate dances that we see performed today involving the intricate plaiting of ribbons were not original to the holiday but arose only as part of the holiday's nineteenth-century revival. Originally it was a simpler ring dance. The dancers were mainly young men and women, so the dance was an exercise in amorous play.[16] In due course Morris dancing became part of the festival, mainly in England.

Having covered traditional non-Christian May Day rituals, we can turn to a Christianized May Day ritual, the Crowning of the Blessed Virgin Mary.

THE RETURN OF THE GODDESS OF MAY DAY

In the Catholic Church's liturgical year the entire month of May became devoted to the veneration of the Virgin Mary. The high point has always been the ritual known as "Crowning an Image of the Blessed Virgin Mary," said to have been initiated by St. Philip Neri in sixteenth-century Italy, after which it quickly gained widespread grass-roots popularity. This ritual is usually performed on May Day, or alternatively on Mother's Day or May 31. Ever since its inception, the ritual has involved a group of young boys and girls proceeding to a statue of Mary and placing a crown of flowers on her head to the accompaniment of a hymn to her. During the ritual she is given various epithets, including Queen of heaven, Queen of the world (also of "all" the world, and "all of the earth), and Queen of the universe.[17] Several Marian hymns and songs also call her Queen of May. One called "Bring Flowers of the Rarest" goes in part,

O Mary! we crown thee with blossoms today,
Queen of the Angels, Queen of the May.[18]

In light of the strength of these traditions, and in the wake of the adoption of the doctrine of the Assumption of the Virgin in 1950, in 1954 Pope Pius XII officially proclaimed the Queenship of Mary.[19]

In church thinking, Mary is called Queen because she is the mother of the Messianic King, Son of David, is the "perfect follower" and companion of Christ the redeemer, and is the "foremost member of the Church."[20] No flowered crown is mentioned in the official account of and instructions for this ritual, but elsewhere the flowers in her crown are said to represent Mary's virtues, and the ritual is in spring because she brought true, eternal life into our world (leaving behind the death associated with original sin); in the ritual she is called the "Mother of all the living,"[21] which was a biblical epithet of Eve drawn from earlier mythology.[22] Indeed, the crown symbolizes such things in New Testament scripture (Jas 1:12 ("crown of life"); 2 Tim 4:8 ("crown of righteousness"); 1 Pet 5:4 ("crown of glory"); Rev 2:10 ("crown of life"); see also Rev 12:1 ("a woman clothed with the sun, with the moon under her feet, and on her head a crown of twelve stars"), which language is invoked in the crowing ritual.[23] The church says the practice of depicting Mary in art with a crown goes back to the in the era of the Council of Ephesus (431 CE), where it is Christ who crowns her, while the ritual practice of church officials crowning her (now with flowers) had become popular by the end of the sixteenth century;[24] so far as we know, St. Philip Neri (d. 1595) was the first to decorate a statue of Mary with flowers in early May. Finally, venerating Mary in May makes sense to Christians because much of May falls within the 50-day Easter season ending with Pentecost—the descent of the Holy Spirit upon the apostles and other followers of Christ—and Mary was with the apostles waiting for the Spirit to descend (Acts 1:12–14).

As a matter of history, the May crowning ritual emerged organically as one of popular devotion to Mary during the period of more traditional pagan May Day celebrations. The Church eventually responded by formally Christianizing and legitimizing the Maytime popular devotions through indulgences. As one Catholic organization explains, "In this way, the Church was able to Christianize the secular feasts which were wont to take place at that time."[25] As for the Crowning ritual in particular, in addition to this ritual's authentic Christian origins, it also has non-Christian roots in traditional May Day mythology, floral rituals of spring, and goddess veneration, as reflected in the crowning of the May Queen ritual described above. It is a later iteration of the perennial early-May goddess traditions in which the mother archetype is expressed in terms of the fertility and fruitfulness of springtime in full swing,[26] which accounts for why it has stood the test of time; it touches something deep inside our psyche. Calling Mary "our mother" reflects an instinctive and universal attachment to her figure, even though it is inevitably difficult for us to consciously articulate the particulars of what this epithet means. Mary is in all of us, which is to say she is important and deserves our attention, whatever one's religious position. Interestingly, in 1563 the Council of Trent, in explaining why the veneration of images of Mary and other figures is not idolatry, states that such images are venerated "because the honor which is shown them is directed to the prototypes that those images represent."[27] Well, there we have it.

CHAPTER 8

National Myth: The Goddess Behind America's Independence Day

Virtually all countries have a national holiday. Such holidays are usually based on the foundation of the nation, or its new form of government (often by revolution or independence), or maybe a famous battle. They are celebrated using national myths that people have fashioned in connection with these events. Some of this mythologizing simply involves rewriting history into a more favorable light, in which case the account can be viewed as a "myth" to the extent it is false. In the Russian Revolution in St. Petersburg, for example, there was never any charge of the Bolsheviks across Palace Square to storm the Winter Palace, even though it became the stuff of legend and was widely depicted in books, art, and films.[1] Similarly, in America's case, historians have shown that many traditional details of the Boston Tea Party, Paul Revere's ride, and other famous events in the American Revolution never happened in the way they have been embraced by the popular imagination.[2] In a more truly mythological sense, however, our national story is expressed using real mythological symbols from the ancient past. Everyone knows that such symbols are not historical, but they are important and stick because they resonate with our psyche, like any good mythological symbol should. In this chapter I'm concerned with myth in this latter sense. I focus not on historical inaccuracies in our national myths and legends, but instead on the background and meaning of the principal mythological symbol of our independence, Lady Liberty, especially her role in the American Revolution and our early national life.

© The Author(s) 2020
A. George, *The Mythology of America's Seasonal Holidays*,
https://doi.org/10.1007/978-3-030-46916-0_8

The Goddess Liberty in Ancient Times

America's official national motto is "In God We Trust,"[3] but actually it was a goddess who stood behind our founding fathers in America's struggle for independence. And she has served as a national symbol ever since then, which continues to irritate some religious conservatives. She appears in the name of our national capital, on coins, in official government seals and medals, and in public art, especially many statues, most famously the Statue of Liberty. These days when questions about the role of religion in our government, legal system, schools, and society as a whole have become especially acute, Independence Day is an opportune time to remember the mythology of our nation's goddess and better understand what it actually represents.

Lady Liberty's name comes from the Roman goddess Libertas, but she had a Greek precursor, the goddess Eleutheria, meaning "freedom" or "liberty" in Greek, which principles she personified. Zeus in his role as protector of political freedom likewise was known as Zeus Eleutherios ("Zeus the Liberator"), in whose name a stoa at the Agora in Athens was built after deliverance from the Persians. Eleutheria actually was an epithet of the goddess Artemis. Although we know many myths about Artemis, none regarding her aspect as Eleutheria survives, only her face on some coins. So we don't know how she was connected with liberty.

The mythology of Libertas is richer. She rose to national prominence in connection with the establishment of the Roman Republic in 509 BCE. She was venerated by and was a symbol of the prominent Junia family. As a symbol she played a role in overthrowing Rome's last king, the tyrannical Tarquinius. After the overthrow of the kingship, resentful nobles hatched a plot to regain power, but it was foiled by Vindicius, a slave of one of these noble families (the Vitellii) who reported the plot to the Senate, and so the new Republic was saved by a slave whose name came to signify liberation. In due course several temples were built in honor of Libertas and her face appeared on coins, but unfortunately none of the temples or statues to her has survived.

Having escorted the Republic into being, her role then evolved into one of overseeing the manumission of slaves. In the city of Rome, the master would take his slave before the temple of Liberty, where a Roman official pronounced the slave free while touching him with a rod, called the *vindicta,* in honor of Vindicius. The freedman then cut his hair and received from his former master a white robe and a brimless wool cap resembling a beehive, called a *pileus*. Accordingly, the symbols of Libertas included a rod (or pole) surmounted by a *pileus*, a broken scepter (symbolizing the overthrow of monarchy), and a cat (symbolizing watchfulness).

MYTHICAL WOMEN AND GODDESSES AS ALLEGORICAL PERSONIFICATIONS OF NATIONS

Ever since ancient times, in myths the Earth has usually been portrayed as feminine in nature, because it generates and regenerates life, for which reason people developed Mother Earth goddesses, such as the Greek Gaia. From this tradition, the continents themselves and many countries in the Americas, Europe, Africa, and Asia came to be represented by allegorical female figures, both goddesses and humans, and dozens of countries still do today.[4]

Why did females personify the continents, and why do mythical females so commonly personify nations? At least for Europeans and Americans, part of the answer comes from the classical tradition. The Romans typically gave feminine names—in the feminine gender in Latin—to major places such as kingdoms, provinces, and cities, and they were portrayed as female, including as goddesses, on Roman coins and medals.[5] Europeans followed suit in the classical revival beginning in the Renaissance. Thus, for example, when Europeans needed a name for the New World, they feminized the first name of the explorer Amerigo Vespucci's first name to produce "America."

But there are deeper, more mythological reasons for this. Idealized female figures have nurturing, motherly, and queenly characteristics, as depicted in myths. They serve as the protectresses of nations over which they preside, whose citizens are visualized as a large family. Such a matron thus serves to unite the nation. Examples of where this matronal aspect predominates include Mother Russia in Russia, Bharat Mata (Mother India), and Ibu Pertiwi (Mother Earth) in Indonesia. As the national protectress, she can also take on martial characteristics as a female warrior, as in the case of Mother Svea in Sweden, commonly portrayed like a Valkyrie.

Apart from their matronal characteristics, such female figures can also unite a country because they come to represent particular virtues to which the nation aspires and around which its people build its national myth. This comes from a long tradition of allegorizing virtues through female figures.[6]

Thus, for example, Thailand is personified by Saraswati, the Hindu goddess of knowledge, wisdom, music, and art. These virtues also can include political virtues and forms of government. Thus, the personification of The Netherlands is the Dutch Maiden, typically portrayed with Liberty's pole and cap to represent the country's traditions of tolerance and freedom; likewise with Brazil's Effigy of the Republic, a woman in a red Phrygian cap (also bay leaves) and bearing a sword, originating in connection with the country's independence from Portugal in 1889, and whose visage still graces the nation's currency. Liberty (often together with Reason) became the face of France in the lead-up to the French Revolution of 1789, and with the establishment of the First Republic in 1792 a variation of her— Marianne in her Phrygian cap—was officially established to personify liberty, reason, democracy, the French Republic, and the French people in general.

These allegorical females usually sport other symbolic trappings, including particular clothing (or lack thereof); certain deities, persons, or animals surrounding them; articles in their hands, on their heads, or placed around them; and symbolic background architecture or landscape. These symbols help to deepen the allegory, and thus contribute to the nation's myth and national unity.

It is important to stress that in all these cases, at least in Europe and America, the use of these female figures is strictly allegorical. They are not invoked in connection with any religion, whether Christian, pagan, or otherwise, even though in the distant past some of them were goddesses who originally had religious importance. Nor do the other allegorical symbols associated with them have religious significance. Accordingly, they are not venerated in any religious manner, nor are they used by particular religions. This point must be stressed because, as we shall see, some people erroneously claim that Lady Liberty is associated with paganism, while others have concocted a myth that our founding fathers intended to create a "Christian nation," a claim belied by the nation's early symbolism discussed in this chapter, as well as by voluminous historical evidence.[7]

THE FEMALE PERSONIFICATION OF AMERICA

Prior to the discovery of the New World, female figures already represented the three continents of the known world, Europe, Africa, and Asia. After America was discovered and was being settled by Europeans, it too came to be symbolized by a female figure, a native "Indian" woman who became known as the "Indian Queen." She was the product of a proliferation of allegorical figures in European art and literature during the fifteenth and sixteenth centuries. The discovery of the New World spawned a new secular symbolism glorifying the progress and greatness of Europe, in which process the Indian Queen played an important role.[8]

The Indian Queen was portrayed as human, not as a deity, and had no religious connotations other than perhaps in connection with being uncivilized (her religion also being presumably primitive in comparison to Christianity). In the early portrayals, she was a portly, matronly woman depicted in a wild Caribbean setting. She was typically semi-naked with bare breasts, bore a feathered headdress, held a club or a bow and arrow, sat or stood among palm trees, and was accompanied by exotic animals such as parrots, alligators, snakes, or an oversized armadillo. Sometimes cannibalism was depicted in the background (Fig. 8.1) This portrayal reflected Europe's fascination with the exotic and mysterious New World.

Fig. 8.1 *Personification of America,* drawing by Marten de Vos, ca. 1590

As such, she symbolized a *place;* the female symbol of America did not yet represent any abstract ideas. And she represented the entire New World, not just North America or the British colonies that would become the United States. She appeared in Europe on maps, in fashionable artwork, and also through actors in live performances, pageants, and parades. She had a sexual, erotic quality to her, the message being one of inviting potential investors and colonists to come exploit her.[9]

In the 13 British colonies of North America, as tensions mounted between the colonists and the Crown in the lead-up to the revolution, a version of her developed known as the "Indian Princess," who became known on both sides of the Atlantic. She typically was bare-breasted, wore a tobacco-leaf skirt and a feathered headdress, and carried a bow and arrow. But gone were the exotic animals around her. Sometimes a cornucopia, an old Earth Goddess symbol (e.g., of Demeter), was beside her symbolizing America's bountiful potential. Her complexion became lighter, and she took on a martial profile as both representation and protector of the colonists. She began to represent ideas and ideals. She often was assisted by Liberty, who by then had become popular in Europe; sometimes Liberty alone was depicted. In either case, she was now accompanied by other symbols of liberty such as the pole and cap, sometimes came to wear a stola, the Roman robe for women corresponding to the men's toga, as in the political cartoon in Fig. 8.2, which is also rich in other mythological imagery. In it, Britannia offers the Stamp Act to the colonies, which Minerva representing wisdom advises not to accept. Here the female allegorical figure is European Liberty, while the American "Indian" aspect is represented by a male. Liberty lies on the ground oppressed by a thistle (the national emblem of Scotland, and so here symbol of the King's chief minister, the Scot Lord Bute) and is attacked by a serpent symbolizing treachery. Mercury/Hermes, representing fair trade and truth, departs from the colonies. And when the Stamp Act was repealed, colonists in New York celebrated by erecting a ship's mast as a Liberty Pole, which was an outgrowth of Libertas's *vindicta.* Another example is a coin that Paul Revere designed and struck in Boston in 1776, which portrays Liberty seated on a globe, holding her rod in one hand and scales on the other, with her cat at her feet, and around the edge the words "Goddess Liberty"; on the reverse side was Janus (his two faces now representing Whigs and Tories) (Fig. 8.3).

The Indian Princess was thought of as the daughter of Britain's own female personification, Britannia, and thus she represented the colonies as

Fig. 8.2 Political cartoon by anonymous British artist, 1765, entitled *The Deplorable State of America*

Fig. 8.3 Paul Revere coin, 1776. Author's photograph of replica

being Britain's progeny. As such, she also came to represent colonial aspirations to the full civil rights of Englishmen (and eventually independence), as well as to unimpaired English-American trade, a goal shared with the merchant class in England. The Indian Princess was especially popular in English political cartoons that catered to the merchant class and were sympathetic to the cause of the colonists. In them the Indian Princess was portrayed as a much-abused maiden, an innocent victim of the King's ministers.[10] Although the colonists were not entirely comfortable with being identified with Indians, for the sake of their cause they too embraced her. Paul Revere produced numerous prints portraying her as a victim of the Crown's actions. In one, she is being pinned to the ground at Boston harbor while the British Prime minister forces her to drink British tea, which she spits back in his face; meanwhile the lord of the admiralty is at her feet lifting her skirt, and Britannia stands by helpless and distraught (Fig. 8.4). In other depictions, however, Britannia tussles with her rebellious daughter, in one example exclaiming, "I'll force you to obedience you rebellious slut" (Fig. 8.5). By the end of the revolution, however, the Princess and Britannia were being portrayed as reconciled *sisters*, marking them as independent from each other.[11]

Over the course of the American Revolution and its aftermath, Liberty superseded the Indian Princess. In the lead-up to the war, Americans

Fig. 8.4 *The Able Doctor,* by Paul Revere, 1774. Alamy stock image

Fig. 8.5   *The Female Combatants*, unknown artist, 1776. Courtesy of the Lewis Walpole Library, Yale University

embraced Liberty because she had reappeared in England during political debates that both edified British liberty and warned of the dangers threatening it. The American colonists in turn embraced her, on the one hand as a symbol of their British heritage, and on the other as a symbol of America's separation and the rights that the colonists were defending.[12]

A symbolic turning point in this transition appeared on the map used in the peace negotiations with Great Britain. During the negotiations in

1782 the Indian Princess appeared in the map's cartouche, but when the same map was reprinted in 1784 she was replaced by Liberty.[13] This change occurred for important substantive reasons. The Indian Princess had served her rebel role, and once the rebellion was over the newly independent nation needed a personification more directly representative of its ideals and system of government. Further, Americans had become uncomfortable with being represented by an Indian. The Princess's semi-naked appearance and dress implied inferiority compared with Europe, some Indians such as the Iroquois had sided with the British during the war, and now there was continued conflict with Indians resulting from Indian Removal policies of which Americans did not want to be reminded.[14] So they chose a classical deity, Liberty, a European woman clothed in a Roman stola and *pileus,* and holding her staff; sometimes her head bore a single plumed feather, the last remnant of the Indian Princess, a fashion that had originated with her and had become popular in Europe. Over time she was portrayed less and less with the *pileus,* however, because it had been worn by freed slaves and thus was offensive to the southern states;[15] the red Phrygian cap associated with the French Revolution, however, to some extent replaced it. Sometimes she wore the helmet of Athena/Minerva, not simply to show that America can defend herself (for which purpose she was also commonly depicted with a sword and/or shield), but more importantly because these were goddesses of wisdom, a virtue essential for a democracy's elected officials in guiding the new nation. Liberty was also often depicted with Hermes/Mercury, the god of trade, and with a cornucopia. With these features in place, she could represent not just a place but also abstract principles which had become enshrined in the new nation and its government; and, Americans thought, better than in Europe. She thus helped the nation build its myth, even though these ideals were not being realized in respect of Native Americans, slaves, and women, among others. (But eventually Liberty was used as a symbol in the anti-slavery and suffrage movements.)

Accordingly, while the Indian Princess did manage to appear on some initial Congressional and diplomatic medals, Liberty quickly took over official public imagery in the United States, reaching its peak during the Madison administration.[16] Our founders avoided depicting real individuals, especially political leaders, for an important reason. In European countries, it was customary to use images of their monarchs on the nation's coinage. But in 1792 Congress, fearing an imperial presidency, decided to put Liberty on our coinage rather than any national leaders; she was replaced by presidents on our currency only in the twentieth century.[17] She appeared on early designs of our Great Seal, and still appears on the state seals of New York, New Jersey, North Carolina, Pennsylvania, and Wyoming. She was prominent in our annual Fourth of July celebrations, most notably in our 1876 centennial. She also became ubiquitous in unofficial contexts, such as frontispieces of magazines and journals; parades and other public displays; textile design; commercial signs and advertisements; souvenirs; political posters; weathervanes; sheet music covers; circus wagons; stoves, culinary goods and utensils; andirons; firefighting equipment; figureheads on ships; and folk art generally.

As Liberty became prominent, another version of her, Columbia, also became popular, and their names were sometimes used interchangeably.[18] Her name is a feminization of Christopher Columbus's name, and so came to symbolize at first the New World and later, beginning before the revolution, American identity. Whereas Liberty appeared as a visual image, Columbia appeared mostly in writings (especially poems), songs, and place names.[19] When images of Columbia did appear, she was less classically attired than Liberty, most notably appearing in red, white, and blue costume, including stars-and-stripes imagery. And while Columbia did represent American liberty and national unity, she connoted America as a *place*, or places within America, more than did Liberty, while Liberty more narrowly symbolized national principles, ideals, and public virtues. Columbia thus appeared in many important place names, including our national capital, The District of Columbia. In 1784 King's College in New York was renamed Columbia College (now University). In 1786 South Carolina named its capital city Columbia. (Today some 30 U.S. cities are named Columbia.) The Columbia River in what is now the state of Washington (and Oregon) was so named in 1792. While Columbia's popularity decreased in the mid-nineteenth century, especially after the Statue of Liberty was erected, she has continued to make spotty appearances into modern times. Examples include Columbia Pictures, the TV network Columbia Broadcasting System (CBS), and a Space Shuttle and several naval ships named Columbia. The song "Hail, Columbia" was used as our de-facto national anthem until 1931, when the "Star-Spangled Banner" officially became the anthem. It was also the Presidential Anthem until it was replaced by "Hail to the Chief" in 1954; today it serves as the Vice Presidential Anthem.

A key usage of Liberty/Columbia as a symbol is in public art and architecture, of which I'll cover just two important examples. In the mid-nineteenth century when the U.S. Capitol was being rebuilt, a statue was needed atop its new dome. For this the sculptor Thomas Crawford designed a 20-foot bronze statue of a female allegorical figure largely the same as Liberty/Columbia, called the Statue of Freedom (or Armed Freedom, or Freedom Triumphant in War and Peace). In Crawford's original design she held a rod reminiscent of the *vindicta* and wore the *pileus*. But the Capitol's reconstruction was in charge of the southerner Jefferson Davis, who would soon become president of the Confederacy. He rejected the *pileus* as an affront to slaveholders; his curious rationale was that such a symbol was "inappropriate to a people who were born free and would not be enslaved." In Crawford's revised design, she became more martial in appearance, holding a sheathed sword instead of a rod and wearing a military helmet reminiscent of Athena/Minerva (Fig. 8.6). The helmet, which featured an eagle's head and a feather arrangement, and also her robe fringed with fur, were also designed to recall the old Indian motifs. When the statue was being installed in 1863 during the Civil War, it was symbolically hoisted up (in pieces) by former slaves.

Liberty most famously appears in the statue entitled "Liberty Enlightening the World," commonly known as the Statue of Liberty. The idea was hatched in 1865 as the American Civil War was ending and America's centennial was looming. At a dinner party in Paris two abolitionists, the law professor and historian of America Édouard René de Laboulaye and the sculptor Frédéric Auguste Bartholdi, together floated the idea of providing a gift to the American people on the centennial of American independence, in which France's friendship and support had been crucial. But what shape this gift would take and when it would be created was delayed by two events. One was the Franco-Prussian War, resulting in the downfall of the repressive regime of Napoleon III (who had supported the Confederacy), followed by efforts to establish a stable new republic, which might benefit from American support. The other was Bartholdi's project to build a lighthouse in Egypt at the entrance to the Suez Canal, which was nearing completion. For that he designed a statue of a woman holding a torch aloft, much like what would become our Statue of Liberty. After that project fell through in 1869, Bartholdi turned his attention to providing a similar monument to America. In 1871 he traveled here to drum up support, and he succeeded. Freemasons were active on both sides of the ocean in funding and organizing the project, and in order to help attract money from them he too became a Freemason in 1875.

Fig. 8.6   Statue of Freedom, by Thomas Crawford, 1863. Alamy Stock Image

Bartholdi's design was a reworking of his earlier Suez vision, but this time the lady was Liberty. Her traditional connection with the freeing of slaves was especially fitting in the aftermath of the Civil War. The statue was not ready by America's centennial as originally hoped, but she was eventually dedicated 1886, in a Masonic ceremony. Some religious conservatives at the time objected to a "pagan goddess" serving in such a role. *The American Catholic Quarterly Review* decried the erection of this "idol of a heathen goddess . . . holding her torch to proclaim that mankind receives true light, not from Christ and Christianity, but from heathenism and its gods."[20] Some fundamentalist Christians raise similar allegations and complaints today, even claiming that she is the devil, as readers can readily discover by searching the Internet.[21]

In fact, however, religion, whether pagan, Christian, or otherwise, had nothing to do with it. There is no evidence that Bartholdi had any religious intentions or was embracing Liberty as a religious figure, nor did the Freemasons who were involved. To the contrary, the Freemasons specifically prohibit discussions of the specifics of the nature of the divinity, so naturally there is no goddess imagery or veneration in Freemasonry,[22] as was the case among the many founding fathers of America who were Freemasons. In our Constitution, early laws, and original national symbols, our founders also kept religion out of our national government and legal system.[23] But at the same time they included freedom of religion (and of no religion) amongst the many other freedoms that they enshrined in our system of government, and which Liberty symbolizes. Our nation embraced Liberty not out of religious motives, but, riding a neoclassicist revival, in order to associate America with classical secular ideals of civil liberty and democracy. Ultimately the statue is a symbol of enlightenment, as her actual name "Liberty Enlightening the World" specifies. The idea was that the American example of enlightened democracy would shine throughout the world, which to a significant extent it has, and the Statue of Liberty as a symbol has played no small symbolic part in that. Lady Liberty has a rightful place in the symbolism of our nation and its holiday, so as we celebrate the Fourth of July we can be thinking about the ideals and rights that she represents, and consider how we can better exercise them in our individual lives and realize them in our national life.

CHAPTER 9

Halloween: Eve of Transformation

Halloween is probably our most confusing holiday, which is evident from what we see and do that evening. We have symbols of the fruits of harvest (cornstalks and corn, pumpkins and other squash) celebrating the fertility of the earth juxtaposed with symbols of decay and death: autumn leaves, skeletons, ghosts, the Grim Reaper, gravestones, Dracula, and the dead rising from their graves in Michael Jackson's *Thriller* music video. It combines both Christian and pagan traditions. Other symbols of the holiday more generally evoke the supernatural, such as haunted houses, fairies, and witches. Kids celebrate by trick or treating and engaging in pranks, while adults go to parades and evening parties in costume, or maybe watch *Rocky Horror* together. And the costumes themselves are a hodgepodge of themes. Some evoke themes of death or of the supernatural, some parody celebrities, some allude to current events, some make social or political statements, and others are sick jokes (such as Tylenol bottle costumes in the wake of the 1982 Tylenol poisonings). We encounter pirates, plants, hot dogs, garbage cans, vending machines, rockets, sperm, tubes of toothpaste, Monica Lewinsky in her stained blue dress—the variety is endless. And the holiday is celebrated universally across the population, regardless of age, gender, religion, nationality, ethnicity, political affiliation, or sexual preference.

How does one get a handle on all this? Normally, we would trace the history. But deciphering the origins of Halloween and its rituals in Europe is vexingly difficult. This is partly because diverse traditions from many

© The Author(s) 2020
A. George, *The Mythology of America's Seasonal Holidays*,
https://doi.org/10.1007/978-3-030-46916-0_9

pre-literate cultures and religions in various places were assimilated over many centuries. Much of Halloween's ritual and meaning comes from the Celts, but the Druids, who were literate, forbade committing the elements of their religion to writing, instead relying on oral education and tradition,[1] so they left us no ancient written record of Celtic myths and rituals. With the spread of Roman religion and culture and then Christianity into Europe, some of the Celtic religious practices, rituals, and myths were recorded by Roman and Christian writers, but they had their own biased perspective on the pagan practices so their accounts were not particularly reliable. And Christianity contributed its own content to what would become Halloween. These factors have led to misunderstandings and "myths" about the origins of the holiday.

On the other hand, understanding the meaning of Halloween is made easier by the archetypal nature of the holiday. It is fair to say that virtually every ancient and modern culture has had some festival or rituals dealing with the dead, together with various troublesome or evil spirits from the supernatural world.[2] As Joseph Campbell observed, the nature of Halloween is based upon archetypal structures within our psyche which evoke themes that underlie our emotional and spiritual life.[3] This process yields the material of myth, although in the case of Celtic cultures we have only later, filtered versions of the myths to go by. In principle, a comparative approach examining various cultures is appropriate here, but given the space limits of this chapter I can only hit some high points.

Today Halloween is popularly traced on the one hand to the Celtic Samhain festival, and on the other to the Christian All Saints' Eve, All Saints' Day, and All Souls' Day—collectively called Allhallowtide—with which the church endeavored to replace Samhain. Allhallowtide, however, also has more ancient roots in the classical Mediterranean world, so that is where we must begin.

GREEK AND ROMAN PRECEDENTS

The Anthesteria in Athens

The ancient Greeks held a three-day festival of the dead at the beginning of spring (around our March 1), the Anthesteria ("flower festival"), which modern scholars consider the rough equivalent of Catholicism's All Souls' Day.[4] Over time, after the god Dionysus became prominent, it also became a wine festival because the new vintage was ready to drink, in cups wreathed with flowers. Except for this, the festival's rituals have little to do with spring flowers, but rather reveal that the festival was concerned with what else was rising then: the spirits of the dead *(keres)*. Before the festival became Dionysian, it was one for placation of ancestral spirits, as was still evidenced in the rituals.

On the first day, wine jars were opened and the drinking and feasting began, but originally the vessels were probably burial urns, from which the *keres* flew out when the lids were taken off (as with Pandora's jar).[5] Originally the presiding god who was honored was Hermes, who in Greek myth was the messenger to the underworld and an intermediary to the *keres* who could enchant and control them with his wand (*rhabdos*, later the caduceus). Thus, during the festival an offering of cooked grain and seeds was made to Hermes, so that through him the Athenians were feasting and placating the *keres*. To further keep the *keres* at bay, people chewed buckthorn (a purgative, as seen above in May Day rituals), pitch was smeared on the doorposts of homes, and buckthorn was fastened to doors. On the third day, the ghosts were summarily dismissed with the formula, "Begone you *keres*! The Anthesteria is over."[6] The streets and homes thus having been cleansed from the taint of death and of threats from the underworld, life could return to normal.

Roman Festivals of the Dead

The Romans had a festival of the dead called the Lemuria. Like the Greek Anthesteria, it was celebrated on three days, but on May 9, 11, and 13, skipping the even days, which the Romans considered unlucky. According to the etiological myth told (and perhaps invented) by Ovid in *Fasti*, after Romulus laid the remains of his brother Remus in his tomb, the latter's ghost visited Faustulus and Acca (who had adopted and raised the brothers) and asked them to have Romulus set aside a holiday in his honor. Romulus complied and called the holiday Remuria. The name was later changed to Lemuria, says Ovid, because "L" is a smooth letter that is easier to pronounce.[7] In fact, the holiday was named after the shades of the restless dead called *lemures*.

The Lemuria originally had both public and private rituals, but the public aspects have been lost to us. The private ritual practiced at home is described by Ovid. In the middle of the night the head of the household would get out of bed and, standing barefoot, throw black beans over his shoulder. He would do this nine times never looking back, each time saying, "These I send. With these beans I redeem me and mine." The spirits of the dead were thought to collect or partake of them, thus being appeased; otherwise, they might make off with a living member of the family out of envy or loneliness. Having so appeased them, he sends them on their way with the second part of the ritual. He touches water and then clatters bronze implements, which (like on New Year's Eve) was thought to drive them away. As he does this, nine times he recites, "Ghosts of my fathers, be gone!" Only then, having duly performed the ritual, may he look back.[8] Because of this festival and its attendant ghosts, Romans were cautious during May, never doing anything important then. In particular, May was considered an unlucky month for marriages,[9] hence our tradition of June brides.

The Lemuria was preceded by similar festival on February 13–21 called the Parentalia, the last day of which was called the Feralia. It was also an occasion for honoring and placating the ghosts of one's dead ancestors, which people felt a need to do lest they be harmed by these spirits. The rituals involved were largely private, conducted within each family. One public aspect of its rituals that has come down to us is that on the first day a Vestal Virgin performed ceremonies in honor of the dead. This too may have had a private origin among the Vestals since the ceremony originally placated the ghost of Tarpeia, a Vestal who had betrayed Rome to the besieging Sabines and was crushed to death for her treachery; so her spirit was likely to be malevolent unless appeased.[10] The other public ritual that we know of occurred on the final day, called the Feralia, probably from the verb *ferre* (cf. Greek *ferō*) meaning to bring or carry, since people carried gifts to the tombs of ancestors on that day. The day also had a dark rite in which an old hag sat with girls and performed the rites of Dea Tacita ("the Silent Goddess"). The ritual involved incense, thread, black beans, wine, and a fish head sealed with pitch and pierced with a bronze needle. It was designed to shut the tongues of the spirits so they could not harm the living; thus, at the end she proclaimed, "We've bound up hostile tongues and unfriendly mouths."[11] Having dealt with the dead, the next day, called Karista (meaning kinsfolk), people held a family reunion devoted to honoring the living members of the family (and also the *Lares* of the household), renewing ties and patching up old quarrels. (Truly wicked members of the family could not attend.) A potluck family meal, which probably originated as a funereal feast, was held to which each attendee brought his or her contribution.[12]

It is sometimes claimed, even in some fairly recent writings about Halloween, that the ancient precedent for Halloween is a Roman festival dedicated to Pomona, the Roman goddess of fruits and orchards.[13] Some claim that it was celebrated on November 1, others that it was part of an August 13 (or 23) festival dedicated to Vertumnus (god of the turning seasons) called the Vertumnalia.[14] In his *Metamorphoses*, Ovid tells a lovely myth about the romance between Vertumnus and Pomona,[15] but in none of his works does he refer to a festival to her.[16] In fact, there is no evidence for a Pomona festival, and probably none ever existed.[17] In modern times, the error seems to go back at least as far as the eighteenth-century English topographer William Hutchinson, who wrote, "The first day of November seems to retain the celebration of a festival to Pomona." This statement was then uncritically repeated going forward.[18] One modern writer suggests that Hutchinson was simply inspired by Ovid's myth,[19] but this would not account for the alleged date since Ovid mentioned no date or even any festival. More likely the error can be traced to a misreading of a passage in Varro's *De Lingua Latina*, which actually specifies August as the month of the Vertumnalia.[20]

ENTER CHRISTIANITY

Christianity developed its own version of a holiday dealing with spirits of the dead. This took a few centuries to jell, and the history is instructive. Halloween can only be understood in connection with All Saints' Day and All Soul's Day, celebrated on November 1 and 2 respectively, and the Christian (Catholic) doctrine underlying them. So it is important to trace their origins, concepts, and historical evolution.

All Saints' Day

Early Christians started celebrating the deaths of their martyrs, on the anniversaries of their deaths. Before long, however, especially after the persecutions of Emperor Diocletian, there were too many martyrs to feasibly honor each of them on these anniversaries, so Christians began honoring them collectively once each year. The earliest mention of this holiday comes from 359 CE, in a hymn by St. Ephraem commemorating all martyrs sung at Edessa, Greece. The date was May 13, the last day of the Lemuria, marking another example of Christians grafting onto pagan holidays.[21]

Subsequent sources from the Eastern Mediterranean and Levant show that martyrs were commemorated annually, though in some locations the date was the Friday after Easter or the First Sunday after Pentecost. Martyrs were commemorated in Rome too, but the feast also came to honor non-martyred saints. On May 13, 609 or 610, after receiving the Pantheon ("to all gods") temple in Rome from the Byzantine Emperor Phocas, Pope Boniface IV converted the building to Christian use, rededicating it to the Virgin Mary and the martyrs. Although the occasion was for martyrs and not yet for all saints, that event is generally considered the origin of All Saints' Day, since thereafter it was celebrated in Rome every year on the anniversary of the dedication, May 13. As Bede, for example, described the event, the stains of idolatry were removed from the building "so that where once the worship not of all the gods but rather of all the demons had taken place, there should thenceforth be a memorial *to all the saints*."[22] The circumstance of the Pantheon's conversion from pagan to Christian use together with dedicating it on the last day of the Lemuria has led some scholars to conclude that the dedication of the Pantheon and establishment of All Saints' Day on that date represented an effort to offset and Christianize the Lemuria tradition.[23] The Roman gods that had been venerated there were replaced by Christianity's god and martyrs, so the sanctuary was renamed that of St. Mary and the Martyrs.

This interpretation accords with Pope Gregory the Great's instructions in his famous letter from few years earlier in 601, in which he instructed Mellitus, Bishop of London, to cleanse pagan shrines of idols and put them to Christian use, and to integrate pagan rituals and customs into those of Christianity. Through such tactics, he argued, it would be easier to convert pagans:

> In this way, we hope that the people, seeing that their temples are not destroyed, may abandon their error and, flocking more readily to their accustomed resorts, may come to know and adore the true God. And since they have a custom of sacrificing many oxen to demons, let some other solemnity be substituted in its place, such as a day of Dedication *or the Festivals of the holy martyrs* whose relics are enshrined there. . . . They are no longer to sacrifice beasts to the Devil, but they may kill them for food to the praise of god, and give thanks to the Giver of all gifts for the plenty they enjoy. If the people are allowed some worldly pleasures in this way, they will more readily come to desire the joys of the spirit. For it is certainly impossible to eradicate all errors from obstinate minds at one stroke . . . .[24]

In fact, Gregory was describing a process that tends to happen anyway, as we will see in the evolution of Christmas at the time of the winter solstice and its connection with the festival of Sol Invictus (p. 231). Here Gregory was simply advocating being proactive about it.

By around 800 a holiday for all the saints came to be celebrated on November 1 in Germany and England, and the church in Rome followed suit.[25] In 732 Pope Gregory III dedicated a new chapel in honor of all saints at Saint Peter's in Rome, and on that occasion formally made the holiday a combined one for all saints as well as all martyrs and also changed the date (at least in Rome) to November 1. In 837 Gregory IV officially changed the date to November 1 for all of Christendom, and instructed the Holy Roman Emperor, Louis the Pious, to enforce this throughout the Carolingian empire. The November 1 date gradually took hold through Western Europe in the ensuing centuries, and by the twelfth century May 13 was no longer used. The reason why the church changed the date is unclear. The twelfth-century theologian Jean Beleth explained that Rome could not support the large numbers of pilgrims arriving for the feast in May, so it was better to hold it after the harvest had come in.[26] It is possible, however, that since the pagan peoples to the north in Europe already celebrated festivals on November 1 (see below), the churches in these lands and eventually the Vatican itself moved to that date in order to Christianize the holiday, in line with Gregory the Great's policy.[27]

Early Christian belief held that the soul survives a person's physical death, at which point it will go straight to either heaven or hell. But in 1245 at the Council of Lyon, the Catholic Church officially adopted the doctrine of Purgatory, an intermediate state in which the souls of people who had committed merely venal rather than mortal sins could undergo final purification before being entitled to enter heaven. The church based this doctrine on certain scriptures and the practice of saying prayers for the dead dating from the beginnings of Christianity.[28] As the notion of Purgatory evolved, All Saints' Day became an occasion not just for honoring and praying for saints, but also for praying to saints to ask them to intercede on behalf of dead souls in Purgatory so that they would be finally saved and go to heaven forthwith.

During the Reformation, Protestants rejected Purgatory as inconsistent with their doctrine of predestination, according to which a soul is predestined for heaven or hell from the very beginning. For them Purgatory was a superfluous concept. For the same reason, praying for dead souls or for saints to intercede on their behalf would be pointless.

All Souls' Day

All Souls' Day is meant to honor, pray for, and come to terms with the souls of dead friends and relatives, especially if their death was recent. It originated in the early Middle Ages when some churches and monasteries began observing an annual feast with prayers dedicated to the souls of the departed, but at varying dates. The eventual choice of November 2 is largely due to St. Odilo, abbot of the monastery at Cluny, who in 998 decreed that all Cluniac monasteries should hold it on the day following All Saints' Day, to pray for souls in Purgatory. Due to Cluny's wide influence, the custom spread across Europe and the day was eventually adopted as a holiday by the Vatican in the thirteenth century.[29]

All Souls' Day developed from a mixture of pagan tradition and Christian doctrine. The date is best explained by the pagan (Celtic) tradition that at this time of year the souls of the dead (as well as various evil spirits, witches, etc.) were active and could appear to the living and harm them, sometimes to rectify wrongs done to them while alive and enforce the obligations of kinship.[30] As a result, there was an element of appeasement and reconciliation involved. Thus, in addition to prayers, offerings of food, flowers, and candles, including on graves, were made to the dead; candles were thought to give light to souls languishing in darkness, possibly also to light their way back home. Church bells were rung to comfort the souls in Purgatory, and in the popular mind also perhaps to ward off demonic spirits.[31]

The saints became involved in this process because people believed that they could intercede on behalf of souls in Purgatory, helping them to move into heaven. What we now call Halloween emerged formally as a church liturgy on the eve of All Saints' Day, known as All Saint's Eve or All Hallows Eve. (The word "hallow" was both a verb meaning "to make sacred" or "holy" and a noun meaning "saint," so Halloween means "Saint's eve" or "holy eve.") It was on this Eve that formal prayers directed to saints asking them to intercede for the souls of the dead commenced. The meanings and rituals of All Saints' Eve, All Saints' Day, and All Souls' Day became linked and intermixed. The three formed a triad known as Allhallowtide.

Allhallowtide was focused on the fate of dead souls rather than on the living. Nevertheless, these holidays were tied to the doctrine of the Communion of Saints, which consists of the spiritual union of all members of the church, both living and dead (including those in Purgatory), headed by Christ. The notion goes back to St. Paul, who wrote that in Christ Christians form a single body.[32] One enters the Communion when one is baptized. For our purposes, the Communion is important because it breaks down barriers between earth and the supernatural realm, and implies a connection between the living and the dead. This enables Catholics to pray to saints for them to intercede to help the *living*.[33] Such openness to the supernatural has transformational possibilities, as discussed below.

Allhallowtide became an important holiday celebrated at all levels of society. In pre-Reformation England All Saint's Eve featured prayers for the dead and saints in church rituals, candle and torch processions. At the end of the liturgy church bells rang for a long time (often until midnight) to comfort souls in Purgatory. The monarch played a key ceremonial role at the national level, while the mayors of towns would put on a feast to entertain local officials, the gentry, and other prominent citizens.[34] When the Reformation came to England it was hard to stamp out these customs; people found ways other than through official church liturgies to pray for and comfort the dead and celebrate the occasion (e.g., bonfires, praying in a circle while burning straw, baking soul cakes).[35] But in Ireland, northern Scotland, and Wales Allhallowtide customs continued and merged with the pre-Christian traditions of Samhain, which we examine next.

THE CELTIC MYTHICAL BACKGROUND: SAMHAIN

In pagan Europe November 1 was a logical time to transition from summer to winter. With the shortening days, falling leaves, and colder temperatures, people sensed decay and death in the air, especially in the more northerly parts of Europe. The harvest was now in and the herds had been brought home from their summer pastures. The cattle and pigs were culled, both to provide winter food and to reduce the number of mouths to feed over the winter. The military campaigning season also was over. People wrapped up their pending affairs and paid off their debts. For these reasons, now was also a good time to hold tribal assemblies to take care of communal business, in Ireland most notably at the Hill of Tara. These were all good reasons to have a festival at that time.

The Celtic peoples[36] divided their year into summer and winter halves, beginning on May 1 and November 1 respectively. As we saw in Chap. 7, May 1st (Beltane) was a liminal time, and so too was November 1, called Samhain (pronounced "sow-in" with the "ow" as in "cow," and meaning "summer's end" or "when summer goes"). Since the Celts began each day at sunset, the Samhain festival began in the evening. It lasted for three days, like the Anthesteria, Lemuria, and the later Allhallowtide. The three-day nature of Samhain reflects the lunar cycle,[37] which is evidenced by the fact that the festival began not precisely on (our) November 1 but on the new moon at around that time.[38] The three-day cycle of the new moon is one of death and renewal, a symbolic mythical motif that we saw in the case of Easter in Chap. 6 (p. 91). And indeed, the Celts viewed Samhain as the occasion of the death of the old year and the beginning of the new.[39] So we can expect that the concepts behind and the myths and rituals of Samhain would resemble those of New Year's elsewhere.[40] As we shall see, the essence of pre-Christian Samhain was thus *to utilize the occasion of the passage from the old year to the new to achieve the regeneration of individuals, their kings, and society, through interaction with the powers and beings of the Otherworld.* It was a festival of transformation, celebrated by using myths and rituals concerning the Otherworld.

When we read descriptions of Samhain, we are typically told that Samhain is a liminal time when "the veils are thin," and that certain supernatural evil spirits and/or spirits of the dead emerge to threaten people, who establish rituals to protect themselves and their possessions.[41] But as we shall see, this characterization appears to be anachronistic because it projects onto pre-Christian Samhain thinking and practices concerning spirits of the dead that emerged only after Allhallowtide. In order to get a more accurate picture of what Samhain was about, it is first necessary to understand more fully how the pre-Christian Celts conceived of the Otherworld and its inhabitants, and how humans could interact with them. This will enable us to determine, as best we can, what elements of Halloween are authentically traceable to Samhain and which are more related to Allhallowtide.

In this analysis, the Celtic myths and legends are key. Indeed, many of the key events in Celtic myths took place during Samhain.[42] Samhain festivities probably included the retelling of these myths, and perhaps also their reenactment.[43] Since key Celtic myths themselves involve Samhain, we should look to these myths and their symbols to understand the meaning of the holiday.

The Otherworld and Its Inhabitants

In Celtic thinking, the cosmos had two parts. The first was on earth where humans and animals lived. All else was called the Otherworld. The heavens seem not to have been of concern, and so divine beings did not reside there. Rather, the Otherworld was quite close, but for most people usually just beyond reach.[44] It mainly consisted of the world just below the Earth's surface, various magical islands (some of them floating, appearing and disappearing, and changing location), and far-away places on Earth. The Otherworld was divine, though physically it resembled the normal earthly world. It was essentially paradisiacal, with only good weather, no diseases, and tasty food that was not filling. In the Otherworld, space and time worked differently. There the normal order of the universe was suspended and somewhat dissolved, as in primordial, mythic time. In comparison to our world, time usually moved much more slowly there, so its dwellers hardly aged and rarely died, but it might also move faster; or, events that usually occur in sequence (through causation) might occur simultaneously. For example, trees could blossom and bear fruit at the same time.[45] Similarly, in one myth the hero Mac Oc was both conceived and born on Samhain in shrunken time (nine months into one day).[46] It was this nullification of ordinary space and time which enabled interaction between the two worlds.[47] Hardly any other mythic tradition plays with time and space in so radical a fashion.[48]

The powers of the Otherworld were thought to work transformations. In the Welsh legend of *Peredur,* even sheep could be transformed: On Samhain night, white sheep crossing an estuary turned black, and black sheep crossing from the other side turned white.[49] As seen below, humans too could be transformed during Samhain.

The portals between this world and the Otherworld were most commonly mounds of earth called *sídhe* (also known as fairy mounds), hills (especially those with old forts on top), the bottoms of lakes, caves, waterfalls, and some streams. On Samhain, these portals were open so that both the inhabitants of this world and those of the Otherworld could go back and forth. So the oft-used term "liminal" means not only that the veils between the two worlds were thin, but that the entrances were actually open.

The principal beings in the Otherworld who were of concern to the Celts were the Tuatha Dé Dannan, which means "the people of Danu." These were former humans, descended from the goddess Danu, who lived in Ireland before the Gaels (Celts) arrived and defeated them in battle. The resulting treaty arrangement was that the Celts would live on the surface world and the Tuatha would live in the Otherworld, where they became divine beings known as the fairy people. Each lived in a *sídhe* or other haunt. They looked like regular humans rather than low-level demons, spirits, witches, or the small elfish creatures in later fairy tales. Many of them emerged on Samhain eve. Thus, in one tale about Finn Mac Cool known as *Finn's Childhood,* "The sun had barely set when the mounds opened. . . . Finn saw a crowd of *people* emerging from the mounds, exchanging joyful speech."[50] These residents of the Otherworld were not spirits of the dead.

Much like the ancient Greek divinities, the Tuatha had the same virtues and flaws as normal humans. Although some of them resented having been defeated by the Celts,[51] generally they held no grudge against humans. Rather, they watched over the surface world and endeavored to keep it balanced and harmonious, intervening when necessary to achieve this.[52] For example, one myth told that the chief god, the Dagda, and a goddess—usually the Morrígan—had intercourse on Samhain eve, which ensured the continued prosperity and well-being of humans, their crops and animals, and their enterprises.[53] And in the above-mentioned *Finn's Childhood,* Finn observed that the people who had emerged from the mounds "brought with them stuff to eat and drink mutually. In appearance everyone seemed to be celebrating, . . . the inhabitants of the mound displayed no hostility toward the people gathered in the meadow."[54] Their generally good nature is reflected in the epithets for them, including "the Good People," "The Good Neighbors," and "The People of Peace."[55] Unlike spirits of the dead or evil spirits, the Tuatha were not fearsome or especially threatening.

Consequently, evil spirits and spirits of dead ancestors do not appear in the myths and legends concerning Samhain.[56] In the historical record, such other beings pop up only in Christianized Celtic culture, where they, together with the fairy people, are demonized as satanic creatures, which is what led to the grotesque characters of Halloween.[57] This was not about true transformation, but a crude effort to make people fear the devil.

Most people most of the time were unable to see or interact with the Otherworld, because they lacked the ability and the conditions were not right. Druids, poets, and a few others who had undergone initiation, however, possessed what was called "second sight," which enabled them to see what was invisible to others.[58] They could behold and interact with the

Otherworld and its beings at will, and also practice divination. The rest of the population could not, except to some degree when the portals to the Otherworld were open at Samhain and Beltane. Thus, in *Finn's Childhood* the marvelous beauty Ele could be seen only on the night of Samhain.[59]

Samhain Myths and Rituals

In any place and age, princes and paupers will celebrate holidays differently. Peasants were concerned with their family, crops, and flocks, while kings had to deal with relations among the tribes, warfare, treaties, the people's prosperity, relations with the priests, and religious rituals. And in Celtic lands the Druids and poets had a near monopoly on literacy. It is they who best knew the religion and mythology, were guardians and preservers of the culture, and moderated the Samhain festivities and rituals of kings and chieftans. There cannot have been Druids and poets in every small village, yet peasants still celebrated Samhain in their own ways, ways that often never made it into the myths and legends. So inevitably, what we know about pre-Christian Samhain comes from the upper crust of the society. But the myths were not written down; that was prohibited. They existed only in an oral tradition, and when Christianity arrived and Druidism was deconstructed, much was lost. As a result, many of the Samhain-related practices that were recorded by monks and historians after Christianity appeared, and which made it into Halloween, came from the peasantry. To a large extent our holiday is a degenerated remainder of what was once more sophisticated and special, but hints of the earlier higher-order rituals still shine through in the myths and legends.

The key pre-Christian Samhain rituals that we can be fairly confident about were:

- the communal bonfire
- feasting on transformational food
- intoxication through a transformational beverage
- divination
- recitations and reenactments of myths

On the pragmatic level, Samhain was also the occasion for a political assembly to make key decisions, judicial proceedings to resolve conflicts, entering into or renewing contracts, and any distribution or redistribution of community property. These adjustments in the society all took place within a symbolic suspension of time.[60]

The Transformational Communal Bonfire

On Samhain evening, as at Beltane, all fires in Ireland were extinguished – a sign that summer had died—and then a bonfire would be lit, by Druids where there were any.[61] The bonfires were communal, around which the celebrants gathered. We cannot be certain what the purpose(s) of the bonfire was and exactly what rituals were held around it, as the evidence of pre-Christian Samhain bonfires is spotty and late, and the rituals are poorly attested in the folklore, myths, and legends.[62]

Theories about the origin and purpose of the bonfires vary. One prosaic explanation was that people had accumulated much refuse over the summer season, so it was convenient to build a communal fire to burn it.[63] Another theory is that, as with Beltane bonfires, the Samhain bonfire was meant to imitate the sun, an effort of sympathetic magic encouraging the sun not to fade further and ensuring that summer will return.[64] Others believe that the bonfire was intended to frighten evil spirits (possibly also the dead) and keep them at bay,[65] but in light of the above discussion of the Otherworld this explanation seems anachronistic.

If we look to the mythology of fire in general, the myths of the Celts involving fire, and the very nature of the Samhain holiday, however, a different picture emerges. To begin with, unlike in the ancient Mediterranean, in northern Europe fire was not one of the primordial elements; rather, it was an agent for transforming the three elements of earth, water, and air,[66] which means people too. Indeed, the mythological symbolism of fire generally regards it as a purging and purifying agent: It incinerates the old to make way for the new, and thus is associated with renewal and transformation.[67] Thus, fire ("sulfur") played this kind of role in alchemy. Psychologically, light and fire symbols often refer to consciousness, in particular to unconscious content becoming conscious,[68] so in this case content from the "Otherworld." In this analysis, it is important that Samhain marks the New Year. As we saw in Chap. 2, the essence of the New Year's is eliminating the old and making way for the new, through rituals of purification and renewal; in some cases the cosmos itself was thought to be recreated, and both deities and kings had to undergo rituals of death and renewal. In Samhain, renewal and transformation was achieved in part through the bonfire ritual, the feast and intoxication, and contact with the Otherworld. These were all complimentary.

The Celtic myths involving fire show that the Celts saw it as transformative, and that the most important transformation (or renewal) was undergone by kings. The Celtic specialist Jean Markale argues that on Samhain the king would undergo some form of death and rebirth ritual, most likely in connection with fire.[69] This is indeed reflected in some myths. In one, known as *The Drunkenness of the Ulstermen*, the hero Cú Chulainn (a mythic double of his king, Concobar Mac Nessa[70]) and his companions are invited to a feast on Samhain hosted by their enemies, the king and queen of Connaught. After they are filled with food and inebriated with drink, they are imprisoned in an iron house, and a fire is started around it in order to roast them alive. Cú Chulainn's companions blame him for their plight. But Culchulain executes a powerful jump and breaks the structure and enables them to escape. Connaught's king, now apologetic, hosts them to another feast in a wooden house. During the feast, challenged by his companions, Cú Chulainn executes yet another jump known as "the leap of the salmon," in which he breaks through the roof of the house, proving that he is now better than ever. The lesson is clear: the transformed Cú Chulainn has emerged from the trial by fire improved and more trusted by his men.[71]

The same kind of ordeal occurs in another story, in which a large, red-haired man and his wife, both from the Otherworld, arrive in King Matholwch's kingdom of Ireland and begin to commit various offenses. To get rid of them, the King's vassals put them and other guests inside an iron house that they had built, and fires are set around it to incinerate them. When it got too hot, the red-haired man gave the house a blow with his shoulder, casting it aside, so he and his wife survived. Having learned his lesson and been transformed through the trial by fire, he is now gracious to the King. He presents Matholwch with a magic cauldron which he had brought with him on his journey, which restores to life the dead who are placed within it.[72] There seems to be a parallel between these iron houses and cauldrons, both of which can transform people (even from the Otherworld) in combination with fire (see below pp. 164–65). So, in this story the king too is transformed by contact with the Otherworld on Samhain.

Finally, in a Celtic story from Brittany known as the *Saga de Yann*, a young man who had been born in miraculous circumstances sets out on an adventure to bring his king a magical object that will enable the king to marry a certain princess, who like the young man is also fantastic. When he succeeds, the princess demands that the young man be burned at the stake, but the magician who had caused his miraculous birth gives him a potion that enables him to emerge from the fire not only unscathed, but also more handsome and intelligent than before, transformed to a higher level of being. Having seen such results, the princess now demands that her king/husband undergo the same, but of course he perishes. The hero and princess get married, so the old king is replaced by someone who has been transformed. The princess exclaims, "It is you who have accomplished the finest exploits. Accordingly, it is you who should be king now, and I the queen."[73]

Feasting on Transformational Food

Another original and important element of the festival was the feast. As already mentioned, cattle and pigs were culled at this time of year.[74] While some beef may have been eaten at this feast, the featured dish was actually pork. The Celts raised pigs in large numbers, and they were a seemingly inexhaustible source of food; the Celts also hunted wild boar. They believed that eating pork at Samhain would give people immortality (in the afterlife).[75] Pigs were associated with the Otherworld and its wisdom.[76] These concepts were reflected in the mythology of the Dagda, who had two immortal pigs. He would regularly have them slaughtered and served at feasts, but by the following morning they were always alive and healthy again.[77] Similarly, Manannán mac Lir, king of the Tuatha Dé Danann, presided over a banquet of immortality for the Tuatha's blacksmith-god, Goibniu, who made weapons for Tuatha warriors. Manannán served his marvelous pigs to the warriors, but they were perpetually reborn, meaning that the food was supernatural.[78] Likewise, in the Irish tale *The Death of Muircertach mad Erca,* warriors fallen in battle were given an enchanted feast of pork and wine, and so were recalled to life.[79] Eating pigs ensured people's immortality.[80] For like reasons, pig bones and heads were placed in Celtic graves.[81] Boar images were also often placed on the swords, shields, and helmets of warriors,[82] not only because boars were fierce but also for protection.

Interestingly, the pork was not roasted directly over the fire but was braised in cauldrons. Why? Because transformations occur in cauldrons, as in witches' brews prepared in them. That is why cauldrons are so prominent as Celtic archeological relics. The Celts thought that cauldrons can restore life, give supernatural knowledge, and enable people to tell lies from the truth and to distinguish the brave from cowards.[83] The Dagda had his own magic cauldron, said to have been brought to him by the Tuatha Dé Danann from mythical islands in the far north, from which no one would go unsatisfied.[84] The effect of cauldrons is also seen in the Welsh myth known as *Branwen Daughter of Llyr.* In that story about a battle between the Welsh and Irish, the Irish have a magic cauldron into which they immerse their slain warriors so that they will rise the next day ready to fight again. The Welsh win only by destroying the cauldron.[85] In the Welsh tale *Peredur,* the hero fell into a trance upon seeing a certain cauldron. A corpse then arrived on a horse, and it was placed into the cauldron where an ointment was rubbed on it, and the hero was revived.[86] As noted above, the cauldron given to King Matholwch also restored people to life. This very idea may be portrayed on the inside of the famous Gundestrup cauldron (Fig. 9.1). It shows a deity dipping a series of wounded or dead warriors in a cauldron, apparently to restore them.[87] So, on Samhain the perceived effect of eating pork braised in a cauldron must have been quite powerful.

Intoxication on Transformational Drink

In Celtic lands, people drank beer, wine, and mead. But wine was a luxury and the beer was iffy. Better was mead, which became the drink of the gods, and was the usual drink at feasts including at Samhain. Celtic tales featuring drunkenness typically were set during Samhain.[88]

Fig. 9.1 Section of the Gundestrup Cauldron, artist(s) unknown, ca. 150 to 1 BCE

In ancient and medieval times, people did not understand the nature of fermentation or how intoxication occurs. Rather, they just saw that grapes, fruit, and honey naturally begin to ferment, and that when one drank fermented beverages one became intoxicated. This was thought to be a magical, supernatural phenomenon. Thus, when people became intoxicated, they thought that they were connecting with and experiencing the divine.[89] Naturally, the gods drank these beverages, and some of them (e.g., Dionysus) became identified with them. Thus, at Samhain the intoxication accompanying the feast was yet another means of accessing the Otherworld and achieving transformation.

Divination

Samhain was the night of the year most focused on divination.[90] This was a logical consequence of the portals to the Otherworld being open at the time. Naturally people wanted to learn what the new year would bring. Some people were thought to be able to see into the future by accessing the Otherworld, which was most readily accomplished on Samhain.

Because we have no written records from pre-Christian times, and due to the influence of Christian Allhallowtide, it is difficult to be sure what were the subjects of divination and what were the original Samhain-specific divination methods and rituals. It is at least evident, however, that fires, both the communal bonfire and private hearth fires, were used. This ritual probably involved tossing stones or other items into the fire or placing them around it and then examining their positions, or markings next to them, the next morning.

Recitations of Poems and Reenactments of Myths

Most likely poets would have attended the major Samhain celebrations and practiced their art at them, reciting myths. It is also possible that some myths were reenacted at the festivities.[91]

No Apparent Focus on Dead Ancestors

Again, due to the absence of records, it is hard to know whether pre-Christian Samhain had any focus on the spirits of dead ancestors. The notion that Samhain was a festival of the dead was popularized by James Frazer in his classic, *The Golden Bough*,[92] and this claim is repeated even today. Cultural historian Ronald Hutton argues that Frazer's notion is anachronistic and that no evidence of Samhain pertaining to the dead exists from before the coming of Allhallowtide;[93] other scholars generally agree that there is no evidence for ancestor veneration at Samhain.[94] As seen above, the Tuatha who emerged from the Otherworld on Samhain were living beings, not spirits of the dead, and were generally friendly. Samhain's rituals were aimed at the *living*. It is not crucial to resolve this issue for purposes of Halloween, however, because the dead became important anyway once Allhallowtide took hold. It is probably to Allhallowtide more than Samhain that Halloween owes its own focus on human death, including its images of skeletons, ghosts, gravestones, and skulls and crossbones.

THE EMERGENCE OF HALLOWEEN IN EUROPE

For the church, formally Allhallowtide had replaced Samhain. Some Samhain traditions continued, but in the Catholic Allhallowtide they took on a Christian flavor. What would become Halloween developed in parallel as an unofficial popular holiday. It became known as Halloween in the eighteenth century.[95]

We owe Halloween mostly to Ireland and neighboring Celtic lands (Wales, Isle of Man, parts of Scotland). This was natural, because Ireland was the heartland of Samhain, and then it became Catholic, so that Samhain traditions could be integrated to some extent with Allhallowtide, with Halloween developing as a popular offshoot. Heavy Irish migration into the Scottish islands and highlands in the early Middle Ages had brought Samhain there.[96] This is important because it was the Irish and Scots who brought Halloween to America. Whether Samhain or a similar festival on November 1 existed in continental Europe is a debated issue,[97] but we need not consider that question here because it was not continental Europeans who brought Halloween to America.

Some Halloween customs may have originated with Samhain, others from Allhallowtide, while others were new. Notably, the Allhallowtide rituals among Christianized Celts did not overtly reflect the older mythology, which was generally suppressed though recorded for posterity by some clerics and historians. In Protestant areas where Allhallowtide was prohibited, especially post-Reformation England, Halloween customs developed more randomly and there was no common set of rituals across the land.[98]

Halloween's focus on the dead comes from All Souls' Day rather than from Samhain. Whereas that Catholic holiday conceived of the dead souls of interest as being in Purgatory, in parallel the notion that restless spirits of the dead were active on earth on Halloween night developed as a popular tradition. Although the Celts thought that the beings of the Otherworld who emerged on that night were alive, looked like ordinary people, and were generally good, as a result of rank superstition and demonization by the church they became grotesque creatures. Some animals were also demonized, such as a black cat being thought of as Satan in disguise. People felt a need to appease dead souls through offerings of newly harvested crops and other food (at the doorstep, by the hearth, etc.) and by other rituals discussed below; other goblins and evil spirits also had to be frightened away to protect people, their livestock, and their crops.

One ritual that carried over from pre-Christian Samhain for some time was the communal bonfire. After the establishment of Allhallowtide, the church in part opposed the bonfire tradition but also sought to give this ritual a new meaning. Thus, at Uisnech in the center of Ireland, St. Patrick replaced the Druids' bonfires with his own, as a sign that Christianity would triumph.[99] Now the bonfires were claimed to give comfort to and beckon the souls of dead ancestors in Purgatory.[100]

People also used devices besides the bonfires to drive away evil spirits and witches. In Scotland people burned effigies of them.[101] In southern Ireland people made a *parshell*, an apotropaic cross of sticks woven with straw placed at the entrance to the home. Some people would leave offerings of food to placate them so they would do no harm. In the Hebridean island of South Uist, homeowners would carry burning peat around the household to protect it, while fishermen in the Hebredies conducted a mixed Christian and pagan ritual to propitiate the powers of the sea, since this was the beginning of the stormy season. Specifically, the fishermen would go to the seashore and recite the Lord's Prayer, then one of them would wade into the sea waist-deep, pour out a bowl of ale as an offering, and ask a being called Shoney (Johnny) for a good catch over the next year.[102] Another practice was to carry around torches and lanterns, and light lamps and candles to ward off evil spirits. Some lanterns were made from hollowed-out turnips or other root vegetables, which eventually became known as Jack o'Lanterns.

The term "Jack o'Lantern" seems to have originated in Ireland. They were made from turnips or other root vegetables; pumpkins were native to North America, not Ireland. In part they served as lanterns for guisers and pranksters who roamed around the villages, but since they also were designed to scare off threatening spirits, some were placed in house windows to protect the home.[103] Once Allhallowtide took hold, the lanterns were thought to represent souls trapped in Purgatory.[104] In later centuries when evil spirits were taken less seriously, the carvings on Jack o'Lanterns still were meant to portray the evil spirits, but were now mocking or parodying them.

The presence of "Jack" in the name seems to have come from the old Irish legend of Stingy Jack. Jack was a miserly drunkard and tough customer, always playing tricks on people. One evening he encountered the Devil in a pub, and asked him to pay for his drink. The Devil obliged by turning himself into a coin, which Jack then pocketed. In his pocket was also a cross, which kept the Devil from turning back into his real form. Jack agreed to free the Devil by getting him to promise not to take Jack's soul for ten years. After the ten years had passed, the Devil came up to Jack while he was walking down a country road, and asked for his soul. Jack pretended to agree, but asked the Devil first to fetch an apple from a nearby apple tree since this would be his last chance to eat one, which he agreed to do. But while the Devil was up the tree Jack carved a cross on the tree trunk, preventing the Devil from coming down. As a condition for his release, the Devil this time agreed *never* to ask for Jack's soul. When Jack died, he approached the Gates of St. Peter, but Peter would not let him in because he had led a bad life. Jack then went over to the Gates of Hell, but the Devil wouldn't let him in there either, keeping his promise to Jack. But he did give Jack an eternally glowing ember from Hell's fire to light his way, which Jack placed into a hollowed-out turnip, which he used as a lantern. Ever since then Jack has been wandering between earth and the netherworld, between good and evil, and he soon became known Jack of the Lantern. The term Jack o'Lantern also became a name for Will o'the Wisps (moving marsh or peat bog flares from methane gas), because they were likened to Jack roving around.

Like at Samhain but unlike in Catholic Allhallowtide, on Halloween people practiced divination. In rural areas, this was done at the bonfire in much the same way as at Samhain. In urban areas, the fire was indoors in the fireplace so divination was practiced there (see Fig. 9.2). In particular, young people, especially eligible young women, used divination on Halloween to learn about their prospects for marriage. This was an important annual occasion, because in the homosocial world of the time,

Fig. 9.2   *Halloween,* Engraving by E. Scriven from painting by J.M. Wright, ca. 1841, after the poem *Halloween* by Robert Burns, 1786

Halloween as a social event provided one of the few opportunities for eligible men and women to interact.[105]

Another Halloween custom that was derived from Samhain and Allhallowtide was the feast. A true feast was the province of wealthier people who could afford it, but differences in wealth in this context led to the development of alternative Halloween customs. One became known as "souling," and featured "soul cakes." The lower classes would seek gifts of food from the rich so that they could have a modest feast of their own. To this end they would go door-to-door performing ditties or singing, in return for which they expected some morsels of food to take with them. For their part, the rich would prepare themselves by baking soul cakes. The idea was that when the poor came to the door, they would be given soul cakes in return for their promise to pray for the souls of the dead, especially those from the household providing the soul cakes. In Protestant areas, this custom served as a partial replacement of the prayers for dead souls in church liturgies on Allhallowtide eve, whereas in Catholic areas this popular custom augmented the church rituals.

One interesting outgrowth of the culling of animals and the feast of pork was that the bladders of the slain animals were extracted, stuffed and sewn up, and used for ball games. Hence the origin of the football season in the autumn, and of the football as a pigskin.[106]

Another custom related to souling was guising. People, mainly young men, would dress in primitive costumes and often blacken their faces with ash. Sometimes they dressed in white. Sometimes men dressed as women. Originally the idea of guising seems to have been to prevent the spirits of the dead from recognizing the guisers, or perhaps to scare the spirits off. As time went on, however, it seems that the guisers dressed so as to imitate the spirits. This could have been meant to scare them away through sympathetic magic, but once the spirits began to be taken less seriously, the guises were meant to parody them. Whatever the intent, the end psychological result of the Halloween masquerade is to break down barriers between the natural and supernatural, and between the living and the dead.

If you are guising yourself as a troublesome evil spirit, it is logical to play pranks on people.[107] So inevitably playing pranks became a Halloween tradition. This was usually done by groups of young men, for whom the exercise provided an opportunity for male bonding.[108] Often their intentions were serious, in that the pranksters meted out rough justice to uncooperative or stingy villagers in an effort to get them to conform.[109] The pranks themselves were often ambitious and elaborate. They included plugging up chimneys, blowing smoke through people's keyholes, letting horses out of stables and barns, and taking gates off their hinges and moving them.[110]

By the eighteenth century, Halloween's link to Allhallowtide had become tenuous, which led to differing customs, especially as it spread to Protestant areas such as England. Particularly in urban areas, the earlier meanings of Halloween had devolved into courtship rituals, costuming that no longer served its original serious purposes, games, and pranks. The holiday was now more concerned with the living than the dead, and to the extent it tapped the supernatural it was to benefit the living. In these latter senses, the traditions of Samhain remained.

HALLOWEEN IN NORTH AMERICA

In England and northern continental Europe Protestantism dominated, which did not honor saints and prohibited Allhallowtide; from what we can tell, Samhain-type traditions were not strong in these lands either. Since the American colonies initially were dominated by puritanical Protestantism, at first there was no basis on which Halloween could gain a foothold in the colonial period or in the young United States. Halloween became popular in America only after the large influx of Irish and Scottish immigrants in the late-nineteenth century. Yet the holiday's popularity grew to the point that it lost its ethnic roots and now is celebrated universally across all sections of our population. As such, it is a homogenizing force in our culture.[111]

Certain elements of Samhain, Allhallowtide, and Halloween in Europe have survived, including the emphasis on otherworldly beings being present on that evening, guising (now known as trick or treat, and no longer done to save souls), Jack o'Lanterns (only now with pumpkins), and playing pranks. Others have not survived, such as bonfires (except in Samhain revivals), feasting, and divination. The Samhain poetry recitations and reenactments of myths have been replaced by Halloween films and music videos. A new custom in some cities is Halloween parades or processions. Now adults also dress up in costumes and go to evening Halloween parties, where they generally don't drink to excess. Halloween has also become an opportunity for free expression on social and political issues. And most importantly, Halloween preserves the original Samhain notion of personal transformation in the course of this magical evening, though not as overtly or in the same way. (By contrast, Allhallowtide never was about personal transformation, or even the living in general.) Accordingly, now we can consider the psychological dimensions of Halloween that Joseph Campbell was describing (above p. 150), because they can make the holiday transformative.

HALLOWEEN AND TRANSFORMATION

The symbols of Halloween relate to realms beyond our everyday conscious life and world. In fact, they emerge from our unconscious, which is the source of our feelings of holiness and the sacred. Ultimately, our psyche refuses to erect a permanent barrier between the profane and the sacred, between our world and the Otherworld (that of the unconscious).

The unconscious will catch up with us sooner or later. The symbols and rituals of Halloween are part of this process.

On Halloween we should not only let this process take its course, but proactively facilitate it. As Campbell advocated, we must be transparent to the transcendent. Our other holidays have become domesticated and institutionalized, whereas Halloween (like Carnival) deliberately invites us to exercise our freedom and creativity. Halloween is the only remaining major American holiday in which people, young and old, can celebrate by taking on alternative roles that exercise their imagination and potential for creative expression and fantasy. It is cathartic. Its archetypal nature came out, for example, in its easy mingling of Christian and pagan elements. It therefore can serve important mythological, creative, and psychological purposes.

Halloween helps enable people to act out their sublimated fantasies. It can help children come to terms with frightening images and characters in dreams, and likewise can help adults deal with nightmares (by confronting and making friends with nightmare characters). In our constrained lives, the rebellious, transgressive aspect of Halloween can be liberating. And it can help us deal with death in a culture that has an uneasy relationship with it and leaves matters of death in the hands of secular specialists who serve no ritual function. Although mocking it can be a willful defense against the unacceptable, merely making it visible is still one path to coming to terms with it.

The Otherworld beings were once helpful, and we can make that so again. It's not so hard, because they are already inside us. The veils are thinner than we realize. We can use Halloween to open them.

CHAPTER 10

Thanksgiving: Our American Mythmaking in Action

Nearly every society has had its etiological myth explaining how the soci-ety originated and why it is special and favored by the gods. The ancient Greeks had a variety of them. In one, told in Plato's *Menexenus*, Socrates explained how the goddess Athena had brought mankind forth from the land of Attica, which gave the Athenians a special nobility and closeness to the gods.[1] The Romans traced their ancestry back to the noble Trojans through Aeneas, and also through Romulus and Remus. Israel traced its origin as the chosen people to the appearance of Abraham and the Exodus from Egypt, guided by Yahweh. So after a brand-new society was estab-lished in North America by people who had abandoned Europe, one could expect our own mythical account of America's cultural and social origins to appear, and that's what we got. Thanksgiving commemorates in mythi-cal, idealized terms the cultural conception of our nation, eventually lead-ing to its political birth in 1776. Other than the Fourth of July, it is the only annual holiday that is uniquely our own and provides a sense of national *communitas*. It holds a special place in the American psyche because it is so tied up with our sense of our mythic past.[2]

We have reshaped this holiday over the centuries according to our evolving self-perception, a mix of our higher ideals and our national shadow. In his most famous book, *The Quest of the Historical Jesus*, Albert Schweitzer showed how each generation of scholars portrayed Jesus in its own image.[3] Thus, during the Enlightenment when human reason was most esteemed, scholars focused on how Jesus could not have performed

© The Author(s) 2020
A. George, *The Mythology of America's Seasonal Holidays*,
https://doi.org/10.1007/978-3-030-46916-0_10

miracles, and naturalistic explanations were proposed for these biblical events. In progressive times when social agendas were prominent, Jesus's own social agenda and ethics were highlighted. He was even called a Marxist.[4] More recently some scholars have argued that he was a feminist,[5] or gay,[6]—a sure sign of our changing times. The story is much the same with how Thanksgiving evolved, meaning that we have been engaged in mythmaking.

THE NATURE OF THE "FIRST THANKSGIVING"

To understand the authentic origins of Thanksgiving, we must look back across the Atlantic to the Puritans in England and Leiden, Holland.[7] The English Puritans who would become the Pilgrims had fled to Leiden to escape religious persecution. Among other things, they refused to celebrate the Church of England's many annual holidays, which they viewed as either pagan in nature or popish inventions.[8] Instead, they developed the twin practices of holding days of fasting and of thanksgiving, always on weekdays rather than on Sundays. When something bad happened and people concluded that they had offended God, or when God's help was particularly needed, the Puritans held a day of fasting, penitence, humiliation, and prayer. When good things happened, they would hold a day of thanksgiving to give thanks to God's providence, which day started in church and ended with a communal meal indoors but without other festivities. These holidays served to regulate behavior within the community, based on how the exercises of God's Providence were interpreted.[9] These solemn days were occasional ("providential") in nature because the exercises of God's providence could not be predicted, so there might be several such days in any given year, or none. These days of fasting and thanksgiving, together with the Sabbath, were the only "holidays" observed by the Leiden Puritans.[10]

The Pilgrims and subsequent Puritan immigrants brought this tradition to America. What became known as the "first Thanksgiving" in 1621, however, was a different kind of affair. Before commenting further on how it compares both with the traditional Puritan thanksgivings and our modern holiday, it is important to quote in full our only eyewitness account of it, in a 1621 letter by the Pilgrim Edward Winslow:

> Our harvest being gotten in, our governor [William Bradford] sent four men on fowling, so that we might after a special manner rejoice together

after we had gathered the fruit of our labors. They four in one day killed as much fowl as, with a little help beside, served the company almost a week. At which time, amongst other recreations, we exercised our arms, many of the Indians coming amongst us, and among the rest their greatest king Massasoit, with some ninety men, whom for three days we entertained and feasted, and they went out and killed five deer, which they brought to the plantation and bestowed on our governor, and upon the captain and others. And although it be not always so plentiful as it was at this time with us, yet by the goodness of God, we are so far from want that we often wish you [Englishmen] partakers of our plenty.[11]

This account is immediately followed by the remark, "We have found the Indians very faithful in their Covenant of Peace with us; very loving and ready to pleasure us: we often go to them, and they come to us," and further comments to the same effect.[12]

The 1622 publication that contained this brief account, entitled *Mourt's Relation*,[13] was a large pamphlet published in London aimed at the investors who were financing Plymouth Colony. In England criticisms of the project were circulating, so this publication was compiled as a promotional tract designed to ensure the continued support of the Pilgrims' financial backers and to attract additional migrants.[14] It painted a rosy picture. This bias is evident from the cover page of the pamphlet, which says that it describes "their *safe* arrival, their *joyful* building of, and *comfortable* planting themselves in the now *well defended*" town of Plymouth.[15] This sales pitch was worthy of a real estate promoter of a Florida swamp. As such, it cannot be relied upon as an objective historical account of what happened. The mythmaking began at the outset. In 1624 Winslow followed this with his book entitled *Good News from New England*, describing events in Plymouth from November 1621 (already after the first Thanksgiving) through the summer of 1623. It was written for the same purpose,[16] as evidenced by its title.

Interestingly, the other eyewitness accounts of the first few years of Plymouth Colony touched upon the period of the first harvest but did not mention any 1621 harvest celebration. These writings included the account of Plymouth's governor at the time, William Bradford, who was the very person who had ordered and organized the event. When describing that harvest period, he mentions that the harvest was small but that the colonists had shot many turkeys.[17] Apparently this feast was not a notable event to the participants themselves, but a version of it was considered interesting for purposes of consumption by Winslow's London audience. In his own account, Bradford mentions that colonists had written back to England about the results of the first growing season, stressing that these were "not feigned but true reports."[18] It thus appears that the reliability of reports coming back from Plymouth Colony (including *Mourt's Relation?*) was being questioned at the time.

After *Mourt's Relation* was published in London in 1622, only a few copies were brought back to America, and they soon disappeared. Fortunately, a copy was discovered in a Philadelphia library in 1820, but it was published in full only in 1841, in which edition the editor, Rev. Alexander Young, in a footnote termed the 1621 event the "first Thanksgiving," without any further explanation. Young's designation stuck. In the 220 years since the event, there had been no published account of it. Before the pamphlet's rediscovery, no one even knew about this "first Thanksgiving." Thus, for example, in the 1760s Thomas Hutchinson, the pre-Revolutionary governor of Massachusetts and historian, erroneously wrote that the Puritans in Massachusetts "constantly" held "in the fall, a day of thanksgiving and public acknowledgement of the favors conferred upon them in the year past. . . . It has continued without interruption, I suppose, in any one instance, down to this day."[19] He not only mischaracterized the actual Puritan thanksgivings but was entirely unaware of the 1621 feast. Thus, until 1841 Thanksgiving evolved in a tortuous fashion and without knowledge or commemoration of the 1621 celebration. There being no solid historical accounts to rely upon to anchor the origins and meaning of the evolving holiday, Thanksgiving was ripe for mythmaking. So the holiday took on an independent body of symbols and historical associations.[20]

But before tracing the mythological evolution of the holiday after 1621, it is important to compare what actually happened with the Pilgrims' own notions of what a thanksgiving was and with some of our modern associations concerning the event.

First, the 1621 event was not a "thanksgiving" in accordance with Puritan definition and custom, so the Pilgrims did not look upon it as such.[21] In their own minds, their first thanksgiving since leaving Leiden was held on July 26, 1623, and it had nothing to do with harvests. Rather, it was celebrated in thanks for relief from a drought and for the safe arrival of new colonists from England.[22] That event, like past providential thanksgivings, was a solemn religious ritual marked mainly by prayer; the meal afterwards was traditional but secondary. The 1621 celebration as described by Winslow, however, differed in several important respects:

- It was three days, whereas actual thanksgivings were only one day long.
- It was outdoors, whereas actual thanksgivings were indoors.
- While the Pilgrim participants probably said prayers on the occasion, it was not a religious holiday by nature.
- The participants engaged in recreations, whereas this was prohibited on true thanksgivings, which were solemn occasions.[23]
- Being held in late September or early October, it had the character of traditional English rural secular harvest festivals.[24] Further, the Wampanoag had their own harvest-related festivals,[25] so they would have understood the event well. A Puritan thanksgiving could not be a harvest festival, because that would make it an annual rather than occasional event; one could never predict whether God's Providence would result in a good harvest.

Lest we lose sight of things, however, an important historical core remains: The Pilgrims were indeed being thankful by holding a feast. This fact was enough to serve as the essential rootstock of the holiday, onto which many fictional embellishments were grafted once the public became aware of the 1621 feast in the mid-nineteenth century.

Second, the participation of the Wampanoag at the event differed from our traditional sentimental perception of it as evidencing warm relations between them and the Pilgrims. Actually, their relationship got off to a rocky start. According to Nathaniel Morton, soon after the Pilgrims' arrival and before the two sides ever met, the Wampanoag shamans, presumably with Massasoit's knowledge and at his urging, conducted a three-day ritual "to curse and execrate them with their conjurations." Morton said this was Satan at work, meaning that the Wampanoag were doing the Devil's bidding.[26] Nevertheless, after this ritual didn't work, when the sides eventually met in March of 1621, they signed a peace treaty, needed by both sides for protection against other threatening tribes. Starting the morning after signing the treaty and over several weeks thereafter, groups of Wampanoag began visiting Plymouth unannounced, including with women and children and sometimes on the Sabbath. This practice taxed the Pilgrims' resources and interfered with their work. It became so "oppressing" to the Pilgrims that in June they sent a delegation to Massasoit to explain that they could no longer afford to offer hospitality to so many frequent groups of visitors, but that if Massasoit wanted to come himself or send his own messengers that would be fine; for this purpose they gave Massasoit a copper chain for his messengers to carry so that the Pilgrims would know whether a person was really sent by Massasoit.[27] But then Massasoit discovered that the chief intermediary between him and the Pilgrims, the English-speaking Squanto (a Patuxet whom Massasoit had essentially been holding prisoner before the Pilgrims arrived), had been playing a double game and asked the Pilgrims to kill him, but they refused.[28] At the "first Thanksgiving" it seems that the Wampanoag again came uninvited, this time *en masse:* their chief Massasoit together with some 90 other men (no women or children this time).[29] Their purpose in coming is not clear, but it was probably political. Winslow's account does not actually say that the Pilgrims were giving thanks to the Wampanoag; presumably, given their theology, any formal thanks would have been given only to God, not to pagans. For their part, the Pilgrims put on a demonstration of their firearms, perhaps to impress Massasoit.

In light of the promotional purpose of Winslow's letter, his account of the Wampanoag visit to the feast is probably overly rosy, leaving negative issues out of the story. In any event, the 1621 feast and any association it may have had with friendship with the natives was soon forgotten. Shortly after the event, the Pilgrims built an eight-foot high, 2700-foot-long palisade around their settlement, and the following spring they built a fort on the hill armed with six cannon.[30] Within two years after the 1621 event, the severed head of a dead Massachusetts Indian together with a cloth splashed with his blood decorated that fort, just in time for Massasoit and his fellow Wampanoag to see it when they arrived for Bradford's marriage celebration.[31] In October 1637 a Thanksgiving was proclaimed by Bradford to celebrate the colonists' victory in their war against the Pequot.[32] If there ever had been any sentimental association between Thanksgivings and friendship with the natives, that surely was enough to end it. Indeed, no idyllic artistic portrayals of the 1621 feast emerged until after the wars with Native Americans across the nation were over, near the end of the nineteenth century.[33] Before that Thanksgiving art usually portrayed Native Americans as a threat, as in Fig. 10.1. Such was the early Thanksgiving tradition concerning Native Americans.

Third, several other details differ from the later Thanksgiving holiday. For one thing, we don't know for sure what was on the menu, except for presumably some kind of fowl and venison, which the Pilgrims and Wampanoag hunted for the occasion.[34] Turkey may well have been on the

Fig. 10.1 *Thanksgiving Day in New England Two Hundred Years Ago,* unknown artist, from *Frank Leslie's Illustrated Newspaper,* November 27, 1869, showing a Puritan family's Thanksgiving dinner being interrupted by a hail of arrows. In the midst of the Indian Wars, the motif of violence between colonists and Native Americans was popular

menu, especially since Bradford mentioned that the Pilgrims hunted many of them during that period,[35] but we can't be certain. There would also have been no cranberry sauce (sugar was lacking) or sweet potatoes (not native to North America). Presumably they did not eat the same food on all three days. The Pilgrims also would not have been dressed in black clothes and hats with buckles; rather, they wore colorful clothing. There were also probably hardly any tables and chairs to accommodate the participants outdoors; most would have sat on the ground.

THE DEVELOPMENT OF THANKSGIVING BEFORE 1841

As the colonial population became less Puritan and expanded beyond the Puritan strongholds, the Puritan worldview eroded, and the original strong tie between church and state became weakened by the end of the seventeenth century. Thanksgivings did not die out; they just changed in character. Changes came readily because the holiday was anchored only in evolving oral tradition, not documented historical events, scripture, church doctrine, or laws. People began to both anticipate and aggregate providential events, so that by the end of the seventeenth century a pattern emerged of regular fasts in the spring (when the fate of the crops was uncertain and God's grace was sought) and Thanksgivings in the autumn,[36] which became more like traditional harvest festivals. Eventually the spring days of fasting faded away, leaving only autumn Thanksgivings, but without the Puritans' original doctrinal baggage. Thanksgiving was no longer dependent on particular acts of God's providence. The dates of Thanksgivings were now mostly proclaimed by the secular authorities of individual colonies and (later) states, and their dates differed.

Whereas Thanksgivings originally were collective affairs observed by the local community as a whole, at both church and at the meal, it became more of a family celebration.[37] As the holiday retreated into the home, it also began to lose its original formal religious character with religious rituals.[38] The holiday now included secular entertainments, often not on the day itself, including Thanksgiving balls. Acts of charity also became popular, especially helping the poor.[39] Even weddings were sometimes celebrated as part of Thanksgiving, as they were often household rather than church affairs.[40] The popular mind came to believe that the holiday had always been customary, seasonal, and in its current form. Notably, between 1676 and 1840 (the year before *Mourt's Relation* was published in America) no colonial or state Thanksgiving proclamation referred to the Pilgrims.[41] Until the Civil War, Thanksgivings were largely restricted to New England and became a regional tradition there.

During the Revolutionary War, the Pilgrims became associated with the American cause, being elevated to the status of our national forefathers, so unsurprisingly it was during this conflict that Thanksgiving was first raised to a national holiday. As tensions with England rose before war began, in 1774, to honor the Pilgrims, much of Plymouth Rock was removed from its bed, taken into the town square, and placed at the foot of a liberty pole.[42] The Pilgrims were thus being wrongly identified with our Founding Fathers' Enlightenment-based secular views on liberty and democracy.[43] The Pilgrims were depicted as Americans rather than Englishmen. The first national Thanksgiving Day was proclaimed by the Continental Congress in 1777, and it had both a religious and military flavor. It was held in December of that year in thanks for the Colonial Army's victory at Saratoga. The proclamation implored God for further blessings, especially to inspire our military commanders with wisdom and fortitude, and also for economic prosperity; it also called upon the people for penitence and confession of sins. Thereafter the Congress proclaimed Thanksgivings each year during 1778–84, all in October, November, or December. After other national Thanksgivings in 1789 and 1795, although many individual states held Thanksgivings on various dates, no further national Thanksgiving was held until the close of the War of 1812, in April 1815.[44] All were similarly military in character, and were not associated with autumn or harvests. The holiday was used politically to pronounce the nation's achievements in trade, industry, and agriculture.[45]

After 1815 no national Thanksgiving was proclaimed until the Civil War. Ironically, the first two of these were proclaimed by the *Confederacy* for July 28, 1861, and September 28, 1862, in celebration of military victories at Bull Run.[46] As for the North, President Lincoln proclaimed the first national Thanksgiving of the Union for April 13, 1862, in thanks for its own military victories. In 1863 he proclaimed two national Thanksgivings, one in August following the battle of Gettysburg, and another on the last Thursday of November. The latter began our unbroken succession of national November Thanksgiving holidays.[47]

Thanksgiving was now consistently tied, if not to the Pilgrims themselves, to an idyllic vision of colonial New England.[48] In Massachusetts Forefathers' Day was celebrated every December 22 to celebrate the Pilgrims' landing. The American Revolution, our victory in it, and also the victory of the Union in the Civil War, were attributed to traditional Yankee values and fortitude, which Thanksgiving came to celebrate. After the Revolution there was a Yankee exodus to territories outside of New England. There the expatriates formed New England societies, and among other things they celebrated Forefathers' Day and Thanksgiving, thus spreading the popularity of Thanksgiving to other territories and states.[49]

THANKSGIVING AFTER THE REDISCOVERY OF THE "FIRST THANKSGIVING"

Before 1841, Thanksgiving was not a nationally self-conscious event. It did not yet commemorate a mythic past or consciously embrace national values and identity, and so was simply a tradition rather than a formal national holiday.[50] This changed following the rediscovery and republication in 1841 of the full version of *Mourt's Relation* including Winslow's account of the 1621 feast in Alexander Young's book, *Chronicles of the Pilgrim Fathers,* which brought public awareness of that feast and for the first time ever called it the "first Thanksgiving." This gave the holiday a commemorative function that it had previously lacked. It thus set in motion a process in which over the remainder of the nineteenth century the essential myth of the holiday was formed and the day became a truly national holiday.

The "first Thanksgiving" gained the attention of Sarah Josepha Hale, the influential editor of a ladies' magazine. Beginning in 1846, she waged a 17-year campaign to make Thanksgiving a national holiday, succeeding when President Lincoln issued his Thanksgiving proclamations. Although Hale had been stimulated by the new information about the Pilgrims and the "first Thanksgiving," her campaign tactic was to stress the current benefits of having such a holiday, particularly in the home. As the savvy editor of a women's magazine who saw that Thanksgiving was a family tradition, Hale in particular campaigned for Thanksgiving as a women's holiday, as a result of which female Pilgrim characters became prominent in legendary accounts of the 1621 feast.[51] (A legend even arose that Mary Chilton was the first Pilgrim to set foot on Plymouth Rock, but actually she was not there that day.[52]) This new feminine focus was reflected in the 1889 novel by Jane G. Austin, entitled *Standish of Standish—A Story of the Pilgrims,* containing a colorful, imaginative account of the first Thanksgiving in which the Pilgrim women preparing the food were the most prominent characters. (The novel's plot was dominated by several romances, it being that era's version of a chick flick.) The book became a national bestseller that went through at least 28 printings.[53] She also wrote other popular stories about the Pilgrims. Just as today's movie audiences wrongly draw on "historical" dramas for iffy information about history, Austin's many readers devoured the various details of her narrative, which helped fix the mythical stereotype of the "first Thanksgiving" in the popular mind.

To be fair, Austin was quite an authority on the Pilgrims (her brother too had written a book about them) and knew a lot about what did and probably did not happen at that feast. But as a novelist she exercised much creative license, beginning with calling it the first Thanksgiving. So, in her telling of the event Bradford invites Massasoit and his subjects, including women. The Pilgrims say prayers. The participants sit at long tables. Winslow dresses in his "festive doublet and hose." Turkey ("more succulent . . . than any I ever saw at home" in England) is on the menu, which is quite extensive and imaginative. It included hasty pudding, "clam chowder with plenty of sea biscuit swimming in the savory broth," great pieces of cold boiled beef (where did cows come from?) with mustard, beechnut dressing, and a "great pewter bowl of plum-porridge with bits of toasted cracker floating upon it." And the "oysters in their scallop shells were a singular success, and so were the mighty venison pasties, and the savory stew compounded of all that flies in the air . . . swimming in a glorious broth cunningly seasoned by Priscilla's anxious hand." But the most impressive event that day was when, to the fanfare of trumpets and drums, a "little army of nineteen men, preceded by the military band," which exercised its firearms, "accented at one point with a tremendous roar from the cannon" at the fort they were constructing. Austin commented, "here stood the nucleus of that power which a century and a half later was to successfully defy and throw off the rule of that magnificent but cruel stepdame [England]; here stood the first American army."[54] Here we see the position of the Pilgrims in America's creation myth.

Standish of Standish was an important source for another influential work about Thanksgiving, Clifford Howard's 1897 article in *Ladies' Home Journal*, entitled "The First Thanksgiving Dinner," which repeated Austin's descriptions more or less as fact. It included W.L. Taylor's illustration of the first Thanksgiving, complete with long tables, Pilgrim men in black dress, white lace collars, and tall steepled hats, and a log cabin in the background (the Pilgrims did not build log cabins). In the fashion of the time, a woman is the focal figure (Fig. 10.2). This illustration was widely reproduced in other publications, further contributing to the stereotype.

Although Winslow's description of the first Thanksgiving was published in 1841, it took until near the end of the century for the Pilgrims to become essentially linked with the holiday. There are at least four reasons for this, deriving from the history of that period, which we need to explore because the Thanksgiving myth evolved based on how we have viewed ourselves at any particular point in time.

First, for most of the nineteenth century we were involved in wars with Native Americans, particularly in the West. During that period, stories and images of the Pilgrims being friends the natives were not appealing. But they did become acceptable once the Indian Wars were over and began to be suppressed and repressed from our national memory.

Second, Thanksgiving was mostly popular in New England. It was generally not observed in the South, where it was perceived as a Yankee holiday. At a time of conflict with the North, for southerners observing

Fig. 10.2   *The First Thanksgiving,* by W.L. Taylor in *Ladies' Home Journal,* 1897

Thanksgiving would be unpatriotic. Besides, the South had an alternative end-of-year holiday, Christmas, because it had never had a Puritan heritage to oppose it. Thus, it was only during postwar Reconstruction and the Progressive era that Thanksgiving could be welcomed in the South.

Third, by the time the public learned of Winslow's account, Americans were already celebrating Thanksgiving in ways much different than did the Puritans. The differences were difficult to confront, as in cases of cognitive dissonance. In order for the Pilgrims to become a fixture in our Thanksgiving, either people would have to start celebrating it more like the Pilgrims did, or we would have to rewrite the Pilgrims' history to fit our tastes. We know which approach won out: The Pilgrims' Calvinism was forgotten, their political views were twisted beyond recognition, and the nature of their Thanksgivings was forgotten so that the holiday was thought of always having been mainly a family event.[55] The Pilgrims were portrayed as holding Enlightenment values and were sharply distinguished from the authoritarian Massachusetts Bay Colony (even though Plymouth was eventually absorbed into it); the Pilgrims were not even thought of as Puritans, instead being called merely "Separatists."[56]

Fourth and finally, it was in the late nineteenth century that we had the most massive immigration into America, and as a result the Pilgrims were elevated to iconic status as ideal immigrants. They were looked upon as inspirational models for the new immigrants. This status drew them further into our national consciousness.[57]

Since, due to our early Puritan heritage, Christmas was hardly celebrated in most of America (except the South) through most of the nineteenth century, Thanksgiving took on an additional role and importance that it no longer has. Thanksgiving rather than Christmas assumed the role of our summing-up, end-of-year holiday of marking the transition into winter and eventually the New Year, somewhat like the Celtic Samhain. This function became more pronounced once the holiday began to be celebrated annually in November. At that point Thanksgiving was no longer a harvest celebration, nor were autumn colors associated with the holiday because the leaves were long off the trees. (It was Halloween that had these associations.) Because of the colder climate at the time, in New England during November snow was often already on the ground and ponds were frozen. Accordingly, sleighing and skating became popular Thanksgiving recreations. This was reflected in the 1844 poem by Lydia Maria Child entitled "The New-England Boy's Song about Thanksgiving Day," popularly known as "Over the River and Through the Wood," famously describing a sleigh ride to a holiday celebration at Grandfather's house. As the title indicates, this holiday was Thanksgiving. But once Christmas became popular and the climate grew warmer, the poem was set to music with slightly modified wording (including changing "Grandfather's" to "Grandmother's") and it became a popular Christmas song instead. Similarly, "Jingle Bells" (composed ca. 1850, published 1857) originally did not concern Christmas, but was composed for Thanksgiving celebrations.[58] Once Christmas in wintry December became popular, Thanksgiving lost its association with these activities and songs about them, and they were utilized instead for Christmas.

Once Christmas was firmly established, Thanksgiving was relieved of its role as our end-of-year winter holiday. This made it easier for the Pilgrims and their "first Thanksgiving" to be given more prominence in the holiday's observance. In parallel, as industrialization and urbanization took over our national economy and work life, a nostalgia for a lost agrarian past developed, so Thanksgiving became a locus for celebrating and vicariously experiencing that idyll. This helped to revive the harvest theme as a lasting element of the holiday.[59]

In a further departure from Pilgrim traditions, in the late nineteenth century on Thanksgiving a college football game between the two leading teams from the season became popular. As we've seen, the Pilgrims did not permit recreation on their Thanksgivings. This game helped popularize Thanksgiving as a national holiday because it featured teams from different states, and so was especially helpful in getting the South to accept the holiday.

Thanksgiving and the Pilgrims were increasingly invoked to serve public policy, political, and educational purposes. In the Reconstruction period, during the campaign to enact the Fifteenth Amendment to our Constitution, which prohibited denial or abridgement of the right to vote based on race, color, or previous condition of servitude, Thomas Nast drew an illustration for the November 20, 1869, issue of *Harper's Weekly* entitled "Uncle Sam's Thanksgiving Dinner." It depicted people of various nationalities and races in their traditional dress, including a Native American and a former slave, sitting peacefully around the Thanksgiving dinner table (Fig. 10.3). Somewhat later, in the Progressive Era, Teddy Roosevelt, as part of his trust busting efforts, invoked the Pilgrims

Fig. 10.3 Uncle Sam's Thanksgiving Dinner, Illustration by Thomas Nast in *Harper's Weekly*, 1869

(actually not so inaccurately) as favoring the regulation of businesses.[60] The Pilgrims and the Thanksgiving story began to be more regularly included in school curricula, thus driving them into our national consciousness and helping to consolidate America's creation myth. A young Russian immigrant around the turn of the twentieth century wrote that she had learned from her textbook that

> America started with a band of Courageous Pilgrims. They had left their native country as I had left mine. . . . I saw that it was the glory of America that it was not yet finished. And I, the last comer, had her share to give, small or great, to the making of America, like those Pilgrims, who came in the *Mayflower*.[61]

All the elements of contemporary Thanksgiving existed by the early twentieth century, but they did not jell together until after WWII. During the patriotic fervor of both world wars, Americans looked to the Pilgrims as a source of American values. WWII was fought to preserve our national values and way of life, and the Pilgrims were held to embody them. Their image became more spiritual; they were the most pure and spiritual of the colonists, and came to be viewed as our national parents. The virtues that they represented were held to have made our victory in WWII possible. And since America emerged from the war as the world's preeminent power and opposed to Communism, the Pilgrims and Thanksgiving became useful for promulgating our values abroad.

The mythmaking continued in the ensuing decades and up to the present day. During the postwar Red Scare the Pilgrims were heralded as anti-Communists. Whereas in the 1940s *Life* magazine had said the Pilgrims epitomized traditional virtues (disciplined, hard-working, and committed to church, home, and family), during the turbulent 1960s *Look* magazine characterized the Pilgrims as anti-establishment counterculture figures, calling them "dissidents" and "commune builders." Lyndon Johnson appealed to the Pilgrims' principles to justify the Vietnam War. The Republican Richard Nixon praised the Pilgrims as rugged individualists, when in fact they were oriented toward the collective. As the Cold War thawed, they were seen as having reached the first détente, in their case with the Native Americans. Bill Clinton said that the spirit of peacemaking between the Pilgrims and Native Americans was a model for Middle East peace negotiations.[62] Doubtlessly, we will see the like in the future. On the other hand, in the wake of modern protests by Native Americans in regard to Thanksgiving, at least at Plymouth Hall Museum a shift has occurred away from the traditional Thanksgiving story of unity with the natives and toward reviving the harvest theme,[63] even though harvest was not necessarily associated with Pilgrim Thanksgivings. Nationwide as well, the Native American perspective on the event is being more widely told.[64]

THANKSGIVING AND HISTORICAL MYTH

As Henry Cabot Lodge once observed, "The historical myth, indeed, would not exist at all if it did not profess to tell something which people for one reason or another, like to believe, and which appeals strongly to some emotion or passion, and so to human nature."[65] While our Fourth of July holiday celebrates our *political* beginnings and civic values, Thanksgiving reaches deeper into who we like to believe we are as a people and what are our essential *cultural* values. But as we have seen, the values projected onto the Pilgrims and the various meanings of Thanksgiving are the ones that we have considered important at each point in our history. This process, in which symbols and rituals are used by overt references to important past events to inculcate norms and values through repetition (as in annual holidays) is called "the invention of tradition."[66] It legitimizes the status quo of the time. As a result, Thanksgiving has come to stand for what we perceive as our national identity, and as such gives us our etiological myth as a people. The Pilgrims are seen not just as the first in many waves of similar immigrants, but as our separate and unique parents. For this myth to work, it had to seamlessly connect then and now. To use a biblical analogy, if our Revolutionary War was like the Exodus and the Conquest of Canaan, the Pilgrims have become our Abraham, our ultimate foundational symbol. The Pilgrims have become so because their mythologized story offers symbols for us to grasp and act upon, first and foremost the 1621 first Thanksgiving in suspended dreamtime on a golden autumn afternoon. We can revisit that moment each year, as it is our own myth of the eternal return, through which each year a community holds a ritual that takes its members back to a mythical golden beginning, *in illo tempore*.[67]

While it is important to be self-aware about the past and determine, to the extent possible, what did and didn't happen in our history, we must also recognize the value contained in this national myth, just as one should have and hold onto one's own personal myth. We know, for example, that the "first Thanksgiving" was not representative of the whole of the Pilgrims' relationship with the Wampanoag, but we can presume that on at least that one occasion they shared friendship and gave thanks. More importantly, the occasion as mythologized does serve as a model for being our best national self. That is worthwhile in itself. The myth can point to how to realize our best national future, for example in celebrating our diversity, ensuring equal rights, accommodating immigrants, maintaining the principles of our democracy, and preserving family values. The continued vibrancy of Thanksgiving suggests that we are continuing to mythologize it. The myth is alive and still functions well for us, as it has in the past in different conditions. And inevitably our vision of our own creation will mirror our mythical, ideal vision of our society at each point in time as it evolves.

CHAPTER 11

Christmas: New Beginnings and the Birth of the Divine Child-Hero

Our annual celebration of the birth of Jesus heralds a new beginning with high hopes for the future, both for individuals in their spiritual lives and for humankind. So it was indeed appropriate for the Catholic Church to begin its liturgical year with the Christmas season, starting with Advent. As we shall see, Christmas can still function in this way for people of all religious and non-religious persuasions, without necessarily having to believe the biblical nativity stories.

This chapter cannot be an exhaustive treatment of all aspects of the birth of Jesus as narrated in the Gospels. Rather, it focuses on the mythological elements of those stories which have become fixtures in our Christmas holiday. These include the virginal conception and incarnation, the action of the Holy Spirit, the birth in Bethlehem, the adorations of the magi and shepherds, the chorus of angels, the ox and donkey at the nativity, the massacre of the innocents and flight to Egypt, the presentation of Jesus in the temple, and the relationship of Jesus's and John the Baptist's conceptions and births. Using a mythological perspective, this chapter details how and why we came to have these Christmas stories that we celebrate. This approach better enables us to understand their meaning, appreciate their continuing spiritual value today, and celebrate Christmas in a spiritually reinvigorated manner.

While the birth of Jesus is the principal mythological basis for Christmas, many European pagan traditions crept in to further define this holiday.

© The Author(s) 2020
A. George, *The Mythology of America's Seasonal Holidays*,
https://doi.org/10.1007/978-3-030-46916-0_11

Myths lie behind those traditions too, and the fact that they have some of the same mythical underpinnings as the Christian myth helps to explain why they were readily assimilated into the holiday. Further, St. Nicholas became a mythologized figure, also acquiring some pagan characteristics.

Our discussion of the "mythology" of Christmas has two steps. The first is to determine how much of the Christmas story is probably historical and how much is likely myth (in the sense of not being factually true), so that we can be as clear as possible about the extent to which the Christmas story is mythologized. The second is to analyze the mythological elements in order to better understand the deeper meaning of the story and of our holiday. I also discuss why early Christians considered it important to celebrate the birth of Christ, as well as their decision to do so on December 25th. Mythology underlies those decisions as well.

Is the Christmas Story a Myth?

Did the Christmas events that we celebrate ever happen? The stories of Jesus's birth abound with extraordinary, miraculous elements having the ring of myth: A royal genealogy. Intervention by God (through the Holy Spirit) causing a virgin to conceive. Revelatory angelic appearances, including in dreams. A new star moving westward across the sky to Jerusalem, then south to Bethlehem, and stopping over the house of Jesus's birth (Mt 2:2–10). Adorations of the wonder child by magi (in Matthew) or shepherds (in Luke). A chorus of angels celebrating his birth, and then rising up into heaven (Lk 2:13–15). Prophecies about his nature and wondrous future. An evil king (Herod) out to kill the wonder child who could oust him. And much more.

Infancy stories of Jesus appear only in the Gospels of Matthew and Luke. There is no mention of Jesus's birth in Mark or John, nor in the writings of St. Paul or the rest of the New Testament. Nor are any circumstances of the nativity referred to in the remainder of either Matthew or Luke. They are self-contained literary units that preface the rest of Matthew and Luke. These Gospels might have done well enough without them, as did Mark and John, but Matthew and Luke included them in order to make particular theological points, which are also largely mythical. I consider in the next section why Matthew and Luke wanted to include them, but for now let's examine to what extent these accounts are history rather than myth.

The Christmas story as portrayed in our modern culture in stories, Christmas carols, Christmas cards, and art, is usually a conflation of elements from Matthew and Luke, but almost without exception each of these elements belongs exclusively to either Matthew or Luke, and is absent from or even contradicted by the other Gospel. We can count on our fingers the elements that they have in common: virginal conception through the Holy Spirit, rather than Joseph being Jesus's biological father; Jesus's birth in Bethlehem, late in the reign of Herod, after his parents have started living together; Joseph's Davidic descent; angels predict his birth, say to name the child Jesus, and predict that he will be the Savior; and Jesus is then brought up in Nazareth.[1]

Otherwise Matthew's and Luke's accounts vary, either in their focus or in squarely contradicting each other.[2] In fact, the two stories don't have a single scene in common.[3] A Hebrew Bible prophecy in Micah 5:2 had predicted that the Messiah will be from Bethlehem, but everyone knew that Jesus had grown up on Nazareth. According to Matthew, Joseph and Mary's original home was in Bethlehem, Jesus was born there, and they moved to Nazareth after their return from Egypt. But in Luke, Joseph and Mary always live in Nazareth, and they visit Bethlehem only to register for tax purposes, when Jesus was born. Matthew has the star, Luke does not. In Matthew Jesus is born in the family house, in Luke in a stranger's out building where there is a manger. In Matthew magi visit Jesus, probably several months after his birth, but in Luke it is humble shepherds from near Bethlehem, on the night of his birth. In Matthew, the family flees Bethlehem for Egypt to escape Herod's massacre of the innocents, but Luke reports no such thing. Rather, in Luke, soon after Jesus's birth, the family travels to the temple in Jerusalem to present Jesus there, after which they return home to Nazareth. Matthew and Luke also each offer genealogies of Jesus, but they are inconsistent with each other. These contradictions are irreconcilable,[4] meaning that in each case one of them can't be true, most likely neither. As the eminent biblical scholar Geza Vermes put it, "To attempt a full reconciliation of the two Infancy Gospels is a patently lost cause: squaring the circle would be easier than reducing the two into a single coherent unity."[5]

Each narrative in many respects also runs counter to known historical facts, in which instances they are also not credible on their own terms.[6] For example, the account in Luke 2:1–4 of the empire-wide Roman census during Herod's reign, which supposedly brought Joseph and Mary to Bethlehem by reason of Joseph's birth there, cannot be true.[7] There would be a record of such an ecumenical census, but there is none; indeed, such a census would have been impractical. Further, Judea was not subject to direct Roman taxation during the reign of Herod when Jesus was born.[8] Rome set up its own taxation system in Judea only in 6 CE when it came under direct Roman rule through a prefect who reported to the governor of Syria. This governor, Quirinius, did initiate a local census as part of setting up that new system, but this was in 6 CE.[9] So if Jesus was born during this census, then he could not have been born during Herod's reign, which had ended some 10 years earlier. But this census covered Judea and its residents, not Galilee, so Joseph and Mary, who Luke has living in Nazareth, would not have been subject to it.[10] And even if they were, by law the registration would have taken place in the district where Joseph was resident — meaning registration in Sepphoris for people from Nazareth — rather than where his ancestor David was born.[11] Nor would Mary have been required to go and appear with her husband to register.[12] Those who believe in the inerrancy of scripture continue to insist that Luke's account must be true, but as the historical Jesus specialist John Meier concluded, "Attempts to reconcile Luke 2:1 with the facts of ancient history are hopelessly contrived."[13]

Another example of historical inaccuracy is Matthew's story of the massacre of the innocents, which (at least as portrayed) would have been such a prominent and infamous event that, in the view of historians, there would have been some historical record of it.[14] (Likewise for the account of the star.[15]) Rather, Matthew invented the incident to get Jesus to Egypt so he could be a new Moses to the people with a new Law, for Matthew 2:15 quoted Hosea 11:1, in which Yahweh said, "out of Egypt I have called my son." But in Hosea "son" referred to the people of Israel as a whole, not any individual who was Yahweh's son;[16] Matthew contrived a new, prophetic meaning for the passage. Further, Matthew equated the massacre with the pharaoh's massacre of the Hebrews' newborn sons in Exodus 1:15–22.[17] In Matthew's story, Jesus's family did not return to Bethlehem ostensibly because Herod's son was now ruling Judea, which made Bethlehem dangerous. But inexplicably they then went to Nazareth in Galilee where Herod's *other son* (Herod Antipas ("the Fox"), who later beheaded John the Baptist) was ruling. From the frying pan into the fire![18]

A third example is Luke's account of Jesus's presentation at the Jerusalem temple (2:21–40). Whereas in Matthew Jesus must be rushed out of Bethlehem and all of Judea once Herod finds out about him, in Luke his parents stay put and take him to Jerusalem 40 days after his birth,

where temple prophets proclaim him the future savior of Israel and proclaim it to all who will listen, this occurring just footsteps from Herod's
palace![19] This episode as reported also contains significant mistakes in
Jewish Law and ritual which render the account doubtful. First, Luke 2:22
says that both Mary and Joseph went for "*their* purification under the Law
of Moses," whereas under the Law only the mother was considered impure
and had to undergo this.[20] Also, purification of the mother and the presentation (and redemption) of the firstborn child were two separate rituals,
but they are conflated by Luke. Finally, there was no requirement to bring
the child to the temple and "present" him there; rather, the parents would
go by themselves and just pay five shekels.[21]

Matthew and Luke could not have based their accounts upon taking
testimony by eyewitnesses, because almost certainly they would have died
by the time these authors wrote almost a century after Jesus's birth, and
both are thought to have lived far from Jerusalem and Bethlehem. If a
uniform and possibly reliable oral or written tradition of Jesus's infancy
had developed, their accounts would have not been so vastly inconsistent.
No two parallel narratives in the Gospels have a higher rate of contradiction.[22] The vast majority of modern biblical scholars outside the funda-
mentalist/evangelical orbit regard these infancy narratives as unhistorical.[23]
Paul never described the nativity, yet as New Testament scholar J.K. Elliot
observed, "the Christmas story provides us with no more real facts about
the historical Jesus than Paul himself does."[24]

In summary, the historical information that we can derive from the
Christmas story is very limited: Jesus was born sometime late in King
Herod's reign, probably between 6 and 4 BCE. His parents were Mary
and (probably) Joseph, Jews of modest means. And as we shall see, the
place of his birth was almost certainly Nazareth rather than Bethlehem,
but the other circumstances of his birth and youth are unknown.[25]

Matthew's and Luke's accounts were written based on a combination
of differing local traditions and the authors' own creative imaginations for
the purpose of creating an appealing myth to make their own theological
points. Let us explore how these evangelists did so.

WHY WERE THE INFANCY MYTHS CREATED?

Since no infancy stories or even references to the extraordinary events of
Jesus's birth appear in Mark, John, or elsewhere in the New Testament, it
is appropriate to ask why Matthew and Luke decided to include such

stories. One reason was simple curiosity among early Christians.[26] There
was an insatiable appetite for more details about Jesus's miraculous life,
starting from its beginning, and such demand created the supply. In the
resulting stories, the extraordinary character of Jesus's life, death, and
reported resurrection was projected backwards to his conception and
birth. (The traditions concerning his birth were probably newer than
those about his life, death, and resurrection,[27] and seem not to have
coalesced into a single, consistent narrative tradition by the time when
Matthew and Luke took up the matter.) Later examples include the
Infancy Gospel of Thomas (end of second century), which described
Jesus's childhood up through his appearance at the temple at age 12
(where Luke picks up); the Protoevangelium of James (late second century), mainly providing details of Mary's background; and finally the
Gospel of Pseudo-Matthew (early seventh century), which combined the
material in Thomas and James and added mythological material of
its own.[28]

But Matthew and Luke had more specific theological reasons for writing their infancy stories. First, Mark, which had no infancy narrative, wrote
that Jesus was declared the Son of God at the time of his baptism (1:11).[29]
Matthew and Luke, however, wanted to show that Jesus's divine nature
existed even earlier, at the time of his conception, which accordingly in
their Gospels occurred through divine means.[30] (Later, the Gospel of John
pushed Jesus's existence and divine nature back to before the creation of
the cosmos (1:1–4).[31]) It was important to enhance Christ's divinity
because these Gospels were written for Mediterranean audiences, both for
Christians and for potential diaspora Jewish and gentile converts.
Accordingly, as in the case of the Easter-related stories (see pp. 88–90,
104–06), the nativity stories utilized stock mythological motifs from the
Mediterranean world that the intended audience would have recognized
and which, therefore, would have had maximum persuasive power in
showing that Jesus was divine.[32] A second goal was to characterize Jesus as
being superior to John the Baptist, since he had a competing following
(see below p. 208). A third goal, especially in Matthew, was to connect the
very appearance of Jesus to the traditions and perceived prophecies of the
Hebrew Bible,[33] in order to give the Jesus story more weight and credibil-
ity. It was useful to show the Jewish diaspora audience how Jesus as the
Messiah had been prophesized in the Hebrew scriptures, while for the
gentile audience it helped to show that the religious background and process leading to the appearance of Jesus had an old, venerable, and

documented background, because gentiles were skeptical of the novel Christian religion and its new divine figure. A fourth reason was that, given that Jesus was generally regarded as being from Nazareth, Matthew and Luke decided to portray Jesus as being born in Bethlehem in order to fulfill the prophecy in Micah 5:2, in order to substantiate the claim that he was the Messiah. This was important because Jews were skeptical about a claimed Messiah coming from Galilee.[34] Finally, many biblical scholars also believe that another reason for these infancy stories (and in particular the virginal conception) was to combat rumors, reflected in the Gospels, that Jesus was an illegitimate child (see pp. 209–12 below).[35]

Thus, we see at work here what mythologists call the "functionalist" character of myths, according to which myths are structured and function to reinforce and further an existing belief system within a community, especially its religion.[36] Beyond this, but along the same lines, the infancy stories were designed to attract converts from both the Jewish and Gentile communities. This purpose was advanced by using a sacred narrative containing miraculous events, appealing to divine sanction and ancient scripture, and taking liberties with the historical background. In other words, it helped to design the stories *in the manner* of myth. This explains, for example, the incorporation of even blatant falsehoods in a story never meant to be an objective historical account, as well as why people didn't mind. Why, for instance, would Luke place Christ's birth in the context of the above-mentioned census that was conducted only years later, and claim that it was worldwide and ordered by Augustus? Early Christians knew why: For them, it carried an evangelical, spiritual truth. As St. Ambrose (ca. 340–397 CE) explained in one of his sermons:

> While the secular census is referred to, the spiritual is implied, a census to be made known, not to the king of the earth but to the king of heaven. It is a profession of faith, an enrollment of souls . . . that you may know that this is of Christ, not of Augustus, the "whole world" is ordered to be enrolled. And who could decree the enrollment of the whole world? Not of Augustus but of the Lord it was said, "The earth is the Lord's and the fullness thereof."[37]

The census thus becomes a metaphor, a building block of the myth. Luke utilizes it to contrast earthly and heavenly authority, the profane and the spiritual. It also showed that Jesus's family, and by implication Jesus himself, was Law abiding.[38] Yet the story is a veiled slap at the Romans: By ordering a worldwide census, Augustus inadvertently triggered the eventual enrollment of followers of Christ throughout the known world.[39] Mythmaking in action.

Ambrose's attention to Rome, and to Augustus in particular, exemplifies a final important reason for Matthew and Luke having infancy stories: The need to compete with and better Roman gods and divine emperors in the Greco-Roman religious marketplace. As detailed below, this purpose helps explain many elements of the infancy accounts, but here let us just set some of the context: When Jesus was born, Augustus Caesar was emperor. He was supposedly the son of a God (Apollo), an omen shortly before his birth had indicated that Rome would have a new king, and when the Senate heard about this it attempted to prevent any newborn sons from being raised over the next year. Once Julius Caesar (who had adopted him) was deified, Augustus took on the additional title *Divi Filius*—"Son of a God." After Caesar died, a comet appeared in the sky, which was considered his divine soul ascending to heaven, marking also the transition to Augustus. Then, to make his point, Augustus issued a coin with his portrait on one side and the comet with the words *Divi Filius* on the other. He defeated Marc Antony and reigned supreme, thereby establishing the *pax Romana*. His adopted name, Augustus, meant "majestic," "exalted," "venerable," "sanctified," "consecrated," and "holy." In the eastern empire, in 9 BCE, just a few years before Jesus's birth, Augustus's birthday (September 23) was declared New Year's Day. In proposing this measure, the governor of Asia, Paulus Fabius Maximus, explained that

> the birthday of the most divine Caesar . . . is the day which we might justly set on a par with the beginning of everything . . . [He]e gave a new look to the whole world. . . . For that reason one might justly take this to be the beginning of life and living. . . .[40]

And in accepting this proposal, the Asian League of Cities remarked that Augustus Caesar

> by his epiphany *exceeded* the hopes of those who prophesized *good tidings*, not only outdoing benefactors of the past, *but also allowing no hope of greater benefactions in the future;* . . . [T]he birthday of the god first brought to the world the *good tidings* residing in him.[41]

John Dominic Crossan noted that the word used for "good tidings" *(euaggelia)* is cognate with the word the Christian evangelists used for "good tidings"/"gospel" *(euaggelion)*;[42] likewise, the verb *euaggelidzō* means "to evangelize," and also "to bring good news," as when the angels announced Jesus's birth to the shepherds (Lk 2:10) When Matthew and Luke wrote, the emperor's cult (discussed below pp. 106–07) was in full swing.

The Christian evangelists had to compete with this when claiming that Christ, not the emperor, was the divine one, the true Lord of heaven and earth, the bringer of real peace, and the authentic savior of all. In order to convince gentiles in the Roman world of this, Christian evangelists had to fight fire with fire. So it helped Matthew's and Luke's cause to place miraculous stories of Jesus's birth at the beginning of their Gospels, stories containing mythical motifs already familiar to a Greco-Roman audience while also using scripture as prophetical proof.

The Underlying Archetypal Mythology of the Christmas Story

Jesus and the "Birth of the Hero" Motif

Myths and legends feature countless hero figures, and even real history features many real people whose lives have been mythologized, being made into heroes. Scholars have long recognized that Jesus is one such heroic figure.[43] In Jesus's case, like many others, this portrayal begins with his ancestry, parentage, conception, and birth. In the field of mythological studies this initial phase of a hero's life is known as the "birth of the hero" motif. It outlines a stereotypical pattern into which the details of the infancy narratives slot.

The most famous elements in this motif are those developed by the psychologist Otto Rank[44] and by Lord Raglan;[45] Joseph Campbell also included the birth and childhood of heroes as part of his hero cycle.[46] No two scholars have come up with exactly the same pattern and number of elements, nor does any single hero myth contain all elements of any one such pattern.[47] Nevertheless, the birth stories of many hero figures, including Jesus, do hit most of the data points, so it is important to examine this motif's application to Jesus.

Several key elements of this archetypal pattern in the Greco-Roman Mediterranean world appear in Jesus's infancy narratives,[48] including:

- An earthly biological or adoptive father who is either a king or in a royal line, as in both Matthew's and Luke's genealogies of Jesus; the Messiah described in the Dead Sea Scrolls is also from the line of David.[49] Other examples include Plato (descended from Solon), Aeneas (son of prince Anchises of Troy), Perseus, Theseus, Asclepius, Oedipus, Heracles, Jason, and Romulus.[50]
- A miraculous conception through divine intervention, as in both Matthew and Luke, so that he could be considered the son of a god (sometimes a goddess), as in all of the Gospels. Other examples include Romulus (fathered by Mars), Aeneas (son of Aphrodite), Heracles (Zeus) Alexander the Great (Zeus), Augustus Caesar (Apollo), Plato (Apollo, also descended from Poseidon), Apollonius of Tyana (Proteus), Pythagoras (Apollo), Asclepius (Apollo), Perseus (Zeus), and Semiramis (by the fish goddess Derceto).[51]
- Thus, he is said to be born divine or semi-divine, as in Matthew, Luke, and John. Other examples include Heracles, Pythagoras, Plato, Asclepius, Epicurus, Augustus Caesar, and Apollonius of Tyana.[52]
- His mother is a virgin (sometimes royal) as of just before such miraculous conception, although Jesus is the only example in which conception does not occur through express or euphemized intercourse. Examples include Danae (mother of Perseus), Rhea Silvia (mother of Romulus and Remus), Koronis (mother of Asclepius), Aethra (mother of Theseus), and Alcmene (mother of Heracles); similarly among divinities Leto (mother of Apollo) and Semele (mother of Dionysus).[53]
- Prophecies, dreams, omens, astral phenomena, or other portents of his coming and future importance and greatness, as in Matthew 2:2, 5–10 and Luke 2:10, 29–38. Other examples include Augustus Caesar, Apollonius of Tyana, Pythagoras, Plato, Alexander the Great (by magi), Aeneas (annunciation by Aphrodite), Cyrus, and Zoroaster.[54]
- Soon after birth the child is abandoned or spirited away, or an attempt is made to kill him, as in Matthew's account of the massacre of the innocents and flight to Egypt, which Campbell calls the motif of "infant exile and return."[55] Other examples include Heracles

(once by his mother and again by Hera), Sargon I, Moses, Jason, Ion, Paris, Augustus Caesar, Zoroaster, Cyrus, Romulus, Semiramis, and Asclepius.[56]

- He is born into and grows up living in modest or primitive, and obscure conditions, as in all of the Gospels; often he is raised by foster parents (Joseph was Jesus's adoptive father) or sometimes even animals; in some cases, little or nothing is said or known of his childhood. Other examples include Perseus, Paris, Jason, Romulus, Cyrus, and Moses;[57] a female example is Semiramis. In Luke, Jesus's humble beginnings are emphasized by his parents being unable to secure accommodations in Bethlehem, his being placed in the manger (presumably among animals), and the adoration by shepherds. Nothing is known of his early childhood.

- Although his early childhood is obscure, later in childhood he displays wisdom and other exceptional qualities, as in Luke 2:46–47, 52. Other examples include Pythagoras, Epicurus, Alexander the Great, Apollonius of Tyana, the Olympic champion Theagenes, Cyrus, and the biblical figures of Moses, Samuel, Solomon, and Daniel.[58]

People in the ancient Greco-Roman Mediterranean world came to expect such characteristics in their heroes, so inevitably myths and legends developed to satisfy these expectations. It is precisely these common elements in their biographies that conform to the hero pattern which are historically suspect, and so are normally regarded as mythical.[59] So too in the case of Jesus.

New Testament scholarship has shown that early Christians were striving to prove to skeptical gentiles and diaspora Jews that Jesus shared in these marks of divinity and hero status, and that he was even superior to the Greco-Roman heroes and gods (including deified emperors).[60] For example, the early church father Justin Martyr famously wrote,

And when we say also that the Word, who is the First-begotten of God, was born for us without sexual union, Jesus Christ our teacher, and that He was crucified and died and rose again and ascended into heaven, we propound nothing new beyond [what you believe] concerning those whom you call sons of Zeus.[61]

Compare, for example, Matthew's infancy story with the birth of one son of Zeus, Alexander the Great, as described by Plutarch. There too a genealogy is given. There too is a betrothed young couple and the woman is a virgin, but Zeus intervenes and fathers the child using his thunderbolt (in Matthew God works through the Holy Spirit). Then ensues drama over the sexual fidelity of the bride, and so too over the legitimacy of the son, as in Matthew. Her account of the conception is not trusted until the groom has a dream that convinces him of her faithfulness, and also predicts greatness for the child, again as in Matthew.[62]

Notwithstanding this kind of parallel, as M. David Litwa stressed in his recent valuable study of Jesus's depiction as a Mediterranean god, the point here is not necessarily to argue for direct influence on Matthew and/or Luke from particular Greco-Roman myths and legends, although this seems plausible in some cases such as Alexander's above in the case of Matthew, and the birth of Aeneas in the case of Luke.[63] Rather, the principal point is that the motifs through which the birth of Jesus was mythologized were part and parcel of Greco-Roman Mediterranean culture, and were applied to Jesus, as recognized by church fathers.[64] It was to this Hellenized Mediterranean audience, after all, to which Matthew's and Luke's Gospels were mainly directed, in order to win converts and grow Christian communities in the face of both traditional pagan beliefs and newer Roman propaganda surrounding the deification of emperors. If Christianity was to gain traction, its hero figure would have to conform to Mediterranean norms and expectations.

The Nature and Role of the Holy Spirit in Jesus's Birth

Both infancy narratives say that Jesus was conceived through the Holy Spirit. The Holy Spirit has a deep theological, mythological, and psychological background which we must unpack in order to understand its place in the Christmas myth.

The wind has a numinous quality to it that lends itself to myths. It is invisible, cannot be grasped, held, or weighed, and is seemingly immaterial. Yet it has tangible effects. It can be heard, felt, and is seen to sway trees and be part of storms. Wind has *power*. Most importantly, the ancients recognized that our breath also is the movement of air, and that it is found only in living beings and leaves us when we die. Hence the concept of the "breath of life," which enters us when we become alive and departs when we die. Accordingly, the movement of air in both wind and breath was thought to be an animating divine force. In Greek and Roman myths, the wind often impregnated animals (mainly mares, hens, and vultures) and sometimes women, thus animating (conceiving) new life.[65] This was one aspect of the wind operating as a mediating agency between the divine on the one hand and earthly matter on the other. The biblical Holy Spirit played a similar animating, creative role, between the divine and earthly realms.

The Hebrew Bible begins with God's spirit or wind as the agency for the creation in Genesis 1. In verse two the "spirit" or "wind" of God moved or hovered over the formless primordial waters as the creation commenced, and so was already at work then. The Hebrew word for this, *ruach*, connotes air in motion, such as wind or the breath, the latter also connoting life, as in the "breath of life" in Genesis 6:17 and 7:15. This word also translates as "spirit," and in this sense is used to refer to the creative force from God which moves the charismatic judges and prophets to do extraordinary things.[66] In the Greco-Roman world the concept of *pneuma*, which in the Septuagint served as the Greek translation for *ruach*, was similar. It could refer to the wind, the breath, the process of breathing, spirit, or divine inspiration.[67] For example, according to one legend, the spirit *(pneuma)* of Heracles was said to have lain with the mother of the Olympic champion Theagenes of Thasos, who was so conceived.[68] In the original Greek New Testament the Holy Spirit is called the *pneuma hagion*. The Holy Spirit was an animating agent that worked in tandem with God's power *(dynamis)* to mediate with earthly matter, including women.[69]

In the Hebrew Bible, the Holy Spirit was the source of life, as well as the source of miracles (as would be the virginal conception), and it was associated with the coming of the Messiah and messianic/end times.[70] Consequently, even before the infancy narratives were written, in early Christian tradition the Holy Spirit was already viewed as having been at work at Jesus's baptism (Mk 1:9), as well as during his resurrection (Rom 1:4). It was therefore a logical step for Matthew and Luke to portray it also as being at work during Jesus's conception, especially since the Hebrew Bible's prophetic tradition had viewed election by God as occurring at the stage of the womb.[71]

As mediating agents, the Holy Spirit and power *(dynamis)* together enabled Yahweh to cause conceptions without tainting his traditional nature as an asexual deity and offending Jewish sensibilities. The Spirit also facilitated the virginal conception,[72] generating a fetus while keeping Mary pure. Interestingly, later during Jesus's ministry, he was said to be working with the Holy Spirit to effect his miracles and other works, but at least in the Synoptic Gospels Jesus himself never mentions this and he never appeals to the Holy Spirit to substantiate his claims;[73] his association with the Holy Spirit (as an independent, external force) appears to have been retrospectively imputed to him by New Testament authors in narratives and in polemic,[74] and hence has the aura of myth.

I discuss the mytho-psychological aspects of the Holy Spirit separately below (pp. 243–45).

The Virginal Conception

Mary conceiving Jesus while remaining a virgin as a result of supernatural intervention is not something that a historian can prove or disprove. For Christians it is simply an article of faith. For them it is crucial to hold that God literally took on the human condition in the fullest possible sense.[75] The two Gospel accounts of how Jesus literally became the God-man was one way to anchor that theological creed. It would be pointless to debate the historicity of this miraculous event here, because, as in the case of the resurrection, the tools of the historian's craft are unable to address it. Instead, my purpose is to analyze this and the other infancy narrative events from a mythological standpoint precisely because the story is *told in the manner* of myth, which gives it the character of a mythological statement that best yields up its meaning through a mythological analysis. Considering the virginal conception in some detail also enables us to observe the process of mythmaking in action.

The notion of Mary conceiving Jesus while remaining a virgin, without Joseph's, any man's, or God's sexual participation, was a novel idea. There is no exact precedent for a virginal conception in the Hebrew Bible or other Jewish writings and traditions.[76] Matthew 1:22–23 invoked scriptural prophecy as precedent, but most biblical scholars (including Jews) agree that the scripture in question, Isaiah 7:14, refers neither to a virgin conceiving nor to the Messiah.[77] Similarly, the potential precedents from Greco-Roman myths all involve virgins having intercourse (express or implied) with a god, so those conceptions were all sexual, though still miraculous because of the involvement of a god.[78] Matthew and Luke wrote against this familiar pagan mythological background, and a major point of theirs in this episode was precisely that Mary did not have sex, thus rendering Jesus's conception an entirely unique and holy event. It was an extraordinary, one-time exercise of Yahweh's creative power using the Holy Spirit, like in the creation itself.[79] By definition it had to be distinct from the examples in pagan myths, and it was. Yahweh was an asexual being, so impregnating Mary in the manner of Zeus would be out of the question. Because of his virginal conception, Jesus could be considered superior to the pagan deities and heroes. While such fine distinctions may have satisfied theologians, they were likely lost on most gentiles, at least initially. As Richard Miller summarized the reception of the Christian religion among pagans, "The Hellenistic Roman world . . . commonly identified the Judeo-Christian deity as indeed being Father Zeus (Jupiter), the supreme god of the classical pantheon, thus interpreting Jesus as agnate to the array of other demigods born of the god's dalliances with mortal women."[80]

How did the novel idea of the virginal conception originate? It is unclear from where or from whom. Obviously, there were no third-party eyewitnesses to the Annunciation in Luke, Joseph's dream in Matthew 1:20–23, or Jesus's conception by the Holy Spirit who could have related the story. There are also signs that the idea did not originate with Mary, Joseph or Jesus's siblings. Indeed, one awkward aspect of the Gospels is that, outside the two infancy narratives themselves (even in Matthew and Luke), Mary evidences no knowledge of this miraculous event or (prior to the resurrection) of Jesus's special identity or divinity, even though according to Matthew and Luke much of this had been explained to her (and Joseph) by angels in connection with his conception and birth; nor do Jesus's brothers or his neighbors in Nazareth display knowledge of this.[81] And, unlike the portrayals in Christian art and our modern Christmas nativity scenes, the Gospels never mention Mary venerating her newborn wonder child. The tradition of the virginal conception may have developed later than the other material contained in Matthew and Luke. The fact that both Matthew and Luke included a virginal conception in the story but with differing details suggests that some such tradition preceded them,[82] but that a uniform version of it had not yet become established.

No one has been able to prove that any single factor can explain the appearance of the idea of the virginal conception. In examining how and why this notion came about, we must consider both the reasons arising from historical developments at the time, which in turn led to mythmaking, as well as the underlying mythological meaning that supports the idea and gives it substance. Most likely the notion arose from a confluence of these factors.

Reasons Arising from Historical Developments

There are at least three possible historical reasons for such a novel idea arising at the time. It is important to consider them because the virginal conception is not strictly attached to or necessary to uphold the theological creed that Jesus was the Son of God.[83] After all, St. Paul and the Gospels of Mark and John made no claim of a virginal conception and did fine without it in upholding Jesus's divinity.

The first historical reason may derive from the complex relationship between Jesus and John the Baptist, both during and after their lives. We know that even after Jesus's death, the Baptist's sect and Jesus's followers disagreed with each other and competed with each other for adherents. Thus, Luke reported that when Paul went to Ephesus, he found some 12 supposed Christians who had not heard of the Holy Spirit and had been baptized only into "John's baptism." He corrected their error and baptized them in the name of Jesus, after which the Holy Spirit came upon them (Acts 19:1–7). Luke also mentions an influential Alexandrian preacher named Appolos, "who knew only the baptism of John" and needed to have some things about "the way of God" explained to him, as a result of which he came to teach that the Christ was Jesus (Acts 18:25–28).[84] Paul, writing earlier, speaks of Apollos as initially a competitor, at least in the minds of a faction of Corinthian Christians (1 Cor 1,12; 2:4–6). Further, the *Pseudo-Clementine Recognitions,* dating from the mid-fourth century but probably containing first-century material and traditions going back even to apostolic times,[85] states that disciples of John thought that he was the Christ.[86] This tense rivalry with John is reflected in all of the Gospels, which go out of their way to show that Jesus was superior to John, who accordingly is portrayed as merely laying the groundwork for the coming of Jesus, the true Messiah. Apparently, stories were circulating among John's followers, who believed that he was the Messiah and perhaps divine, about his special nature and deeds. He too had died at the hands of the authorities because of his teachings and beliefs. Had John's followers prevailed over those of Jesus, we would have no Christianity or Christmas as we know them. The mythologized stories about John and his deeds presumably were suppressed, and have been lost to history.

Judging from Luke, stories were circulating about John's miraculous conception, because he reports one, modeled on the Hebrew Bible story of Abraham and his barren wife Sarah. Luke writes that John's mother

Elizabeth was barren, and while his father Zechariah was in the temple offering incense the archangel Gabriel appeared to him and announced that he would have a son who will be filled with the Holy Spirit *even before his birth* (Lk 1:8–15). Elizabeth acknowledges that "this is what the Lord has done for me" (1:25), although it is still presumed that Zechariah is the biological father through intercourse. Gabriel then makes the parallel Annunciation to Mary that God has favored her, so that she will conceive in her womb and bear a child who will be called Son of the Most High, and who will hold David's throne and reign forever in a kingdom of which there will be no end.[87] When Mary asks how this could happen since she is a virgin, Gabriel explains, "The Holy Spirit will come upon you, and the power [*dynamis*] of the Most High will overshadow you, and therefore the begotten one will be holy and be called the Son of God." Then to persuade her further he invokes the miracle of Elizabeth conceiving (1:35–37). Mary then visits Elizabeth, and when Mary greets her the fetus John leaps in her womb, signifying that the Holy Spirit has entered John as Gabriel had predicted (1:39–42). The Spirit's entering John thus occurs through the presence of the unborn Jesus, who already had acquired it his very conception. Then, after Elizabeth addresses Mary as the "mother of my Lord," Mary breaks out into song, singing a hymn that we have come to know as the *Magnificat,* which in Luke's version magnifies the status of Mary and by implication that of her son. So now both the fetus John and Elizabeth have recognized Jesus as Lord. Then so does his father Zechariah, who says to the unborn John, "And you, child, will be called the prophet of the Most High, for you will go before the Lord [Jesus] to prepare his ways" (Lk 1:76). Many New Testament scholars consider the *Magnificat* to have been a traditional hymn, which was perhaps first utilized by followers of John and put on the lips of Elizabeth, before Luke took it up and made it Mary's.[88] This story serves to establish Jesus as superior to John in every respect, and the key part is the virginal conception. Jesus's superiority to John also is portrayed in the other Gospels.

The second historical reason for the virginal conception story may have been to refute charges that Jesus was born out of wedlock (i.e., was illegitimate), and that Mary therefore had been scorned. A detailed examination of this issue is not possible here, but it is worth summarizing the issues in order to illuminate the process of constructing myths. The first clear, datable documentation of the charge of illegitimacy is actually quite late, coming in Origen's *Against Celsus* (ca. 248 CE),[89] but this presumably reflects charges that had been circulating for some time. The current state of the evidence does not allow us to fill the gap backward between Origen and Jesus's birth. Many scholars, however, argue that the Gospels themselves contain evidence that such charges were circulating among Jews at the time,[90] citing the following main reasons:

- To begin with, Matthew felt a need to squarely confront the issue. Joseph learns that Mary has become pregnant without his participation, outside of wedlock. He believes that she is an adulteress until the archangel Gabriel persuades him to the contrary (1:18–25). There is no alternative explanation for the pregnancy except for a miracle. According to the stark logic of Matthew's account, if one does not accept the miracle, then Jesus was illegitimate, and neither was he divine (at least until his baptism as in Mark). Did Matthew need to go out on this limb? Apparently so, for it appears that the conclusion that Mary's pregnancy was out of wedlock was a contemporary deduction from known facts. Otherwise, merely raising the issue and putting his story out for public consumption just to make a theological point might have been a great tactical blunder; indeed, the story itself has fueled centuries of charges that Jesus was illegitimate.[91] At the time, however, Matthew knew that the story fell into line with the many Greco-Roman myths about the miraculous births of heroes.
- Second, Matthew took the unusual step of including four prominent women from the Hebrew Bible in Jesus's genealogy. In Judaism genealogy is typically rendered through the father, as Luke did with Jesus. The women in question (Tamar, Rahab, Ruth, and Uriah's wife Bathsheba) were either sinners or otherwise at fault (or at least beset with rumors), and were in irregular, even scandalous, marital situations. But Yahweh ended up blessing each of them,[92] and their marriages ultimately resulted, through lineage and Yahweh's Providence and grace, in the coming of Jesus the Messiah. Some scholars see in Matthew's inclusion of these women a prefiguration of Mary's own irregular situation,[93] for the purpose of demonstrating either that Mary had not sinned or that, even if rumors about her scandalous pregnancy were true, through Yahweh's grace she could still be worthy of bearing the Messiah. Just as anyone slandering these four women would have been slandering someone Yahweh had blessed, so too would anyone condemning Mary and Jesus.[94]

- Third, the figure of Joseph is problematic. An earthly father of Jesus was needed for purposes of adoptive Davidic sonship, but Joseph plays virtually no other role. He hardly appears outside the infancy narratives and is conspicuously not mentioned in the New Testament passages that mention Mary and Jesus's brothers, where one would expect the father to be mentioned too, even if he were no longer alive. In Judaism the usual (though not exclusive) practice was to describe a man as the son of his father using the father's name (as in Luke), but in Mark 6:3 he is called only the "son of Mary," which may very well be a slur,[95] and in the parallel passage of Matthew 13:55 again only Mary is referred to as his parent by name. Some New Testament scholars suspect that Jesus's illegitimacy (father unknown) may lie behind the phraseology of Mark 6.3.[96] Indeed, apparently because of the scandalous nature of this phrase, later redactions of Mark revised it to read, "son of the carpenter and Mary."[97]

- Fourth, in John 8:31–59 Jesus is engaged in a testy dispute with some Jews which gets personal, with each side assaulting the other's character. Without referring to the circumstances of his own birth, Jesus repeatedly claims that God is *his* Father, while the Jews maintain that Abraham is *their* father (in the ancestral sense), and then say, "*We* were not born of fornication; *we* have one father, God himself" (8:41). The pronoun "we," which according to the Greek syntax is there for emphasis and contrast,[98] has been read by many scholars as marking a contrast with Jesus, who is the one born of fornication.[99] Other scholars disagree, arguing that this is just a crude insult not directed at his actual status (cf. "You bastard!"),[100] or that the discussion was about spiritual not biological legitimacy.[101]

- Finally, in *Against Celsus,* Origen opposes a claim that Mary had been convicted of adultery with a soldier named Panthera (a common name among Roman soldiers[102]) and that Jesus was their son, pointing to the virginal conception as his defense.[103] There may be some historical basis for this claim because of events around the time Jesus's conception and birth.[104] As reported by Josephus, when Herod died in 4 BCE, in and around Sepphoris (an hour's walk (6 kilometers) from Nazareth and where many Nazarenes probably worked and shopped), a revolt broke out which the Romans put down brutally by burning the city and enslaving its inhabitants.[105] In such a situation, women (especially young ones) who were not able to flee or hide were typically raped. The children born nine months later would have been reminders of this awful humiliation by the Romans, and they and their mothers were the objects of scorn. The virginal conception, together with placing Jesus's birth in the reign of Herod, would be a useful way to deflect allegations that Mary was such a mother (cf. Rhea Silvia above).

A third historical reason behind the virginal conception could be the influence of the apocalyptic Qumran community, which could have influenced John the Baptist and through him Jesus and his followers. According to one of the Dead Sea Scrolls, God would "father" the Messiah, who as in both Matthew and Luke would also be a descendant of David (again the birth of the hero motif).[106]

Theological Reasons for the Virginal Conception
In addition to historical circumstances, conceptual theological reasons also lie behind the virginal conception. First and foremost was a christological purpose to make Jesus the Son of God as of his very creation, as opposed to at his baptism or resurrection.[107] As seen above, this higher Christology served in part to make Jesus superior to John the Baptist, but it also makes Jesus compare favorably with Greco-Roman heroes and gods.

A related theological reason may have been to prove his messiahship, since in the Jewish apocalyptic tradition the Holy Spirit would be associated with the Messiah and messianic times. The Messiah would be anointed by and work through the Holy Spirit, and so it was not a stretch that he would be conceived through the Holy Spirit since, as discussed above, it is a creative force. Conception through the Holy Spirit would serve to avoid offending Jewish sensibilities about the asexual nature of Yahweh, emphasize the sacred and unique nature of the event, and possibly also portray Jesus as being born untainted by original sin,[108] which was thought to be passed on through heredity.

In analyzing this story as mythmaking, it is important to note that, in the myths and legends of the ancient Mediterranean world, the divine birth of men actually was not the most important hallmark of divinity. Rather, it was their great works benefiting humanity — the example that they set during their lives — which proved this. Divine conception was then projected back into the biographies of such great men who already had earned the indicia of divinity.[109] As Origen recognized, people reasoned that someone so extraordinary must have had divine seeds.[110] Such retroactive divinization by followers occurred in the case of many other great teachers, such as Plato, Pythagoras, Apollonius of Tyana, and others with whom Jesus was inevitably compared. The growing tendency to make Jesus divine at an earlier point in time can be seen in the evolution of Christology in the New Testament. The earliest view was that Jesus became divine at his resurrection, then in Mark Jesus became divine at his baptism, Matthew and Luke made him divine as of his conception, while at the farthest extreme in John Jesus exists as a divine being in heaven before the creation of the cosmos.[111]

Having seen how the myth of the virginal conception originated, we can now turn to its general mythological (as opposed to theological) meaning.

The Mythological Meaning of the Virginal Conception

As we have seen, Matthew's and Luke's theological reason for including the virginal conception story was not only to show that Jesus was the Son of God, but that he had acquired this divine status at his very conception. In the Gospel of John, in which Jesus was created by God as a divine being even before the creation of the cosmos, Jesus still would need to be incarnated as a fetus in Mary's womb, but John skips over how this happened; that would have led to confusion.[112] He simply says that the Word became flesh (1.14). So in John we have no Christmas event. Interestingly, even as early Christianity was coming to embrace John's higher Christology, in parallel the evolving Christmas holiday utilized that of Matthew and Luke. We still live with this mixed message.

Be that as it may, a concern in John's Gospel was to show that for people to experience salvation they had to go through both a physical birth and a spiritual birth. This is seen most dramatically in Jesus's discourse with the Pharisee Nicodemus in 3:1–15 where Jesus taught that one must be born again, from "above"[113] in addition to first having been born on earth below. Jesus says, "What is born of flesh is flesh, and what is born of the [Holy] Spirit is spirit" (3:6) and then analogizes the Holy Spirit *(pneuma hagion)* to the wind *(pneuma)* which might cause a spiritual birth at any moment. So despite their christological differences, John did complement Matthew's and Luke's distinction between the spiritual and fleshly birth of Jesus, the Christmas message being that the same can occur in all of us.

The more general mythological meaning of the virginal conception and birth is much the same as in John. Joseph Campbell explained that the virginal conception is a symbol of a spiritual birth, a birth of spiritual man out of the animal man. He saw the same meaning in the myth about Buddha's birth, according to which he was born not in the usual way but out of his mother's side, at the level of the heart chakra.[114] As for Matthew and Luke, such a spiritual message (as opposed to just acquisition of divinity at that point) may have been another reason for utilizing the miraculous birth motif, but this is hard to demonstrate since such a message is generally absent in the Greco-Roman examples of miraculous births discussed above.

The Star

As mentioned above, an element of the "birth of the hero" mythological motif is omens or other divine portents marking the hero's birth. In the ancient Greco-Roman world, stars, comets, and other phenomena in the sky were commonly viewed as conveying messages from heaven, and in particular as portending the coming of a new king.[115] A bolt of lightning was said to have appeared at the moment of the birth of Apollonius of Tyana.[116] In Virgil's *Aeneid*, in an episode reminiscent of the magi following the star of Bethlehem, the god Jupiter sent a "star" to show the way for travelers, Aeneas and his father, so they could escape Troy when it was overrun by the Greeks.[117] After Caesar was killed in 44 BCE, a comet reportedly appeared and was said to have marked his ascension into heaven, it being his soul.[118] In 42 BCE, when the Senate declared Julius Caesar a god, Virgil wrote, "Behold, the star of Caesar came forth as a sign,"[119] which became a popular image symbolizing his divinity.[120] Thus, in about 24 BCE the Roman poet Horace wrote, "The Julian star outshines all others just as the Moon outshines the lesser lights."[121] After Augustus became emperor in 27 BCE, he issued coinage which portrayed Julius Caesar's comet together with the legend, "Divine Julius," thus promoting himself as the son of a god.[122] As for Augustus himself, according to Suetonius, a few months before Augustus was born a prodigy was observed in Rome which indicated that nature would soon give birth to a king for the Roman people.[123] The death of Nero (and consequent coming of a new emperor) also was said to have been marked by a comet.[124] In summary, the star calls attention to something new and important, behind which lie divine heavenly powers.

In light of this mythical tradition, Matthew's audience would not have found unusual the claim that a star heralded the birth of the King of the Jews.[125] Matthew must have been aware of the above Mediterranean mythical traditions and again felt a need to have Jesus win the competition with Roman emperors and heroes by writing an analogous but better myth. By using the celestial body motif commonly applied to Roman emperors to symbolize their divinity, Matthew's story was designed to show that Jesus rather than the Roman emperor was the true divine son of God and the true king.[126] Thus, Matthew portrays the magi as explicitly linking the appearance of the star with the birth of the King of the Jews (2:2, 9). Indeed, Suetonius and Tacitus both reported that at that time there was abroad the expectation of a world-ruler to come from Judea,[127] and Josephus mentioned Jewish scripture inspiring such an expectation at the time of the Jewish War.[128] Matthew may have been playing upon such notions.

In addition to this royal imagery, early Christians saw in the star of Bethlehem the coming of *spiritual* light to humankind, beside which the aforementioned stars of famous men pale in comparison.[129] The appearance of a star or comet also marks the births of spiritual leaders. Thus, the appearance of a comet was said to have coincided with the conception of Lao-Tze, while a star fell from the sky when he was born. A star also supposedly arose on the night of Mohammed's birth, and in Islamic tradition Moses has his own birth star.[130]

The star symbol also conferred cosmic qualities to the birth of Jesus, making him ruler of nature and the universe, and served Matthew in his effort to discredit astrology. This was stated well by Clement of Alexandria, who argued that the star signified the end of people looking to astrology to learn their fate, and the dawn of a new path to salvation:

> Therefore, a strange and new star arose doing away with the old astral decree, shining with a new unearthly light, which revolved on a new path of salvation, as the Lord himself, men's guide, who came down to earth to transfer from Fate to his providence those who believed in Christ.[131]

Similarly, St. Augustine explained in an Epiphany sermon:

> For it happened that Christ appeared, not under the star's rule but as its
> Ruler; because that star did not keep to the ways of the stars in the sky but
> showed the men who were seeking Christ the way to the place where he had
> been born. . . . He himself, when born of his mother, made a new star appear
> in heaven and showed it to the earth. . . . At his birth a new light was
> revealed in the star, and at his death the sun's ancient light was veiled.[132]

His star moved unlike any other heavenly body had before, and so directed
the magi to Jesus. The magi were astrologers who had looked to the heavenly bodies for knowledge, but they bowed to Jesus as their master.

Matthew as usual also utilized Hebrew Bible prophecy to buttress this
story. Specifically, he drew from the mythical story of Balaam in Numbers
22–24.[133] In that tale, the king of Moab retained a foreign seer, Balaam,
to pronounce a curse on the Israelites who were about to invade the land.
But a sword-wielding angel and a persuasive talking donkey, both backed
by Yahweh, made him change his mind. So he blessed rather than cursed
Israel, and also prophesized, "A star will come forth from Jacob, and a
scepter will rise from Israel" (24:17). In fact, the story was about a par-
ticular military situation in its own day and had nothing to do with any
Messiah centuries later, but the association gained traction and stuck.
Thus, this connection was portrayed in a medieval painting showing
Balaam pointing out the star to the magi so that they can find Jesus
(Fig. 11.1).

Ignatius, Bishop of Antioch, a generation after Matthew (ca.107–08 CE),
expanded on the star symbolism in his letter to the Ephesians, written
while being taken to Rome to be martyred:

> How was Jesus revealed to the ages?
> A star shone in heaven
> brighter than all the stars,
> and its light was indescribable,
> and its novelty caused astonishment.
> All the other stars
> together with the sun and moon
> formed a ring around it,
> and yet it outshone them all with its light.[134]

Biblical scholars find no evidence that Ignatius was aware of or using
Matthew's Gospel,[135] which indicates that there was an independent tradition of the star story that may have predated Matthew and which both

Fig. 11.1 Nativity Attributed to Khach'atur of Khizan, ca. 1434 CE, now at Metropolitan Museum of Art, New York

writers used. Here the star's "novelty" matches Matthew's portrayal of the star as unique. Portraying it as brighter than everything else in the sky and having the sun, moon, and the other stars move to form a ring about it in a way that defies observation and natural law (as in Matthew) makes the event sacred, and signifies the star's and thus Jesus's superiority.

Matthew too wanted to describe something truly miraculous and unique. Thus, the magi moved westward toward Jerusalem following the star, then it stopped while they were meeting with Herod, after which it started moving south to Bethlehem (only about 6 miles), and then stopped and hovered over the house where Jesus was born (Mt 2:9). Since heavenly bodies don't move in such an unnatural way, the story is mythical, meant to show that divine guiding forces were at work.

The Magi, the Massacre of the Innocents, and the Flight to Egypt

Most New Testament scholars do not regard the stories of the magi, the massacre of the innocents, and the flight to Egypt as historical,[136] so in this sense they are myth. But they are also mythical in the sense of conveying sacred truths.

Historical events may have inspired the magi story. In 66 CE, the Armenian King Tiridates I, who also was a Zoroastrian priest and magus, traveled from the east to Rome accompanied by other magi to pay homage to Nero and vow fidelity to him, and Nero held a coronation ceremony for him. Matthew again may be setting up a parallel contrast and competition between the Roman emperors and Jesus, as part of his portrayal of Jesus as the true king.[137] The hint here may arise from the fact that Tiridates and his magi took a different route home;[138] Matthew 2:12 specifies that the magi did the same.

Since Matthew's audience was gentiles and diaspora Jews, it was important that his Gospel resonate with them and embrace them in the story. One way in which he did this was to place gentiles (the magi) in his adoration story, in order to show that important and wise gentiles had recognized Jesus as king and savior. The episode also serves as a Christian culmination of a line of postexilic Jewish stories (e.g., Esther, Bel and the Dragon) designed to demonstrate the superiority of Judaism over Persian religion and culture.[139] The story thus calls upon Matthew's audience to follow the magi's example.

Matthew structured this story using rich mythological traditions from the Hebrew Bible. First, at the very beginning of his Gospel, (1:1–2) Matthew is keen to portray Jesus as the son (descendant) of Abraham and so to connect Abrahamic traditions with Jesus.[140] (In contrast, Luke's genealogy of Jesus doesn't come until after the infancy narrative, in 3:23–38.) After Abraham had shown his willingness to sacrifice his son Isaac to Yahweh, Yahweh told Abraham, "by your offspring[141] shall all the nations of the earth gain blessing for themselves, because you have obeyed my voice" (Gen 22:18). For Matthew, Jesus was the means through which this was to happen, and the magi story served to set up this idea.[142] Matthew later had Abraham's "son" Jesus carry this idea forward, promising, "I tell you, many will come from east and west and will eat with Abraham and Isaac and Jacob in the kingdom of heaven."[143]

Second, Matthew appears to have relied on Hebrew Bible prophecy. Isaiah 60:3, 6, 10, prophesized that gentile nations shall come to Zion bearing gold and frankincense, praise Yahweh, and submit to its king, much as foreign royalty had given gifts (including gold and myrrh) and honors to Solomon. Also, Psalm 72:11 prophesized that three kings from three places will bring gifts to the Israelite king and fall down before him, saying, "May all kings all fall down before him, all nations give him service." Matthew thus shows that scripture has been fulfilled, with Jesus as this king. His scene of the magi submitting to the baby Jesus demonstrated that eastern religions were being surpassed by Christianity. Further, this event constituted what Davies and Allison called "an inaugurated eschatology," because the above-mentioned movement of nations had now commenced, implying that the promise of Micah 5:2 has been fulfilled and that the end times have dawned.[144] Their gifts to Jesus thus mark the culmination of the magi's trip, representing the "first fruits" of the eschatological pilgrimage of the gentile nations.[145] Interesting in this regard too is an analogous detail from a pagan source, Plutarch's account of Alexander the Great's birth. On the day of Alexander's birth, the magnificent temple to Artemis in Ephesus (then within the Persian Empire) burned to the ground. Magi were there that day, who interpreted the event as portending the end of the empire and the coming of a new kingdom, which turned out to be Alexander's.[146] In Matthew too, the magi saw Jesus as the newborn future king who would overturn the existing order.

A third Hebrew Bible tradition that inspired the magi story was the story of Balaam, already mentioned above in connection with the star.

Balaam, who was considered a magus,[147] also traveled from the east, in his case at the invitation of the Moabite king Balak to destroy Moses. But instead he ended up embracing Yahweh and blessing the Israelites, thus saving Moses and his people. By alluding to the magus Balaam, Matthew again showed how gentiles can become converts, and how the way of Jesus is superior to eastern wisdom, religion, and astrology.

Do the gifts that the magi presented to the baby Jesus hold their own symbolism? The usual explanation, which developed early in Christianity, is that the gold represented Jesus's kingship (it was commonly paid as tribute), frankincense (a form of incense used in religious ritual) represented his divinity, and myrrh (a spice used in burials, including for Jesus in John 19:39) represented his death.[148] But many or most New Testament scholars now oppose this traditional view. For one thing, Matthew has no myrrh in the crucifixion; rather, he changed Mark's "wine mixed with myrrh" (Mk 15:23) to "wine mixed with gall" (Mt 27:34), thus shifting away from any possible connection between myrrh in the adoration of the magi and in the passion.[149] Further, as noted in Chap. 6 (p. 78), unlike Mark and Luke, Matthew does not report that the women at Christ's tomb brought spices to anoint the body, so there is no link to myrrh in connection with the resurrection either. Instead, the gifts, being rare and expensive, probably had a more general significance as showing the momentous nature of Jesus's coming and his supreme status. Placed in the context of magi gentiles at the culmination of their eschatological pilgrimage, the gifts also symbolized the "first fruits" of the movement and of gentile movement toward Christianity.[150]

Matthew's story of the massacre of the innocents and flight to Egypt are meant to parallel the episode in Exodus 1:22–2:10 where Moses was saved by spiriting him away in a floating basket after Pharaoh had ordered the murder of all Hebrew baby boys. Moses eventually leads the Hebrews out of Egypt, and as we have seen, in Hosea 11:1 Yahweh says, "out of Egypt I have called my son." Matthew thus likened the evil Herod to Pharaoh, and drew a parallel between Moses and Yahweh's son Jesus: In the story of the flight to Egypt, Matthew gets Jesus to Egypt so that he can come out of Egypt in fulfillment of scripture. As we have seen, in mythological terms, the attempt to kill the newly born hero and then spiriting him away are standard elements of "the birth of the hero" motif.

The story also may have been intended to portray Jesus favorably against Augustus, who was emperor when Jesus was born. According to Suetonius, after the prodigy appeared in Rome indicating that a new king of the Romans would be born, the Senate became alarmed and decreed that no child born that year should be raised (i.e., they would be killed).[151] Fortunately, those senators with pregnant wives did not want their children killed and hoped that the prodigy was about their own son, so they were able block the decree from being registered in the treasury and so from becoming legally effective. So the attempt was thwarted, like in Matthew and generally in the "birth of the hero" motif. The stories of the star and the massacre of the innocents enabled Jesus to compare well with the divine emperor, the son of Apollo.

Matthew's infancy story is artfully constructed both as literature and as myth because of how well it conveys sacred truths. It is the place where the Hebrew Bible and New Testament meet, so that the most important story in human history can begin. The story incorporates perennially resonant characters and motifs, and its figures and symbols carry spiritual ideas. It is no wonder that this story remains popular and central to our culture, and that it helped inspire our Christmas holiday.

The Shepherds and Angelic Choir in Luke

Luke's adoration scene features shepherds rather than magi, and it occurs on the night of Jesus's birth rather than months afterwards as in Matthew. Biblical scholars generally agree that the story is not historical.[152] There is no clear consensus regarding why Luke chose shepherds for this role. It helps to begin by looking at Luke's overall message in the scene; then we can see better why shepherds fit in.

The scene opens with shepherds tending their flock at night when they see an angel standing before them, who announces that he is bringing "to you good news of great joy for all the people: to you is born this day in the city of David a savior, who is the Messiah, the Lord" (2:10–11). Here we have heavenly witness and recognition of Jesus's birth that parallels the earthly witnesses. Then the angel and the multitude of the heavenly host break out into song, singing, "Glory to God in the highest heaven, and on earth peace among *those whom he favors,*"[153] again placing heaven and earth in parallel. This rings of apocalyptic thinking. According to that view, the evil forces and unrepentant people in the world would be overthrown and the Kingdom of God would be established on earth, in which the good people who follow God and believe in Christ as their savior will live in peace.[154] Under this approach, while potentially all people are eligible to be elected on judgment day, only the repentant and humble who love God with all their heart (i.e., "the people that he favors" in the song) will enter the kingdom, while the rich and the Romans will be excluded. Gentiles can be among the elect. They must be gathered (converted) as flocks of sheep are gathered by shepherds. St. Ambrose thus preached in a sermon about the nativity, "Christ is born, and the shepherds begin their watch; those who will gather the flocks of the gentiles, before living as untended beasts, into the Fold of the Lord."[155]

By raising this eschatological theme in the shepherd story, Luke seems to be drawing a contrast between the *pax Romana* imposed by force and the coming Kingdom of God in which people will live in true peace.[156] In an ironic twist, the angels' announcement appears to be modeled after civic proclamations of praise for the Roman emperor.[157] From the apocalyptic perspective of the time as well as that of later Christianity, in Jesus's day there was no true peace on earth; the world was all wrong and in disarray. This idea was later reflected in European paintings of the nativity showing the surroundings in disrepair or ruin, especially ruined classical architectural structures with vegetation growing out of the cracks (Figs. 11.2 and 11.4).[158]

They symbolized the chaos of the world into which Jesus was born, the end of classical culture and religion, and the beginning of the new era. This artistic motif was inspired by a medieval myth, told in Jacobus de Varagine's hagiography aptly titled *The Golden Legend* (ca. 1260). According to the story, the Romans built a Temple of Peace and asked Apollo how long it will endure. The god answered that it will last until a maiden bears a child. Thinking that such an event was impossible, the Romans thought it would stand forever. But on the night Mary bore Jesus, the temple collapsed to the ground.[159] Indeed, Christianity's ultimate earthly goal as a counter-cultural movement was nothing less than to dismantle the classical Greco-Roman political, social, and religious order.[160]

Another dimension of Luke's shepherd story comes from the social status and reputation of shepherds. For the most part, shepherds were ordinary, humble people of modest means. As St. Ambrose preached in a sermon, "Because the shepherds are people of humble stature, we should not esteem lightly the testimony of their faith. For the more humble the testimony appears to human wisdom, the more precious it is to the eyes of faith."[161] In saying that he was bringing good tidings "to you," Gabriel conveyed that Jesus will be the savior of the humble and poor, as Jesus later proclaimed in Luke 4:18. On the other hand, shepherds also had a

Fig. 11.2 Adoration of the Magi, Leonardo da Vinci, 1481–82. Alamy stock image

dubious reputation for being tricky and dishonest, and hence were viewed as sinners.[162] Jesus attracted sinners to his flock during his ministry, and redeemed sinners were poised to enter the Kingdom of God. The shepherds symbolized this well.

A final connection with the shepherds lies with David. Luke first has Mary and Joseph travel to "the city of David called Bethlehem, because he was descended from the house and family of David" (2:4). The angel then announces to the shepherds that Jesus has just been born "in the city of David." David was a shepherd in Bethlehem. In fact, it is only as a shepherd that the Hebrew Bible connects David to Bethlehem, and this happens in the scene where he is anointed as king, at which moment the spirit of God came upon him, and remained with him from that day forward (1 Sam 16:1–13), much as happened with Jesus from his conception. Thus, Luke's shepherd story serves to identify Jesus with David and supports the notion of Jesus both being born in Bethlehem and being recognized as the Messiah and King of the Jews.

Luke has thus composed a beautiful mythological scene in which ordinary people come into contact with symbols of the sacred, pointing the way to their salvation.

THE ENDING OF LUKE'S INFANCY STORY

Luke ends his infancy narrative with the presentation of Jesus at the Jerusalem temple and then his visit to the temple at age 12. Most biblical scholars do not consider these episodes historical; the problems with the presentation story were already noted above (pp. 196–97). Rather, they were written to make important theological points that are also mythical in nature.

The Presentation of Jesus in the Temple

Luke 2:22–38 describes the presentation of the infant Jesus in the temple 40 days after his birth and the recognition of his status as Son of God there, thus confirming what Mary had been told during the Annunciation.[163] Having fulfilled prophecy by being born in Bethlehem and being recognized as the Messiah there, now he must get to Jerusalem and be similarly recognized as the Son of God in the temple itself, his Father's house. The scene contrasts the presentation of the circumcised John the Baptist only to his relatives and neighbors, where it is proclaimed that he will prepare the way for Christ (Lk 1.59–79). As a literary structuring device, it also bookends the story of Jesus's long journey to Jerusalem and events there occupying the whole second half of Luke's Gospel. As mentioned earlier (p. 196), this story conflicts with Matthew's infancy narrative, in which the family must flee Judea after Jesus's birth.

This story is modeled on the Hebrew Bible story of Elkanah and Hannah and their son Samuel (1 Sam 1:1–2:26). There the formerly barren Hannah conceives and bears Samuel through Yahweh's intervention, and once the boy is weaned, he is taken up to the temple in Shiloh (then the main temple in the land) on the family's annual pilgrimage there for sacrifice. While there, Hannah prays and breaks into a song of praise and thanks, which may have been Luke's inspiration for Mary's *Magnificat*. As the firstborn, Samuel is offered into the service of the Lord, as a Nazirite, and his parents leave him there. The boy is then said to grow up in the presence of the Lord, and to grow in stature and favor with the Lord (2:21, 26). The similarities with Luke's presentation scene, his descriptions of Jesus maturing, and with the subsequent scene of the young Jesus staying at the temple when his parents leave for home, are obvious. Jesus's life, like Samuel's, is to be dedicated to the service of God.

But Luke is saying more than this about Jesus: He is to be greater than Samuel. Thus, at the temple Jesus encounters the prophets Simeon and Anna, who recognize him as the Messiah, the savior of Israel as well as of gentiles.

Jesus in the Temple at Age Twelve

Luke's final story in his infancy narrative (2:41-51) again places Jesus at the temple, this time during the family's annual pilgrimage there during Passover. At the tender age of 12, he stays behind when his parents depart for Nazareth, in order to engage in discussions with teachers of the Law at the temple, who are amazed by his knowledge and understanding. Mary and Joseph discover his absence and return to collect him. They find him after three days, perhaps a parallel to the resurrection on the third day.[164] Once they find him, they ask why he did this: "Child, why have you treated us like this? Look, *your father* and I have been searching for you in great anxiety." He answers, "Did you not know that I must be in *my Father's house?*" Thus, Luke contrasts Jesus's earthly and (real) heavenly father, and shows his true loyalty, as well as some understanding of who he is and his mission. This may help explain Joseph's disappearance from Luke's Gospel after this point.

Part of Luke's purpose in this story is to show that Jesus had remarkable abilities at a young age, especially in understanding the Law, an important point because the Pharisees accuse him of breaking it. Under the Jewish Law, a boy assumes certain adult responsibilities at age 13, signified in modern Judaism by the bar mitzvah; before then the parents are responsible for the boy's actions. So, by having Jesus break away from his parents and show remarkable understanding of the Law before he turns 13, Luke may have been showing that Jesus was ahead of the norm. As mentioned above, having remarkable abilities and qualities at a young age is an element of the "birth of the hero" mythological motif.[165]

Luke's ultimate purpose in this story, however, was to show that Jesus, as the Son of God, must do the work of his real Father at the expense of even his own earthly family obligations, just as later during his ministry he would expect much the same from his followers. This is the first time that we see Jesus understand his purpose, his calling. Whereas in the earlier presentation scene at the temple Luke's *audience* is reminded of who Jesus is, now we see Jesus *himself* coming to understand who he really is. Here again, Luke may have had the Samuel example in mind, for Josephus too reported what probably was a tradition, namely that at age 12 Samuel began to prophesize and, together with the high priest, realized that God had called him.[166]

This event corresponds to the stage in the mythological hero cycle when the budding hero hears "the call" to his hero's journey. In this stage, the protagonist, still in the everyday world of everyday people, is stimulated and recognizes the call to adventure that promises to take him out of that world and onto his hero's journey.[167] In Luke, this episode marks only the beginning of the call phase because Jesus is still too young to act upon it. This phase ends and the next two typical stages, "supernatural aid" and "the crossing of the threshold,"[168] transpire together in the very next event that Luke narrates, Jesus's baptism, at which moment the Holy Spirit descends on Jesus in the form of a dove, setting him on his hero's journey, in the form of his ministry and beyond.

What we celebrate each Christmas is the birth of a mythologized Christ figure, in that he was built up by Matthew and Luke to be larger than life using a number of standard mythological motifs, molding or making up details to fit them. By the end of the events that we celebrate at Christmas, the figure of Jesus is developing into a mythical hero in much the normal manner. But since mythological narratives are designed to convey sacred truths, Christmas is also a celebration and reaffirmation of the sacred truths that Jesus taught, stood for, and (quite literally) embodied.

WHY DID CHRISTIANS DECIDE TO CELEBRATE JESUS'S BIRTH WITH A HOLIDAY, AND TO HOLD IT ON DECEMBER 25?

Rather than celebrate Jesus's physical birth (the nativity), early Christians could have decided to celebrate other potentially more significant events marking the divine Messiah's coming into the world, such as his miraculous conception (as told in Matthew and Luke), the visitation of the magi (eventually celebrated as Epiphany), or his baptism (the establishing event in the Gospel of Mark). The early Christian festivals of the apostles and martyrs were associated with their deaths, not their births, and at first so too in the case of Christ, with his death and resurrection (Easter) becoming the primary Christian festival. There was also a practical difficulty in celebrating his birth, because the actual birth dates of Jesus and virtually all other Christian figures were not known, and still aren't, whereas the dates of their deaths were better known.

Our oldest Gospel, that of Mark, contains no account of the birth of Jesus. Rather, it begins with his baptism by John the Baptist, which Mark obviously considered the pivotal event. In the baptism scene the Holy Spirit descends as a dove upon Jesus, and a voice from heaven declares, "You are my Son" (Mark 1:10–11). In Mark's view, apparently, this was when Jesus became the divine Son of God.[169] St. Paul, in his epistles written several years before Mark, never mentions the birth of Jesus, saying only that he was descended from David according to the flesh and was born of a woman under the Law (Rom 1:3–4). These earliest writings suggest no awareness of any story of Jesus's birth; apparently, the earliest Christians did not consider this important. The four Gospels take varying positions on when Jesus became divine, but in no case does this happen on his birthday. As we shall see, although early Christians speculated about the date of Jesus's birth at least as early as the late second century, there is no evidence that Christians celebrated the nativity with a holiday until late in the reign of Constantine. Why was his birth date originally considered unimportant?

There were basically three reasons. First, early Christians considered their *true* birth to be the date of their death, when the faithful would enter into eternal bliss in heaven. This belief was especially important in the context of persecution and martyrdom. And it was already the main Christian feast, Easter, which celebrated resurrection and eternal life. Second, and correspondingly, early Christians held the body in low esteem, with some sects holding extreme views in this regard. The Docetists thought that Jesus was not human but pure spirit, so in their view his physical birth was a mere appearance, not a reality. The Gnostics considered the material world and the physical body profane, and therefore viewed Jesus's physical birth as unimportant, so they focused instead on his teachings. Third, Christians such as Origen opposed the celebration of birthdays because they considered the practice a pagan affectation, notably among Roman emperors and officials.[170] Indeed, scripture had given birthdays a bad rap: On his birthday the Egyptian pharaoh hanged his baker (Gen 40:22), and the birthday party of Herod Antipas had cost John the Baptist his life. But in a peculiar way, as we shall see, in the end the Roman tradition of observing birthdays helped bring about the Feast of the Nativity.

In this situation, given that Easter celebrated the Messiah's *exit* from the earthly world, Christians sought a doctrinally acceptable way to celebrate his earlier *entry* into our world, in particular the initial manifestation and recognition of his divinity and identity. Conceptually, the main possibilities here were:

- His miraculous conception (incarnation) making him divine, marked by the Annunciation in Luke
- The nativity, given that on the occasion a chorus of angels had recognized him as savior, and that the magi did much the same shortly thereafter
- His baptism, when the Holy Spirit descended upon him as a dove, and God proclaimed him "my Son," as described just above
- The first manifestation of his identity and divinity at the start of his ministry, which in the Gospel of John was the miracle of turning water into wine at Cana

Jesus's conception never became the subject of an entire festival, but as we shall see, it helped give us the December 25 date for our holiday. The first of the above events to occasion a festival was Jesus's baptism. This developed in Alexandria, where initially Mark's Gospel (which has no nativity or Cana miracle) seems to have been most influential.[171] Clement of Alexandria reported that one Christian group there celebrated the baptism early in the second century.[172] This feast was called Epiphany (from the Greek *epiphaneia,* meaning "appearing," "appearance," or "manifestation") because Jesus acquired and first manifested his divinity at his baptism. Before long, the festival also came to celebrate other manifestations of Jesus's identity and divinity, including the star and the adoration of the magi, the miracle at Cana, the feeding of the multitude, and his birth.[173] As the church matured, the baptism and everything else dropped out of Epiphany except for the star and the adoration of the magi; and the festival's date settled on January 6.[174] Baptism dropped out because the Council of Nicaea in 325 CE ruled that any doctrine that God became incarnate in Jesus after his birth (e.g., at baptism) was heretical.[175]

This leads us to ask why Christians didn't simply celebrate Epiphany. Why add a feast of the nativity? There were two main reasons. One was practical and strategic, as a means of attracting converts, solidifying the religion, and overcoming pagan beliefs and practices, even at the expense of absorbing some of them. The other was doctrinal.

As for historical and strategic factors, Matthew's and Luke's Gospels were written approximately 10–15 years after the Jewish War of 66–70 CE, after which Jerusalem's Jews were dispersed and hopes of an imminent eschaton dimmed. As a result, Christianity shook off much of its Jewishness, and it became even more oriented toward gentiles in the larger Greco-Roman world. This afforded Christians flexibility, but it also posed a challenge: Christians had to focus on convincing pagans that Jesus was an extraordinary and divine being worthy of their veneration, and to the exclusion of their traditional gods and divine emperors. Also, as discussed above and evidenced in the Gospels themselves, the followers of Jesus were competing with those of John the Baptist.

As we have seen, in the ancient Mediterranean world, myths of heroes and gods having miraculous births were common and popular, most importantly those about Augustus Caesar. So if Christianity was to make headway in the Mediterranean world, it would be most helpful to show that the birth of Jesus also was miraculous, using mythological motifs familiar to that audience. Matthew's and Luke's taking this approach seems to have had an impact along these lines, because debates subsequently arose between early church fathers such as Origen and Justin Martyr on the one hand and pagans and Jews on the other about whether the Christian infancy narrative imitated pagan motifs.[176] As discussed below, the Christian use of pagan motifs to further their case came to include adopting solar symbolism, which led them to the winter solstice, observed on December 25th.

The doctrinal reasons behind the importance of Jesus's conception and birth, and eventually of celebrating it, go back to our earlier discussions of why Matthew and Luke wrote the infancy stories, including the evolution of christological doctrine to render Jesus divine at an earlier stage (pp. 106–07). Further, as noted, the Council of Nicaea had shot down the notion that Jesus became divine at his baptism. The story of the magi, however, was important because, as discussed (pp. 218–21), it was a model for pagans recognizing Jesus Christ as their savior, which is what Christians wanted pagans (gentiles) to do. The popularity of this story raised the profile of Jesus's birth. It showed that that Jesus was recognized as special from his very birth, for which purpose a festival celebrating it would be useful.[177]

Further, St. Paul had written that Jesus was the new, second Adam, who through his sacrifice on behalf of humankind undid the curse on humankind arising from the sin of the first Adam, enabling us all to be saved (Rom 5:12–21; 1 Cor 15:21, 45). For Christians adhering to this doctrine, the *creation* of Jesus was important, because to them it made sense that Jesus came into being as a human on the anniversary of the original creation of the world, when Adam was created and sinned. Because of the traditional mythological symbolism of spring as a time of creation, the creation of the cosmos was thought to have occurred in the spring, with the first day in the Genesis 1 creation myth occurring on what would be the spring equinox, then considered to be on March 25. (Some noted that, since the sun (needed for an equinox) was not created until the fourth day, the date should be March 28th, the 25th being inclusive in accordance with ancient practice.[178]) But the church father Sextus Julius Africanus (ca. 160-ca. 240 CE) argued that it was Jesus's *conception* that occurred on March 25, which meant that he was born nine months later, on December 25.[179] His rationale was that the real and important creation of Jesus was on the date of his incarnation as divine (virginal conception), not that of his subsequent earthly birth. It was this December 25 date for Jesus's birth which took hold and endured. Why?

This idea conveniently put Jesus's birth right on the winter solstice, which in Rome under the Julian calendar was observed on December 25th.[180] The ancients viewed the winter solstice as the birthday of the sun, because it marks the annual turnaround when the sun, like a newborn child, begins to grow,[181] and points toward spring and renewal. Further, Roman Emperors in this period identified themselves with the sun, often depicting this relationship on coins showing the emperor's profile with a radiate crown.

Christians played upon solar symbolism when portraying Christ, which became important in the Feast of the Nativity catching on, and on the solstice. Solar imagery of Christ was fueled by scripture. For instance, Christians considered him to be the "sun of righteousness" referenced in Malachi 4:2 who would arrive to overthrow the forces of evil in the world, Matthew 17:2 said that Jesus's transfigured face shone like the sun, and Revelation 1:13–16 said that the Son of Man's (i.e., Christ's) face was like the sun shining. Correspondingly, when Jesus died the sun disappeared and darkness overcame the land (Mk 15:33; Mt 27:45). And Jesus himself reportedly claimed, "I am the light of the world. Whoever follows me will never walk in darkness but will have the light of life" (Jn 8:12). A late third-century mosaic in the necropolis under St. Peter's at the Vatican portrays Christ as Sol (or Apollo-Helios) wearing a radiate crown and driving a chariot, thus adopting the old mythological motif of the sun crossing the sky in a chariot (Fig. 11.3). Jesus was acquiring the traits of a solar hero.

It was taking some time for a celebration of Jesus's birth, and on December 25, to develop, but in the third century came a fortuitous development on the part of the Romans: Sun worship became more popular in the Roman empire. The emperor Elagabalus (reigned 218–22 CE), a Syrian who had been a priest of the Syrian sun god, Sol Invictus, established this deity's cult as the chief cult in Rome. After Elagabalus was assassinated, attempts were made to suppress the cult, but it survived. The emperor Aurelian (reigned 270–75 CE) furthered the cult, in 274 proclaiming Sol to be the exclusive official divine protector of the empire and the emperor.[182] Scholars traditionally have held that Aurelian formally established December 25 as the birthday of Sol Invictus and instituted a festival of the god on that day, but there is no record of this, so some scholars challenge that notion.[183] This lack of documentation hardly matters, however, because astronomically and mythologically for the Romans his birthday being on December 25 was a foregone conclusion. Indeed, one fourth-century observer reported that Romans lit candles on this day to celebrate the sun's birthday.[184]

In the early fourth century, the converted Christian emperor Constantine used solar symbolism to popularize Christ and Christianity. In doing so, he merged pagan and Christian ideas and practices in order to make Christianity more appealing to what was still the large pagan majority of the population. For example, whereas Christians had called their Sabbath the Lord's Day, in 321 Constantine changed its name to Sunday ("day of the Sun"), for it coincided with a day dedicated to the sun god, and made it an official day of rest.[185] This helped put pagan sun worship into acceptable Christian form. Then, after celebrating Jesus's

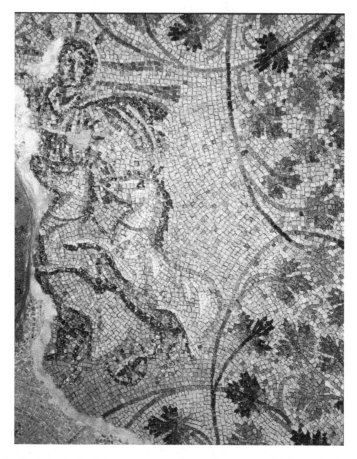

Fig. 11.3 Mosaic depicting Christ wearing radiate crown driving a chariot in the sky. Unknown artist, late third century CE. Located at St. Peter's, Vatican, Rome. Alamy stock image

baptism was declared heretical at Constantine Council of Nicaea, Christians were drawn more naturally to the pagan solar (equinox) celebrations.[186] As one would expect, it was indeed in the new pro-Christian climate established by Emperor Constantine that the Feast of the Nativity on December 25 took off. It was during this new era when we first see the Feast first attested, in 336 CE, near the end of Constantine's reign.[187]

Solar symbolism then became ingrained in Christmas. For example, in a Christmas sermon, St. Ambrose preached:

Well do Christian people call this holy day, on which our Lord was born, the day of the new sun; and they assert it so insistently that even Jews and pagans agree with them in using that name for it. We are happy to accept and maintain this view, because with the dayspring of the Savior, not only is the salvation of mankind renewed, but also the splendor of the sun. . . . For if the sun withdrew its light when Christ suffered, it must shine at his birth with greater splendor than ever before.[188]

Pope Leo I, in office 440–61, likewise praised the link between Jesus and the sun, yet was vexed by Christians bowing to the rising sun before entering church.[189]

As Christianity grew and Rome declined, the Feast of the Nativity took over as the December 25 winter solstice holiday in the Mediterranean and eventually Europe, with the characteristics of the Roman and Christian celebrations in that holiday season becoming combined. While it is popularly claimed that the Christians simply took over a pagan holiday, the reality was more complex. As seen above, the Christians already had their own good theological reasons for celebrating the Feast of the Nativity on December 25, including their own solar symbolism based in scripture. The eventual syncretism resulted from the actions of Constantine. Whereas Aurelian had sought to unify the empire under a universal pagan religion of the sun, Constantine achieved the same through Christianity, by combining aspects of both. In the minds of Roman converts, Sol Invictus was superseded by Christ.

In establishing the new holiday, it also helped that the Roman Saturnalia festival was held on December 17–23, which holiday the Feast of the Nativity also subsumed. As we shall see, some of our Christmas rituals originated with the Saturnalia. The holiday would first be called Christmas beginning only in mid-eleventh-century England. (Nevertheless, for simplicity, in this book I usually use the term "Christmas," even where the events in question preceded the adoption of that name.)

How Christmas Mythology and Ritual Evolved to What We Have Today

Not only have the biblical Christmas stories endured until today, but they have been enhanced, which is to say further mythologized. Also, in some respects either Matthew's or Luke's version has prevailed, while in others the two accounts have been combined and conflated. Thus, Matthew's magi story remains a standard image in Christmas cards and nativity scenes largely at the expense of Luke's shepherds, yet Luke's story of Jesus lying in the manger prevailed over Matthew's scene of Jesus being born in the family house. As a result, our modern conflated Christmas imagery typically portrays the magi visiting the newborn Jesus lying in the manger, though sometimes with shepherds and their sheep also in attendance. Matthew did not say how many magi there were, but over time they became three to match the number of gifts. They also came to be thought of as kings, through reliance on Isaiah 60:3, 6 and Psalm 72:10–11 discussed earlier (p. 219). And they acquired names and descriptions: the young and shaven Caspar, the bearded old Melchior, and the black Balthasar. The tradition also arose that they rode camels, which later sometimes were included in nativity scenes; Matthew had not specified their means of transport.

Traditions also developed about particular animals being near Jesus as he lay in the manger, which made their way into European nativity art as stock images. An ass and an ox, humble animals who serve people, were usually present to symbolize Jesus's humble beginnings. Their presence also alludes to the prophecy in Isaiah 1:3, which reads, "An ox knows its owner, and the ass its master's manger, but Israel does not know, my people do not understand."[190] Since even these lowly animals at the nativity know that Jesus is Lord, the implied question is, "Will people recognize this too?" In Christian thinking, also related was the prophecy in Habakkuk 3.2 (LXX) that "between two animals you shall become known,"[191] which was interpreted to mean the ox and ass of Isaiah. Thus, the magi's (and animals') recognizing Jesus's divinity (Epiphany) was held to be predicted by Hebrew Bible scripture. Perhaps Isaiah's prophecy is also why Luke used a manger in the story. The figure of the ass may also look forward to when Jesus rode an ass into Jerusalem to meet his fate. The ox, as well as sheep (especially the lamb), were also included because both were sacrificial animals, and thus were a symbol of Christ's sacrifice. Sheep also symbolize Christ's flock of followers, as noted earlier

Fig. 11.4   *Adoration of the Magi* by Fra Angelico and Fra Filippo Lippi, ca. 1492. Alamy stock image

(pp. 222–23). Sometimes even peacocks became included in nativity scenes, as in the *Adoration of the Magi* by Fra Angelico and Filippo Lippi (Fig. 11.4), because they symbolize immortality.[192] They are linked to the phoenix, which comes back to life, and to the sun.[193]

Once the infancy narratives about Jesus started to circulate, Christians developed an insatiable appetite for more details about his miraculous life, and such demand created the supply. Thus appeared in the late second century the Infancy Gospel of Thomas, recounting legendary episodes from Jesus's childhood, the Protoevangelium of James (late second century), mainly providing details of Mary's background, and later Pseudo-Matthew (early seventh century), which combined the material in the Infancy Gospel and Protoevangelium and added mythological material of its own. The Protoevangelium is interesting because it portrayed Jesus as being born in a cave (near Bethlehem) (18.1; 21:3); Justin Martyr, Origen, and Eusebius also claimed this.[194] Inevitably, a suitable cave was identified near Bethlehem, and the Empress Helena (Constantine's mother) built the Church of the Nativity over it around 325–30 CE. Soon pilgrims were visiting it. Eventually this motif was portrayed in art, both in Orthodox Christian icons, where it became the norm,[195] as well as in Western European art, including famous nativities by Giorgione, Botticelli, and Antoniazzo Romano.[196]

Why did early Christians depart from the Gospels and use the cave (or grotto) motif in portraying Christ's birth, and why did it endure? Inevitably, a scriptural basis in the Hebrew Bible was sought and found; Justin relied on Isaiah 33:15–16's prophecy about a savior, which in the Septuagint says that "he will dwell in a high cave of a strong rock." But this is a stretch, and in any event does little to explain why Christians became interested in portraying a cave in the first place. Another possibility is that the cave motif was borrowed from Mithraism, since Mithras was held to have been born from a rock or (possibly) in a cave.[197] He was also said to have killed the bull in a cave, and his mystery rites were performed in a structure representing a cave, the Mithraeum. Beginning in the second century CE Christianity came into competition with Mithraism, so it would have been useful to appropriate some of its mythology to make Jesus compare well. After Christianity prevailed Christians did, after all, build churches atop old Mithraea to symbolize the triumph of light over darkness.[198] A Mithraic origin to the nativity's cave motif has not yet been proven, however. Another possibility is that the cave prefigures Jesus's eventual entombment, but the Christians' focus was on the resurrection, not entombment.

In light of the above, it is probably more fruitful to focus instead on the mythological meaning of a cave and a birth in it. Caves often symbolize the dark, undifferentiated, timeless, primordial state before the creation occurred and hence become the place of creation, including birth, especially since they resemble the womb and were often thought of as such. Similarly, as we saw in Chap. 3, they are places of re-creation and transformation, which is why religious rituals have been conducted in caves since prehistoric times. In particular, the initiation rites of Greek and Roman mystery cults were held in cave-like underground chambers. The cave is therefore a place of a spiritual quest and rebirth. The image of Jesus's birth in it thus further symbolizes a spiritual birth, and spiritual potential for anyone. Finally, as noted previously, Jesus was portrayed as the light that overcomes darkness, for which purpose a cave motif works well.

Other extensions of the infancy myth were designed to accommodate church doctrine. For example, the Immaculate Conception of Mary, according to which through God's intervention she was born free of original sin, was developed to ensure that Jesus too was born sinless, since church doctrine taught that the taint of original sin is hereditary going back to Adam. For his part, Joseph came to be portrayed often as an old man[199] in order to reinforce the claim of Mary being a virgin, in particular to support the church's argument that Jesus's siblings reported in the Bible were from the widower Joseph's prior marriage, thus supporting the doctrine of Mary's perpetual virginity.

Another legend or myth arising from church history in late ancient times and which became associated with Christmas was that of St. Nicholas, to which we now turn.

The Mythmaking Behind St. Nicholas and Santa Claus

St. Nicholas provides another interesting example of how Christmas mythology has developed. We know very little about the real person; most traditions about him are myth and legend.

We do know that he was born in the mid-third century, became Bishop of Myra, a seaport in Lycia, Asia Minor, and attended the Council of Nicaea, signing onto the Nicene Creed. According to tradition, while at the Council he became so incensed at Arius that he struck him in the face. (Imagine Santa Claus punching out a churchman!) He was a Confessor (i.e., remained faithful and confessed Christ publicly during persecution) and was imprisoned during Diocletian's persecutions of Christians. He probably would have been martyred, but he was released after Constantine became emperor. He was buried in Myra, where his tomb became a popular pilgrimage destination. Myra eventually fell under Muslim rule, so in order to protect St. Nicholas's remains, in 1087 sailors from Bari, Italy (then in the Venetian empire) stole most of his remains and transported them to Bari. During the First Crusade they were moved to Venice, where the church of St. Nicholas was built in his honor and where the remains still lie. His feast day is on December 6, traditionally the date of his death.

Judging from what little we know about Nicholas's life, including why he was canonized, he might easily have become lost to history. Yet stories circulated about his good deeds and miracles, and his legend grew. The Byzantine Emperor Justinian I built a church in his honor in Constantinople, and Nicholas's contemporary, St. John Chrysostom, spoke favorably of Nicholas in a sermon. Since Myra was a seaport, unsurprisingly the first evidence of Nicholas's cult was among sailors looking to him for a safe voyage;[200] he was said to have saved mariners during a storm. This may explain why the Venetians (a maritime empire) were so keen on obtaining his relics. By the high Middle Ages, Nicholas had acquired some of Poseidon's characteristics, such as riding on a white horse symbolizing the crest of a wave. The Saint's protection was sought not only for the sailors but for their ship's cargo, especially grain. Stories arose that he even paid for grain that some people could not afford.[201] Eventually he became popular throughout Europe, especially once his remains were transferred to Italy and his name was included in *The Golden Legend*.

The legend that seems to have ensured his lasting fame, first known from the eighth century, concerned the three daughters of a poor man who could not afford a dowry for them, meaning that they were having trouble getting married. It seemed that they might be forced into prostitution, sold into slavery, or have to marry undesirable husbands. But one night St. Nick came to the house secretly with a gift in a sack: gold coins for the oldest daughter's dowry, which he tossed through the window (some came to say down the chimney). As the story was embellished over time, the gold was said to have landed in stockings or shoes hung by the fireplace to dry. Nicholas later did the same for the other two daughters, so he acquired a reputation as a gift giver, to children in particular. Eventually this led to the custom of children hanging stockings or putting out shoes hoping for gifts from Nicholas on his feast day, December 6. In another story, Nicholas, through prayer resulting in God's intervention, restored the lives of three murdered theology students, and likewise in the case of three small children who had been captured and killed by an evil butcher who planned to sell the meat. He was also said to have intervened to save the lives of condemned innocents (he knew who had been naughty and nice!), once even grabbing and stopping an executioner's sword. Naturally, St. Nicholas became a patron saint of children, though also for sailors, other travelers, merchants, and bakers.

St. Nicholas's feast was celebrated by giving gifts on St. Nicholas Eve, December 5th. As a bishop, St. Nicholas would have worn a pointed red hat called a miter and a red robe, which carried over into Dutch version of the Saint, Sinterklass, and so is the origin of Santa's red costume. Sinterklass was an elderly, stately man with long white hair and long beard. He also carried a large red book in which he recorded which children have been good or naughty over the past year. The Dutch name Sinterklass is a shortening of that of the saint, in English becoming Santa (=Saint) Claus (=Ni-*cholas*).[202] In Holland he traditionally rode a white horse, perhaps a carryover from the Poseidon imagery. St. Nicholas naturally was the patron saint of the Dutch immigrants who sailed across the Atlantic to settle in New Amsterdam, which became New York City.

Norse mythology and the Norse Yule festival also appear to have influenced the development of the Santa Claus figure. Yule was the winter solstice holiday in Nordic countries, featuring a feast in which pig was eaten, representing the mythical pig Sarine who was eaten daily in Valhalla and who resurrected overnight only to be eaten again the next day,[203] as in the Samhain myths discussed earlier (p. 164). People placed a pair of straw goat figures in front of their homes, representing Thor's two goats, Tannprisnir and Tanngnjostr, who pulled his chariot across the sky. Until the nineteenth century it was these goats who were thought to deliver Yule gifts to children. (In Finland, the Santa/Father Christmas figure is still called Joulupukki, which means "Yule goat.") The god Odin also played a role in Yule festivities. At this time of year he rode his eight-legged horse Sleipnir across the sky visiting people's homes. While some influence of Odin and perhaps Thor on the figure of Sinterklass seems likely, the idea that Sleipnir is the origin of Santa's eight reindeer has not yet been proven. For one thing, when Washington Irving portrayed the celebration of St. Nicholas's day among the Dutch immigrants who had settled in New Amsterdam, the Saint traveled not on a sleigh pulled by reindeer but by horse and wagon. It was in the 1821 story, "A Visit from St. Nicholas" (which became known as "The Night Before Christmas"), generally attributed to Clement Clark Moore, that the eight reindeer first appeared, and we don't know from where he got them. That story also cemented the link between St. Nicholas and modern Christmas. Previously in American tradition, St. Nicholas had delivered his gifts on December 5, the eve of his own holiday celebrated on December 6. But in Moore's story St. Nicholas came on Christmas Eve, not in connection with his own holiday, and that became our tradition.[204]

The Evolution of Christmas Myth and Ritual in Europe and the United States

The post-Roman history of Christmas parallels the usual fate of myth and ritual in holidays, by reflecting the varying cultures in which the holiday came to be observed. Thus, the story of Christmas was one of the integration of the original Christian idea behind the holiday with the religions, myths, and rituals of the pagan cultures of Europe. The result was the amalgam of Christian and pagan elements that we still see today.

Since the indigenous European peoples were not literate, much of their mythology and ritual that is now associated with Christmas, as well as their own potentially analogous holidays, have been lost to us. Also, it is not possible within the scope of this chapter to trace the evolution of Christmas in the many cultures in which it came to be celebrated. Therefore, below I simply summarize some key developments not already covered.

First, since Rome had dominated much of Europe and influenced its indigenous cultures, aspects of Roman Christmas, as well as other Roman holidays that influenced Christmas, continued in Europe. Most important was the legacy of the Saturnalia, already discussed in Chap. 5 (pp. 64–65). Held on December 17–23 near Rome's winter solstice, it was an end-of-year festival of dissolution of the type discussed in Chaps. 2 and 5. Accordingly, it featured a carnival atmosphere of revelry, role reversals, and (within each household) the appointment of a mock king *(Saturnalicius princeps)* to preside over the festivities, much like the later Twelfth Night tradition of choosing a King Bean and Queen Pea for the evening's festivities.[205] Some of its rituals and customs carried over to Christmas, including gift giving, especially to children (this tradition comes from the Saturnalia, not the example of the magi[206]), feasting, taking the day off from work, adorning the entrances of temples with new green foliage symbolizing the continuation of life and fertility (an antecedent to our Christmas wreaths, trees, mistletoe, holly, etc.),[207] and the burning and giving of wax candles, symbolizing the returning power of the sun's light. The Roman Kalendae of January 1–3, a New Year's festival, had some similar customs, especially gift-giving and decorating entrances with greenery. Christmas eventually both absorbed and extinguished the Saturnalia.

Second, just as Christmas in the Roman world was linked to the winter solstice traditions and Christ acquired solar imagery, so too Christmas in post-Roman Europe took on characteristics of pagan winter solstice festivals. As Clement Miles summarized this process,

Christmas, indeed, regarded in all its aspects, is a microcosm of European religion. It reflects almost every phase of thought and feeling from crude magic and superstition to the speculative mysticism of Eckhart, from mere delight in physical indulgence to the exquisite spirituality and tenderness of St. Francis. . . . It is a river into which have flowed tributaries from every side, from Oriental religion, from Greek and Roman civilization, from Celtic, Teutonic, Slav, and probably pre-Aryan, society, mingling their waters so that it is often hard to discover the far-away springs.[208]

And because we don't have an extensive or reliable picture of what pre-Christian European mythology contributed to the evolution of Christmas, we are left with a set of interrelated pagan symbols and rituals that over the centuries attached themselves to the holiday: the Yule log that protects the household; candles; holly; mistletoe; and eventually whole Christmas trees. They have nothing to do with the birth of Jesus[209] and everything to do with pagan winter solstice festivals, symbolizing the continuation of life and the sun through the winter.[210] So, for example:

- Many Christian leaders initially opposed green decoration at Christmas because of its connection with ancient Rome and pagan Europe, but these traditions proved to be too strong, and eventually greenery found its way even into churches.[211]
- Other pagan practices were accepted more readily, as compromises in accordance with Gregory the Great's accommodation policy (see pp. 154–55). A traditional pagan solstice procession might now have a crucifix carried by clergy rather than an idol at the front of it,[212] while the participants probably did not appreciate a meaningful difference.
- Some bizarre superstitious pagan rituals and beliefs continued, but now as part of Christmas. For example, in parts of Germany, on Christmas morning before the cattle were watered, a dog was thrown into their water to protect the cattle from the mange. In Bohemia a black cat was caught, boiled, and buried by night under a tree to keep evil spirits away from the fields. In France and the British Isles people hunted and killed a wren because it was considered a magical bird that brings good fortune, and they paraded it around town and from house to house to confer good luck.[213]
- Many pagan beliefs that mark the solstice as a liminal time carried over into Christmas. These beliefs (or superstitions) include, in various places, that Christmas Eve (like Beltane and Samhain) is a good

time for divination; that animals gain the power of speech at midnight on Christmas Eve; that trolls and other uncanny beings are out and about on Christmas Eve, so one should not go outside; and finally one that might have some scriptural basis: that water turns into wine at midnight on Christmas Eve.[214] Such beliefs naturally led to performing rites of purification (including wassailing and fire rites), and in Christian terms blessing.[215]

Third, the feasting and drinking that was typical of the Roman and pagan end-of year/solstice holiday continued as part of Christmas. In practice, it was a winter solstice party with a Christian veneer on top.[216] In medieval times the festivities likewise took on the characteristics of a festival of dissolution, with a Lord of Misrule or similar figure presiding over the revels. Within churches, the Christmas season also included the Feast of Fools, and in France, Switzerland and other areas the temporary appointment of a choir boy as Boy Bishop on December 28 (Holy Innocents' Day, marking the massacre of the innocents) to take on adult roles in the church.[217] This riotous tradition reappeared in America in non-Puritan circles. One minister complained in 1758 that Christmastime had become a time for "sinning, sexuality, luxury, and various forms of extravagance, as though men were not celebrating the birth of the holy Jesus but of Venus, or Bacchus."[218]

Fourth, attempts were made to ban Christmas, either because of its pagan characteristics or because it was considered a popish invention with no scriptural basis (Jesus's date of birth not being stated in the Bible), but they all failed. These attempts occurred mainly during the Reformation, especially among the Puritans.[219] This resulted in Christmas hardly being celebrated in colonial America and the young United States, since Puritans dominated early colonization.

Both in Europe and America, the Christmas holiday has survived and continues to flourish, in both its Christian and pagan aspects, although the grossest pagan superstitious elements and raucous practices have fallen away. On the one hand, the Christian nativity myth endures, while on the other hand the pagan symbols continue to generate warmth and comfort during the cold season and promise us spring. Witness, for example, the annual Christmas television broadcasts consisting only of a burning fireplace surrounded by green decoration, to the sound of holiday music. The continued vibrancy of the holiday is an indication that there is something archetypal about it which resonates with our psyches. Therefore, by paying due attention to these psychological aspects, we can conceptualize and celebrate the holiday in a modernized spiritual way that enriches our holiday experience.

PSYCHOLOGICAL AND MODERN SPIRITUAL ASPECTS OF THE CHRISTMAS MYTH

As discussed in Chap. 6 (p. 113), the Christ figure can be understood as representing the integration of our total psyche (the "Self"), specifically the integration of the unconscious part of our psyche with ego consciousness (the "self"),[220] a process that Carl Jung called individuation. As a symbol of the Self, Christ represents both the dynamic *process* of integration as well as the substantive *result*, the more integrated Self. This endeavor can be considered "religious" because the unconscious is the source of our numinous experiences of "divinity," upon which the integration process draws.

The Holy Spirit and the Incarnation

In Matthew and Luke, the Christmas story begins when Mary becomes pregnant, known as the incarnation. Jesus was both human and divine as of this moment of his conception in the womb. In both Gospel accounts, this happened through the action of the Holy Spirit. Thus, in order to understand the incarnation (and so too the Christmas event) from a mytho-psychological perspective, we first must understand the Holy Spirit from that perspective.

As discussed earlier (pp. 204–06), the Holy Spirit is a creative divine force or energy that acts as a mediating agent between God and the cosmos, especially humans. Not only prophets but other important figures such as Moses, Joshua, charismatic judges, Saul, David, and Solomon received their capabilities and powers through the Holy Spirit. Of course, the Messiah too would be endowed with the Holy Spirit, and could transmit it to others on behalf of God.[221] In short, the Holy Spirit is a link to God and yields an experience of the divine.

Jesus was baptized through the Holy Spirit. He performed his miracles through it (e.g., Mt 12:28; Lk 11:20; Acts 10:38), and conferred it upon his disciples when commissioning them to preach and perform healings (Mt 10:1, 20; 28:16–20; Lk 9:1–2). It descended upon the disciples at

Pentecost, which enabled them to proclaim the gospel, including in foreign tongues (Acts 2:1–13). St. Paul spread the gospel through it, and he said that it dwells within Christians, so they can live as Christs (e.g., Rom 8:9–11). The Spirit was intended to have a continuing effect and provide ongoing guidance, in the form of the Paraclete (Jn 14:16–17, 26). The Spirit has a deifying effect, which is noticeable to others. This was exemplified when Paul and Barnabas, who carried the Spirit, were mistaken for gods (Zeus and Hermes). Observers remarked, "The gods have come down to us in the likeness of men" (Acts 14:11).

In psychological terms, the Holy Spirit is the psychic energy (libido) that brings "divine" archetypal unconscious content into ego consciousness. Technically it is not the substantive unconscious content itself, but is the carrier of that content; yet the content and the psychic energy hit ego consciousness together, so in practice and effect the two are inseparable and operationally synonymous.[222] It is literally felt somatically, in the body, indeed an in*carn*ation. The result is an overwhelming numinous experience. When this content and spirit incarnate, they take on a personally meaningful quality that psychologists call "soul." Soul has a lasting effect on ego consciousness and also grows over time as more and more content is integrated, which is why the Christian myth can speak of the Paraclete. On the other hand, to the extent a person fails to integrate archetypal unconscious content, he or she is said to suffer a loss (or lack) of soul (see pp. 115–16). This is characterized by a lack of energy and motivation, listlessness, and some degree of depression, because one's ego consciousness has no inspiration or inner guide.

More technically, these archetypal contents and spirit form the core of complexes that structure our personality.[223] This means that what we know as the "divine" is key in forming our psyches, and hence also the character of what we perceive and think of as the external world. In particular, when archetypal content is experienced by ego consciousness, it feels like something "other," as if it is from the external world, when actually it is external only to ego consciousness, not to our entire Self. Hence the appearance of external divine beings, including the God-man. When we perceive the "Holy Spirit" as something external affecting someone else, we are projecting this psychic energy onto heroic figures (Jesus, Paul), often using solar imagery.[224] Idealized people are seen as the carriers (or even the source) of spirit,[225] and in sometimes as being divine themselves. This brings us to the Divine Child figure, to be considered shortly below.

While in Matthew and Luke Christ's incarnation was literalized as a one-time historical event, mythologically and psychologically the implication is that incarnation can occur in any and all of us, and repeatedly. St. Paul's teachings come close to this. Further, we see other versions of such incarnation in various mythical and religious traditions, which evidences that the process of incarnation of the "divine" is an archetypal psychic process. Thus, in ancient Egypt the king was the god Horus born to a mortal woman, and in India Vishnu incarnated at times of need, while a Bodhisattva incarnates in order to liberate humanity.[226] The archetypal nature of the Christ story is also evidenced by Christianity's spread and acceptance in the many cultures of the Mediterranean. As Jung put it,

> Christ would never have made the impression he did on his followers if he had not expressed something that was alive and at work in their unconscious. Christianity itself would never have spread through the pagan world with such astonishing rapidity had its ideas not found an analogous psychic readiness to receive them.[227]

As a result, Christians were able to live more spiritually integrated lives. More specifically from the mythological standpoint, the incarnation of Jesus was considered a kind of second creation. As we've seen, the first creation marked the emergence of ego consciousness, through which we are able to see opposites, as seen by Adam and Eve gaining the "knowledge of good and evil" in the Eden myth. Jesus was viewed as the second Adam (Rom 5:12–14; 1 Cor 15:21–22, 45). Jesus as the second Adam works mythologically because he represents a yet higher, more integrated consciousness, and therefore also a more evolved God-image. As discussed above (pp. 116–17), the incarnation of the divine in Jesus marks the dawn of this higher consciousness, resulting quite literally in a spiritual birth; he is thus available as a symbol of the Self. With that understanding, we can now consider the meaning of the baby Jesus exemplifying the Divine Child.

The Birth of Jesus and the Divine Child Motif

The archetypal figure of the "Divine Child" has great importance in myth and psychology. The child archetype is an emanation from the collective unconscious,[228] meaning that "divine" child figures arise from it, in miraculous births. Within us, the Divine Child represents the "preconscious, childhood aspect of the collective psyche,"[229] meaning content of the collective unconscious that is not yet integrated with ego consciousness. The Divine Child is a "symbol of unity" to be born from the tension of opposites,[230] representing the "potential future,"[231] giving hope of change for the better. Hence, he is a savior figure who promises to provoke that change and redeem us.

But the Divine Child does more than represent potential: His coming actually initiates (or reinvigorates) the individuation process. The Divine Child is a numinous symbol resulting from the affect of this moment, representing the wholeness that will result. Since in this moment humans feel the divine, it is only natural that it will be mythologized, historicized, and eventually celebrated through a sacred holiday.

Unconscious content rises up because it needs to be recognized and accepted by ego consciousness in order to be integrated and embodied as soul. Thus, when the Divine Child appears, he must be recognized, accepted, and adored. In the Christmas story, we see this process at work in the accounts of the adorations of the magi and the shepherds, and the chorus of angels.[232] This also appears to be happening when the fetus John the Baptist leaps in his mother's womb just as the pregnant Mary appears before John's mother Elizabeth (Lk 1:41).

But as discussed in Chap. 5 (pp. 117–18), when confronted with such powerful unconscious material, ego consciousness will suffer. When the Divine Child appears, inevitably he will clash with "the establishment" of our ego consciousness — the Pharisees, scribes, priesthood, and Romans of our self — which will oppose and reject him in order to preserve the status quo (i.e., the ego's dominant position). This is why in the "birth of the hero" motif attempts are made to kill the special child, or he is abandoned back to nature (i.e., back to the unconscious), often to be brought up by animals or otherwise in primitive conditions (pp. 202–03) until he is ready to come forth, reveal himself, and begin his quest. This same process is reflected in the story of Herod and the massacre of the innocents and the flight to Egypt. Herod, the reigning King of the Jews, fears Jesus as a threat to his kingship; he and the Romans are ego consciousness running rampant.[233] Such is the precariousness of individuation. But the nature of culture heroes is to overcome this opposition in order to bring benefits to humankind, including higher consciousness. So, the child-hero inevitably breaks free and evolves toward independence, and so in the "birth of the hero" motif he is often described as gaining in wisdom and accomplishing extraordinary deeds at a young age, like Jesus as discussed above.

The Divine Child figure can accomplish this because in a young child the ego is only budding, not yet dominant, and so is naturally more integrated with the unconscious; the opposites are not yet sharply contrasted. Being in such a state, a child appropriately represents not merely the potential for wholeness of the Self, but *the way* to achieve this. He is well-suited for the task because he is carried by powerful numinous spirit (psychic energy), yet as a child he is less threatening than much other archetypal content.

Accordingly, Jesus uses child imagery in his teachings. This is why Jesus says in Matthew 18:4 that "unless you change and become as little children, you will never enter the kingdom of heaven."[234] And St. Paul said, "God sent his Son . . . so that we might receive adoption as children. And because you are children, God has sent the Spirit of his Son into our hearts" (Gal 4:4–6). Mark's Gospel provides a larger narrative context for this metaphor of integration. The enacted "parable of the child amongst" in Mark 9:33–37 can be read according to this psychological framework. In verse 34 the disciples' egos are driving their behavior, so they are competing with each other for greatness and preeminence, which hinders their spiritual growth. Accordingly, Jesus teaches them that if anyone would be first, initially he must be last, as a humble servant. (In the ancient household, where this scene takes place, a child had the lowest status.) Thus, as Jesus the God-man physically embraces a child in a house, he teaches that a person first must identify oneself with a child and in an important sense become mentally like one, with the ego having no pretensions to greatness. Psychologically, the story shows the need to tame ego consciousness by becoming like a child so that self-aware individuation can occur. This can establish a new pattern for human relationships that will leave no occasion for strife, which is what at the beginning of this story had been occurring among the disciples.

The goal of the individuation process in New Testament terms is the Kingdom of God. Psychologically speaking, this is the point where the Self has become integrated. This is why, for example, Jesus can say that there is no marriage in the Kingdom of God; instead, people will exist there like angels in heaven (Mark 12:25). The opposites, in this example the masculine and feminine principles, will have been resolved and integrated. The idea is similar in religions worldwide. In Hinduism, for example, the Divine Child Ganesha is born from the spirit of his father Shiva and part of the body (earth) of his mother Parvati. He is a unity not only of male and female, but also of spirit and matter, and of heaven and earth. As such, he represents the integration of opposites in the psyche and the path toward spiritual enlightenment.

In summary, the miraculous conception and birth of the Divine Child represent the incarnation of the divine within ourselves and potential for our better future. Recognizing and accepting him, as the magi did, results in integration. His birth is a spiritual birth, potentially ours too. Christians concretized this in terms of the future realization of the Kingdom of God or salvation by going to heaven in an afterlife. Psychologically, however, this is an internal affair. Jesus himself spoke in such terms, telling the Pharisees that "the kingdom of God is within you" (Lk 17:21). Similarly, according to the Gospel of Thomas, he taught:

- "When you give rise to that which is in you, what you have will save you. If you do not give rise to it, what you do not have will destroy you."[235]
- "The kingdom is within you. . . . When you know yourselves, . . . you will know that you are the sons of the living Father."[236]

Observing Christmas offers us the chance to focus on our own incarnation by celebrating the Divine Child within us. We each can have our individual way of "putting Christ back into Christmas."

NOTES

CHAPTER 1

1. Deities: Tuesday after Tyr; Wednesday after Wotan (Odin); Thursday after Thor; and Friday after Frigg/Freya. Heavenly bodies: Saturday after Saturn; Sunday after the sun; and Monday after the Moon.
2. The connection of April, May, and June with Aphrodite, Maia, and Juno respectively is not entirely certain and is still debated.
3. Bradshaw and Hoffman 1999b, p. 2.
4. Originally, they represented the lunar cycle ("year") of the waxing, full, and waning moon, also three phases. Harrison 1969, pp. 189–90.
5. See Philostratus the Elder, *Imagines* 2.34.
6. See Harrison 1969, pp. 186–90. Plato's *Cratylus* 410c, suggests a point of connection between the two triads. He argues that the word "horae"—Greek *horai* with a roughened long ō (omega)—is best understood by reference to what he calls the "old Attic" rendition of the word, *horai* (with roughened short o (omicron)), derived from the verb *horidzō*, which means to discern, distinguish, determine, mark out, draw boundaries, delimit, separate, and divide. Plato's point here, regardless of whether his etymology is correct, is that he considers the essence of the Horae to be distinguishers, which function can be applied in various contexts and situations. Thus, in the case of the initial triad, they represent the separate seasons. In the case of the second triad, they distinguish between justice and injustice, war and peace, and good laws vs. lawlessness.

© The Author(s) 2020
A. George, *The Mythology of America's Seasonal Holidays*,
https://doi.org/10.1007/978-3-030-46916-0

7. *Theogony* 903.
8. Harrison 1969, pp. 517–18.
9. Cf. Eliade 1978a, pp. 261–63.
10. Graves 1960, pp. 125–26.
11. Eliade 1991b, p. 21.
12. Campbell 1949, p. 384.
13. Eliade 1987, pp. 14–18.
14. This happened so long before literate society came about that it is difficult to speculate about why this trait became part of our nature. In this book, therefore, I take this trait simply as an empirical fact and proceed from there. If I had to speculate, my guess is that it was valuable from the evolutionary standpoint because it generates positive psychic energy (libido) which enabled people to function more effectively, such as getting psychologically charged before the hunt, or battle, or in competing for a mate.
15. Aveni 2003, p. 28.
16. See Hillman 1983 and 1992.
17. See Corbett 1996.
18. For example, the biblical garden of Eden story takes the form of myth, but scholars have been unable to identify any corresponding rituals associated with it. Likewise with Noah's flood. The seven-day creation story in Genesis 1 may reflect an Israelite liturgical ritual concerning the enthronement of Yahweh, but it is difficult to know whether the myth or the ritual came first.
19. Wulff 1997; Fuller 1994.

CHAPTER 2

1. Actually, in Mesopotamia at first time was reckoned in terms of six-month equinox years, because there were both spring and fall rains separated by "chaos" periods of summer parching and winter withering. Accordingly, festivals equivalent to the "new year" were celebrated every six months in the spring and autumn. See Wensinck 1922, pp. 188, 195; Cohen 1993, pp. 400–1, 406, 437.
2. Ovid, *Fasti* 1.177.
3. Altheim 1938, p. 194.
4. *Fasti* 1.125.
5. Ovid, *Fasti* 1.185–226.
6. *Fasti* 1.102–114.
7. Hesiod, *Theogony* 116ff
8. *ANET*, p. 72 (Tablet VII, lines 132–34).

9. Wensinck 1922.
10. Franz 1995, pp. 2–4.
11. George and George 2014, p. 323 n. 10.
12. Franz 1995, p. 5.
13. Eliade 1991b.
14. These ideas are discussed in more detail in Eliade 1987; Eliade 1991b; Wensinck 1922, pp. 169, 192.
15. Wensinck 1922, p. 169 (memorializing vs. repeating); Mack 2001, p. 73 (reenactment vs. replication).
16. Harrison 1991, p. 53.
17. Aveni 2003, p. 24.
18. Santino 1994, p. 208.
19. Aveni 2003, p. 19.
20. Aveni 2003, p. 24.
21. See generally George and George 2014, pp. 106–14.
22. Frankfort 1978, p. 410 n. 14.
23. Black and Green 1992, p. 153.
24. For purposes of this ritual, it does not matter that for other ritual purposes Marduk still is confined to the underworld. The Babylonians would not have seen a contradiction here.
25. Frankfort 1978, p. 409 n. 14; Wensinck 1922, pp. 176–77, 181, 184–85.
26. The Akitu festival takes its name from the Akitu House. The etymology and meaning of Akitu is largely unknown, but it has been suggested that "Akitu House" may mean something like "the house where the god temporarily dwells on earth," making it a primordial residence outside the created cosmos inhabited before the god chose (established) his city. See Cohen 1993, p. 405.
27. Lambert 1968, p. 107.
28. Eventually, in 30 BCE Egyptians fixed the New Year at our August 29, even though it did not exactly match the date of Sirius's rising. Aveni 2003, p. 13.
29. Parker 1950, p. 47.
30. Parker 1950, p. 47.
31. Aveni 2003, p. 21.
32. Aldred 1969, pp. 77.
33. Frankfort 1978, pp. 193–94. In years when the king died, Osiris's internment also marked the final internment of the dead king, carried out at the same time.
34. Aldred 1969, p. 77; Parker 1950, p. 62 (§ 314).
35. As explained below, the kas in question are those of Horus and Osiris which are joined to living and deceased kings. Frankfort 1978, p. 104.
36. E.g., Job 26:12–13; Ps 74:13–14, 89:9–10; Is 27:1, 51:9. See generally George and George 2014, pp. 88–90.
37. E.g., Anderson 1987, pp. 72–73.
38. Walton 2009, pp. 87–92.

39. There were variations in other ancient Greek city-states, but space does not allow for discussion of them.
40. In terms of the solar year, the day varied because Athens used a lunar year of 354 days and adjusted by intercalating a month every eight years.
41. Some festivals at other times of the year also involved purifications, just as in other cultures.
42. This holiday is a good example of combining agricultural and urban aspects mentioned above. Its timing reflects reaping the first fruits (here grain) before the main harvest, so the festival traditionally had offering (sacrifice) rituals. But the *pharmakos* ritual discussed here has an urban character. See Burkert 1985, p. 265.
43. Originally, it seems that a particularly ugly or disfigured man was selected and the ritual may have been a true human sacrifice, and the practice of using an already condemned criminal arose once human sacrifice became unaccept-able. Also, originally two such persons may have been selected, one for men and one for women. See Burkert 1985, pp. 82–83.
44. Stringing together the worst-smelling vegetables (garlic, onion, cabbages) helped ward off destructive insects, Aveni 2003, p. 96, so apparently people thought this would work in the case of evil spirits as well.
45. Later each year married women carried out essentially the same ritual during the Thesmophoria festival. See descriptions in James 1961, pp. 135–37; Burkert 1985, pp. 242–56; Harrison 1991, pp. 120–31.
46. See Harrison 1991, pp. 133–34; Burkert 1985, p. 229.
47. Quoted in Scullard 1981, p. 84.
48. *Fasti* 3.97–98.
49. Ovid, *Fasti* 2.19–34; Harrison 1991, pp. 50–51.
50. Scullard 1981, p. 75; James 1961, p. 174.
51. Scullard 1981, p. 76; James 1961, p. 180. The tradition that Gelasius sup-pressed it has been persuasively challenged. See discussions in Chap. 4, pp. 61–62, Green 1931, and Holleman 1974.
52. Scullard 1981, p. 76.
53. See Scullard 1981, pp. 81–82.
54. Scullard 1981, p. 86.
55. Scullard 1981, p. 87.
56. Hutton 1996, p. 3.
57. Hutton 1996, p. 3. The January 1 holiday is now named the Solemnity of Mary, Mother of God.
58. See discussion in Hutton 1996, p. 49.
59. Harrowven 1996, p. 176.
60. As quoted in Hutton 1996, p. 47.
61. Harrowven 1996, p. 176.
62. Some psychological aspects of this opportunity are discussed at the end of the chapters on Easter and Christmas, and should be considered in connection with New Year's as well.

CHAPTER 3

1. Hutton 1996, p. 134.
2. Hutton 1996, p. 145; Aveni 2003, p. 38.
3. See descriptions in Hutton 1996, pp. 135–38.
4. Danaher 1972, pp. 13–14.
5. Lk 2:22–24, discussed in Chap. 11, pp. 196–97, 224–25. Luke does not specify 40 days but this is the period prescribed by Leviticus 12:2–4 in the case of a male child, which law they were following.
6. When the feast began in the Eastern Mediterranean, the Feast of the Nativity (later Christmas) was on January 6, so the Feast of the Presentation fell on February 14. After the date of Christmas became December 25, the Feast of the Presentation was correspondingly moved to February 2, by Emperor Justinian in 542. In the West it was always on February 2, but became associated with the purification of the Virgin only in the seventh century. James 1961, p. 232.
7. Lk 2:32.
8. Danaher 1972, p. 38.
9. Hutton 1996, p. 140 (speaking of northern Europe).
10. See Aveni 2003, p. 35; Yoder 2003, pp. 49–50.
11. Hutton 1996, p. 143; Aveni 2003, p. 35.
12. Hutton 1996, p. 143.
13. See further Dames 1992, pp. 252–54.
14. Aveni 2003, p. 38.
15. Carpenter 1946, pp. 112–56; Leach 1972, p. 124; see Yoder 2003, pp. 53–54 (quoting Carpenter).
16. This was Linnaeus's 1758 classification name. The modern name is *marmota monax*. *Arctomys* comes from the Greek words *arktos*, meaning bear, and *mys*, meaning mouse. *Arctos* also yields "arctic," because of the extreme North's association with bears, hence also *Ursa Major* and *Ursa Minor* ("Great Bear" and "Little Bear") as our most northerly (polar) constellations.
17. Campbell 2015, p. 127.
18. See generally Shepard and Sanders 1985, who treat this in detail.
19. Becker 1992, p. 37.
20. Edwards 2014; Shepard and Sanders 1985, p. 102.
21. Eliade 1978b, p. 29.
22. Edwards 2014.
23. Jung 1959d, p. 187; Jung 1969d, p. 226.
24. Jung 1953, pp. 178–79 and fig. 90; Shepard and Sanders 1985, p. 103.
25. Ronnberg 2010, p. 272.
26. Ronnberg 2010, p. 272.
27. Shepard and Sanders 1985, p. 137.

28. *Moral Epistles,* Epistle 41.3, as quoted in Ustinova 2009, p. 32.
29. See generally Ustinova 2009.
30. Ustinova 2009, pp. 2, 256.
31. Ustinova 2009, p. 239.
32. Ustinova 2009, p. 158.
33. Ustinova 2009, p. 189.
34. Shepard and Sanders 1985, pp. 104–07.
35. Herodotus, *Histories* 4.94–96; Strabo, *Geography* 7.3.5. See discussions in Eliade 1978b and Carpenter 1946, pp. 112–16.
36. Carpenter 1946, p. 114.
37. Carpenter 1946, p. 115.
38. Herodotus, *Histories* 4.94. In this context, Herodotus describes a human sacrifice ritual practiced every four years, in which a person was told messages (wishes) to be given to Zalmoxis and then sacrificed so he could convey these messages (since he didn't really die). Strabo, writing some half a millennium later, does not mention this rite, so perhaps it had been abandoned by then. See Carpenter 1946, p. 113.
39. Strabo, *Geography* 7.3.5; Carpenter 1946, p. 115.
40. Ustinova 2009, pp. 91–92.
41. Pausanias, *Description of Greece* 9.39.
42. The story is told in Plutarch, *On the Daimon of Socrates* 590B-592F.
43. Philostratus, *The Life of Apollonius of Tyana* 8.19.
44. Eliade 1978b, p. 27.
45. Diogenes Laertius, *Lives of the Eminent Philosophers* 109; Carpenter 1946, pp. 132–33.
46. Porphyry, *Life of Pythagoras* 8.3.
47. Eliade 1978b, p. 26.
48. Shepard and Sanders 1985, p. 131.
49. *Life of Constantine* 3.43.

Chapter 4

1. Harrison 1991, p. 630.
2. Lines 116–23.
3. *Elegiac Poems* 1275–78, as translated in Harrison 1991, p. 633.
4. Harrison 1991, pp. 633–35.
5. 178b.
6. 211e–212a.
7. Harrison 1991, pp. 640–45.
8. Kelly 1986, pp. 48–50; *OCT,* p. 77.

9. Kelly 1986, p. 50; *OCT*, p. 77. See also comparison in Oruch 1981, pp. 536–38;
10. Oruch 1981, p. 538.
11. Kelly 1986, pp. 49–50, about Valentine of Rome. In another account, it was Valentine of Terni who cured a boy (probably of epilepsy), the family converted, and the Roman authorities then executed him. Oruch 1981, pp. 537–38.
12. Travers 2006, 1:55.
13. In fact, the prohibition seems not to have originated with Claudius, since he attempted to mitigate it. Campbell 1978, p. 153.
14. This story is retold, e.g., in Aveni 2003, p. 40.
15. Oruch 1981, p. 565.
16. Lines 386–90.
17. Kelly 1986; Oruch 1981.
18. Oruch 1981, p. 550
19. Available in Scattergood, V.J., "*The Boke of Cupide* – An Edition," *English Philological Studies* 9:47–83 (1965).
20. Oruch 1981, p. 559.
21. As modernized from original text quoted in Oruch 1981, p. 560.
22. Kelly 1986, pp. 49–50, 59.
23. Green 1931, p. 60. In the Western empire, a date of February 15 for the feast of the Presentation of the Virgin Mary would be impossible, because 40 days after Christmas (December 25 in the West) was February 2, as discussed in Chap. 3. See Oruch 1981, pp. 540–41.
24. See, e.g., description in Santino 1994, p. 70, claiming that in the Lupercalia male youths drew the names of girls from a box and then would escort them, and that this is the antecedent of the exchange of love notes on Valentine's Day.
25. Kelly 1986, pp. 59–62; Oruch 1981, p. 539–40; Green 1931.
26. Originally, the Lupercalia was a festival of purification and fertility in preparation for the coming of spring, the purification element being carried out through sacrifices. The part relating to human fertility involved noble youths *(luperci)* scantily dressed in goatskins (thus operating as *Fauni)* running around the Palatine carrying *februa* (goat leather straps). Females desiring to conceive would line the route and hold their hands out to be slapped by the *februa* by the *luperci* as they ran by. But there is no evidence that this fertility ritual evolved into matchmaking, romance, love notes, etc. Pagan worship became illegal in 382 CE, after which at least officially the holiday lost its pagan religious function. By the time of Pope Gelasius, the holiday ritual had deteriorated and changed such that the fertility element had been lost. Rather, by that time the ritual entailed women being flogged in the nude (or by at least with exposed backs) for sexual sin. There were still runners, but they were no longer nobles and were not involved in the flogging itself; rather, they ran around singing about the scandals for which the women were being

punished. This was thus a ritual of purification. It ran directly *against* encouraging lovemaking and, hence, human fertility in the cases at hand. See Holleman 1974; see also Green 1931, pp. 62–69.

27. *OCT*, p. 80, noting that Gelasius attempted to have it suppressed, but that the Senate refused to comply, arguing that it was a harmless ancient custom with no (longer) any pagan religious overtones.

28. E.g., Aveni 2003, p. 39–40; Santino 1994, p. 70.

29. Travers 2006, 1:56. He wrote the letter shortly before leaving England for America.

30. Travers 2006, 1:57.

31. Alternatively, when red and white are combined, red can symbolize the man and white the woman. Becker 1992, p. 329.

32. Santino 1994, p. 67.

33. See discussion in Santino 1994, p. 73.

CHAPTER 5

1. As in the original Kronia festival in Ancient Greece (covered immediately below). Burkert 1985, p. 231; Frazer 1996, p. 328. Also, in ancient Persia, at the Sacaea festival a condemned prisoner was made mock king for five days and could do what he wanted; even to lie with the real king's concubines, precisely because he was going to be killed. Frazer 1996, p. 328; *OCD*, p. 942.

2. As told in York 1986, p. 231.

3. Burkert 1985, pp. 231–32.

4. Harrison 1991, p. 110.

5. Since this year was shorter than the actual solar year, the calendar would quickly get out of sync relative to the seasons unless adjustments were made from time to time. The Romans made the adjustment by inserting an extra intercalary ("leap") month called Mercedinus into the calendar when necessary. This intercalation was accomplished by splitting February into two parts: The intercalary month was inserted after February 23, and February's epagomenal days were added onto Mercedinus as the last days of that month. In such a case, the two epagomenal holidays, the Regifugium normally on February 24th and the Equirria normally on the 27th, now were moved to near the end of Mercedinus so as to still occur on the requisite number of days before March 1 (e.g., the Regifugium being the sixth day before, counting inclusively as was the custom then). See Scullard 1981, p. 81, using the Regifugium as the example.

6. York 1986, p. 18.

7. Intercalation is the addition of a week or month. Epagomenal days are added days which together do not constitute up a week or month.

8. York 1986, p. 17.

9. Scullard 1981, p. 81; Frazer 1996, p. 182.
10. York 1986, p. 235.
11. During the Republic, since there was no longer a king and Rome was much larger, such a hiatus grew impractical and was compromised, and the status of each of these days became varied. February 25th and 28th were *dies comitiales* in which popular assemblies *(comitia)* could meet, and the 26th was a hybrid day in which the morning was reserved for religious rituals and the rest of the day was ordinary. The 24th was the Regifugium, designated as *nefasti*, meaning that court proceedings and meetings of *comitia* were banned but other business was apparently permitted. The Equirria on the 27th was a full public holiday of rest and recreation. See York 1986, pp. 7–14 and Table for February calendar between pp. 48 and 49; Scullard 1981, pp. 44–45.
12. Aveni 2003, p. 74.
13. Scullard 1981, p. 82.
14. Scullard 1981, p. 82.
15. York 1986, p. 238.
16. Virgil, *Aeneid* 8.320–25.
17. Virgil, *Aeneid* 8,320–30; Frazer 1996, pp. 676, 679.
18. Scullard 1981, p. 207.
19. Harrowven 1996, p. 10.
20. *OCY,* p. 603.
21. Santino 1994, p. 87.

CHAPTER 6

1. Watts 1950, p. 21.
2. E.g., Jn 1:29, 36–37; 1 Pet 1:19. In John, Christ dies while the paschal lambs for the feast are being slaughtered. The analogy is driven home by the fact that Jesus's legs are not broken on the cross as is usual, because he is already dead (Jn 19:32–33), which is symbolically important because the Law forbids breaking the bones of the paschal lamb. Exod 12:46; Num 9:12.
3. E.g., *Odyssey* 12.8; *Iliad* 24.776.
4. We still encounter claims that Easter derives from Ishtar, the Mesopotamian goddess. This claim is nonsense on both etymological and historical grounds.
5. Bede 2012, p. 54.
6. Ganz 2008, p. 38; GardenStone 2015, p. 25.
7. See description of these writings in GardenStone 2015, pp. 42–72.
8. Karl Georg Friedrich Goes, *The decline of public cult in the Middle Ages* (Sulzbach, Germany, 1820), as quoted in GardenStone 2015, p. 60.
9. Quoted in Shaw 2011, pp. 51–52.

10. Shaw 2011, pp. 52, 69.
11. See discussion in Newall 1971, pp. 384–86; Hutton 1996, p. 180.
12. Hutton 1996, p. 180.
13. Hutton 1996, p. 180.
14. Shaw 2011, pp. 52, 61.
15. Shaw 2011, p. 61; GardenStone 2015, pp. 29–31.
16. See the descriptions in GardenStone 2015, pp. 40–71. These include: the Ostara rune stone (pp. 40–41); Ostara sanctuary near Osterholz (p. 43); temple of Ostara (46); grove of Ostara at Osterode (p. 49); veneration of Ostara at the Externsteine stone formation (p. 51); an idol of Ostara (p. 57); a sacred stone at Elstra (p. 59); and the Oster stone altar at Blankenburg (pp. 60–62).
17. GardenStone 2015, pp. 62–70, including the Corvey field blessing (pp. 62–70) and the Aecerbot Ritual with which it appears to be related (pp. 67–70); and the Oster stone and field name at Gambach (pp. 70–71).
18. Shaw 2011, pp. 58–61, 64; GardenStone 2015, pp. 72–74.
19. Shaw 2011, p. 69.
20. Shaw 2011, p. 69.
21. For background information on Q, see Kloppenborg 1987 and 2000, and Mack 1993.
22. Mack 1995, p. 49. Regarding such stratification of Q see also Crossan 1991, p. 429; Kloppenborg 1987.
23. Mack 1995, p. 47.
24. Q 14:27, in Robinson et al. 2000, p. 454; also Mack 1993, p. 79.
25. Mack 1993, p. 139. See surrounding Q^1 text in Mack 1993, p. 99. Mack sees this as late Q^1 material prior to the stage of Q^2. Mack 1993, p. 138. Further, being crucified is used to describe one dying to one's former self. Paul's usage of the term "crucified" when referring to his old self, his travails, the flesh, and the world has this kind of idiomatic connotation. E.g., Rom 6:6; 1 Cor 1:13; Gal 2:19; 5:24; 6:14.
26. See comparable statements in Mark 8:34, Matthew 10:38 and 16:24, and Luke 9:23 and 14:27, where the evangelists are presumably alluding to the crucifixion.
27. Kloppenborg 2000, pp. 420–32; Mack 2001, pp. 41–56; Mack 1993, pp. 45–46; Mack 1988, pp. 183–84. The Cynics were popular philosophers who had countercultural ideas and lifestyles, and propounded their ideas through witty and ironic stories, pronouncements, and argumentation, and expressed their ideas by their simple lifestyle. They operated as individuals and formed no organized school, whereas the Q people formed a social and religious group that produced the Q document. For more detail see Kloppenborg and Mack above.
28. Mack 1993 and 1995.

29. This earliest information is from Paul in his letter to the Galatians.
30. Mack 1988.
31. Mack 1995, p. 75.
32. Mack 1995, pp. 78–82, 140, 158.
33. Mack 1995, p. 89.
34. Paul in Philippians 2:6–11 utilizes an earlier hymn of praise to Christ that mentions Christ's death on a cross, but most scholars agree that this detail was added by Paul. Mack 1995, p. 92. The hymn does not otherwise mention anything in the Easter story.
35. Q 22:28, 30, in Robinson et al. 2000, pp. 558–60; also Mack 1993, p. 102.
36. The above summary follows that in Mack 1988.
37. E.g., Aslan 2013, pp. 153–54; Ehrman 1999, pp. 215, 220–22.
38. Mk 15:27; Mt. 27:38.The term *lestēs*, often translated as "bandit," also refers to a violent revolutionary insurrectionist (guerrilla). *BDAG*, p. 594. See, e.g., references in Mt 26:55; Mk 14:48; and Lk 22:52. The charge of sedition (treason) for which Rome convicted him suggests that the Romans viewed him as such.
39. Mk 15:7; Lk 23:19.
40. E.g., Brandon 1967.
41. Late in the twentieth century, various non-apocalyptic interpretations of the historical Jesus emerged, for example that he was a revolutionary (Brandon 1967), a magician (Smith 1978), a proto-Marxist (Horsley 1987), a proto-feminist (Schüssler-Fiorenze 1994), or, as already discussed above (p. 74), like a Cynic popular philosopher and sage. In contrast to the Gospel of Mark, which portrays an apocalyptic Jesus, the evidence from the earliest Palestinian Jesus movements, especially but not limited to Q^1, does not seem to evidence an apocalyptic Jesus. Space does not allow me to discuss here the complex issues involved. For a general introduction see the exchanges of views in Miller 2001 and in Beilby and Eddy 2009. For apocalypticist viewpoints, see, e.g., Allison 1998; Ehrman 1999; Fredricksen 1999; and Aslan 2013. Burton Mack best elaborates the case for a non-apocalyptic Jesus based on Q^1, and argues that the figure of an apocalyptic Jesus emerged probably in the 50s CE. See Mack 1988, 1993, and 1995.
42. Ehrman 1999, p. x.
43. Mt 19:28; Lk 22:29–30; see Ehrman 1999, pp. 186–87.
44. Mack 1995, p. 109.
45. Mack 1995, pp. 109–12.
46. Aslan 2013, p. 150.
47. Ehrman 2014, pp. 214–15.
48. Nickelsburg 1980; *ABD* 5:172–73. For further discussion of this model in the context of the passion, see Crossan 1991, pp. 384–91, and Mack 1988, 106–8, 265–68.
49. In *NOAB*, pp. 1548–51.

50. The Wisdom of Solomon is particularly important because it is a Hellenistic form of the wisdom tale, probably written in Antioch, where the idea of Jesus's martyrdom (crucifixion) and resurrection may have first arisen. See Mack 1988, p. 110 n. 9.
51. *HBD,* p. 703 (entry for Mordecai).
52. Nickelsburg 1980; Mack 1988, pp. 106–07, 265–68; *ABD* 5:172–77.
53. *NOAB,* note to 49:3; Ehrman 1999, p. 236. Thus, Nickelsburg does not include the suffering servant among the stories that fit his template. See Nickelsburg 1980, pp. 158–59.
54. Ehrman 1999, p. 236.
55. Mk 11:2, 4, 7; Lk 19:30–33, 35; Jn 12:14.
56. His confusion may have come from the Septuagint translation of Zechariah 9:9, which disrupts the original parallelism and indeed refers to "a donkey and a young colt [*upozugion kai polon neon*]." But this did not confuse the other evangelists.
57. As with Isaiah 53 discussed above.
58. E.g., the language quoted in Luke 11:49 does not exist in any known text. *NOAB,* note to 11:49; Elliott 1982, p. 67. In Luke 24:27 Jesus is said to interpret scriptures to this effect, but none is specified. So does Paul in 1 Corinthians 15:4, but again nothing is specified; this appears simply to be a recitation of an early creed.
59. Sanders 1993, p. 260; Ehrman 1999, pp. 212–13.
60. Mk 11:17; Mt. 22:21; Lk 20:25; Gospel of Thomas 100. This saying appears to be authentic, but its original context is uncertain.
61. Sanders 1993, p. 273.
62. *Pro Rabirio Postuma,* 5.16.
63. In the Eden story humans (represented by Adam and Eve) were never cursed, only the ground was. Their transgression was never called a sin; the first sin was by Cain. The transgression was due to a chaotic aspect of human nature that we had at from time of our creation in the garden. This is the standard Jewish doctrine accounting for the origin and nature of sin, called the *yezer hara* ("impulse to evil"). Thus, our sinful nature was not the *result* of the transgression in the garden, but was the *cause* of the transgression in the first place. According to the Hebrew Bible, the way to deal with this aspect of our nature was by applying the knowledge of good and evil acquired in the garden of Eden to control that nature. This was also a purpose of the Law. Adam and Eve did not have this knowledge as of when they transgressed; rather, they were in the position of minors who lack legal capacity, and thus at the time were incapable of sin. See George and George 2014, pp. 246–74.
64. Ehrman 2012, p. 215.
65. Litwa 2014, p. 20.

66. Litwa 2014, p. 173.
67. *First Apology*, 21.
68. In Christian times, the Dioscuri were superseded by the pair of Jesus Christ and his "twin," Judas Thomas. Barnard 1997, p. 153.
69. *First Apology* 54.
70. *Against Celsus* 2:55.
71. MacDonald 2000, 2014, and 2015.
72. Miller 2015, p. 162.
73. The standard discussion of the noble death concept as applied to Christ is Seeley 1990. Shorter discussions can be found in Mack 1988, pp. 106–08, and Mack 1995, pp. 80, 140, 158.
74. Genesis Rabbah 100.7; Leviticus Rabbah 18.1. See Raphael 2019, p. 110. Alternatively seven days.
75. Mettinger 2001, p. 214.
76. *NOAB*, note to Hosea 6:2.
77. The movements of the sun around the winter solstice (on December 22–25), may also be relevant, because the rising and setting sun visibly stops moving south for three days, and then on December 25th begins moving north again, marking the definitive return of the sun and the promise of spring, and giving cause for celebration, and mythmaking. On the spring equinox, the sun finally overcomes darkness, as the days are now longer than the nights.
78. Cashford 2002, pp. 130, 244.
79. He dies on the 17th day of the month and is found again on the 19th of the same month. *Isis and Osiris* 13C, 39F.
80. Mettinger 2001, p. 214.
81. *CCC*, 632.
82. Leeming 2005, pp. 98–99.
83. Apollodorus, *Library* 3.5.3; Pausanias, *Description of Greece* 2.31.2.
84. E.g., Ehrman 2014, p. 213; Elliott 1982, p. 90; Charlesworth et al. 2006, p. 225.
85. Nickelsburg 1980, p. 175.
86. Miller 2010, pp. 761–66 lists over 20 examples; Miller 2015 lists 77.
87. The classic description of this standard cycle is in Campbell 1949.
88. Miller 2015, p. 35.
89. Ehrman 2014, p. 186.
90. Vermes 2008, xvi, 9, 30.
91. Ehrman 2014, p. 176.
92. *ABD*, 5:691.; Ehrman 2014, pp. 168–69. This logic would not apply in the case of Matthew's Gospel, however, because in it the angel rolls the stone aside only to reveal a tomb that is already empty (Mt 28:2). Also, in John 20:19–20, 26 the resurrected Christ walks through a door or wall.
93. Apollodorus, *Library* 2.5.12; Graves 1960, p. 516 (134.d).

94. Hengel 1977, p. 87; Ehrman 2014, pp. 157–58.
95. Crossan 1994, ch. 6.
96. Philo, *Flaccus* 83. See discussions in Ehrman 2014, pp. 158–59, and Crossan 1994, p. 159.
97. Ehrman 2014, pp. 156–68.
98. Keener 2003, 2:1182.
99. Miller 2015, pp. 39, 76.
100. Miller 2010.
101. The classic study on cognitive dissonance reduction is Festinger 1957.
102. Dein 2001; Komarnitsky 2014. Dein had infiltrated the movement and thus was able to follow and report on the developments from the inside.
103. Festinger et al. 1956. These three social psychologists had infiltrated the movement and so were able to follow and report the developments from the inside.
104. Jung 1969b, p. 121.
105. Miller 2010, p. 774. For Romulus, see below pp. 104–6. The Senator Livius Geminus was said to have seen both the resurrected emperor Claudius on the Via Appia, and the resurrected Drusilla, sister of Gaius, who was consecrated as Panthea. Seneca, *Apocolocyntosis* 1. The body of Aristeas supposedly disappeared right after he died, and he later reappeared and wrote a poem before disappearing for good. Herodotus, *Histories* 4.14.
106. Thompson 1955–58. Motif A192 is "Death or departure of the gods." Motif A193 is "Resurrection of gods." Motif A192.3 is "Expected return of deity." A580 is "Culture hero's (divinity's) expected return. Divinity or hero is expected to return at the proper time and rescue his people from their misfortunes." Interestingly, the combination of dying and rising is not a separate motif, perhaps reflecting the scholarly debate.
107. Frazer 1935, 4.1: 256. For examples of such claims and discussion, see Doherty 2013, pp. 167–73; Price 2011, pp. 18, 44–46, 391, 401–2; Ehrman 2012, pp. 221–30. In order to shore up that theory, some of its more recent proponents have shifted the ground, and argue that the dying-and-rising gods evolved into initiation-based mystery cults, point to Christianity's connection with mystery cults, and on that basis claim an ultimate connection between Christianity and the old dying-and-rising god myths. E.g., Price 2011, pp. 44, 402. There are indeed correspondences between early Christianity and such Greco-Roman mystery cults, but there is no need to invoke the old agricultural myths. Discussion of any relationships between such myths and mystery cults would take us well beyond the scope of this book.
108. Smith 2005; Rudolph 2005; Smith 1998.
109. *NOAB*, note to verse 8:1.
110. Smith 1990, pp. 112–13.

111. Mettinger 2001, pp. 172–75.
112. When the notion that Christ had resurrected first developed, the higher christological ideas of him being a divinity since the beginning of time (as in the Gospel of John) or as of his conception (as in the infancy stories in Matthew and Luke) had not yet developed. Rather, he was exalted and became divine upon his resurrection. See Ehrman 2014.
113. Teeter 2011, pp. 58–66.
114. Aslan 2013, p. 165.
115. E.g., 2 Mac 7:1–41, and the apocryphal Testament of Judah 25:4, in Charlesworth 1983, 1:802. See generally Vermes 2008, pp. 29–38.
116. Acts 23:8, thus according to Luke; *ABD*, 5:688. For discussion see Vermes 2008, pp. 45–48.
117. E.g., Mt 22:23–33; Mk 12:18–27; Lk 14:14; 20:27–40); likewise St. Paul (e.g., 1 Cor 15:12–35) and other apostles (e.g., Acts 4:2).
118. Beard et al. 1998, 1:384–88. Note, however, that Mithras seems not to have died. Originally in Asia Minor, Attis may not have been a dying god, but he was so in the ritual in Rome.
119. The Hilaria festival is discussed in more detail in Chap. 7, pp. 122–23.
120. Watts 1950, pp. 61–62.
121. Jung 1959a, p. 117 (describing in that case Osiris).
122. Jung 1969a.
123. E.g., Frankfort 1951, pp. 20–22.
124. Ovid, *Metamorphoses* 14.808–22; Livy, *History of Rome* 1.16; Plutarch, *Romulus* 26.27.
125. See discussion in MacDonald 2015, pp. 135–38.
126. Litwa 2014, p. 166.
127. Plutarch, *Romulus* 27.6–7; Ovid, *Fasti* 4.492–96. While such dark cosmic phenomena are normally symbolic of death, it is not entirely clear whether Romulus died and immediately resurrected or was simply taken up and turned divine. See Litwa 2014, pp. 172.
128. Livy, *History of Rome* 1.16.
129. Plutarch, *Romulus* 27.5–6; Diodorus of Halicarnassus, *Roman Histories* 2.63.3–4.
130. Plutarch, *Romulus* 27.8.
131. Dionysus of Halicarnassus, *Roman Histories* 2.56.5; Plutarch, *Romulus* 29.2; Miller 2010, p. 768.
132. Miller 2010, p. 768.
133. Plutarch, *Romulus* 27.7–8; Ovid, *Metamorphoses* 14.808–28; Litwa 2014, p. 168.
134. Plutarch, *Romulus* 28.1–3. In Ovid's *Fasti* 2.499–505, Proculus also encounters Romulus while traveling on the road.

135. Another example is Livius Geminus claiming to see the postmortem Claudius on the Via Appia. Miller 2015, pp. 74–75.
136. Plutarch, *Romulus* 28.2. In Ovid's *Fasti* 2.505–09, he gives orders.
137. Plutarch, *Romulus* 28.7; Acts 1:9.
138. Litwa 2014, p. 164, 166–67. For Romulus's case, see Livy, *History of Rome* 1.16.
139. Plutarch, *Romulus* 28.4–6.
140. *Apology* 21.23.
141. Actually the practice started with Julius Caesar, who was dictator but not technically an emperor.
142. Ehrman 2014, p. 49.
143. I am not arguing that this is the only reason for this evolution in Christology; there were others.
144. See generally Ehrman 2014, particularly pp. 236–37.
145. James 1961, p. 216.
146. See James 1961, p. 216; Frazer 1996, pp. 705–15.
147. See examples listed in Frazer 1996, p. 711.
148. Frazer 1996, pp. 713–14.
149. Frazer 1996, p. 714.
150. James 1961, p. 216.
151. Gimbutas 1989, p. 213.
152. Eliade 1996, p. 415; Chevalier and Gheerbrant 1996, p. 340.
153. Chevalier and Gheerbrant 1996, p. 338.
154. 1:233–40.
155. Ronnberg 2010, p. 14.; Chevalier and Gheerbrant 1996, p. 339.
156. Eliade 1996, p. 414.
157. Newall 1967, p. 14.
158. Eliade 1996, pp. 414–15.
159. Gimbutas 1989, p. 218 (with illustrations).
160. Newall 1967, p. 20.
161. See Newall 1967, pp. 22–23.
162. Morrill 2006, p. 119.
163. Newall 1971, pp. 177–206 (giving numerous examples).
164. Newall 1967, p. 13.
165. Newall 1967, p. 23.
166. Newall 1967, p. 8.
167. Cooper 1992, p. 121.
168. Ferguson 1954, p. 20.
169. Cross 2004, p. 100.
170. Watts 1950, p. 105–6.
171. Harrowven 1996, p. 39.
172. Morrill 2006, pp. 123–24.

173. Morrill 2006, pp. 121–22.
174. Jung 1976a, pp. 193–94.
175. See Corbett 1996; Jung 1959a, 1959c, 1969a, and 1969c.
176. Jung 1969c, p. 429.
177. Jung 1969c.
178. Jung 1969c, p. 372.
179. Jung 1969c. As explained in my earlier book, *The Mythology of Eden,* originally the Israelite God-image included a feminine element in the form of the goddess Asherah, who was Yahweh's wife. The official monotheist movement largely eliminated her, thus driving the feminine aspect of the God-image underground, into the unconscious. George and George 2014, pp. 41–80, 215–37. The appearance of Sophia, and later Mary mother of Jesus, to some extent marks the reappearance of the feminine principle in the God-image.
180. Jung 1969c, p. 391.
181. Quaternity symbols have a design incorporating the number four, such as in many mandalas, and the cross. A quaternity (e.g., the four directions of the compass) represents totality, integration, and wholeness.
182. Jung 1969a, pp. 419–29.
183. Jung 1959a, pp. 119–20, 138–39; Jung 1969c, p. 429.
184. Jung 1959a, pp. 119–20, 139.
185. Campbell 2015, pp. 149–69.
186. Jung 1976b, p. 694.
187. Jung 1976a, p. 179; Jung 1959a, pp. 141–42.
188. Jung 1959a, p. 142; Jung 1976b, p. 695.
189. Jung 1959a, p. 121.
190. Jung 1976b, p. 695.
191. Jung 1969a.
192. Cf. 1 Tim 2:5 ("there is also one mediator between God and humankind, Jesus Christ").
193. Corbett 1996, pp. 128–30; Jung 1969c.
194. Jung 1969b, p. 157.
195. As translated in Barnstone and Meyer 2009, pp. 44–45. The final line appears only in one manuscript, the Greek Papyrus Oxyrhnchus 654, but I have included it here because from the psychological perspective it provides a logical closure to the process being described. From the psychological standpoint, "rule" would be self-mastery, and "rest" would be the integrated state of the psyche, both of which come after the suffering ("trouble") has run its course.
196. As quoted in Corbett 1996, p. 134.
197. Jung 1976b, pp. 694–95.

198. Edinger 1992, pp. 135–38, listing many examples from Matthew. There are many more from the other canonical Gospels.
199. Saying 70, as translated in Barnstone and Meyer 2009, p. 62.
200. Edinger 1992, pp. 135, 143
201. Watts 1950, p. 65.
202. See Miller 2015, pp. 94–96, 123, 130–2 (regarding the need to mythologize the historical Jesus, though not necessarily from the perspective of depth psychology).
203. Jung 1959a; Dundes 1990. See also discussion in Chap. 11, pp. 201–4.
204. Litwa 2014, pp. 169–70.
205. Wilson 1990, 1:224–25.
206. Campbell 2001, pp. 111–12.
207. Campbell 1964, p. 114.
208. In one example, neuroscientists compared meditation by Tibetan Buddhist monks with Franciscan nuns doing meditative centering prayers. The neuroscientists found that the brain patterns of the two groups were essentially the same, except that in the case of the nuns their language centers were slightly activated because their meditative prayer involved muttering some words at the outset about opening themselves to God's presence. The only real difference between the two groups, not neurological in nature, was in their *interpretation* of what was happening. The nuns thought they were in communion with God, while the Buddhists thought of it as joining universal consciousness. See Newberg and d'Aquili 2001, pp. 6–8.
209. Lane 1974, p. 575 n. 79.

CHAPTER 7

1. Hutton 1996, p. 237.
2. Originally, in Asia Minor, Attis seems not to have been a rising (resurrecting) god. See Mettinger 2001, pp. 157–59.
3. *Fasti* 5.195–228.
4. *Georgics* 2.330–1.
5. Matthews 2001, pp. 47–48; Frazer 1996, pp. 145–51.
6. Hutton 1996, p. 233.
7. Hutton 1996, p. 225.
8. Kirk et al. 2007, pp. 197–203; Cirlot 1971, p. 105.

9. The Roman references to Pales are inconsistent and confusing, so it is not entirely clear whether Pales is male, female, two deities, or male and female (androgynous). See Scullard 1981, p. 104.
10. *Fasti* 4.721–807. See also the description in Scullard 1981, pp. 104–5.
11. Hutton 1996, p. 224.
12. For further details on tree mythology, see George and George 2014, pp. 139–76.
13. Hutton 1996, pp. 233–34.
14. Malory 1969, pp. 427–28 (Book XIX, chs. 1–2).
15. Eliade 1996, pp. 312–13.
16. Hutton 1996, p. 235.
17. National Conference of Catholic Bishops 1991, pp. 459–77.
18. Full text available at https://en.wikipedia.org/wiki/Bring_Flowers_of_the_ Rarest, last accessed December 24, 2019.
19. *Ad Caeli Reginam, Encyclical of Pope Pius XII on Proclaiming the Queenship of Mary.* Available on the Vatican website at: http://w2.vatican.va/content/ pius-xii/en/encyclicals/documents/hf_p-xii_enc_11101954_ad-caeli-regi- nam.html, last accessed December 24, 2019.
20. National Conference of Catholic Bishops 1991, pp. 454–55.
21. National Conference of Catholic Bishops 1991, pp. 458, 474. Use of this epithet apparently serves the idea of Christ as the second Adam.
22. Gen 3:20. For a discussion of the earlier mythical background to this epithet and of Eve as a goddess figure, see George and George 2014, pp. 224–28.
23. National Conference of Catholic Bishops 1991, p. 471.
24. National Conference of Catholic Bishops 1991, p. 454.
25. https://www.catholicculture.org/culture/liturgicalyear/overviews/ months/05_1.cfm, last accessed December 24, 2019. Pope Pius VII granted a partial indulgence in 1815, and Pius IX granted a plenary indulgence in 1859. As a result of the Church's wholesale revision of indulgences in 1966, this Maytime Marian veneration no longer carries an indulgence.
26. See Jung 1959b, pp. 81–82.
27. Session 25, Second Decree, *On the Invocation, Veneration, and Relics of Saints, and on Sacred Images,* available at www.thecounciloftrent.com/ch25. htm, last accessed December 24, 2019. The Council said this by way of clari- fying that the images themselves are not holy, as if any divinity resides within them, but rather that they are representative of a prototype. My point here is that, to a modern mythologist, the Council's statement also calls attention to the common archetypal aspects of Mary and the goddesses in relation to the coming of spring and summer discussed in this chapter.

CHAPTER 8

1. George and George 2003, pp. 447–48.
2. Documented, for example, in Raphael 2014. For instance, Revere was only one of many riders, and he never shouted, "The British are coming!" because his mission depended on secrecy and he was riding through an area full of British loyalists. And contrary to tradition, there is no evidence that Samuel Adams instigated the Boston Tea Party (although he immediately supported it after the fact), and only a few of the participants were dressed as Indians.
3. As our *official* motto it is relatively new, from an act of Congress in 1956 at the height of the Cold War, aimed at differentiating America from godless Communism. This was only two years after Congress had added "under God" to the Pledge of Allegiance for the same reasons. The earlier official motto, *E Pluribus Unum* ("from many one"), had been in place since 1792.
4. Fleming 1965, pp. 67–69 (regarding continents). Regarding individual countries, see the list in the Wikipedia article "National Personification" at https://en.wikipedia.org/wiki/National_personification, last accessed on December 24, 2019.
5. Higham 1990, p. 48.
6. Hieronimus and Cortner 2016, p. 87.
7. See Green 2010 and 2015.
8. Higham 1990, p. 46.
9. Hieronimus and Cortner 2016, pp. 150–51.
10. Higham 1990, pp. 52–55; Hieronimus and Cortner 2016, p. 61.
11. Hieronimus and Cortner 2016, p. 93.
12. Higham 1990, p. 59.
13. Hieronimus and Cortner 2016, p. 94.
14. Higham 1990, p. 59; Hieronimus and Cortner 2016, pp. 52–53.
15. Hieronimus and Cortner 2016, pp. 90–92.
16. Hieronimus and Cortner 2016, pp. 65–67, 94.
17. Higham 1990, p. 63; Hieronimus and Cortner 2016, p. 95.
18. Fox 1986, p. 6.
19. Higham 1990, p. 63; Hieronimus and Cortner 2016, pp. 106–7.
20. "Our Great Goddess and Her Coming Idol," *American Catholic Quarterly Review* 5:597 (no attributed author).
21. Hieronimus and Cortner 2016, pp. 174–208.
22. Hieronimus and Cortner 2016, p. 197.
23. See generally Green 2010 and 2015, refuting the "myth" that America as a polity has Christian foundations.

CHAPTER 9

1. Caesar, 6.14.
2. See, e.g., the many examples given in Tylor 2010, vol. 2, chs. 12–13.
3. Campbell, Joseph. "Trick or Treat," lecture delivered at Fountain Street Church, Grand Rapids, Michigan, on October 21, 1981, available at http://www.thedailybeast.com/articles/2014/10/31/joseph-campbell-on-the-roots-of-halloween.html, last accessed on December 24, 2019.
4. Harrison 1991, p. 36; James 1961, p. 141.
5. Harrison 1991, pp. 43–46. Pandora's "jar" was actually the same kind of urn *(pithos)*.
6. James 1961, p. 141. Harrison 1991, p. 35; Burkert 1985, 240.
7. *Fasti* 5.451–84.
8. *Fasti* 5.429–43; Aveni 2003, pp. 129–30.
9. Ovid, *Fasti* 5.485–90.
10. Scullard 1981, p. 75; James 1961, p. 174.
11. Described in Ovid, *Fasti* 2.572–82. See Scullard 1981, p. 75.
12. Ovid, *Fasti* 2.617–34; Scullard 1981, pp. 74–76; James 1961, pp. 174–75.
13. E.g., Bannatyne 1990, pp. 6–7; Kelley 1919, pp. 12–13.
14. Kelley 1919, p. 13, claims that the Pomona festival was on November 1, and that the Vertumnalia was on August 23.
15. 14.626–771.
16. Since Ovid's *Fasti* covers only January–June, it does not shed light on whether such festival existed.
17. Morton 2012, pp. 12, 17–18. No Pomona festival is mentioned in the leading modern scholarly work on Roman festivals, Scullard 1981, although Pomona herself is mentioned briefly (pp. 16, 28).
18. E.g., in Pakenham, J.A.G., "Pagan Rites and Christian Festivals," *The Canadian Monthly and National Review* 10:525–33, at p. 530 (July–December, 1876), and in the December 12, 1903, weekly issue of *The Churchman*, p. 751.
19. Morton 2012, pp. 17–18.
20. The passage in question (6.20–21) first describes certain festivals in August, and then in a separate sentence says that the Vertumnalia is observed "at that time" without further specifying a date. The sentence after that goes on to describe a festival in October, the Meditrinalia. The phrase "at that time" refers to August, but it is possible that some readers mistakenly thought it refers to October. See the Italian Wikipedia page on the Vertumnalia, at https://it.wikipedia.org/wiki/Vertumnalia, last accessed December 24, 2019. That article traces the mistake back to 1696 in book by Laurentius

Begerus, available at https://arachne.uni-koeln.de/Tei-Viewer/cgi-bin/
teiviewer.php?scan=BOOK-thesaurusbrandenburgicus03-0601_163496,
last accessed December 24, 2019.

21. See Aveni 2003, pp. 129–30.
22. Bede, 2012, p. 227 (523) (emphasis added).
23. See *NCE*, p. 289.
24. Bede 1990, 1:30, pp. 91–93 (emphasis added).
25. Hutton 1996, p. 364.
26. *NCE*, p. 289.
27. *NCE*, pp. 289–90.
28. *CCC*, 1031–1032.
29. *NCE*, p. 290.
30. Rogers 2002, p. 23.
31. Rogers 2002, p. 23.
32. Rom 12:4–13, 1 Cor 12:12–27.
33. See *CCC*, 956–58; Olson, Matthew, "Is it Biblical to Ask Saints to Pray for
    Us?," *Ignitum Today* (2013), at http://www.ignitumtoday.
    com/2013/09/15/its-biblical-to-ask-saints-to-pray-for-us/, last accessed
    December 24, 2019.
34. Hutton 1996, p. 371.
35. Hutton 1996, pp. 372–76.
36. Since Halloween came from Ireland, parts of Scotland, and to some extent
    Wales, all references to "Celts," as well as my use of the adjective "Celtic,"
    should be understood to be limited to these locations and do not include
    continental Europe. I do not purport to make any "pan-Celtic" statements.
37. See generally Cashford 2002, pp. 128–31.
38. MacLeod 2012, p. 97.
39. Koch 2006, 7:1556.
40. An apparent difference, in connection with the New Year being a repetition
    of the creation as told in myths (see Chap. 2), is that no Celtic creation
    myths have come down to us. But presumably they had at least one.
    Rolleston 1990, p. 94.
41. See, e.g., the Wikipedia article on Samhain, at https://en.wikipedia.org/
    wiki/Samhain.
42. Rogers 2002, p. 20; Markale 1999, p. 165.
43. Markale 1999, p. 166.
44. Monaghan 2008, p. 371.
45. Monaghan 2008, p. 371.
46. Markale 1999, p. 165.
47. Markale 1999, p. 165.
48. Markale 2000, p. 74.
49. Markale 2000, p. 63.
50. Quoted in Markale 2000, p. 64 (emphasis added).

51. Markale 2000, p. 68.
52. Markale 2000, pp. 36, 71.
53. Cunliffe 1997, p. 189.
54. Quoted in Markale 2000, p. 64.
55. Epithets listed in MacLeod 2012, p. 34.
56. Arguably, we are entitled to assume that this is the case based on evidence from other cultures across geography and time, but space limitations do not permit a discussion of this here.
57. Markale 2000, pp. 68, 118.
58. MacLeod 2012, pp. 412–13. The poets included, in ascending order of rank: bards, fili (in seven ranks), and the satirists. These jobs required years of training and demanded familiarity with altered states, and the best were thought to have the ability to "shape-shift" (change their form, such as into an animal). They could also prophesize and cast spells. MacLeod 2012, pp. 35–36, 187, 368.
59. Markale 2000, p. 64.
60. Markale 2000, p. 79.
61. Markale 1999, p. 165.
62. Hutton 1996, pp. 366–70.
63. Harrowven 1996, p. 85.
64. Aveni 2003, p. 127;
65. Rogers 2002, p. 12; Aveni 2003, p. 126; Harrowven 1996, p. 85.
66. Markale 2000, pp. 47, 95–96.
67. Becker 1992; pp. 112–13; Cirlot 1971, pp. 105–6; Ronnberg 2010, p. 84.
68. Jung 1967, p. 150 n. 77.
69. Markale 2000, pp. 51, 62, 107.
70. Monaghan 2008, pp. 107–8.
71. Markale 2000, pp. 45–47.
72. Markale 2000, pp. 44–45.
73. The tale is contained in full in Markale 1984, pp. 148–68 (quote on p. 168, my translation from French), and is summarized in Markale 2000, p. 123.
74. Rogers 2002, p. 19.
75. Markale 1999, p. 165. Ancient Greek mythology and practice gives some insight into why pigs are important. Pigs were featured at the Eleusinian Mysteries and at the Athenian Thesmophoria festival, also in connection with transformation. On the second day of the Eleusinian Mysteries the initiates carried piglets down to the sea, where they washed and sacrificed them as an act of purification. Bowden 2010, p. 33. The Thesmophoria was held among married women in honor of Demeter after the autumn sowing to ensure fertility of the crop. It commemorated Kore's (Persephone's) annual return to Demeter from Hades at this time of year, which ensured

fertility in the land. The women sacrificed piglets and then threw them into deep clefts in the earth; some of the women descended the clefts and brought up decayed piglet remains from the prior year, which were then mixed on altars with seeds, from which farmers would take and spread them on their fields to ensure germination of the crops. The role of pigs was explained by an etiological myth saying that the swineherd Euboleus was feeding his swine when and where Kore was abducted into Hades, and that his pigs also fell into that chasm in the earth after her. For further details, see Burkert 1985, pp. 242–46; Harrison 1991, pp. 120–31.

76. Davidson 1988, p. 48.
77. Monaghan 2008, p. 380.
78. Markale 1999, p. 110–11, 117; Cooper 1992, p. 234. According to the mythology, this was in the times before the Tuatha were defeated by the Gaels and retreated to the Otherworld.
79. Davidson 1988, p. 46.
80. Markale 2000, pp. 26–27.
81. Davidson 1988, p. 48.
82. Davidson 1988, p. 48 and Plate 2c.
83. Koch 2006, 1:358–60.
84. MacCana 1970, p. 58; Markale 2000, pp. 43–44.
85. MacCana 1970, p. 76.
86. Markale 2000, p. 42.
87. Davidson 1988, p. 47; Markale 2000, p. 42. This is the prevailing interpretation of this image. The other principal interpretation is that it represents death by drowning, which appears in some Irish tales. For general discussion see Koch 2006, 3:854–57, with annotations.
88. Monaghan 2008, p. 407.
89. For more detail on these ideas, see the author's upcoming book *The Mythology of Wine,* and also his initial blog post on the mythology of wine, "The Mythology of Wine – A First Sip," July 31, 2018, at https://mythologymatters.wordpress.com/2018/07/31/the-mythology-of-wine-a-first-sip, last accessed December 24, 2019.
90. Hutton 1996, p. 380; Rogers 2002, p. 20; Markale 2000, pp. 54–63 (reenactments); Monaghan 2008, p. 407 (divination).
91. Markale 1999, p. 166; Markale 2000, pp. 54–63
92. Frazer 1935, 10:225–26.
93. Hutton 1996, p. 370; likewise Rogers 2002, p. 19.
94. E.g., MacLeod 2012, p. 174.
95. Rogers 2002, p. 31.
96. Hutton 1996, p. 362.
97. See, e.g., Hutton 1996, pp. 362–63.
98. Rogers 2002, p. 32.

99. Chevalier and Gheerbrant 1996, p. 380.
100. See Aveni 2003, p. 127; Harrowven 1996, p. 85.
101. Harrowven 1996, p. 86.
102. Hutton 1996, p. 369.
103. Rogers 2002, pp. 31–32; Hutton 1996, p. 380; Harrowven 1996, p. 86.
104. Rogers 2002, p. 29.
105. Rogers 2002, pp. 43–44.
106. Rogers 2002, p. 24.
107. Hutton 1996, p. 382.
108. Rogers 2002, p. 43.
109. Rogers 2002, p. 42.
110. Hutton 1996, p. 382.
111. Rogers 2002, p. 136.

CHAPTER 10

1. 237a–238b.
2. Gomes, Peter, Foreword to Baker 2009, p. ix.
3. Schweitzer 2005.
4. E.g., Arel, Dan, "Sorry Republicans But Jesus Was a Marxist," *Huffington Post*, December 3, 2014, available at https://www.huffingtonpost.com/dan-arel/sorry-republicans-but-jes_b_5916564.html,   last   accessed December 24, 2019.
5. E.g., Wright 2004.
6. E.g., Oestreicher, Paul, "Was Jesus Gay? Probably," *The Guardian*, April 20, 2012,   available   at   https://www.theguardian.com/commentisfree/belief/2012/apr/20/was-jesus-gay-probably,   last   accessed December 24, 2019.
7. Baker 2009, p. 17.
8. Baker 2009, p. 18.
9. Baker 2009, p. 22.
10. McKenzie 2013, p. 138.
11. Heath 1963, p. 82.
12. Heath 1963, p. 82.
13. Heath 1963.
14. McKenzie 2013, p. 32.
15. Heath 1963, p. 1 (emphasis added).
16. McKenzie 2013, p. 32.
17. Bradford 2006, p. 58.

18. Bradford 2006, p. 58. The first reports would have come to England aboard the ship *Fortune*, which arrived in Plymouth around the ninth of November, 1621, and left for England about two weeks later. Morton 1669, p. 47. This would have included the materials compiled for *Mourt's Relation*, but also must have included private correspondence.
19. Quoted in Baker 2009, p. 32.
20. Baker 2009, p. 16.
21. Baker 2009, pp. 26, 111, 176.
22. McKenzie 2013, pp. 141–44.
23. Baker 2009, pp. 23, 29.
24. Baker 2009, p. 37.
25. Grace and Bruchac 2001, p. 37.
26. Morton 1669, p. 43.
27. Heath 1963, pp. 58–62.
28. McKenzie 2013, pp. 136–37.
29. McKenzie 2013, p. 135.
30. McKenzie 2013, p. 137.
31. McKenzie 2013, pp. 137–38.
32. McKenzie 2013, p. 144. They were also thankful for the resolution of conflicts among certain of their ministers. Baker 2009, p. 28.
33. Baker 2009, pp. 10–11.
34. Heath 1963, p. 82.
35. Bradford 2006, p. 58.
36. Baker 2009, p. 30; McKenzie 2013, p. 149.
37. Baker 2009, pp. 29, 43–44.
38. McKenzie 2013, p. 161.
39. Baker 2009, pp. 34–35.
40. Baker 2009, p. 44.
41. McKenzie 2013, p. 149.
42. Baker 2009, p. 99.
43. McKenzie 2013, pp. 104–5, 118.
44. Baker 2009, pp. 33–34 & n. 2.
45. Baker 2009, p. 16.
46. Baker 2009, p. 70.
47. Baker 2009, pp. 70–71.
48. Gomes, Peter, Foreword to Baker 2009, p. x.
49. Baker 2009, pp. 62–63.
50. Baker 2009, p. 36.
51. McKenzie 2013, p. 161.
52. Baker 2009, p. 101.
53. McKenzie 2013, p. 128.
54. Austin 1889, pp. 280–86.

55. McKenzie 2013, pp. 160–63.
56. Baker 2009, pp. 99, 104. In England the groups of Puritans were called "Separatists" (short for "separating Puritans") because they had separated from the Church of England to establish their own congregations. Thus, to distinguish Separatists from Puritans is inaccurate. See McKenzie 2013, p. 49.
57. McKenzie 2013, pp. 154–57, 165.
58. Strauss, Valerie, "'Jingle Bells' – Written for Thanksgiving?", *Washington Post*, Dec. 24, 2013; see also https://www.snopes.com/fact-check/jingle-bells-thanksgiving-carol/, last accessed December 24, 2019.
59. Baker 2009, pp. 37–38.
60. McKenzie 2013, pp. 167–68. Regarding the Plymouth Colony's extensive regulation of business, see McKenzie 2013, pp. 113–17.
61. Dennis 2005, pp. 109–10.
62. McKenzie 2013, pp. 168–69. Nixon was wrong because the Pilgrims formed a tight collective with shared responsibilities. They were guided by the biblical concept of covenant, which emphasized shared responsibilities to the collective (family, church, civil community) over individual rights. McKenzie 2013, pp. 106–7.
63. Baker 2009, p. 7.
64. E.g., Hobsbawm and Ranger 2012.
65. Quoted in Baker 2009, p. 1.
66. Hobsbawm and Ranger 2012, p. 1.
67. See the discussion of this concept of Mircea Eliade on pp. 19–20. See generally Eliade 1991b.

Chapter 11

1. Brown 1977, pp. 34–35; Miller 2003, p. 13.
2. Brown 1977, p. 36; Miller 2003, pp. 11–12; Vermes 2006, pp. 10–12.
3. Miller 2003, p. 11.
4. Miller 2003, pp. 12–13.
5. Vermes 2006, p. 12.
6. Ehrman 1999, p. 40.
7. Brown 1977, p. 549.
8. Josephus, *Antiquities* 17.2.2 (§ 27); Vermes 2006, p. 85; Brown 1977, p. 551.
9. Josephus, *Antiquities* 18.1.1 (§§ 1–3).
10. Meier 1991, p. 213.
11. Brown 1977, p. 549; Vermes 2006, p. 86.
12. Vermes 2006, p. 86; Meier 1991, p. 213.

13. Meier 1991, p. 213; likewise Miller 2003, p. 12.
14. E.g., Brown 1977, p. 36.
15. Brown 1977, p. 36.
16. *NOAB*, note to Hos 11:1. This is apparent from the full verse, which utilizes traditional synonymous parallelism: "When Israel was a child, I loved him, and out of Egypt I called my son." Accordingly, the Septuagint translated the term as "children," as in the common phrase "the children of Israel." But Matthew altered the meaning to refer to a single male individual, in order to support his flight to Egypt story. Vermes 2006, p. 107.
17. Vermes 2006, pp. 110–11.
18. Meier 1991, p. 212.
19. Meier 1991, p. 213.
20. The postpartum purification requirements are set forth in Leviticus 12:2–8, which specifies a purification period of 40 days in the case of a male child. At the end of the period, the mother must bring an offering to the priest at the tent of the meeting (the tabernacle, later the temple in Jerusalem) and the priest shall make atonement on her behalf. According to Leviticus 12:6–8, this is in part a sin offering, which in the context of Mary and Christianity raises interesting questions in relation to the doctrine of the Immaculate Conception, according to which Mary was born free of original sin and remained sinless.
21. Meier 1991, p. 210.
22. Miller 2003, p. 12.
23. E.g., Freed 2001, pp. 16–17; Ehrman 1999, pp. 36–40; Miller 2003, pp. 175–77; Kelly 2008, pp. 1–8; Aslan 2013, p. 33. Meier and Brown take a skeptical view of the historical claims in the infancy narratives. Meier 1991, pp. 209–12; Brown 1977, pp. 32–38. Interestingly, the last book ever put on the church's *Index of Forbidden Books* was Jean Stienmann's *La Vie de Jésus* (1959), because it rejected the historicity of the infancy narratives.
24. Elliott 1982, p. 17.
25. See Meier 1991, p. 229.
26. Brown 1977, p. 28.
27. Freed 2001, p. 11.
28. James and Thomas can be found in Wilson 1990, pp. 421–39 and 439–51 respectively. Pseudo-Matthew can be found in Ehrman and Pleše 2014, pp. 37–57.
29. Ehrman 2014, pp. 236–39.
30. Brown 1977, pp. 29–32, 311–16; Meier 1991, p. 213 & n. 34; Ehrman 2014, pp. 236–46.
31. Ehrman 2014, p. 236.
32. See generally Litwa 2014; Ehrman 2014.
33. Brown 1977, p. 37.

34. Brown 1977, p. 28; see, e.g., Jn 1:46; 7:41–42, 52.
35. Brown 1977, pp. 28–29, 534–42; Freed 2001, pp. 32–37. For a detailed treatment of this issue, see Schaberg 2006.
36. For further background on the functionalist character of myths, see George and George 2014, p. xix.
37. Quoted in Kelly 2014, pp. 139–40. Ambrose is quoting Psalm 24:1.
38. Kelly 2008, pp. 83, 88. Luke wanted to assure Rome that Christians are not lawbreakers, and also show that Jesus obeyed Roman and Jewish law. Showing that Jesus was innocent of any crime was important in converting both Jews and gentiles, because to them worshiping a convicted and crucified criminal as a divinity was considered scandalous and was a roadblock to spreading the religion. Thus, Luke told the story of Jesus saying that it was acceptable to pay taxes to Caesar, since taxes are only of this world (Lk 20:21–25; likewise Mt 22:17–21; Mk 12:14–17). Luke also portrayed Pilate as believing Jesus was innocent. (23:1–25).
39. Kelly 2014, p. 140.
40. As quoted in Crossan 2007, p. 147.
41. As quoted in Crossan 2007, p. 148 (emphasis added).
42. Crossan 2007, pp. 148–49.
43. Rank 1990; Dundes 1990; Campbell 1949, p. 319.
44. Rank 1990.
45. Raglan 1990.
46. Campbell 1949, pp. 318–34.
47. Neither Rank nor Campbell came up with a specific number of elements; Raglan had 22, but they went beyond the birth stage.
48. Rank 1990, pp. 39–43; Dundes 1990. Rank, Raglan, and Campbell discuss many other parallel examples from European and Asian myths, but any direct influence from them is unlikely and space considerations prohibit covering them. The Greco-Roman examples given below should suffice.
49. *DSS*, p. 144.
50. Miller 2003, pp. 146–47 (Plato and Asclepius); Raglan 140–41 (Heracles, Perseus, Jason).
51. Miller 2003, pp. 145–150 (Plato, Apollonius, Pythagoras); Rank 1990, p. 34 (Romulus); Litwa 2014, p. 53 (Plato, Alexander); MacDonald 2015, pp. 14–17 (Aeneas); Diodorus Siculus, *Historical Library* 2.4 (Semiramis). According to Dio Cassius, before Augustus was born his mother Attia dreamed "that her womb was lifted to the heavens and spread over all the earth. That same night her husband Octavius thought that the sun rose from between her thighs." She believed that her child had been fathered by Apollo. *History of Rome* 45.1.2–3, quoted in Miller 2003, pp. 140–41. A Chinese example is Fu Hsi. Campbell 1949, p. 316.

52. Miller 2003, pp. 140 (Augustus), 148–49 (Apollonius), 151 (Pythagoras); Litwa 2014, pp. 106–7 (Epicurus).
53. Raglan 1990, pp. 139 (Theseus), 139–40 (Romulus), 140 (Heracles and Perseus), 142 (Asclepius).
54. Miller 2003, pp. 139 (Alexander, quoting Plutarch's *Alexander*); 141–43 (Augustus, quoting Dio Cassius's *History of Rome* and Suetonius's *The Twelve Caesars*), 146 (Plato, quoting Diogenes Laertius's *Lives of Eminent Philosophers*), 148–49 (Apollonius, quoting Philostratus's *Life of Apollonius of Tyana*), 150 (Pythagoras, quoting from Imamblichus's *The Pythagorean Life*), 319–21 (Aeneas, quoting Homer's *Hymn to Aphrodite,* showing parallels with Luke's text*);* MacDonald 2015, pp. 14–17 (Aeneas, showing parallels in texts of Homer and Luke); Rank 1990, p. 42 (Zoroaster); Herodotus 1.107–08 (Cyrus), Philostratus, *Life of Apollonius of Tyana* 1.5 (lightning appeared at the moment of his birth).
55. Campbell 1949, p. 323.
56. Rank 1990, pp. 13 (Sargon), 14–15 (Moses), 16–17 (Ion), 19 (Paris), 34 (Romulus), 42–43 (Zoroaster); Miller 2003, pp. 126–28, (Moses, Sargon), 141 (Augustus, quoting Dio Cassius's *History of Rome*), 153 (Heracles, quoting Diodorus Siculus); Raglan 1990, pp. 141 (Jason), 142 (Asclepius, in whose case the attempt was to kill his mother while he was still in her womb); Herodotus, *Histories* 1.107–13 (Cyrus); Suetonius, *Augustus* 94.3 (Augustus). For Semiramis, see Diodorus Siculus, *Historical Library* 2.4. Outside the Mediterranean, good examples are the baby Krishna being threatened with death by King Kamsa, and the father of the African hero Mwindo trying to kill him after learning of his birth.
57. Rank 1990, p. 34 (Romulus); Herodotus, *Histories* 1:113 (Cyrus). See generally Campbell 1949, p. 326. After being saved from a plot to kill him, Jason was entrusted to the centaur Chiron to be educated; so was Asclepius, to whom Chiron also taught healing. Pindar, *Nemean Ode* 3.53–54; Pindar, *Pythian Ode* 3:43–46.
58. Nolland 1989, p. 129; Miller 2003, pp. 136–37 (Theagenes), 151 (Pythagoras). For Apollonius of Tyana, see Philostratus, *Life of Apollonius of Tyana* 1.5, 7. For Theagenes, see Pausanius, *Description of Greece* 6.11.2–3. See generally Campbell 1949, p. 327. Examples outside the Mediterranean include Buddha, Krishna, the Polynesian Maui, and the Irish hero Cuchulainn. Campbell 1949, p. 327, 330–31.
59. Dundes 1990, p. 180.
60. Litwa 2014; Ehrman 2014, p. 358 (regarding the emperor).
61. *First Apology* 21.1. He goes on to list many examples.
62. Plutarch, *Alexander* 2.1–4; see discussion in Miller 2015, pp. 124–29.
63. For Aeneas see the *Homeric Hymn to Aphrodite* and the discussion in MacDonald 2015, pp. 13–17.

64. Litwa 2014, pp. 20, 37–67 (especially pp. 42, 62), 215–23; see likewise Ehrman 2012, p. 215.
65. Zirkle 1936. For example, according to Ovid's *Fasti* (5.195–203), the virgin nymph Chloris was taken by the West Wind, personalized as Zephyrus, after which she was known as the goddess Flora.
66. *ABD*, 3:262–63.
67. *LSJ*, p. 1424.
68. Pausanius, *Description of Greece* 6.11.2.
69. See discussion in Litwa 2014, pp. 51–61.
70. Davies and Allison 1988, p. 201 (giving examples); *ABD*, 3:265, 267 (called the "spirit-filled Messiah").
71. Davies and Allison 1988, pp. 200–1.
72. Mt 1:18; Lk 1:35. In Matthew only the Holy Spirit was involved, whereas in Luke both the Holy Spirit and the power *(dynamis)* of God were at work.
73. *ABD*, 3:267 ("not one synoptic word concerning the spirit . . . can be positively claimed as Jesus' own").
74. *ABD*, 3:267–68.
75. Welburn 2006, p. 16.
76. Vermes 2006, p. 54.
77. Welburn 2006, pp. 10–14; Ehrman 2014, p. 242; Freed 2001, pp. 72–75. In summary, in Isaiah 7:14 the operative word in Hebrew is *almah*, which does not mean "virgin" but simply refers to a young woman, normally one of marriageable age, who is normally but not always a virgin; when virginity was implied, the term *betulah* was used. Davies and Allison 1988, p. 215; Miller 2003, pp. 190–91; Vermes 2006, pp. 58–59. The word *almah* occurs only nine times in the Hebrew Bible, and Isaiah 7:14 is the only time it gets translated as "virgin" in English language Bibles; in the other cases it is translated as "girl" or "young woman," so one suspects that doctrinal motives are at work here. Miller 2003, p. 191. In the Septuagint *almah* was translated into Greek as *parthenos,* which sometimes means virgin (think of the virgin goddess Athena Parthenos, after whom the Parthenon is named), but not necessarily so. For example, in the Septuagint it was even used to refer to widows, Miller 2003, p. 190 (citing, e.g., Joel 1.8 (LXX)), and in Genesis 34:3 (LXX) it was used to describe Dinah's state some time *after* she had been raped. See *LSJ*, p. 1339 definition 2, for other examples of using this word to refer to non-virgins. The other problem with invoking Isaiah 7:14 is contextual: The passage was written during the Syro-Ephraimite War (735–33 BCE), as part of Isaiah's effort to persuade King Ahaz not to ally with Assyria against Israel and Syria. In the prophecy, the young woman in question was a particular eighth-century BCE woman who was already someone's wife (most likely King Ahaz's wife, though possibly Isaiah's), *NOAB*, note to 7:14, so obviously she was not a virgin; moreover,

she may have been already pregnant (the Hebrew is unclear; the NRSV translates in present tense: "the young woman is with child"; the LXX Greek uses the future tense). According to the prophecy, the son would soon grow up eating luxurious foods because Israel and Syria will have given up their war against Judah, so that Judah will have returned to prosperity. The passage cannot fairly be read as a prophecy about a future woman or a virgin. The prophecy was aimed at resolving Judah's immediate military plight and had nothing to do with predicting a future messiah. In light of this specific context, it is no wonder that there is no evidence that Jews ever interpreted this passage to refer to a virgin. Meier 1991, pp. 221–22.

78. It is not feasible to cover all the examples here, but just to mention some of the better-known ones. Romulus was conceived by the vestal virgin Rhea Silvia and the god Mars during their tryst in his sacred grove. Zeus impregnated the virgin Danae with a golden shower to produce Perseus, but the shower is just a euphemism for sex and semen, Chevalier and Gheerbrant 1996, pp. 783–83, meaning that she is no longer a virgin when she gives birth. In the rape of the Phoenician virgin Europa, Zeus takes the form of a bull and copulates with her to produce King Minos of Crete. In the cases where the god is not his normal self, it seems that he takes a different, mediating form so as not to tarnish his usual divine form, which as we have seen has an analogy in the case of the Holy Spirit. There are also examples of non-virgins being impregnated by such transformed gods, such as in the myth of Leda and the Swan, but that takes us further afield.

79. Brown 1977, p. 531.

80. Miller 2015, p. 8.

81. Freed 2001, p. 30; Meier 1991, p. 221; Brown 1977, pp. 525–26. A possible exception is Mary in the miracle at Cana.

82. Meier 1991, p. 221.

83. See Brown 1977, p. 529.

84. Perhaps Luke was papering over the differences here, as he was prone to do elsewhere in Acts.

85. *ABD*, 1:1062; see also Kelly 2008, p. 17.

86. *Recognitions* chs. 54 and 60.

87. In contrast, Gabriel had told Elizabeth lesser things about John: that he would be filled with the Holy Spirit, that he would bring Israelites to God, and make the people ready for Jesus. Lk 1:15–17.

88. Some of the ancient manuscripts of Luke have Elizabeth singing this, so perhaps putting "Mary" in verse 1:46 was a post-Lucan redaction. The question of who really sang this hymn (including in pre-Lucan tradition) and about whom has been controversial and has generated extensive scholarly debate. In 1912, the Catholic Church's Pontifical Biblical Commission had to issue a decree clarifying the church's position that Mary sang it. For

a detailed discussion of this controversy including references to the literature, see Brown 1977, pp. 334–66. In my view, Elizabeth singing some version of it before it was attributed to Mary is more logical because, in the immediate lead-up, it is Elizabeth who is excited about the Holy Spirit just having entered John in her womb; the Spirit being in Jesus was already history. If the song was appropriated by Jesus's followers from John's, this would be yet another example of Jesus's followers making him superior to John.

89. Meier 1991, p. 223.
90. These issues and the competing scholarly claims are discussed in Schaberg 2006; Miller 2003, pp. 211–22; Brown 1977, pp. 534–42; Meier 1991, pp. 222–29; Vermes 2006, pp. 73–75; Freed 2001, pp. 32–37; and Davies and Allison 1988, p. 220 & n. 68.
91. Brown 1977, p. 143.
92. Specifically, the pregnant Tamar was rumored to be an adulteress, but she was proven innocent and vindicated (Gen 38:6–26). Rahab was a prostitute in Jericho who saved the lives of two Hebrew spies that Joshua had sent there because she was loyal to Yahweh, and in return she and her family were saved when Joshua razed Jericho and killed its inhabitants (Josh 2:1–24; 6:17–25). Ruth was a Moabite childless widow living in Bethlehem, and thus in an irregular and dire situation for a woman, but she behaved honorably one night together with Boaz, not having sex, and honored Yahweh, and as a result ended up marrying Boaz, being blessed by Yahweh, and being honored by the villagers who previously had ignored her (Ruth 1:1–4:22). Bathsheba was summoned to have sex with King David soon after David had spied her bathing, and got pregnant. David then murdered her husband Uriah by sending him to his death in battle, and married her. Yahweh struck their first child so conceived dead, but soon they had Solomon. 2 Sam 11:1–12:25.
93. Freed 2001, pp. 31–52; Schaberg 2006, p. 41.
94. See Davies and Allison 1988, pp. 171–72; Brown 1977, pp. 71–74, 143. The other common denominator among the four women was that they were all non-Jews who had faith in and honored Yahweh, so an alternative explanation for their presence may be that Matthew was emphasizing the potential salvation of gentiles. Davies and Allison 1988, p. 171.
95. Lane 1974, pp. 202–3; Aslan 2013, p. 37; see also Vermes 2006, p. 73. Apparently because of the scandalous nature of this phrase, later redactions of Mark revised it to read, "son of the carpenter and Mary." Vermes 2006, p. 73; Aslan 2013, p. 37. Similar is Matthew 13:55, perhaps for the same reason.
96. See Lane 1974, p. 203; Freed 2001, p. 34. The absence of Joseph also fits the idea that the infancy narratives were self-contained, newer units that

were dropped into the main narratives in Matthew and Luke, which naturally would not have included a Joseph figure.

97. Vermes 2006, p. 73; Aslan 2013, p. 37.

98. This is called the "exclusive" use of *we*, here meaning "we not including you [Jesus]." For a discussion of the relevant syntax, see Wallace 1996, pp. 397–98. He comments on John 8:53 as being an example of the "exclusive" *we*, and in that connection relies on a parallel interpretation of 8:41, which he says contains an allegation of Jesus's illegitimate birth, adding that the issue of paternity is key to the entire pericope.

99. Freed 2001, pp. 35–36; Keener 2003, p. 759 & n. 547 (citing various scholars who take this view).

100. E.g., Miller 2003, pp. 214–15.

101. Meier 1991, p. 227–29.

102. Brown 1977, p. 537 n. 14; Miller 2003, p. 216.

103. *Against Celsus* 1.28, 32, 37.

104. See discussion in Miller 2003, pp. 220–21.

105. Josephus, *Antiquities* 17.10.9 (§§ 288–89); *Jewish War* 2.5.1 (§ 68); *ABD*, 5:1091.

106. 1QSa 2:11–12, in *DSS* 143–47.

107. Ehrman 2014, pp. 236–37.

108. There is no direct evidence in Matthew or Luke of sensitivity to such a possible taint, Brown 1977, p. 530, but Paul's doctrine of original sin (according to which the taint is passed down genealogically) had existed for a couple decades before Matthew and Luke wrote, so they presumably were aware of it.

109. Litwa 2014, pp. 65–66. See also Litwa's Chapter 3 (pp. 78–109), elaborating on how in the Mediterranean world a figure's divinity was proved by his beneficial works conferred on humanity.

110. *Against Celsus* 1.37, using Plato as the example and calling his divine birth a myth. Using this logic, in a later passage (1.67), Celsus argued that Jesus could not be divine because (in his view) he had not accomplished great works benefiting humanity. Origen's response was at that level of argumentation, claiming that Jesus had accomplished more than the Greco-Roman exemplars.

111. Ehrman 2014, pp. 236–37. For the details of this developing Christology, see Ehrman 2014.

112. Freed 2001, pp. 15–16.

113. Jn 3:3, 7. John is engaging in wordplay here, because the Greek word in question *(anōthen)* means both "above" and "again" or "anew." The pun does not work in Aramaic, the language in which this conversation would have taken place, so it appears that we have mythmaking here.

114. Campbell with Moyers 1988, pp. 173–75.

115. Miller 2001, p. 102; Davies and Allison 1988, p. 233.
116. Philostratus, *Life of Apollonius of Tyana* 1.5.
117. *Aeneid* 2.680–705.
118. Suetonius, *Julius Caesar* 88.
119. *Ecologue* 9.47.
120. Funk et al. 1998, p. 128.
121. *Odes* 1.12.46–48.
122. Funk et al. 1998, p. 128.
123. *Augustus* 94.3.
124. Tacitus, *Annals* 14.22.
125. Brown 1977, p. 170.
126. See Ehrman 2014, pp. 49, 234–35.
127. Davies and Allison 1988, p. 233.
128. *Jewish War* 6.5.4 (§ 312).
129. E.g., Eusebius, *Demonstration of the Gospel* 9.1: "In the case of . . . remarkable and famous men we know that strange stars have appeared . . . But what event could be greater or more important for the whole universe than the spiritual light coming to all men through the saviour's advent . . . ?"
130. Davies and Allison 1988, p. 234.
131. *Excerpta ex Theodoto,* para 74.
132. As quoted in Kelly 2014, p. 142.
133. Davies and Allison 1988, pp. 234–35; Brown 1977, pp. 190–96.
134. *Ephesians* 19.2, as quoted in Miller 2003, p. 103.
135. Miller 2003, p. 103.
136. Miller 2003, p. 100; Maier 1998, pp. 170–71 (recognizing that the weight of scholarly opinion is against historicity, but arguing for historicity); see also Brown 1977, p. 227 ("There are serious reasons for thinking that the flight to Egypt and the massacre at Bethlehem may not be historical.")
137. The story is in Dio Cassius, *Roman History* 63.1–1; Suetonius, *Nero* 13; Pliny the Elder in his *Natural History* describes both Tiridates and his companions as magi (30.6). For scholarly analysis, see Brown 1977, pp. 174, 192; Davies and Allison 1988, p. 252.
138. Dio Cassius, *Roman History* 63.7 ("by another way"). See Miller 2003, p. 108; Davies and Allison 1988, p. 252.
139. This even though contemporary Jewish thinking owed a large debt to Persian religious thought, including the notion of cosmic resurrection. See discussion in Miller 2015, pp. 154–58. But since the magi would have believed in immortality, their visit to the newborn Jesus implied looking forward to his resurrection. Miller 2015, p. 156.
140. Brown 1977, pp. 181, 184.
141. Of Abraham's offspring, the Jews came from Isaac, and the Ishmaelites from Ishmael; the Edomites came from his grandson Esau.

142. Brown 1977, p. 184.
143. 8:11. See Brown 1977, pp. 181, 184.
144. Davies and Allison 1988, p. 253.
145. Davies and Allison 1988, pp. 249–50.
146. *Alexander* 3.5–7.
147. E.g., Philo, *On the Life of Moses* 1:50 (§ 276) (also a "prophet"); see Brown 1977, p. 193.
148. E.g., Kelly 2008, p. 47.
149. Davies and Allison 1988, p. 249.
150. Davies and Allison 1988, p. 249.
151. *Augustus* 94.3
152. Freed 2001, p. 136.
153. 2:14 (NRSV translation). An acceptable alternative for the italicized phrase would be "in which he is well-pleased" (cf. Lk 3:22). See *BDAG*, p. 404. Our culture still bears the legacy of the King James Version's translation "good will toward men" at the end of this chorus, but that rendering is not the scholarly consensus. The question turns on the meaning of the word *eydokia* and on what case it is in. This word can mean either (a) the state or condition of being favored or having pleased someone, or (b) the state or condition of feeling good will toward others. *BDAG*, p. 404. The committee producing the KJV had before it a manuscript that had *eydokia* in the nominative case, in which instance the latter meaning is possible ("good will among people"). However, the nominative is poorly attested among the manuscripts and the scholarship favors those manuscripts having the word in the genitive case *(eydokias)*. Nolland 1989, p. 109. When the genitive is used, possible translations include "among the people of [God's] good favor," "among those with whom God is well pleased," or "among those whom he has favored." Most English language translations of verse 14 and commentaries thereon now adopt some such variant conveying that meaning. See commentary in Brown 1977, pp. 393, 403–5; Nolland 1989, p. 109; Freed 2001, p. 142.
154. See generally Ehrman 1999.
155. Quoted in Kelly 2014, p. 139.
156. Horsley 1989, pp. 28–29.
157. Miller 2003, p. 58.
158. Other examples include Fra Angelico's and Filippo Lippi's *Adoration of the Magi* (see Fig. 11.4), Botticelli's *Adoration of the Magi* (ca 1475–76), Nicolas Poussin's *Adoration of the Shepherds* (1633–34), and several nativities of Francesco di Giorgio Martini.
159. Available at Fordham University's Internet History Soucebooks Project, https://sourcebooks.fordham.edu/basis/goldenlegend/GL-vol1-nativity.asp, last accessed December 13, 2019. The collapse of the temple is not

described, but rather is implied. Apollo was one of the few deities shared by both Greece and Rome having the same name.

160. Miller 2015.
161. Quoted in Kelly 2014, p. 139.
162. Freed 2001, pp. 137–38.
163. Brown 1977, p. 479.
164. Kelly 2008, p. 94. Contra is Nolland 1989, p. 131, who argues that the three days serve only to intensify Mary's rebuke of him in 2:48. As mentioned in Chap. 6, three days may simply signify a short period of time.
165. See summary with sources in Nolland 1989, p. 129. For Apollonius of Tyana, see Philostratus, *Life of Apollonius of Tyana* 1.7. For Theagenes, see Pausanius, *Description of Greece* 6.11.2–3.
166. *Antiquities* 5.2.4 (§§ 348–49).
167. See generally Campbell 1949, pp. 49–58.
168. Regarding these stages of the hero cycle, see Campbell 1949, pp. 69–89.
169. Ehrman 2014, pp. 237–38.
170. Origen, *Commentary on Matthew* 10.22; Kelly 2014, p. 66.
171. Talley 1991, p. 123.
172. *Stromateis* 1.21.
173. Cullmann 1956, p. 26.
174. The origins of the January 6 date are complex and still debated, and discussing the issues would go well beyond the scope of the book. For background on the issues, see Roll 1995, Talley 1991, and Cullmann 1956.
175. Cullmann 1956, p. 30.
176. E.g., Origen, *Against Celsus* 1.37; Justin Martyr, *First Apology* 21.1; 60.1.
177. Forbes 2007, p. 31. Although, as discussed, the Gospel of John posited a still higher Christology, it would hardly have been feasible give a holiday date to Jesus's creation in that Gospel, since it occurred even before the creation of the cosmos.
178. Roll 1995, p. 82.
179. Kelly 2010, p. 16.
180. Scullard 1981, p. 212.
181. Kelly 2010, p. 17.
182. Roll 1995, p. 113.
183. E.g., Hijmans 2003, pp. 384–85.
184. Aveni 2003, p. 152.
185. Cullmann 1956, pp. 31–32.
186. Cullmann 1956, p. 32.
187. Scullard 1981, p. 207; Cullmann 1956, p. 29; Roll 1995, pp. 84–86.
188. As translated and quoted in Cullmann 1956, p. 36. I have Americanized the spellings from this British translation.
189. Talley 1991, pp. 100–1; Forbes 2007, p. 31.

190. The link to this prophecy was made in the *Gospel of Pseudo-Matthew*, Chapter 14, although the adoration by the ox and ass occurred on the third day after Jesus's birth, after Mary had relocated the babe from the cave to a stable. This device enabled the author to remain somewhat consistent with Luke's account.

191. This passage appears only in the Septuagint (LXX), not in the Masoretic (Hebrew) text and so does not appear in English translations of the Hebrew Bible. But it is the Greek that the vast majority of literate Christians would have read in ancient times, thus bringing the passage into tradition.

192. Ferguson 1954, pp. 11, 22–23.; Hall 1974, pp. 231, 238.

193. Aveni 2003, pp. 66–67.

194. Justin, *Trypho* 78; Origen, *Against Celsus* 1.51; Eusebius, *Life of Constantine* 3.44.

195. E.g., *The Pskov Nativity* at the Pskov Museum, Pskov, Russia. Available at http://www.christianiconography.info/Wikimedia%20Commons/nativityPskov.html, last accessed December 13, 2019.

196. Giorgione, *Adoration of the Shepherds* (1500); Botticelli, *The Mystical Nativity* (ca. 1500–01); Antoniazzo Romano, *The Nativity* (ca. 1480s).

197. Commodian, *Instructions* 13. Being born of a rock could have left a hole ("cave"), so he could have been born in a cave at least in that sense.

198. *ABD*, 4:878.

199. In paintings, for example, in Georgione's *Adoration of the Shepherds*, and Domenico Ghirlandaio's *Nativity*.

200. Kelly 2014, p. 125.

201. Kelly 2014, pp. 125–26.

202. Kelly 2014, p. 127.

203. Alternatively, the celebrants feasted on Hildisvini, the boar that the goddess Freya rode.

204. Forbes 2007, pp. 87, 113–14.

205. Scullard 1981, p. 207.

206. Matthews 1998, p. 23.

207. Aveni 2003, p. 154.

208. Miles 1976, p. 358.

209. The red berries and thorns on mistletoe were understood by some to symbolize the Passion, Miles 1976, p. 275, but that relates to Easter not Christmas.

210. Forbes 2007, p. 5.

211. Miles 1976, p. 272; Hutton 1996, p. 34.

212. Miles 1976, p. 183.

213. Miles 1976, pp. 292–93; Hutton 1996, pp. 96–99 (regarding the wren).

214. Miles 1976, pp. 233–37.

215. See discussion in Hutton 1996, pp. 42–53.

216. Forbes 2007, p. 141.
217. Miles 1976, pp. 298–308; Hutton 1996, pp. 95–111.
218. Quoted in Forbes 2007, p. 59.
219. Forbes 2007, pp. 54–60.
220. See Corbett 1996; Jung 1959a, 1959c, 1969a, and 1969c.
221. *ABD*, 3:262–65.
222. Corbett 1996, p. 15.
223. Corbett 1996, p. 60.
224. See Jung 1956, pp. 201–2.
225. Corbett 1996, pp. 150–51.
226. Corbett 1996, p. 128.
227. Jung 1969c, p. 441.
228. See generally Jung 1959c.
229. Jung 1959c, p. 161.
230. Jung 1969a, p. 31.
231. Jung 1959c, p. 164.
232. Corbett 1996, p. 149.
233. See Campbell 1949, p. 308 (regarding Herod as the tenacious ego usurping the Self).
234. Likewise, Mk 10:15; Lk 18:17; Gospel of Thomas 22, 46.2.
235. Saying 70.
236. Saying 3.

WORKS CITED AND BIBLIOGRAPHY

Aldred, Cyril. 1969. "The 'New Year' Gifts to the Pharaoh," *JEA* 55:73–81.

Allison, Dale. 1998. *Jesus of Nazareth: Millenarian Prophet.* Minneapolis: Fortress Press.

Altheim, Franz. 1938. *A History of Roman Religion.* London: Methuen & Co.

Anderson, Bernhard. 1987. *Creation versus Chaos: The Reinterpretation of Mythical Symbolism in the Bible.* Philadelphia: Fortress Press.

Aslan, Reza. 2013. *Zealot: The Life and Times of Jesus of Nazareth.* New York: Random House.

Austin, Jane. 1889. *Standish of Standish – A Story of the Pilgrims.* 7th ed. Boston and New York: Houghton Mifflin. Available on GoogleBooks at https://www.google.com/books/edition/Standish_of_Standish/ANA-AAAAYAAJ?hl=en&gbpv=1&dq=standish+of+standish&printsec=frontcover

Aveni, Anthony. 2003. *The Book of the Year: A Brief History of our Seasonal Holidays.* New York: Oxford University Press.

Baker, James. 2009. *Thanksgiving: The Biography of an American Holiday.* Durham, N.H.: University of New Hampshire Press.

Bannatyne, Lesley. 1990. *Halloween: An American Holiday, an American History.* Gretna, Louisiana: Pelican.

Barnard, Leslie, ed. and trans. 1997. *St. Justin Martyr: The First and Second Apologies.* NewYork/Mahwah, New Jersey: Paulist Press.

Barnstone, Willis, and Marvin Meyer, eds. and trans. 2009. *The Gnostic Bible.* Rev. ed. Boston: Shambala.

Beard, Mary, John North and Simon Price. 1998. *Religions of Rome.* 2 vols. Cambridge: Cambridge University Press.

© The Author(s) 2020
A. George, *The Mythology of America's Seasonal Holidays*,
https://doi.org/10.1007/978-3-030-46916-0

Becker, Udo. 1992. *The Continuum Encyclopedia of Symbols*. New York: Continuum.

Bede. 1990. *The Ecclesiastical History of the English People*. Trans. Leo Sherley-Price, rev. by R.E. Latham. London: Penguin, 1990.

———. 2012. *The Reckoning of Time*. Faith Wallis, trans. and ed. Liverpool: Liverpool University Press, 2012.

Beilby, James, and Paul Eddy, eds. 2009. *The Historical Jesus: Five Views*. Downers Grove, Ill.: IVP Academic.

Biedermann, Hans. 1994. *Dictionary of Symbolism: Cultural Icons and the Meanings behind Them*. New York: Meridian.

Black, Jeremy and Anthony Green. 1992. *Gods, Demons and Symbols of Ancient Mesopotamia: An Illustrated Dictionary*. Austin, Texas: University of Texas Press.

Blackburn, Bonnie, and Leofranc Holford-Strevens. 1999. *The Oxford Companion to the Year*. Oxford: Oxford University Press.

Bleeker, C.J. 1967. *Egyptian Festivals: Enactments of Religious Renewal*. Leiden: Brill.

Bowden, Hugh. 2010. *Mystery Cults of the Ancient World*. Princeton and Oxford: Princeton University Press.

Bradford, William. 2006. *Of Plymouth Plantation*. Mineola, New York: Dover.

Bradshaw, Paul. 1999a. "Easter in Christian Tradition," in Bradshaw and Hoffman 1999a, pp. 1–7.

———. 1999b. "The Origins of Easter," in Bradshaw and Hoffman 1999a, pp. 81–97.

Bradshaw, Paul, and Lawrence Hoffman, eds. 1999a. *Passover and Easter: Origin and History to Modern Times*. Notre Dame, Indiana: University of Notre Dame Press.

———, 1999b. *Passover and Easter: The Symbolic Structuring of Sacred Seasons*. Notre Dame, Indiana: University of Notre Dame Press.

———, eds. 1999c. "Passover and Easter: The Symbolic Shaping of Time and Meaning," in Bradshaw and Hoffman 1999b, pp. 1–12.

Brandon, S.G.F. 1967. *Jesus and the Zealots*. Manchester, UK: Manchester University Press.

Brown, Raymond. 1977. *The Birth of the Messiah: A Commentary on the Infancy Narratives in Matthew and Luke*. Garden City/New York: Doubleday.

Burkert, Walter. 1985. *Greek Religion*. John Raffan, trans. Cambridge, Mass.: Harvard University Press.

Campbell, Brian. 1978. "The Marriage of Soldiers Under the Empire," *Journal of Roman Studies* 68:153–66.

Campbell, Joseph. 1949. *The Hero with a Thousand Faces*. New York: MJF Books.

———. 1964. *The Masks of God: Occidental Mythology*. New York: Penguin.

———. 1981. "Trick or Treat," lecture delivered at Fountain Street Church, Grand Rapids, Michigan, on October 25, 1981, available at http://www.the-dailybeast.com/articles/2014/10/31/joseph-campbell-on-the-roots-of-hal-loween.html

————. 2001. *Thou Art That: Transforming Religious Metaphor.* Novato, Calif.: New World Library.

————. 2015. *Romance of the Grail: The Magic and Mystery of Arthurian Myth.* Novato, California: New World Library.

Campbell, Joseph with Bill Moyers. 1988. *The Power of Myth.* New York: Doubleday.

Carpenter, Rhys. 1946. *Folktale, Fiction, and Saga in the Homeric Epics.* Berkeley and Los Angeles: University of California Press.

Cashford, Jules. 2002. *The Moon: Myth and Image.* New York: Four Walls Eight Windows.

Charlesworth, James. 2008. *The Historical Jesus.* Nashville: Abington Press.

————, et al. 2006. *Resurrection: The Origin and Future of a Biblical Doctrine.* New York: T&T Clark.

————, ed. 1983. *The Old Testament Pseudepigrapha.* 2 vols. Peabody, Massachusetts: Hendrickson Publishers.

Chevalier, Jean, and Alain Gheerbrant. 1996. *The Penguin Dictionary of Symbols.* 2nd ed. London: Penguin Books.

Cirlot, J.E. 1971. *A Dictionary of Symbols.* 2nd ed. New York: Philosophical Library.

Cohen, Mark. 1993. *The Cultic Calendars of the Ancient Near East.* Bethesda, Md.: CDL Press.

Collis, John. 2003. *The Celts: Origins, Myths, Inventions.* The Mill, Gloustershire, England: Tempus.

Cooper, J.C. 1992. *Dictionary of Symbolic & Mythological Animals.* London: Thorsons.

Corbett, Lionel. 1996. *The Religious Function of the Psyche.* Routledge: New York.

Cross, Gary. 2004. *The Cute and the Cool: Wondrous Innocence and Modern American Children's Culture.* New York: Oxford University Press.

Crossan, John Dominic. 1991. *The Historical Jesus: The Life of a Jewish Mediterranean Peasant.* New York: HarperOne.

————. 1994. *Jesus: A Revolutionary Biography.* San Francisco, HarperOne.

————. 2007. *God & Empire: Jesus Against Rome: Then and Now.* New York: HarperOne.

Cullmann, Oscar. 1956. *The Early Church: Studies in Early Christian History and Theology.* Philadelphia: Westminster Press.

Cunliffe, Barry. 1997. *The Ancient Celts.* London: Penguin.

Dames, Michael. 1992. *Mythic Ireland.* London: Thames and Hudson.

Danaher, Kevin. 1972. *The Year in Ireland.* Cork, Ireland: Mercier Press.

Davidson, H.R. Ellis. 1988. *Myths and Symbols in Pagan Europe: Early Scandinavian and Celtic Religions.* Syracuse: Syracuse University Press.

Davies, W., and Dale Allison. 1988. *A Critical and Exegetical Commentary on the Gospel According to Saint Matthew,* Vol. 1, *Matthew 1–7.* New York: T&T Clark.

Dein, Simon. 2001. "What Really Happens When Prophecy Fails: The Case of Lubavitch," *SR* 62:383–401.

Dennis, Matthew. 2005. *Red, White, and Blue Letter Days: An American Calendar.* Ithaca, New York: Cornell University Press.

Doherty, Earl. 2013. "'Mythicist Inventions' Creating the Mythical Christ from the Pagan Mystery Cults," in Zindler, Frank, and Robert Price, eds. *Bart Ehrman and the Quest of the Historical Jesus of Nazareth.* Cranford, N.J.: American Athiest Press, pp. 167–82.

Downing, Gerald. 1988. *Christ and the Cynics: Jesus and Other Radical Preachers in First-Century Tradition.* Sheffield, UK: JSOT.

Dundes, Alan. 1990. "The Hero Pattern and the Life of Jesus," in Segal 1990, pp. 179–223.

Edinger, Edward. 1992. *Ego and Archetype: Individuation and the Religious Function of the Psyche.* Boston and London: Shambala.

Edwards, Eric. 2014. "Bear Worship and Bear Cults," *Musings of an Active Mind* (blog), March 10, 2014, https://ericedwards.wordpress.com/2014/03/10/bear-cultsand-bear-worship. Last accessed December 19, 2019.

Ehrman, Bart. 1999. *Jesus: Apocalyptic Prophet of the New Millennium.* New York: Oxford University Press.

———. 2012. *Did Jesus Exist? The Historical Argument for Jesus of Nazareth.* New York: HarperOne.

———. 2014. *How Jesus Became God: The Exaltation of a Jewish Preacher from Galilee.* New York: HarperOne.

———. 2018. *The Triumph of Christianity: How a Forbidden Religion Swept the World.* New York: Simon & Schuster.

Ehrman, Bart, and Pleše, Zlatako. 2014. *The Other Gospels: Accounts of Jesus from Outside the New Testament.* New York: Oxford University Press.

Eliade, Mircea. 1978a. *A History of Religious Ideas.* Vol. 1: *From the Stone Age to the Eleusinian Mysteries.* Chicago: University of Chicago Press.

———. 1978b. *Zalmoxis, the Vanishing God: Comparative Studies in the Religions and Folklore of Dacia and Eastern Europe.* Chicago: University of Chicago Press.

———. 1987. *The Sacred and the Profane.* Orlando, Florida: Harcourt.

———. 1991a. *Images and Symbols: Studies in Religious Symbolism.* Princeton: Princeton University Press.

———. 1991b. *The Myth of the Eternal Return.* Princeton: Princeton University Press.

———. 1996. *Patterns in Comparative Religion.* Lincoln, Nebraska: University of Nebraska Press.

Elliott, J.K. 1982. *Questioning Christian Origins.* London: SCM Press.

Ferguson, George. 1954. *Signs and Symbols in Christian Art.* New York: Oxford University Press.

Festinger, Leon. 1957. *A Theory of Cognitive Dissonance.* Stanford, Calif.: Stanford University Press.

Festinger, Leon, Henry Riecken, and Stanley Schachter. 1956. *When Prophecy Fails: A Social and Psychological Study of a Modern Group that Predicted the Destruction of the World.* Mansfield Centre, Ct.: Martino Publishing, repr. 2012.

Fleming, E. McClung. 1965. "The American Image as Indian Princess 1765–1783," *Winterthur Portfolio* 2:65–81.

Forbes, Bruce. 2007. *Christmas: A Candid History.* Berkeley: University of California Press.

———. 2015. *America's Favorite Holidays: Candid Histories.* Berkeley: University of California Press.

Fox, Nancy Jo. 1986. *Liberties with Liberty: The Fascinating History of America's Proudest Symbol.* New York: E.P. Dutton.

Frankfort, Henri. 1951. *The Problem of Similarity in Ancient Near Eastern Religions.* Oxford: Clarendon Press.

———. 1978. *Kingship and the Gods: A Study of Ancient Near Eastern Religion as the Integration of Society and Nature.* Chicago: University of Chicago Press.

Franz, Marie-Louise von. 1995. *Creation Myths.* Rev. ed. Boston: Shambhala.

———. 1999. *Archetypal Dimensions of the Psyche.* Boston: Shambhala.

Frazer, James. 1996. *The Golden Bough.* Reprint, New York: Simon & Schuster (single volume abridged edition).

———.1935. *The Golden Bough.* 3rd ed. 13 vols. New York: Macmillan.

Fredricksen, Paula. 1999. *Jesus of Nazareth, King of the Jews: A Jewish Life and the Emergence of Christianity.* New York: Alfred A. Knopf.

Freed, Edwin. 2001. *The Stories of Jesus' Birth: A Critical Introduction.* Sheffield, UK: Sheffield Academic Press.

Fuller, Andrew. 1994. *Psychology & Religion: Eight Points of View.* 3rd ed. Lanham, Md.: Rowman & Littlefield.

Funk, Robert, and The Jesus Seminar. 1998. *The Acts of Jesus: What Did Jesus Really Do?* New York: Polebridge Press.

Ganz, David, trans. 2008. *Two Lives of Charlemagne.* London: Penguin.

GardenStone. 2015. *Eostre Ostara Eostar: Facts, assumptions, conjectures, speculations, guesses and nonsense.* Norderstedt, Germany: Books on Demand.

George, Arthur, and Elena George. 2003. *St. Petersburg: Russia's Window to the Future – The First Three Centuries.* Lantham, Maryland: Taylor Trade Press.

———. 2014. *The Mythology of Eden.* Lanham, Maryland: Hamilton Books.

Gimbutas, Marija. 1989. *The Language of the Goddess.* New York: Harper & Row.

Grace, Catherine O'Neill, and Margaret Bruchac. 2001. *1621: A New Look at Thanksgiving.* Washington, D.C.: National Geographic.

Graves, Robert. 1960. *The Greek Myths.* London: Penguin.

Green, Steven. 2010. "Understanding the 'Christian Nation' Myth," *Cardozo Law Review de novo* 2010:245–70.

———. 2015. *Inventing a Christian America: The Myth of Religious Founding.* New York: Oxford University Press.

Green, William. 1931. "The Lupercalia in the Fifth Century," *Classical Philology* 26.1:60–69.

Hall, James. 1974. *Hall's Dictionary of Subjects & Symbols in Art.* London: John Murray.

Hansen, William. 2002. *Ariadne's Thread: A Guide to International Tales Found in Classical Literature.* Ithaca, New York: Cornell University Press.

Harrison, Jane. 1969. *Themis: A Study of the Social Origins of Greek Religion.* 2nd ed. Cleveland and New York: World Publishing. First published in 1927.

———. 1991. *Prolegomena to the Study of Greek Religion.* 3rd ed. Princeton: Princeton University Press. First published in 1922.

Harrowven, Jean. 1996. *Origins of Festivals and Feasts.* Whitstable, United Kingdom: Pryor Publications.

Heath, Dwight, ed. 1963. *Mourt's Relation: A Journal of the Pilgrims at Plymouth.* Bedford, Massachusetts: Applewood Books. First published in 1622.

Heinz, Donald. 2010. *Christmas: Festival of Incarnation.* Minneapolis: Fortress Press.

Hengel, Martin. 1977. *Crucifixion.* Philadelphia: Fortress Press.

Hieronimus, Robert, and Cortner, Laura. 2016. *The Secret Life of Lady Liberty: Goddess in the New World.* Rochester, Vermont: Destiny Books.

Higham, John. 1990. "The Indian Princess and Roman Goddess: The First Female Symbols of America," *Proceedings of the American Antiquarian Society* 100: 45–79.

Hijmans, Steven. 2003. "Sol Invictus, the Winter Solstice, and the Origins of Christmas," *Mouseion,* Series III, 3:377–98.

Hillman, James. 1983. *Archetypal Psychology: A Brief Account.* Dallas, Tex.: Spring Publications.

———. 1992. *Re-Visioning Psychology.* New York: Harper.

Hobsbawm, Eric, and Ranger, Terence, eds. 2012. *The Invention of Tradition.* Cambridge, United Kingdom: Cambridge University Press.

Holleman, A.W.J. 1974. *Pope Gelasius I and the Lupercalia.* Amsterdam: Adolf Hakkert.

Horsley, Richard. 1989. *The Liberation of Christmas: The Infancy Narratives in Social Context.* Eugene, Oregon: Wipf & Stock.

———. 1987. *Jesus and the Spiral of Violence: Popular Jewish Resistance in Roman Palestine.* Minneapolis: Fortress Press.

Hutton, Ronald. 1996. *The Stations of the Sun: A History of the Ritual Year in Britain.* Oxford: Oxford University Press.

James, Edwin. 1961. *Seasonal Feasts and Festivals.* London: Thames and Hudson.

Jung, Carl. 1953. *Psychology and Alchemy. CW,* vol. 12.

———. 1956. *Symbols of Transformation, CW,* vol. 5.

———. 1959a. "Concerning Rebirth," in *The Archetypes and the Collective Unconscious. CW*, vol. 9.1, pp. 111–47.

———. 1959b. "Psychological Aspects of the Mother Archetype," in *The Archetypes and the Collective Unconscious. CW*, vol. 9.1, pp. 73–110.

———. 1959c. "The Psychology of the Child Archetype," in *The Archetypes and the Collective Unconscious. CW*, vol. 9.1, pp. 149–81.

———. 1959d. "The Psychological Aspects of the Kore," in *The Archetypes and the Collective Unconscious. CW*, vol. 9.1, pp. 182–203.

———. 1967. *Alchemical Studies. CW*, vol. 13.

———. 1969a. "Christ, a Symbol of the Self," in *Aion: Researches into the Phenomenology of the Self.* 2nd ed. *CW*, vol. 9.2, pp. 36–71.

———. 1969b. "A Psychological Approach to the Trinity," in *Psychology and Religion: East and West.* 2nd ed. *CW*, vol. 11, pp. 107–200.

———. 1969c. "Answer to Job," in *Psychology and Religion: West and East. CW*, vol. 11, pp. 355–470.

———. 1969d. "The Structure and Dynamics of the Self," in *Aion: Researches into the Phenomenology of the Self. CW*, vol. 9.2, pp. 222–65.

———. 1976a. "The Type Problem in Poetry," in *Psychological Types. CW*, vol. 6, pp. 166–272.

———. 1976b. "On Resurrection," in *The Symbolic Life. CW*, vol. 18, pp. 692–96.

Keener, Craig. 2003. *The Gospel of John: A Commentary.* 2 vols. Grand Rapids: Baker Academic.

Kelley, Ruth. 1919. *The Book of Hallowe'en: the History of Allhallows Eve.* Boston: Lothrop, Lee, & Shepard.

Kelly, Henry. 1986. *Chaucer and the Cult of St. Valentine.* Leiden, The Netherlands: Brill.

Kelly, Joseph. 2008. *The Birth of Jesus According to the Gospels.* Collegeville, Minn.: Liturgical Press.

———. 2010. *The Feast of Christmas.* Collegeville, Minn.: Liturgical Press.

———. 2014. *The Origins of Christmas,* 2nd ed. Collegeville, Minn.: Liturgical Press.

Kirk, G. S., J. E. Raven, and M. Schofield. 2007. *The Presocratic Philosophers.* 2nd ed. Cambridge, Cambridge University Press.

Kloppenborg, John. 1987. *The Formation of Q: Trajectories in Ancient Wisdom Collections.* Minneapolis: Fortress Press.

———. 2000. *Excavating Q: The History and Setting of the Sayings Gospel.* Minneapolis: Fortress Press.

Koch, John, ed. 2006. *Celtic Culture: A Historical Encyclopedia.* 5 vols. Santa Barbara, Calif.: ABC-CLIO.

Komarnitsky, Kris. 2014. "Cognitive Dissonance and the Resurrection of Jesus," *The Fourth R* 27.5:7–10, 20–22.

Lambert, W.G. 1963. "The Great Battle of the Mesopotamian Religious Year – The Conflict in the Akitu House (A Summary)," *Iraq* 25:189–90.

———. 1968. "Myth and Ritual as Conceived by the Babylonians," *JSS* 13:104–12.

Lane, William. 1974. *The Gospel according to Mark: The English Text with Introduction, Exposition, and Notes.* Grand Rapids: Eerdmans.

Leach, Maria, ed. 1972. *Funk & Wagnalls Standard Dictionary of Folklore, Myth, and Legend.* New York: HarperSanFrancisco.

Leeming, David. 2005. *The Oxford Companion to World Mythology.* New York: Oxford University Press.

Litwa, M. David. 2014. *Jesus Deus: The Early Christian Depiction of Jesus as a Mediterranean God.* Minneapolis: Fortress Press.

Love, William. 1895. *Fast and Thanksgiving Days of New England.* Boston: Houghton, Mifflin. Available on GoogleBooks.

MacCana, Proinsias. 1970. *Celtic Mythology.* London: Hamlyn Publishing.

MacDonald, Dennis. 2000. *The Homeric Epics and the Gospel of Mark.* New Haven: Yale University Press.

———. 2014. *The Gospels and Homer: Imitations of Greek Epic in Mark and Luke-Acts.* Lanham, Maryland: Rowman & Littlefield.

———. 2015. *Mythologizing Jesus: From Jewish Teacher to Epic Hero.* Lanham, Maryland: Rowman & Littlefield.

Mack, Burton. 1988. *A Myth of Innocence: Mark and Christian Origins.* Philadelphia: Fortress Press.

———. 1993. *The Lost Gospel: The Book of Q and Christian Origins.* New York: HarperCollins.

———. 1995. *Who Wrote the New Testament?: The Making of the Christian Myth.* New York: HarperCollins.

———. 2001. *The Christian Myth: Origins, Logic, and Legacy.* New York: Continuum International Publishing.

MacLeod, Sharon. 2012. *Celtic Myth and Religion.* Jefferson, North Carolina, and London: McFarland & Company.

Maier, Paul. 1998. "Herod and the Infants of Bethlehem," in Vardaman, Jerry, ed., *Chronos, Kairos, Christos II: Chronological, Nativity, and Religious Studies in Memory of Ray Summers.* Macon, Georgia: Mercer University Press, pp. 169–89.

Malory, Thomas. 1969. *Le Morte D'Arthur.* London: Penguin.

Markale, Jean. 1984. *La tradition celtique en Bretagne armoricaine.* Paris: Payot.

———. 1999. *The Druids: Celtic Priests of Nature.* Rochester, Vermont: Inner Traditions International.

———. 2000. *The Pagan Mysteries of Halloween.* Rochester, Vermont: Inner Traditions.

Matthews, John. 1998. *The Winter Solstice: The Sacred Traditions of Christmas.* Wheaton, Illinois: Quest Books.

———. 2001. *The Quest for the Green Man.* Wheaton, Illinois: Quest Books.

McKenzie, Robert. 2013. *The First Thanksgiving*. Downers Grove, Illinois: InterVarsity Press.

Meier, John. 1991. *A Marginal Jew*, vol. 1: *The Roots of the Problem and the Person*. New York: Doubleday.

Mettinger, Tryggve. 2001. *The Riddle of Resurrection: "Dying and Rising Gods" in the Ancient Near East*. Stockholm: Almqvist & Wiksell.

Michels, Agnes. 1967. *The Calendar of the Roman Republic*. Princeton: Princeton Univeristy Press.

Miles, Clement. 1976. *Christmas Customs and Traditions: Their History and Significance*. New York: Dover Publications. Facsimile of original 1912 edition.

Miller, Richard. 2010. "Mark's Empty Tomb and Other Translation Fables in Classical Antiquity," *JBL* 129:759–76.

———. 2015. *Resurrection and Reception in Early Christianity*. New York and London: Routledge.

Miller, Robert. 2003. *Born Divine: The Births of Jesus & Other Sons of God*. Salem, Oregon: Polebridge Press.

———, ed. 2001. *The Apocalyptic Jesus: A Debate*. Santa Rosa, Calif.: Polebridge Press.

Monaghan, Patricia. 2008. *The Encyclopedia of Celtic Mythology and Folklore*. New York: Checkmark Books.

Moor, Johannes C. de. 1972. *New Year with Canaanites and Israelites*. 2 vols. The Netherlands: Kamper Cahiers.

Morrill, Bruce. 2006. "Easter," in Travers 2006, pp. 113–34.

Morton, Lisa. 2012. *trick or treat: a history of halloween*. London: Reaction Books.

Morton, Nathaniel. 1669. *The New England's Memorial*. Cambridge, Massachusetts: Printed by S.G. and M.J. for John Usher of Boston.

National Conference of Catholic Bishops. 1991. Order of Crowning an Image of the Blessed Virgin Mary, in National Conference of Catholic Bishops, in *Rites of the Catholic Church*, vol. 2. Collegeville, Minnesota: Liturgical Press, pp. 449–78.

Newall, Venetia. 1967. "Easter Eggs," *JAF* 80:3–32.

———. 1971. *An Egg at Easter: A Folklore Study*. Bloomington, Indiana: University of Indiana Press.

Newberg, Andrew, and d'Acquili, Eugene. 2001. *Why God Won't Go Away: Brain Science and the Biology of Belief*. New York: Ballantine Books.

Nickelsburg, George. 1980. "The Genre and Function of the Markan Passion Narrative," *HTR* 73:154–84.

Nolland, John. 1989. *Luke 1–9:20*. Dallas: Word Books.

Oruch, Jack. 1981. "St. Valentine, Chaucer, and Spring in February," *Speculum* 56.3: 534–65.

Parker, Richard. 1950. *The Calendars of Ancient Egypt*. Chicago: University of Chicago Press.

Pennick, Nigel. 1997. *The Sacred World of the Celts.* Rochester, Vermont: Inner Traditions International.

Price, Robert. 2011. *The Christ-Myth Theory and its Problems.* Cranford, N.J., American Atheist Press.

Raglan, Lord. 1990. *The Hero: A Study in Tradition, Myth, and Drama, Part II*, in Segal 1990, pp. 89–175. First published 1936.

Rank, Otto. 1990. *The Myth of the Birth of the Hero: A Psychological Interpretation of Mythology*, in Segal 1990, pp. 3–86. First published 1914.

Raphael, Ray. 2014. *Founding Myths: Stories that Hide our Patriotic Past.* New York: The New Press.

Raphael, Simcha Paull. 2019. *Jewish Views of the Afterlife.* 3rd ed. Lanham, Md.: Rowman & Littlefield.

Rhoades, Richard. 2013. *Lady Liberty: The Ancient Goddess of America.* Bloomington, Indiana: iUniverse.

Robinson, James, et al., eds. 2000. *The Critical Edition of Q.* Minneapolis: Fortress Press.

Rogers, Nicholas. 2002. *Halloween: From Pagan Ritual to Party Night.* New York: Oxford University Press.

Roll, Susan. 1995. *Toward the Origins of Christmas.* Kampen, The Netherlands: Kok Pharos Publishing House.

Rolleston, T.W. 1990. *Celtic Myths and Legends.* Mineola, N.Y.: Dover Publications. Facsimile of 1917 2nd and revised edition.

Rollins, Wayne. 1983. *Jung and the Bible.* Atlanta: John Knox Press.

Ronnberg, Ami, ed. 2010. *The Book of Symbols.* Cologne, Germany: Taschen.

Rudolph, Kurt. 2005. "Mystery Religions," *ER* 9:6326–34.

Sanders, E.P. 1993. *The Historical Figure of Jesus.* London: Allen Lane/Penguin.

Santino, Jack. 1994. *All Around the Year: Holidays and Celebrations in American Life.* Urbana and Chicago: University of Illinois Press.

Schaberg, Jane. 2006. *The Illegitimacy of Jesus: A Feminist Theological Interpretation of the Infancy Narratives.* Sheffield, UK: Sheffield Phoenix Press.

Schüssler-Fiorenze, Elisabeth. 1994. *In Memory of Her: A Feminist Theological Reconstruction of Christian Origins.* New York: Herder and Herder.

Schweitzer, Albert. 2005. *The Quest of the Historical Jesus.* Mineola, New York: Dover. First published 1911.

Scullard, H.H. 1981. *Festivals and Ceremonies of the Roman Republic.* Ithaca, N.Y.: Cornell University Press.

Seeley, David. 1990. *Graeco-Roman Martyrology and Paul's Concept of Salvation.* Sheffield, UK: Sheffield Academic Press.

Segal, Robert, ed. 1990. *In Quest of the Hero.* Princeton: Princeton University Press.

Shaw, Philip. 2011. *Pagan Goddesses in the Early Germanic World: Eostre, Hreda and the Cult of Matrons.* London: Bloomsbury Classical Press.

Shepard, Paul, and Sanders, Barry. 1985. *The Sacred Paw: The Bear in Nature, Myth, and Literature.* New York: Viking Penguin.

Smith, Jonathan. 1990. *Drudgery Divine: On the Comparison of Early Christianities and the Religions of Late Antiquity.* Chicago: University of Chicago Press.

———. 2005. "Dying and Rising Gods," *ER* 4:2535–40.

Smith, Mark. 1998. "The Death of 'Dying and Rising Gods' in the Biblical World: An Update with Special Reference to the Baal Cycle," *SJOT* 12:257–313.

Smith, Morton. 1978. *Jesus the Magician.* New York: Harper & Row.

Snaith, Norman. 1947. *The Jewish New Year Festival.* London: Society for Promoting Christian Knowledge.

Spalinger, Anthony. 1992. *Three Studies on Egyptian Feasts and their Chronological Implications.* Baltimore: Halgo.

Steves, Rick. 2018. *Travel as a Political Act: How to Leave your Baggage Behind.* Berkeley, California: Avalon Travel.

Talley, Thomas. 1991. *The Origins of the Liturgical Year.* 2nd ed. Collegeville, Minnesota: The Liturgical Press.

Teeter, Emily. 2011. *Religion and Ritual in Ancient Egypt.* New York: Cambridge University Press.

Thompson, Stith. 1955–58. *The Motif-Index of Folk Literature.* 2nd ed. 6 vols. Bloomington, Indiana: University of Indiana Press.

Travers, Len, ed. 2006. *Encyclopedia of American Holidays and National Days.* 2 vols. Westport, Connecticut: Greenwood Press.

Tylor, Edward. 2010. *Primitive Culture: Researches into the Development of Mythology, Philosophy, Religion, Art, and Custom.* Cambridge, United Kingdom: Cambridge University Press. Facsimile of 1871 edition.

Ustinova, Yulia. 2009. *Caves and the Ancient Greek Mind: Descending Underground in the Search for Ultimate Truth.* Oxford: Oxford University Press.

Vermes, Geza. 2006. *The Nativity: History and Legend.* New York: Doubleday.

———. 2008. *The Resurrection.* New York: Doubleday.

Wallace, Daniel. 1996. *Greek Grammar Beyond the Basics.* Grand Rapids, Michigan: Zondervan.

Walton, John. 2009. *The Lost World of Genesis One.* Downers Grove, Illinois: InterVarsity Press.

Watts, Alan. 1950. *Easter: Its Story and Meaning.* New York: Henry Schuman.

Welburn, Andrew. 2006. *The Myth of the Nativity: The Virgin Birth Reexamined.* Edinburgh: Floris Books.

Wensinck, Arent. 1922. "The Semitic New Year and the Origin of Eschatology," *Acta Orientalia* 1:158–99.

Wilson, R., ed. and trans. 1990. *The New Testament Apocrypha.* 2 vols. Louisville: Westminster John Knox Press.

Wright, N.T. 2004. *Luke for Everyone.* Louisville: Westminster John Knox Press.

Wulff, David. 1997. *Psychology of Religion: Classic and Contemporary.* 2nd ed. Hoboken, N.J.: John Wiley & Sons.

Yoder, Don. 2003. *Groundhog Day.* Mechanicsburg, Pennsylvania: Stackpole Books.

York, Michael. 1986. *The Roman Festival Calendar of Numa Pompilius.* New York: Peter Lang.

Zirkle, Conway. 1936. "Animals Impregnated by the Wind," *Isis* 25: 95–130.

INDEX[1]

[1] Note: Page numbers followed by 'n' refer to notes.

CPSIA information can be obtained
at www.ICGtesting.com
Printed in the USA
BVHW011839270820
587485BV00003B/23

9 783030 469153